JOHN RAY

APPLE VISION PRO
for CREATORS

A Beginner's Guide to Building **Immersive Experiences**

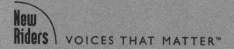

New Riders | VOICES THAT MATTER™

Apple Vision Pro for Creators:
A Beginner's Guide to Building Immersive Experiences

John Ray

New Riders
www.peachpit.com
Copyright © 2025 by Pearson Education, Inc. or its affiliates. All Rights Reserved.

New Riders is an imprint of Pearson Education, Inc.
To report errors, please send a note to errata@peachpit.com

Text Figure Credits
1.3-1.54, 2.2, 2.4-2.26, 2.27a-c, 2.28-2.32, 2.34-2.37, 3.1-3.22a-b, 3.23-3.41, 4.1-4.40, 4.43-4.51, 4.53-4.71, 5.1-5.20, 6.1-6.24, 7.1-7.21, 8.1, 8.3, 8.4, 8.6, 9.1-9.24, 9.26-9.30, 10.1-10.11, 11.1, 11.2, 11.5-11.12, 12.1-12.4, 12.6-12.62: Apple Inc

Executive Editor: Laura Norman
Editorial Services: Charlotte Kughen
Associate/Sponsoring Editor: Anshul Sharma
Senior Production Editor: Tracey Croom
Compositor: Bronkella Publishing, LLC
Proofreader: The Wordsmithery LLC
Indexer: Johnna VanHoose Dinse
Cover Design: Chuti Prasertsith
Chapter Opener Illustration: ZinetroN/Shutterstock
Cover Art: AlpakaVideo/Shutterstock and frantic00/Shutterstock
Interior Graphics: tj graham art

ISBN-13:   978-0-13-836022-1
ISBN-10:   0-13-836022-7

1 2024

This book is dedicated to those who seek new knowledge and try new things. You are a rare breed, and I'm honored to have you as a reader.

TABLE OF CONTENTS

ABOUT THE AUTHOR

John Ray is a lifelong Apple enthusiast and developer. He created a handwriting recognition engine at 15, published his first commercial application at 16, and continues contributing to development projects today. Over the past 25 years, John has written books on macOS, iOS, and iPadOS development, Linux, web development, networking, and computer security. He currently serves as the Senior Director of the Office of Research Information Systems at The Ohio State University. When John isn't writing, editing, or directing he is either re-creating a marine disaster in his living room or over-engineering apps and embedded systems for home automation and device integration.

ACKNOWLEDGMENTS

Many thanks to the Pearson team that made this book possible—Anshul Sharma, Charlotte Kughen, Laura Norman, Anne Groves, and everyone else behind the scenes. Writing is *much* more work than putting words on a page (that's the easy part!). Keeping me on track, making sense of my gibberish, and making sure that what I've written actually *works* is hard. Trust me, I've met myself.

INTRODUCTION

Welcome to *Apple Vision Pro for Creators*, a guide for learning how to create spatial computing experiences on the Apple Vision Pro. If you're reading this book, you probably have an idea of what Apple's headset *is*, but you might not fully appreciate how it fits in with the dozens of virtual reality headsets, augmented reality glasses, and other "tools of the future" that you can buy on the Internet. What advantage does a $3500 headset offer over a $150 pair of glasses or competitors' high-end gear like the Microsoft HoloLens?

To answer the question, we must first take a trip through the industry jargon that has sprung up as companies struggle to find some way *not* to use the words *virtual reality* or *augmented reality* with their products.

WHAT ARE VIRTUAL REALITY AND AUGMENTED REALITY?

These terms describe interactions with objects that do not exist in the real world—also known as *physical reality*. Virtual reality is typically a "replacement" for physical reality: computer generated environments where you can move and interact with items that aren't present. In virtual reality, the laws of physics (and nature itself) can be altered to present the user with otherwise impossible experiences, like flying, visiting distant planets, or just touring faraway and inaccessible places.

Augmented reality is a bit different in that it allows virtual objects and information to be mixed with physical objects. Users can interact with both physical reality and virtual reality at the same time. Augmented reality has been around in different forms for quite some time. Viewfinders on cameras that display lighting conditions, distances, and shutter speed are an example of augmented reality that we take for granted. Cars with heads-up windshield displays are another example where we can see physical reality (the road, signs, and so on) combined with virtual reality (gauges, navigation prompts, and more).

THE JARGON

When virtual reality headsets, such as the Oculus Rift DK1, initially started shipping to consumers, those of us lucky enough to obtain and develop on these devices were given a very limited set of tools. You essentially had two screens sitting on someone's face—the basic requirements for stereoscopic vision—and very little else. The way you interacted with the system varied by application, and there was rarely consistency in how you did *anything*.

It's been over a decade since these consumer headsets first appeared, and while some things have improved, many have stayed the same. There is some semblance of interface consistency on popular platforms like the Oculus Quest family, but developers are still forcing users to shift their expectations of how to work and play in three dimensions as they move between applications.

Over time, virtual reality headsets added external cameras for tracking and understanding a user's environment (some even adding quite awful "pass-thru" video to mingle the real world with virtual reality). Marketing departments were delighted to create new terms for each minor tweak introduced–hybrid reality, mixed reality, and extended reality, for example— despite no real changes from a user standpoint.

Products like Microsoft HoloLens, Google Glass, and Magic Lens *have* moved the state-of-the-art forward with augmented reality, but each have serious limitations in what they can display and how well it "mixes" with physical reality. Microsoft's HoloLens has a very limited area where virtual objects can be displayed; turn or tilt your head and they're gone. Google Glasses, on the other hand, are more like information overlays. Yes, you can see information projected into your view of the physical world, but they lack the ability to create virtual objects or immersive environments.

Recent consumer products like the XReal Air AR glasses do little more than place a flat 2D screen in front of the user. It's a relatively low-res, jittery, and poorly anchored monitor that all but obscures the physical world anyway, but hey, *it's floating in front of you!*

To call this industry and the state of AR/VR solutions "chaotic" is charitable. There are dozens of devices, each making different claims, each offering different interactivity, and each with a complete lack of consistency in experience. This confusion is frustrating for consumers and developers, and—in my opinion—it has led to a market where technology terms are thrown around with little regard to customer expectations.

THE APPLE APPROACH

Apple has entered the world of AR and VR explosively and (strangely) extremely cautiously. Rather than leaning on the various marketing terms that have been watered-down to almost no meaning, Apple is embracing the concept of *spatial computing*. Spatial computing, a term coined in the early 2000s, describes the convergence of the physical and virtual worlds. In spatial computing, there is an expectation that the headset understands the user's environment—what objects are in it, their sizes, what portions of a user's view (or other objects) are obstructed, and so on. This information is collected through myriad sensors and used to blend the physical with virtual in a way that feels natural, accounting for elements such as lighting and shadows to seamlessly meld the real and virtual.

Apple has also purposefully leaned into the *computing* portion of spatial computing, enabling the platform to run hundreds of thousands of apps at launch, while presenting a consistent user experience throughout. Other devices focus on games or niche use cases; the "vision" of the Apple Vision Pro is to create an all-in-one computer that you can use for productivity, entertainment, and gaming. It just happens to reside on your head, rather than your desktop.

What about the price? A $3500 price tag isn't far from a traditional high-end computer setup. My first personal "large" computer purchase was a G4 Cube with an Apple Cinema Display, which cost similar to *two* Apple Vision Pros. Apple isn't pinning the future of the Vision Pro on a $3500 device; they're offering it as an entry point into a new Apple platform that will expand in the coming years with cheaper, and also probably more expensive, options. This is a long-term effort, not a declaration that a single device is the pinnacle of spatial computing. This book, while specific to the Apple Vision Pro, is more about building a foundation in creating applications and experiences for the underlying operating system: visionOS. Today visionOS powers only the Vision Pro, shown in **FIGURE I.1**. Tomorrow? Who knows?

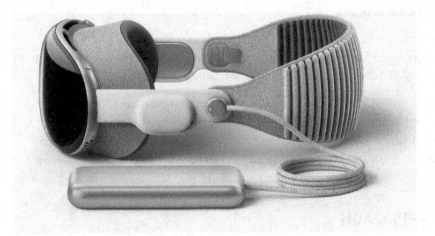

FIGURE I.1 The Apple Vision Pro

NOTE Yes, Apple itself has a tremendous marketing machine and has been known to use industry jargon and magical words in its product descriptions. The original name for visionOS was xrOS (something you may still see in Xcode and visionOS documentation.) XR is the abbreviation for "extended reality," so it's clear Apple was originally going to adopt one of the same terms as its competitors.

THE DEVICE

So, what is the Apple Vision Pro? Augmented reality headsets (such as HoloLens) use advanced transparent optics to create lenses that work like glasses, but with the ability to project virtual objects that overlap and obscure the real world. Apple has done something different.

Instead of combining the physical with the virtual through optical means, Apple has gone the route of pure virtual reality. What?! How is that possible if you can see and interact with the real world? The answer is extremely high-quality pass-thru video. You aren't seeing *through* the device; instead, you're looking at tiny screens that are mirroring the real world to your eyes. With 23 million pixels representing the world, Apple is betting that users of the Vision Pro will not even notice that they're looking at a screen.

Taking the illusion to another level, the Vision Pro has a front-facing 3D lenticular display that projects a rendering of your eyes to the outside of the device, making it appear transparent to those observing the wearer. This feature, dubbed EyeSight, provides greater engagement with the physical world and helps eliminate the isolation of wearing a headset that completely covers the eyes. The outcome is a product that *appears* to be a pair of transparent goggles, but in reality, they completely obscure the user's vision. It remains to be seen if this is the long-term approach for the visionOS platform, but as an initial product, it is a truly a unique approach to achieving the best of VR and AR worlds.

The Apple Vision Pro uses a total of 12 cameras on the inside and outside of the device for eye tracking, pass-thru video, and hand and world tracking. Speaking of which, the headset lacks dedicated controllers; the user experience relies entirely on eye-tracking, hand tracking, and gestures. This includes individual finger tracking—no giant motions or full-hand movements needed. Cameras also authenticate you to the device using eye-scanning to identify the owner of the headset.

To mix the physical and virtual, the headset includes a LiDAR sensor that measures depth by reading the time it takes for light emitted by a laser to be reflected. This can instantly create a mesh (a digital representation of physical surfaces using polygons) of the user's environment, as shown in **FIGURE I.2**. The device also uses six microphones to map how audio interacts with the objects in the environment. The result is that virtual objects can be appropriately lit in the environment, generate shadows, and be hidden by (or hide) physical objects in the room (this is known as occlusion). If the object generates audio, the sound generated considers the different surfaces in the environment to create a spatial audio experience that feels natural and mixes perfectly with the physical world.

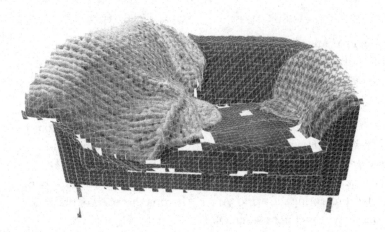

FIGURE I.2 A partial mesh of my living room loveseat (with blankets), captured by an iPhone 15 Pro LiDAR sensor

NOTE When setting up the Apple Vision Pro, you can scan your ears so that your individual ear shape is considered by the device's audio engine. Talk about thorough!

There is even more on the feature list, such as foveated rendering (using eye position to determine a user's point of interest to focus rendering power in that area), high-end Apple Silicon Processors (the R1 and M2), OLED and MicroLED technology, and on and on. Apple has packed a tremendous amount of tech into a small wearable package.

THE SOFTWARE

The raw hardware of the Apple Vision Pro is a dream for many developers, but having to deal with the dozens of sensors and cameras would be a nightmare by any measure. In typical Apple fashion, they've leveraged years of augmented reality work on the iPhone and iPad, as well as their macOS and iOS operating system experience, to create a new operating system, vision OS, that makes both using and developing for the device accessible by anyone with an interest and an ounce of motivation

Using visionOS, you gain access to all the features of the Apple Vision Pro without needing to delve into the complexities that make it work. If you want to display an object in your environment, you load the object and display it. Want to interact with the object? Attach a gesture and interact away. In Chapter 1, "Understanding the visionOS Toolkit," you'll begin by learning the Xcode development environment and a touch of the Swift programming language. By the end of Chapter 2, "From Traditional Applications to Spatial Workspaces with SwiftUI," you will have written an interactive app that displays a three-dimensional model.

The specific software and digital technologies that this book focuses on include

- **Xcode:** The platform for Apple development. Whether you're creating for a Mac or a Vision Pro, you'll be spending most of your time building your projects in Xcode.

- **Swift:** Apple's programming language for the entire Apple ecosystem. It isn't a stretch to say that once you know how to develop for the Apple Vision Pro, you can develop for *any* Apple device.

- **SwiftUI:** A Swift extension for defining user interfaces in code. Similar in some respects to HTML, SwiftUI enables you to quickly define controls, windows, and other objects for user interaction regardless of whether you're creating for iOS, iPadOS, tvOS, macOS, or visionOS.

- **Simulator:** The Simulator application lets you test your creations on your Mac without needing a headset (or an iPhone, iPad, and so on). You use the Simulator to build and test your apps and then fine-tune them on a physical device.

- **RealityKit:** This framework is the workhorse behind the capabilities of the Apple Vision Pro. It offers 3D rendering capabilities but does so with augmented reality at the forefront. It makes use of Apple's existing augmented framework (ARKit) and builds upon it with gestures and other means of interaction.

NOTE A *framework* is a collection of related functions that developers can use for a specific purpose. Apple platforms have frameworks for audio, web interactions, and, in the case of the Apple Vision Pro, augmented and virtual reality.

- **Windows, volumes, and spaces:** These three components make up the different scenarios you can create with visionOS. Windows are simply 2D application windows—nothing terribly special. Volumes are three-dimensional virtual objects added to the environment. Spaces, on the other hand, are entire 3D scenes that can (but don't have to) replace the physical reality entirely.

- **USD files:** Universal Scene Description files are used extensively in this book and in your projects. This file format, created by Pixar, provides a means of describing objects, materials, and even animations. Apple has standardized on these files for 3D development on its platforms. You'll most frequently encounter USDA (USD ASCII) and USDZ (USD zipped) files in the wild.

- **Reality Composer Pro:** An application for building 3D scenes in a point-and-click manner. This can be a great starting point for many projects, and you can even visualize your scenes directly on the Vision Pro without writing any code.

- **Object Capture:** An application and a collection of technologies that use photos of real-world objects to construct a virtual facsimile that you can use in your creations.

- **Materials:** A digital representation of the composition of an object, such as rubber, metal, glass, denim, fuzz, and so on.

- **Shaders:** A description, usually based on mathematical algorithms, of how light interacts with the surface of an object. Imagine an object with ridges in the surface. It would be nightmarish to create all your 3D objects with tiny ridges on their surface. A "ridge" shader might create this effect automatically so that it can be applied to any object you'd like.

- **Spatial Audio:** Audio that can be positioned in three dimensions that tracks your position and movement. Spatial audio gives the user the ability to move around different virtual audio sources and realistically changes the audio to match.

- **Scene reconstruction:** The Vision Pro enables the user to see their environment as if they were looking through glasses. Scene reconstruction takes that environment and recreates it digitally so that virtual objects can interact naturally with the real world.

This sounds like a lot, doesn't it? It is (and there's more), but it's something that you (yes, you!) can do without spending the next few years reading and watching development tutorials.

THE EXPECTATIONS

For you to get the most out of this book, we need to agree on what you can expect. First, you need the motivation to read chapters from start to finish. Concepts are introduced and reinforced through hands-on exercises. If you don't practice (even the simple stuff), you'll find it difficult to see how the different components work together. You do *not* need to be a developer, but you shouldn't be afraid of having to type a few lines of code to make a project work. Most importantly (life lesson time), this should be a topic that excites you. If it isn't, find something that does and do that instead! Watching my first projects come to life made me giddy, and I hope they do the same for you.

You don't have to do difficult math or geometry, but you should understand the difference between 2D and 3D and how coordinates are defined in three dimensions—(x, y, and z), as shown in **FIGURE I.3**. When wearing the Apple Vision Pro, the x-axis gives us positioning to the left and right and the y-axis up and down. The z-axis (the third dimension) moves objects toward and away from you. I cover these topics in more detail throughout the book, but if this makes sense to you, you're good to go! If you'd like a nice introduction to 3D concepts,

Adobe has published an excellent tutorial at https://blog.adobe.com/en/publish/2020/11/09/start-3d-an-introduction-to-key-3d-concepts.

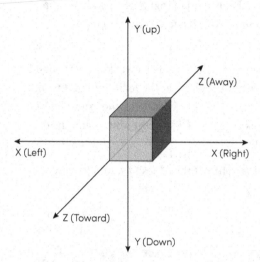

FIGURE I.3 The three axes (x, y, and z) used to define 3D positions

Regardless of your skill-level, you need at least one thing to be a successful creator: an Apple Silicon Mac. Xcode is only available on macOS, and Vision Pro development requires an M1 or later processor. It would be beneficial if you had access to a headset for testing, but this isn't required to get started. Additionally, I cover tools for the iPhone and iPad in Chapter 4, "Creating and Customizing Models and Materials," that can help with your development workflow. These devices aren't necessary to be successful, but they can help supplement the tools available on macOS.

THE PHILOSOPHY

I have spent more than three decades developing for platforms big and small, esoteric and mainstream. In recent years, I've noticed a trend of development being turned into a mundane engineering exercise. Web development, which was once something that many people enjoyed as a hobby, has become so convoluted that even small websites take months to design, debug, secure, and make accessible. Experimentation and exploration are gone—replaced with strict rules and rigidity.

Development, like art, can be a platform for self-expression and creativity. There will always be business to conduct and boring code to write, but shouldn't there be time to just *play*? I think so.

I've been thinking recently about a discussion where a peer mused "imagine what amazing creations we'd have if developers weren't obsessed with creating the perfect unimpeachable code." This cuts the crux of the problem. We've been trained that perfect code is more important than anything else, even if it affects the user experience, makes development tedious, and maintenance problematic.

My philosophy is to make things that work but to give developers the leeway to "color outside the lines". I encourage you to progress through this book looking at the techniques being presented and thinking about how you might use them for your projects. Take the examples and change them, substitute your own files and controls in place of what I present. If you think something can be done differently or better, do it!

You're in possession of the tools to bring new worlds to life. If that doesn't sound like an opportunity for fun, I don't know what does!

Let's play!

> **NOTE** Project files and corrections for this book are available at https://visionproforcreators.com/ and www.peachpit.com/visionpro. I prompt you to download each chapter's files before you get started. Be aware that visionOS is in active development and Apple is tweaking their tools constantly, so some figures and files may have changed before you read this.
>
> If you have questions, you can get in touch with me through the visionproforcreators.com site or via Mastodon at @johnemeryray@wisdomhole.com.

CHAPTER 1

Understanding the visionOS Toolkit

With great power comes a bunch of complicated tools. The Apple Vision Pro and visionOS use the same development environment as Apple's other platforms. This is great news if you're already developing for another Apple device. However, if you're not, it can feel overwhelming.

At the core of Apple's development suite is **Xcode**—software for writing, testing, and distributing applications on the App Store. Bundled with Xcode is **Simulator**—a powerful utility that can run your code on an emulated Apple device of your choice. This guide delves into many more tools, but starting with Xcode and Simulator provides a solid jumping off point.

Development tools are fine and dandy, but they can't do anything without *you*, the creator, providing content. A good portion of that content is in the form of code in the Swift programming language. I've included a short Swift overview at the end of this chapter so that you'll be ready to tackle your first coding project. Don't worry, you won't need a deep dive to get started–just a brief swim.

My aim with this book is to provide you with an enjoyable experience where you spend much of your time experimenting with your Apple Vision Pro and learning how a little bit of code can make (virtual) magic. Before you can achieve that, you need to get your toolbox in order.

In this chapter, you install and configure Xcode, set up sample projects, and test them in the simulator as well as an actual device. You gain hands-on practice with

- **Xcode:** Xcode is the integrated development environment (IDE) for Apple platforms. Explore Xcode installation, required configuration, and basic use. Learn how to add platforms, log into your developer account, and get ready to code.

- **visionOS Projects:** Not all Vision Pro projects are the same. Discover the different types of projects that you can build for the visionOS Pro and begin using Apple's application templates.

- **Simulator:** Simulator is an integrated tool for testing your creations on any of Apple's platforms without the need for a physical device (except a Mac). Learn how to go from Project to Simulator and then navigate the controls to emulate a spatial computing session.

- **Swift:** The Swift programming language was developed by Apple and released in 2014. In the last decade, it has evolved into the standard language for Apple platforms.

This information is foundational, which some might say translates to "kinda boring." Don't we all want to be staring at virtual worlds in our headsets? Of course! But unless you want an endless stream of error messages or to scare your neighbors with exasperated screams, I recommend following along. Let's get started!

SETTING UP XCODE

Xcode will be your best friend, and possibly worst enemy, during your foray into Apple Vision Pro programming. Xcode is the cornerstone of Apple development. It provides your editor, project management tools, file organization, and much more. If this is the first time you've seen it, you may start to question Apple's ability to make simple, easy-to-use, software. Xcode is shown in **FIGURE 1.1**.

Despite the apparent complexity, Xcode can be easy to navigate. I've been using Xcode for more than 15 years, and I use only a tiny subset of the available tools. With Apple's documentation at the ready (https://developer.apple.com/documentation/xcode), there's little need to memorize every single feature.

Let's download and start exploring Xcode. You need an Apple Silicon (M1, M2, or M3) Mac running Sonoma (14.x) and an Apple ID to continue.

FIGURE 1.1 The Xcode interface can be... let's go with "busy."

Downloading Xcode

Xcode is a free download directly from the App Store. To download the application, open the App Store and search for *Xcode* in the search field in the upper left of the window. Click the Get button beside the Xcode icon that appears.

 Depending on the network connection, I've seen the download take minutes to hours. Be patient. Once completed, the Xcode icon is in Launchpad and your Applications folder. Unfortunately, you need to download several more items before you can use Xcode.

TIP The App Store version of Xcode is perfectly fine and works great, but it's rarely the latest version. When Apple announces new operating systems and devices, development for those platforms happens using beta versions of Xcode. Download the latest beta on the developer site at https://developer.apple.com/download/applications/. You can access the download using just your Apple ID—no paid membership needed.

Adding Development Platforms at First Use

Xcode requires additional components, including the Apple Vision Pro simulator and visionOS operating system, to be downloaded before you can start creating. Xcode typically manages this process when it launches for the first time. Go ahead and launch Xcode from the Applications folder or Launchpad now.

When Xcode launches, it asks you to agree to Apple's software development kit (SDK) license.

Click Agree. After a few seconds, you'll be prompted with a list of the platforms you can use for development. Choose Apple Vision Pro, as shown in **FIGURE 1.2**. I recommend also installing iOS. You can always add others later.

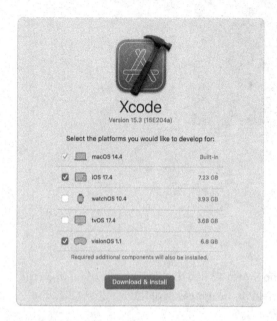

FIGURE 1.2 Picking the platforms you want to use

Click Download and Install to continue. Xcode first downloads some *other* components and then commences with downloading the additional files required to support your chosen platforms, as shown in **FIGURE 1.3**.

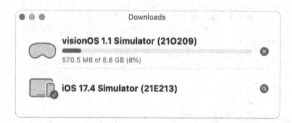

FIGURE 1.3 Waiting while Xcode downloads everything else you need for development

This can take a good deal of time, but it conveniently happens in the background. You can proceed with setting up Xcode while you wait.

Manually Adding Platform Support

If you (like me) are excited to get into Xcode and *maybe* opened it before reading the previous section, you may find yourself needing to add platform support after Xcode is already up and running. No worries, you can modify the platforms supported in your copy of Xcode at any time.

To add or remove a platform, open Xcode and then choose Xcode, Settings from the menu bar. When the Settings window appears, choose the Platforms icon in the upper right. Your screen should now resemble **FIGURE 1.4**.

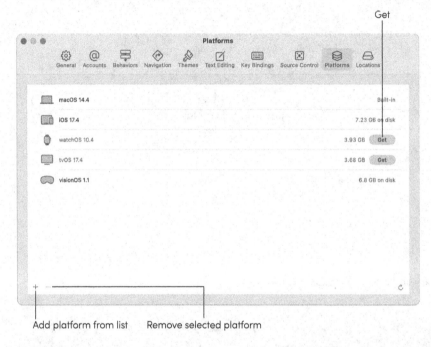

FIGURE 1.4 Using the Platform Settings to remove or add development platforms

Use the + symbol (Add Platform from List) to choose from a list of different platforms and *many* versions of the operating systems. If you're just interested in the latest version of a platform, just choose it from the list and click Get.

To remove a platform, select it in the list, and then click –. This can be quite helpful on machines with a limited amount of storage. The visionOS 1.0 and Apple Vision Pro simulator occupies over 7GB alone!

Configuring Xcode with Your Apple ID

You should now have Xcode installed and *almost* ready. The last configuration step is to add your Apple ID to Xcode, which helps configure the software to build and launch projects and even set you up to submit to the App Store in the future.

Open Xcode and then choose Xcode, Settings from the menu bar. When the Setting window appears, click Accounts. From this panel, shown in **FIGURE 1.5**, you can add and remove accounts that you want to use with Xcode. You're working solely with your Apple ID in this case, so that's what you need to add.

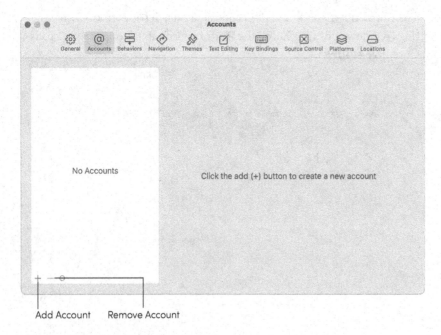

FIGURE 1.5 Adding your Apple ID to Xcode

NOTE You don't need a paid developer account for anything we do in this book. Development opportunities must be open to everyone, and thankfully that's a sentiment Apple shares. Even so, I recommend a paid account if you're able. A paid developer subscription gives you access to additional resources, longer testing durations on physical hardware, and the ability to offer your finished experiences through the App Store. Learn more at https://developer.apple.com/programs/.

To set up your account, click +. You're prompted for the type of account, as shown in **FIGURE 1.6**. Choose Apple ID and click Continue.

Next, log in with the email or phone number associated with your Apple ID. The Accounts Settings refresh to show your account, as demonstrated in **FIGURE 1.7**. You will now be able to close the Settings window and give yourself a thumbs-up. You're done with the initial setup and are ready to create a new project!

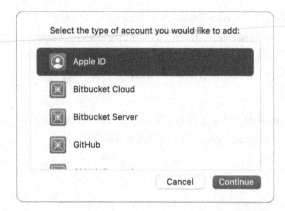

FIGURE 1.6 Selecting to use your Apple ID

FIGURE 1.7 Xcode is now ready to go!

NOTE Assuming you are using a free developer account, the settings reflect a Team with your name and the label Personal Team as well as a Role of User.

My paid membership shows up differently with just my name and the role of Admin. You can learn more about the different roles and services available in paid memberships a: https://developer.apple.com/support/articles/.

CREATING A PROJECT

In Xcode, a **project** is a collection of all the different files that make up an application. This includes Xcode configuration information, code, images, sound, 3D models, icons, and so on. All of this is stored in a folder structure that I'm referring to as the *project folder*.

You're here for the Apple Vision Pro, but it's not too bad if you learn how to create applications that run on multiple Apple Platforms, right? Well, if you don't object, let's look at the two project types that you'll use to deliver both multiplatform applications and unique visionOS creations. In this section, you create a Hello World application for use throughout the chapter.

Start by opening Xcode. After the initial installation, each time Xcode opens, it gives you the option of creating a project directly from the startup screen, as shown in **FIGURE 1.8**.

FIGURE 1.8 When Xcode starts, you have the option of creating a new project.

Click Create New Project. If Xcode is already running and you don't see this dialog box, choose New, Project from the File menu.

You're prompted to choose a template for your new project, shown in the dialog boxes of **FIGURE 1.9**. This is the first decision point that you need to tackle—whether you want to target just visionOS or the full range of Apple platforms. In Chapter 2, "From Traditional Applications to Spatial Workspaces with SwiftUI," you build something that can run on macOS, iOS, iPadOS, and visionOS—that is, a multiplatform application.

In my opinion, if you're setting out to build a nontraditional application that relies heavily on features of the Apple Vision Pro, you shouldn't hinder your efforts by cutting corners to make your code work on other devices. If, however, you're building something traditional—relying heavily on two-dimensional elements (windows, text, and so on)—then absolutely make it multiplatform.

To choose what you're going to be building, click either Multiplatform or visionOS from the selections at the top of the dialog. Both options are shown in Figure 1.9.

In either case, once you've made your decision, you'll want to click the App icon to tell Xcode we're going to be building an application. For this exercise, choose Multiplatform and then App; then click Next.

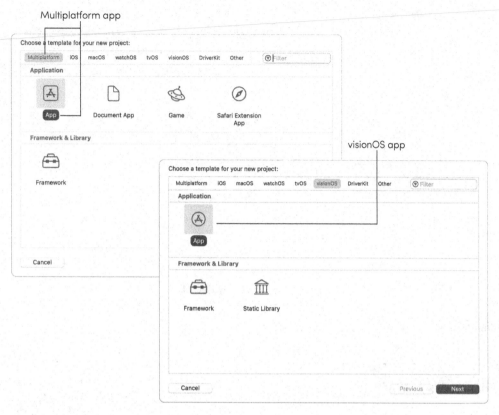

FIGURE 1.9 Deciding whether you're going to create an application for multiple Apple platforms or just the Vision Pro

You should now see the project options screen, shown in **FIGURE 1.10**. This is going to require more explanation, so be aware that there are some "rules" as to what you enter here.

The **Product Name** is the name of the amazing application you're going to build. By default, this is the name of the application as it appears on the App Store, so make it short and sweet. Enter Hello World for the example you're working with here.

> **TIP** The settings you're making now (aside from the Product Name) will be carried through to subsequent projects. If you set your Team and Organizational Identifier properly now, you may never need to touch it again.

Next, choose your **Team**. Unless you're an established developer and have created/joined multiple enterprise development teams, you should see a single option under Team–your name. This indicates that you are the sole developer, and your identity will be used to "**sign**" the application when it is built.

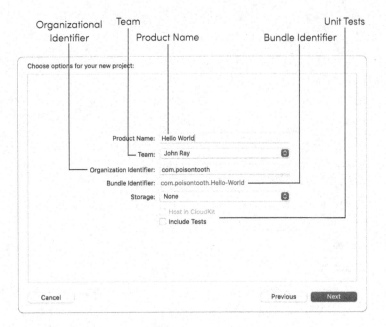

FIGURE 1.10 Choosing the options for your project

WHAT IS SIGNING?

Application signing is the process of attaching an identity to a piece of software. This establishes trust between your creation, Apple, and your users. Once an application is signed, it can't be modified by third parties and is owned by your developer account. This is the horrible awful walled garden that everyone loves to complain about–while willfully ignoring the security benefits it brings.

Now, turn your attention to the **Organizational Identifier.** This is written as a domain name in reverse order. Many people choose to use com.<my name>—for example, com.johneray— except *your* name, not *my* name! This should be a unique identifier throughout Apple's ecosystem. I recommend using a domain name you own or obtaining a new domain name just for your development. I own poisontooth.com so I typically use com.poisontooth as my organization. Until the point you submit to the App Store, the organizational identifier doesn't really matter, so don't fret; you can just mash your keyboard a few times and some random letters will work just fine.

As you enter your Product Name and Organizational Identifier, you're going to see the **Bundle Identifier** fill-in. This is a string that will uniquely identify your application among the millions of other apps on the App Store. Unless this is unique, your app won't be accepted. Again, not a big concern until you submit it to the App Store—just something you should be aware of.

If you're planning on using any of Apple's Storage frameworks, you can select from the Storage dropdown. You don't do this in this book, so you can leave it as None. Host in CloudKit enables storing data via iCloud, so it will remain grayed out unless you choose a Storage option.

Finally, make sure Include Tests is *unchecked*. When checked, the project will include **unit tests**. Unit Tests are a great way to automate testing of core functionality in your applications but require effort to build and use. You don't ever *need* to include unit tests, but as your projects get more complex and include multiple developers, you may want to review unit tests further. Learn more by visiting

https://developer.apple.com/documentation/xcode/testing-your-apps-in-xcode

Click Next. You're *almost* done creating your first project!

The last step is choosing where to save your project. You might be thinking, "Come on, John. I've used a computer. I don't need a screenshot for this!" That's a reasonable attitude, but I *do* need to cover one other option that appears in the Create dialog, shown in **FIGURE 1.11**.

FIGURE 1.11 Disable source control unless you are familiar with its use.

Uncheck the Create Git Repository on My Mac checkbox. **Git** is a form of **source control** and provides a way to track modifications to your code, plan and write new functionality in an application without "breaking" the main code, revert to previous versions if problems occur, and collaborate on a software project with multiple other developers. In short, it's great!

So why are you turning it off? Git (and source control in general) is a big topic to which I cannot do justice in the space of this book. I highly recommend reading Apple's documentation at

https://developer.apple.com/documentation/xcode/
configuring-your-xcode-project-to-use-source-control

for assistance on getting started with Git in Xcode. It isn't a required part of development, and you may find you don't need it, but it *can* be a powerful tool as your development projects grow.

After unchecking the Git checkbox, choose a location to save your project, then Click Create.

> **TIP** I use macOS to sync my Documents folder with iCloud, and I store my projects within Documents. This enables me to move between different Macs and keep working on my projects. It also gives me the ability to browse and review code directly from the Files app on my iPad.

Congratulations! You've created your first project. Xcode now opens the project workspace.

EXPLORING THE XCODE WORKSPACE

Xcode is not a tiny application, as you can probably see by looking at **FIGURE 1.12**. There are icons and various other controls all over the screen. Maybe not quite as many as a Microsoft Office application, but nonetheless, it's complex. The good news is that you need to use only a subset of these tools during your development. I've been using Xcode since its initial release, and I still haven't touched every setting.

Let's become familiar with the core components of the workspace.

> **NOTE** Depending on your screen size and whether you've poked around Xcode before, your display may look different than mine. The screenshot was taken from a fresh installation of Xcode. I review the controls that you need to help you find what might be missing in your environment.

Along the top of the Xcode window is a toolbar with a few simple controls for managing your project and workspace. The Hide/Show buttons show or collapse the right and left panels (Navigators and Inspectors, respectively). Play and Stop buttons are used to start and end your application. The Simulator dropdown chooses what type of device (Mac, Apple Vision Pro, iPad, etc.) will be running your code.

Xcode status messages are displayed in the center field to give insight into what Xcode is doing at any moment. Compiling code to make a piece of software is relatively intensive, so Xcode can occasionally become unresponsive. The status can help keep you patient by showing exactly what action Xcode is taking.

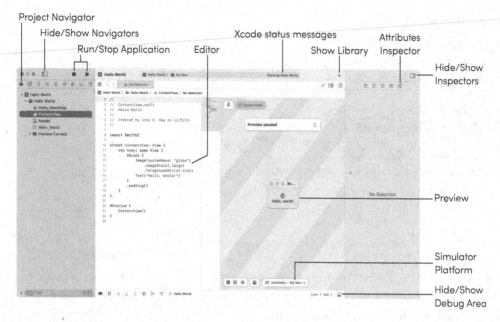

FIGURE 1.12 The Xcode workspace is vast.

Lastly, the + button displays the Library, which holds code snippets that can be inserted into your project.

Below the Xcode toolbar lies the meat of the application—different panels of information used to configure your project, edit your code, fix errors, and more.

Navigators

On the left side of your Xcode window is a selected folder icon and a list of the files and folders that make up your project. This area is the **Navigator** panel, which helps you navigate "stuff" across your entire project. If this is *not* visible, click the Hide/Show Navigators button to make the area visible.

Project Navigator

When opening a project, by default, the navigators will be visible, and the folder icon will be selected. This places you in the aptly named Project Navigator, as shown in **FIGURE 1.13**.

This is the navigator you'll be using the most during your development efforts, so it's critical to understand what you're seeing.

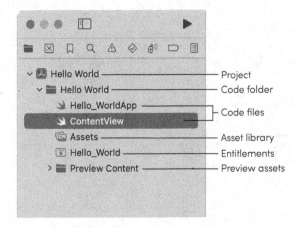

FIGURE 1.13 The Project Navigator helps you find your way around your project files.

The top-level item in the Project Navigator is your project file. This contains the settings for your project, the platforms it supports, the app type, and so on. You can use this to tweak the Team, Organizational Identifier, and more. This corresponds to the .xcodeproj file you see in the Finder.

Next, the Code folder contains all the code and assets (images, icons, etc.) that are used in the project. Clicking on a filename shows its contents in the area to the right—the editor. You'll use the project navigator primarily to choose which file you want to code within.

The second-to-last icon within the code folder (named after your project) represents the project **Entitlements**. Entitlements define the various features that you want the application to be able to use that are "special" in some way—usually involving the transmission of information over a network. For example, if you want "Sign in with Apple", Siri, or Maps, you'd need to list the features in the entitlements file. Doing this ensures that Apple grants the proper permissions to the application and that the user knows exactly what the application will access before downloading from the App Store.

> **TIP** If you click and view the entitlements file, Xcode decides that you changed it. You're likely to see an error message stating that the file was modified during the build. This is rather ridiculous, but can be easily rectified by choosing Product, Clean Build Folder from the menu bar. This removes the error flags set by Xcode and gets you back to an error-free state.

Finally, the Preview Content folder is a place to put assets that should only be used during development. This isn't commonly used, so don't worry if you never touch this feature.

As you can tell by the list of icons at the top of the navigator panel, there are more navigators that you can access for different insights into your project. You're welcome to click through them all, but you'll discover that several relate to unit tests, source control, and other esoteric features that we don't need right now. Let's focus on two that can help you right away.

Search Navigator

You activate the Search Navigator by clicking the magnifying glass. Use this navigator to quickly search *all* your project files for arbitrary text. The results (in this case, searching for *World* across the Hello World project) are shown in a list below the search term. Clicking a result opens the editor to the location where the search term appears. You can see the Search Navigator in action in **FIGURE 1.14.**

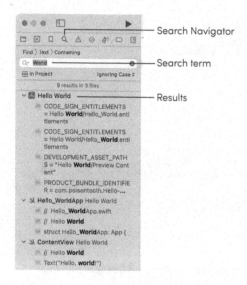

FIGURE 1.14 Using the Search Navigator to search across all the files in your project

Issue Navigator

Another useful navigator is the Issue Navigator, represented by a caution sign, and shown in **FIGURE 1.15.** The Issue Navigator displays any errors in your project across all the project files. You'll also see errors highlighted in your code, but this is a one-stop shop to see everything that is considered a potential problem in your application.

In Figure 1.15, you can see that there is an error `Cannot find 'thisIsAnError' in scope`. This is because I typed `thisIsAnError()` into the ContentView source file and Xcode has no clue what that means. If I click on the error, I'll be taken to the line in the code that is causing the problem, so I can correct it. I talk more about correcting errors later in the section "Detecting and Correcting Code Issues."

Issue Navigator   Error

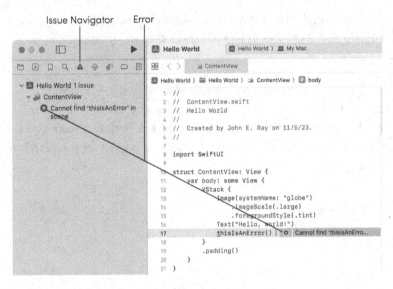

FIGURE 1.15 Browsing your errors in the Issue Navigator

TIP If you look closely at Figure 1.18, you can see that the error message visible in the Issue Navigator is identical to that shown directly in the code. The trouble with the inline errors is by default they're truncated to fit in the editor panel, and you only see errors in the file you're currently viewing. The Issue Navigator always shows the full message and any other messages generated by files throughout your project.

The Xcode Editor

The Xcode editor appears to the right of the navigators and is where you'll be entering code. To open a file for editing, highlight it in the Project Navigator. For many projects in this book, you work directly in ContentView.swift, so open the Project Navigator and then click the ContentView file within the Hello World project.

WHAT IS THE <PROJECT NAME>APP.SWIFT FILE?

When Xcode creates your project, it sets you up to start coding immediately in ContentView.swift. It also creates a file named after your project and appended with "App." The code in this file sets up the application for execution, telling the system that it should begin by running the code in ContentView.swift. This is frequently all you need, and you won't modify the "App" file. Occasionally, you'll make some adjustments, but usually you can just ignore the file.

If the file wasn't already selected, you see the editor refresh with the code listing, and a new tab appears above the editor with the filename, as shown in **FIGURE 1.16**.

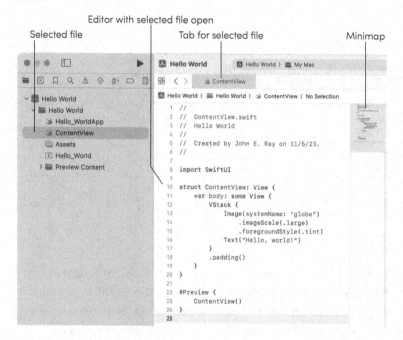

FIGURE 1.16 Choosing a file in the Project Navigator and edit it within the editor

You can use the editor like any other text editor. Type and delete code, copy, paste, and so on. To the right of the editor panel is a preview thumbnail of the file—called the **Minimap**. You can click within the Minimap to quickly jump between different sections of code. This becomes useful when your code is longer than a few lines. For the Hello World example, it's overkill. You can disable the Minimap by deselecting Minimap from the Editor menu.

If you open another file from the Project Navigator, you'll see a new tab appear at the top of the editor. You can jump between different files using the tabs, or just click them again in the Project Navigator.

Code Completion

If you've worked in a code editor before, you may be familiar with the concept of **code completion**. Code completion occurs when Xcode thinks it may have an idea of what you intend to type. When it does, the editor displays a list of possible options. For example, open the ContentView file in the Xcode editor and place your cursor on a blank line, then type **Text**. As you are typing, you're going to see a variety of autocompletion options appear, as demonstrated in **FIGURE 1.17**.

```
 8  import SwiftUI
 9
10  struct ContentView: View {
11      var body: some View {
12          VStack {
13              Image(systemName: "globe")
14                  .imageScale(.large)
15                  .foregroundStyle(.tint)
16              Text("Hello, world!")
17              Text|
18          ┌──────────────────────────────────────────────────────┐
19          │ S  Text                                                │
20      }   │ I  Text(_ content:)                              >     │
21  }       │ I  Text(_ date:style:)                                 │
22          │ I  Text(verbatim:)                                     │
23  #Previe │ I  Text(_ input:format:)                               │
24      Con │ I  Text(_ subject:formatter:)                          │
25  }       │ I  Text(_ key:tableName:bundle:comment:)         >     │
26          │ I  Text(timerInterval:pauseTime:countsDown:showsHours:) > │
            │ S  TextField                                           │
            ├──────────────────────────────────────────────────────┤
            │ Text                                                   │
            │ A view that displays one or more lines of read-only text. │
            └──────────────────────────────────────────────────────┘
```

FIGURE 1.17 Using code completion to ensure your syntax is correct

If you were writing real code, you would pick the form of the Text keyword that matches what you want, double-click it in the list to add it to your code file, and then fill in any other required information when prompted. You can choose to use this throughout the exercises... or not. All that matters is that the *right* code is entered, not how you choose to enter it.

Library Assets

Another way to speed up your coding process is to make use of Xcode's library of coding assets—named Library. In addition to useful code snippets, the library includes a collection of thousands of free-to-use symbols. To use Library, click the + icon in the right center of the Xcode toolbar. A window appears, as shown in **FIGURE 1.18**.

When you find an asset or code snippet you think might be useful, you can click it for more information or double-click to insert it directly into the editor.

I think it's best to begin by coding by hand to build some muscle memory, but the library holds more than my brain ever will, so it's a useful piece of the coding toolkit regardless.

Before moving on, delete any code that you may have entered in the project. You don't want any pesky error messages showing up to clutter your workspace.

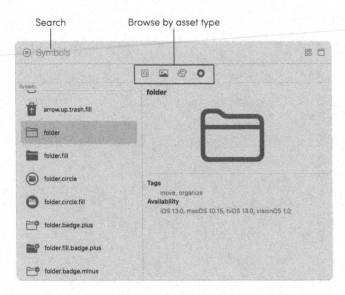

Search   Browse by asset type

FIGURE 1.18 Using the Library to find code and insert it into your project

Getting More Help

Another helpful coding tool is the built-in Xcode documentation. This is useful for research-ing code and learning more about the various features that Swift provides. For example, consider the line in ContentView that begins with Image. Image is used to (guess what?!) display images, but how do we know how it works and how to use it? Jump to a reference of that information by holding down Option, positioning the mouse over the word Image (the **cursor** will change to a question mark [?]), and then clicking, as demonstrated in **FIGURE 1.19**.

A popover with help information appears; it includes code and a real-world example of how Image can and *should* be used. The help also cross-links to other related topics that may be worth exploring.

You can also access developer documentation as a complete browsable and searchable reference. To do this, choose Developer Documentation from the Help menu. The reference documentation appears in a compact window, shown in **FIGURE 1.19**.

Browse topics of interest or drill down to individual functions using the table of contents. Use the search field to search for specific information. For example, searching for *Image* takes you to the same documentation you found when holding down Option and clicking the Image keyword in the code.

> **NOTE** Image (and other Swift keywords) can be used in different ways, and each form has different docu-mentation. When you search for an ambiguous term like Image, you'll first see a long list of possible options to choose from, including a suggested result. For **FIGURE 1.20**, I've chosen the suggested result, and—ta-da—the Image documentation appears.

FIGURE 1.19 Holding down Option and clicking your code to display contextual documentation

FIGURE 1.20 Searching across the entirety of the Xcode documentation instantly

If you want to share documentation with a fellow developer or even just message yourself a link for future reference, click the Share button in the upper-right corner of the window.

If two ways of accessing documentation aren't enough, believe it or not, Xcode provides a third *easier* way to view documentation automatically as you work through your projects. This happens by way of an **Inspector**.

Inspectors

Inspectors are tools that display information about your files and code, and, in some cases, let you modify code without even having to type. By default, the Inspector panel is visible and located on the right side of the Xcode window. If it's not visible in your environment, click the Hide/Show Inspectors button in the upper-right corner of the Xcode window. Please reference Figure 1.12 if you have trouble locating it.

Like the Navigator panel, you switch between different inspectors using the icons at the top of the panel. We will only be accessing three inspectors, as the other two (source control and previews) aren't relevant to this book.

File Inspector

The first inspector—the File Inspector—is represented by a File icon and is shown in **FIGURE 1.21**. This is used to show and edit details about the file you are currently viewing.

Using the text settings section in File Inspector, you can change how indents are handled (tabs or spaces), whether text wraps, and other attributes. It is unlikely you'll *need* to change these settings, but if you're a stickler for using tabs rather than spaces, this is where you can tell Xcode how to behave.

Help Inspector

The Help Inspector, opened by clicking the circle with a question mark, is the third way to view help information, and possibly the best. As shown in **FIGURE 1.22**, the Help Inspector displays help information for wherever your cursor happens to be in the editor.

Test this by clicking between the different lines in the ContentView file. As you click the different pieces of code that make up the file, the Help Inspector immediately refreshes with information about that code, including (again) sample code and (in many cases) examples of how the feature should be used. This is a fun tool to just leave open while editing. It allows you to code freely without having to remember the exact syntax for features. You have real-time feedback and instruction as you code!

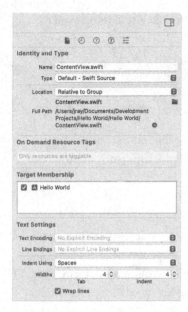
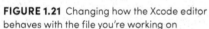

FIGURE 1.21 Changing how the Xcode editor behaves with the file you're working on

FIGURE 1.22 Using the Help Inspector for real-time help

Attributes Inspector

The last inspector may become your favorite while creating user interfaces. Everything you've seen so far would lead you to believe that you're going to be writing code and that you'll need to remember *a lot*. The Attributes Inspector frees you from quite a bit of memorization by giving you the ability to edit attributes of code through a point-and-click interface. It's not "code-free," but it's a great way to give your fingers a break.

To use the Attributes Inspector, first select something you want to inspect in your code. For example, click or highlight the word Text in the editor. The inspector will refresh and show a panel of settings (attributes) that can be used to change the appearance of the "Hello, world!" text. This is demonstrated in **FIGURE 1.23**.

You'll be using the Attributes Inspector in a Chapter 2 project, so you'll be seeing this again very soon.

> **TIP** The Inspectors in Xcode work just fine, but you might find that they frequently end up in a state where they simply don't refresh. It doesn't matter how many times you select a piece of text—the panel just stays the same. To get around this annoying bug, just click to open a different inspector and then click back to the one you wanted. Problem solved.

FIGURE 1.23 In the Attributes Inspector, changing settings on the right updates the code on the left.

Detecting and Correcting Code Issues

You're going to make mistakes, and you're going to get errors and warnings. In Xcode, a majority of the errors your keyboard randomly inserts in your perfect code will be identified before you ever run your application. Xcode constantly analyzes your code and identifies errors (which *must* be corrected before your app will run) and warnings (that *may* be corrected.)

> **NOTE** I've intentionally added some errors to my Hello World project to illustrate the concepts in this section. You can add them to your own Hello World code if you'd like. We're not quite done with Hello World yet, so you'll need to remove the errors or create a fresh version of the project later.

Errors

Errors are frequently caused by mistyping, using pieces of code somewhere you shouldn't, and leaving out something that Xcode expects to be present.

For example, **FIGURE 1.24** shows an error detected for a line of code that reads `Texts("Hello, world!")`.

This error (`Cannot find 'Texts' in scope.`) occurred because `Texts` isn't an actual keyword in Swift, and Xcode doesn't know what to do with it. Changing `Texts` to `Text` will resolve the error.

```
10  struct ContentView: View {
11      var body: some View {
12          VStack {
13              Image(systemName: "globe")
14                  .imageScale(.large)
15                  .foregroundStyle(.tint)
16              Text("Hello, world!")
17              Texts("Hello, world!")          ⊘ Cannot find 'Texts' in scope
18          }
19          .padding()
20      }
21  }
22
```

FIGURE 1.24 Errors *must* be corrected before an application can run.

Warnings

At times, Xcode warns you of an unusual condition, rather than an error. As shown in **FIGURE 1.25**, a warning doesn't prevent your application from running but is likely something you didn't intend to do or forgot to complete. Here, the warning is saying that we created a **variable** named neverUsed and then didn't use it.

> **NOTE** I talk more about development basics later. If variable is a word you're not familiar with, I'll catch you up shortly. For now, just know that a variable stores information in memory, like a name, a date, or even a 3D object.

```
10  struct ContentView: View {
11      var body: some View {
12          VStack {
13              var neverUsed: String    △ Variable 'neverUsed' was never used; consider replacing with '_' or removing it
14              Image(systemName: "globe")
15                  .imageScale(.large)
16                  .foregroundStyle(.tint)
17              Text("Hello, world!")
18          }
19          .padding()
20      }
21  }
```

FIGURE 1.25 Warnings don't *require* correction but may alert you to something you didn't intend.

Making Corrections

To correct an error or a warning, you edit your code to fix the problem—right? Yes, but you can also take advantage of a nifty Xcode feature that can fix common mistakes for you. When you click the left side of an error or warning, you get an expanded view of the message, including potential fixes. You can even let Xcode fix the problem itself by clicking the Fix button, as shown in **FIGURE 1.26**.

> **TIP** When Xcode fixes code for you, frequently it does a great job, but sometimes it breaks your code even further. Xcode has no way of determining your intent or the purpose of a piece of code; it makes its best guess as to the right thing to do. When updating your code with the Fix button, be sure to verify the results and confirm that the "fix" is appropriate for your project.

```
10  struct ContentView: View {
11      var body: some View {
12          VStack {
13              var neverUsed: String
14              Image(systemName: ┌─────────────────────────────────────────────────────────────┐
15                  .imageScale(.l│ ⚠ Variable 'neverUsed' was never used; consider replacing with '_' or removing it ⊗ │
16                  .foregroundSty│ Replace 'neverUsed' with '_'                            [ Fix ] │
17              Text("Hello, world!")└─────────────────────────────────────────────────────────────┘
18          }
19          .padding()
20      }
21  }
```

FIGURE 1.26 Letting Xcode fix errors and warnings for you

Debugging Runtime Errors

The most frustrating type of error that you might encounter as a creator are those that occur while your application is executing: **runtime errors**. These are logic errors or problems that cannot be detected before an application is running. Unfortunately, there's nothing I can do or say to keep these from happening or tell you when they *will* happen. The code in this book has been tested, so you won't really encounter these problems as you learn, but you should be prepared when they do occur down the road.

Runtime errors might not be fatal to your application. In other words, in some cases, the application keeps running despite the error. The "gotcha" here is that these errors might be occurring without your knowledge, affecting the performance and reliability of your application.

The Debug Area

To view runtime errors, use the Debug area. If an error causes your application to quit, the Debug area is shown automatically, as shown in **FIGURE 1.27**. If it *doesn't* appear, you can show the area using the Hide/Show Debug area button.

FIGURE 1.27 The Debug area displays errors occurring while your application is running.

Notice that the Debug area is split into two halves. The left half enables you to see the current values stored in your application, while the right half displays runtime errors in the console log. This belies just a tiny portion of the features available in the Xcode Debugger.

The Xcode Debugger

A **debugger** is an application that gives visibility into your code while it is running. It can be used to trace problems in your application, even if it quits unexpectedly. The Xcode debugger is built into Xcode and available any time you may need it to investigate a problem.

The debugger may be used proactively to just "check under the hood" if you aren't sure your application is behaving properly. You can do this by setting **breakpoints**—places in the code where you'd like the application to stop so you can check the state of your variables or just step more slowly through the execution.

Set breakpoints by clicking on the line numbers you see in your Xcode files. This will highlight the line number, as shown in **FIGURE 1.28**.

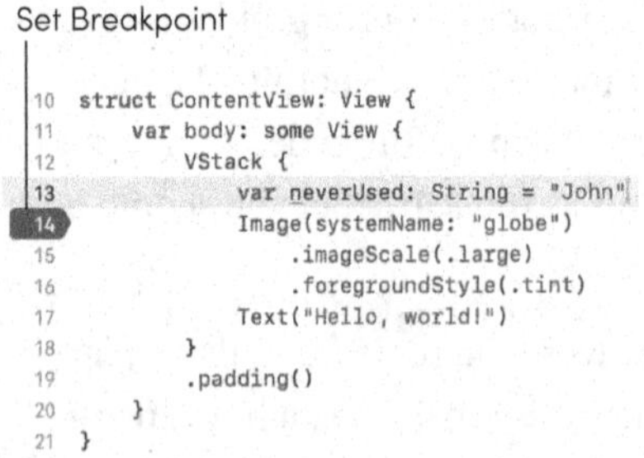

Set Breakpoint

```
10   struct ContentView: View {
11       var body: some View {
12           VStack {
13               var neverUsed: String = "John"
14               Image(systemName: "globe")
15                   .imageScale(.large)
16                   .foregroundStyle(.tint)
17               Text("Hello, world!")
18           }
19           .padding()
20       }
21   }
```

FIGURE 1.28 Breakpoints help you diagnose issues by stopping your code at predefined points.

When you run your application and it reaches a breakpoint, it acts just like it does when encountering an error. The Debug area is displayed, and the application is paused. You can then use the Debug area to check what is stored in your application's variables. Alternatively, simply hover over a variable in your code to view the same details about the variable under your pointer.

The controls at the top left of the Debug area, shown in **FIGURE 1.29**, are used to continue running the application or move through its execution one step at a time.

The Disable/Enable All Breakpoints button, as expected, disables any breakpoints you've set in your application. You can do this on an individual basis by clicking an existing breakpoint—turning it gray (disabled). You can remove breakpoints entirely by right-clicking and choosing Delete Breakpoint.

The Continue/Pause button continues the execution of your application until it encounters another breakpoint or an error. This button can also be used to pause your application while running—as if you had set a breakpoint.

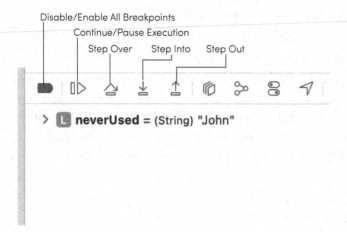

Disable/Enable All Breakpoints
Continue/Pause Execution
Step Over   Step Into   Step Out

> **L** **neverUsed** = (String) "John"

FIGURE 1.29 Use these controls to navigate your code in an application that has stopped at an error or a breakpoint.

When your code execution is paused, use the Step Over button to continue executing the code on the next line. This is used to move through your code line by line and see what is happening at each step. The Step Over function, however, doesn't move the debugger into code outside of the current block you are running. If you reach a function (a block of code that performs an action outside of the current code), Step Over just executes the code and moves to the next line of your current code, not letting you see anything that happens in that function.

To monitor what is happening in functions, you can use the Step Into button instead. This effectively moves you line by line through *all* the code that is being executed regardless of where it is. In large applications, this can be incredibly time-consuming, so the Step Out button is also included. Step Out exits any function that is executing and moves to the next line in your main code block.

Yes, these tools can be confusing (especially when you haven't written any code!), so I highly recommend testing them out in the projects throughout this book. You're not going to *need* them per se, but you *will* find them handy on your projects. You can learn more in the official Apple documentation at https://developer.apple.com/documentation/xcode/debugging.

Adding the Apple Vision Pro Platform

One last skill that you'll need *immediately* in Xcode is understanding how to add additional platforms to a project. The reason? Even though we started this section by creating a project based on Xcode's multiplatform App template, it isn't quite multiplatform enough. It doesn't include support for the Apple Vision Pro. (You know—the whole reason we're here!)

By default, *multiplatform* to Apple means Mac, iPhone, and iPad. If you intend your project to run on other devices, you must first modify the supported platforms in your project. To do this, you return to the Project Navigator.

As you learned earlier, the top line in the Project Navigator represents your project and can be edited to change attributes about the project, including what platforms it will support. For the Hello World project, this should be a blue icon with the text Hello World. Click that line to open the project settings, as shown in **FIGURE 1.30**. If your screen looks (much) different, make sure you're viewing the General settings by clicking General at the top of the editor.

FIGURE 1.30 Select the top line in the Project Navigator to open the project settings.

The Supported Destinations section displays all the platforms that you can support with this project. As you saw in Figure 1.30, Apple Vision Pro is not one of them. Let's fix that oversight now.

Click the + directly under the Supported Destinations list, as shown in **FIGURE 1.31**.

Choose Apple Vision from the dropdown list that appears. This will reveal a submenu with two additional options: Apple Vision and Designed for iPad. If you happen to have an existing iPad application (or are considering the iPad as your primary platform), you can quickly get Vision Pro support using the Designed for iPad option. This will enable your code to run on visionOS with no modifications. It won't gain many of the advantages of spatial computing, but it will work with almost no effort.

We want full visionOS support, so we'll choose Apple Vision from the options. Xcode prompts for a confirmation to Enable Destination Support, visible in **FIGURE 1.32**. Click Enable, and you're done. The project is updated to support Apple's new platform, and you now have access to the full range of features in visionOS.

Time to take stock of your Xcode introduction. You should have a decent idea of how to create projects and how to find the different pieces in Xcode that can help you code. I showed you where errors appear and even a few basics of runtime debugging. What's missing?

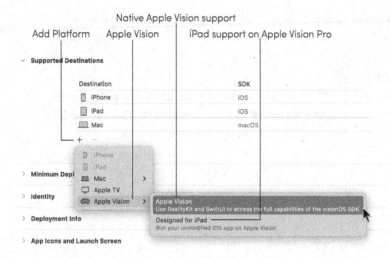

FIGURE 1.31 Editing the Supported Destinations to include Apple Vision Pro

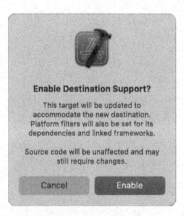

FIGURE 1.32 Enabling support for the newly added platform

If you've opened Xcode and created a project, you've likely noticed I've avoided a *major* feature of Xcode: the preview of your app. I also haven't showed you how to finally *run* an application on a real Vision Pro. That's because these topics deserve their own section, which is exactly what you're about to read!

PREVIEWING AND RUNNING APPLICATIONS WITH XCODE

Chapter 2 covers how to build application interfaces for Apple Vision Pro, and you're going to see me pontificating on the "old days" when we used a tool called Interface Builder to lay out applications graphically. Although Apple doesn't provide a tool to design visionOS interfaces directly, they *do* provide a rather amazing Preview feature that enables you to see your application interface and visualize how changes to code affect what is displayed in the headset.

Previewing Your Application

When you created the Hello World project, you may have noticed a preview panel became visible in the Xcode workspace, as shown in **FIGURE 1.33**; this is called the *Canvas*. By default, the Canvas shows how the application will appear when running on macOS.

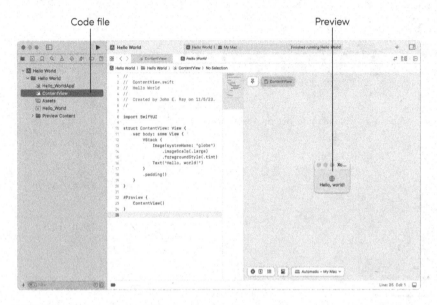

FIGURE 1.33 Previewing your application directly in Xcode

> **TIP** If your Xcode workspace does not have a preview visible, first make sure that ContentView is selected in the Project Navigator. This is the file that contains the application interface that generates the preview. Next, verify that Canvas is selected in the Editor menu. If you complete those two steps, you should have the preview panel (aka Canvas) displayed.

Okay, so I have a preview. Now what? I want to *run* the application, darn it! It may be surprising, but when you're previewing your application, you *are* running it! You can interact with the preview, click buttons, enter text, and so on—it just works. Behind the scenes, Xcode is running a copy of Simulator for your platform and simply passing input and output to the simulator via the Canvas.

The good news is that if you can see a preview, your app is working! The bad news is that this is a sledgehammer approach to generating previews. Although the preview is quite accurate, it can take a while for it to appear, and it does get bogged down at times on lower-end systems.

When you preview applications for Apple's *traditional* platforms, you point and click and use the previewed app exactly as you'd expect. I won't waste anyone's time going into the details of how to click a button or type into a field. The Apple Vision Pro, however, is a different beast with different controls, and that's where we're going to focus our attention now.

> **TIP** Depending on what operations Xcode is carrying out, sometimes the Canvas preview pauses with a Preview Paused message and a Refresh icon in the middle of the Canvas. If this happens, just click Refresh, and the simulation will continue.

Changing the Preview Platform

If you've chosen to build a Multiplatform app, chances are that Xcode has picked *anything but* the Apple Vision Pro platform for the preview. To change the preview platform, click the Preview Device popup menu at the bottom-left corner of the Canvas, as shown in **FIGURE 1.34**. Choose from the available Apple platforms. (You may need to pick More to see the Apple Vision Pro.)

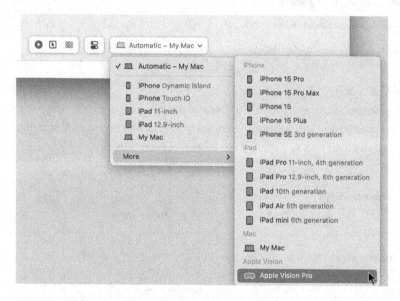

FIGURE 1.34 Selecting the Apple Vision Pro to start previewing applications directly in visionOS

After a minute or two the Canvas will take on the appearance of a room and the app should appear, as shown in **FIGURE 1.35**. What you're seeing is a single image displaying (as best it can) what your Apple Vision Pro would be beaming into your eyes if you were standing in the virtual room.

> **NOTE** The Canvas preview can take minutes to appear when first switching to the Apple Vision Pro. In the background, the simulator is starting up, booting visionOS, and then running your app. It can be a time-consuming process.

FIGURE 1.35 The Canvas displays your app within a virtual room.

Interacting with the Canvas

When an application is launched, it appears directly in front of you at an appropriate viewing distance—just as it does in your Vision Pro headset. Make sure that the Interact with Content button is selected, as shown in **FIGURE 1.36**.

Interact with Content

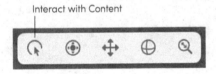

FIGURE 1.36 Make sure that the Interact with Content button is selected.

Using your mouse and keyboard, you can click, drag, and otherwise interact with your application (and visionOS itself) as you would in the headset. Sorta. There's a big difference between sitting at a desktop where you can point and click in an interface and having that interface appear in your room that you can physically move around. The Apple Vision Pro also relies heavily on your gaze and hand gestures. The result is that while the simulator does a good job simulating the application, with so many caveats, it's far more convoluted than using the physical device.

There are so many controls in the simulator that your keyboard and trackpad (or mouse) perform double-duty in many scenarios, making it far easier to go walking through the walls or end up staring at the ceiling than you'd hope.

Use these keyboard/trackpad shortcuts to interact with your application:

- **Clicks, double-clicks, drags:** Use your mouse or trackpad as you normally would with any application. No surprises here!

- **Forward/backward movements:** Remember that in spatial computing, you can use depth to move beyond a traditional 2D desktop. To move objects away from you, hold Shift and then click and drag up. To move objects toward you, again hold Shift but click and drag down.

- **Two-handed gestures:** The Vision Pro can track your hands, and the simulator can pretend (pretty poorly) to do the same. Hold down Option to display two points (representing your index finger on each hand). Use your cursor to move the two points to form gestures. You can change the offset of the points by holding Option and Shift and then dragging the points to where you want them.

- **Gaze:** The mouse pointer controls where your gaze would be in the headset.

> **TIP** Many components (such as gestures) of the simulator feel half-baked. Don't expect to be running the simulator and have it react as easily or smoothly as an actual device. You can develop using the simulator just fine, but it's no replacement for actual hardware.

Moving Yourself (or at Least Your Eyeballs)

With the Vision Pro, you aren't bound to a single position within your environment; you're free to move around. In the simulator, you can move the "camera" (aka "you") to look at the scene from different places and different angles.

If you're a gamer, you'll feel at home using the WSAD keys (or the arrow keys) to move forward, backward, left, and right for basic navigation. The Q and E keys move down and up, respectively. You can also perform these motions with the trackpad; unpinch and pinch to move forward and back, or scroll up, down, left, and right to move in those directions.

Now, keyboard and trackpad controls are fine, but trying to use them (at least for me) isn't a piece of cake. I prefer to use the camera controls in the lower-right corner of the Canvas. These icons, which are shown in **FIGURE 1.37**, represent four actions that are activated via a click-and-drag.

To use these controls, choose the type you want, then click within the Canvas and drag. If you'd like to jump to a particular angle (such as looking at a window from the top or the bottom), use the Camera presets popup menu, shown in **FIGURE 1.38**, to jump to a predefined viewing location.

> **TIP** If you get frustrated using the Simulator controls, there's a nifty "hidden" feature that can make it much easier. If you have a spare Xbox or PlayStation controller lying around, you can pair it with your Mac and use the thumbsticks to control your movement and where you're looking. For many gamers, this turns the Simulator control experience into something more natural.

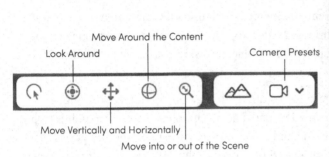

Look Around

Move Around the Content

Camera Presets

Move Vertically and Horizontally

Move into or out of the Scene

FIGURE 1.37 Use the camera controls to make changes to your position.

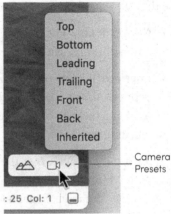

Top
Bottom
Leading
Trailing
Front
Back
Inherited

Camera Presets

: 25 Col: 1

FIGURE 1.38 Camera presets take you quickly to a predefined location/angle.

Changing the Environment

Different applications excel in different (physical) settings. If you're writing a cooking app, you may want to test it in a kitchen. If you're writing something that includes lots of augmented reality features, it would be wise to try it in cluttered or dark environments. To that end, the Simulator includes the ability to swap out the 3D scene used in previews.

To do this, click the Simulated Scene icon (a mountain), as shown in **FIGURE 1.39**.

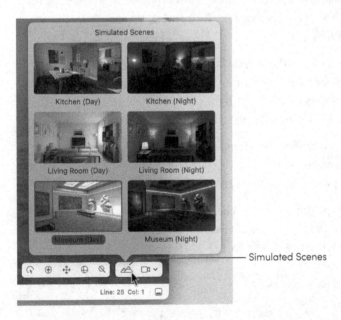

Simulated Scenes

Kitchen (Day)   Kitchen (Night)

Living Room (Day)   Living Room (Night)

Museum (Day)   Museum (Night)

Simulated Scenes

Line: 25 Col: 1

FIGURE 1.39 Picking a new environment from the Apple-provided list

Choose a new scene from the list that appears. After a few seconds, the Canvas refreshes with the new virtual environment.

Using the Selectable View

You're used to seeing the Live view of the Canvas, but there is an alternative option—Selectable—that strips away the 3D environment and gives you a wireframe of your application interface. Switch the Hello World application to the Selectable view, as shown in **FIGURE 1.40**.

In the Selectable view, the application is not running—no interaction is possible. Instead, you can use the camera controls to view the interface from any angle without the nuisance of the real world peeking through. You're also given dimensions for your objects, providing a sense of their size when viewed alongside real-world objects.

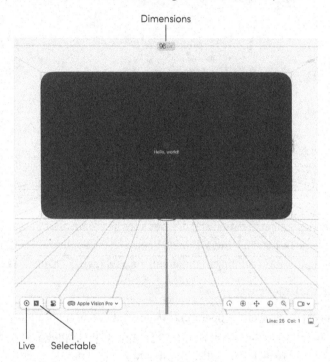

FIGURE 1.40 Using the Selectable view to see a wireframe of your application interface

Lastly, as the name suggests, in this view, components in your interface are selectable—meaning you can click text or other objects and jump to the code that defines them.

Using the Simulator Directly

By using the Canvas in Xcode, you're in turn using the Simulator, but you can also use the Simulator directly. Doing so provides a few additional features and, in my experience, slightly better reliability, performance, and appearance. Most of the screenshots in this book have been taken directly from the Simulator.

To launch the Simulator, choose the device (much as you did for the preview) by clicking the Device menu in the Xcode toolbar. In the Hello World project, change the device to visionOS Simulator for Apple Vision Pro, as shown in **FIGURE 1.41**.

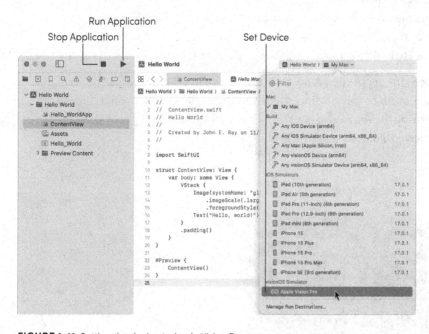

FIGURE 1.41 Setting the device to Apple Vision Pro

Now, click the Run button. Xcode compiles your application and deploys it to the visionOS simulator. This may take a few minutes, so please be patient while visionOS boots and the application is launched. After a brief wait, you see the application running in the simulator, as shown in **FIGURE 1.42**.

There are a few new controls added to the experience:

- **The Home button:** This is a simulation of the entire operating system (not just an application), so you can use the Home button to return to the Home Screen on your simulated Apple Vision Pro headset. It also gives you the ability to make OS-wide settings and access common apps within visionOS (Safari, Photos, and so on), as shown in **FIGURE 1.43**.

- **Save Screen control:** Use this to create screenshots of the Simulator view without the clutter of the onscreen buttons.

- **Capture Pointer and/or Capture Keyboard:** Use one of these options to pass mouse/trackpad movements and keystrokes directly into the Simulator (your gaze). Press Escape to exit these modes and return to normal (shared) input. This is used to simulate hardware connected directly to the Vision Pro rather than hardware shared between the Simulator and your Mac.

Save Screen ⌐ ⌐ Capture Pointer
Home ⌐ ⌐ Capture Keyboard

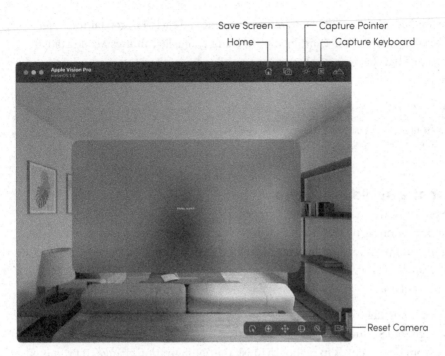

Reset Camera

FIGURE 1.42 The Simulator opens and launches your app.

- **Reset Camera:** The mountain icon takes on a slightly different purpose from the Canvas preview. In the Simulator, it returns your view to the default location within the simulated scene.

FIGURE 1.43 Using the Simulator as a fully emulated Apple Vision Pro

When you are finished using the Simulator, return to Xcode and click the Stop button (refer to Figure 1.41) to exit the application. Quitting the Simulator manually confuses Xcode a tad. It won't hurt anything, but you see several errors because Xcode wasn't expecting the Simulator to just disappear.

> **NOTE** You can launch the Simulator and use it directly without running your application. This is nice for getting a feel for visionOS and how it performs in the Simulator. To do this, choose Xcode, Open Developer Tool, Simulator from the menu bar.

Running on the Apple Vision Pro

For those of you who have an Apple Vision Pro in hand, you're probably chomping at the bit to get your code running on the physical headset. The Simulator is a handy tool for when you're separated from your headset, but running directly on your device is the best way to test your projects. Launching on your device is just *slightly* different (process-wise) than clicking Run to use the Simulator.

To begin, I'm assuming that you've already set up your Apple Vision Pro, and it's working. On your device, go into Settings, Privacy & Security and turn on Developer mode, as shown in **FIGURE 1.44**. Your device needs to reboot to finish the configuration change. If prompted again to enable Developer Mode, choose Enable and be patient.

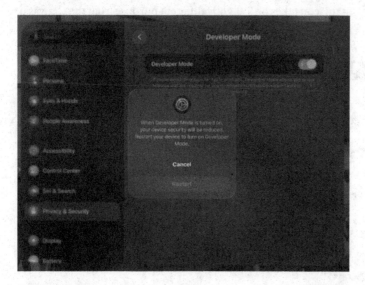

FIGURE 1.44 Enabling developer mode on your headset

Next, on your Vision Pro, navigate to Settings, General, Remote Devices. You see the Ready to Pair message as shown in **FIGURE 1.45**. If you already see a paired computer here, you need to activate the Clear button in the upper-right corner to remove it. This is only visible if you have previously paired the device.

FIGURE 1.45 Navigating to the Remote Devices screen

Now, make sure that Xcode is running on your development Mac, and choose Windows, Devices and Simulators from the menu bar. If your Mac and Vision Pro are on the same network, you see the headset appear with a Pair button underneath it, as shown in **FIGURE 1.46**. Click Pair to continue.

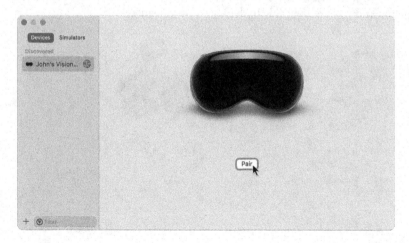

FIGURE 1.46 Pairing the Apple Vision Pro

Return your attention to the Vision Pro. You see it displaying a pairing number you must enter into Xcode. **FIGURE 1.47** shows the code I need to enter into my laptop "Nitrous" to finish the pairing process.

Enter the code into Xcode (yes, you need to switch back to your Mac again!) and click Connect, as demonstrated in Figure 1.47.

FIGURE 1.47 Getting the pairing code and entering it into Xcode to finish the pairing process

After a few minutes of processing between your Mac and the Vision Pro, the Devices and Simulators window should update to resemble **FIGURE 1.48**. This indicates that the setup process has been completed and you are now able to deploy to your headset!

FIGURE 1.48 All set up and ready to deploy applications to the Apple Vision Pro

With the setup process complete, you can run applications directly on your headset by choosing it from the Device dropdown menu, and then clicking Run, just as you did when choosing a Simulator. The difference is that now a visionOS Device category with your physical hardware—not just simulators—is listed, as shown in **FIGURE 1.49**.

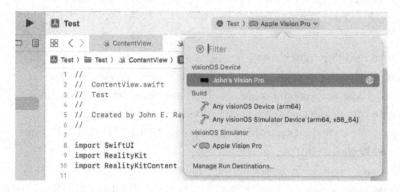

FIGURE 1.49 The physical device available to run projects

As you work with the headset in development mode, you can return to the Xcode Devices and Simulators screen if you want to check to see what development applications are installed, review any errors that have occurred, or unpair the device. This is a good place to check for errors if for some reason your Apple Vision Pro isn't showing up or working properly in Xcode.

Whew—what a trip this has been! You've just finished learning how to set up a rather complex development environment, seen how to create projects, discovered how to add the Apple Vision Pro as a supported platform, and, finally, dabbled in testing code in the Canvas, Simulator, and on an actual device. What more could there be? Well, I've talked about the core software tools you'll be using to create Apple Vision Pro applications, but I need to tell you about Swift—the language that enables you to express what you want an application to *do*. Please take the time to read through Appendix A, "Introducing Swift," before continuing to Chapter 2.

SUMMARY

Chapter 1 has introduced you to the tools you can expect to use each time you code for your Apple Vision Pro. You've learned about Xcode and how to set it up from scratch, create new visionOS projects, and find your way around the various panels and controls that comprise Apple's development environment. You explored the Canvas and Simulator for previewing your creations and learned how to use your traditional macOS devices to control the simulated Vision Pro experience. Lastly, you got a taste of Swift, Apple's development language, and the language basics that you'll be using from here on out.

Please remember that I want you to *learn by doing*. I repeat complex topics where needed and give you more background on Swift, Xcode, and other tools as you read along. I'm not a fan of traditional reference books that make you flip back and forth between chapters to find relevant instructions. I do, however, expect that as you finish up with this reading, you have Xcode installed, configured, and ready to go so that you can get to work on your first project.

Go Further

The most important thing to be doing right now is playing around in Xcode, clicking around, and making sure that you can find the tools you need, such as the Project Navigator, Attributes Inspector, and Editor. Explore the available documentation—either within Xcode or in your browser—starting with https://developer.apple.com/documentation/xcode. Try running the Simulator (without any code) and accustom yourself to navigating in visionOS using your mouse or trackpad and keyboard (https://developer.apple.com/documentation/xcode/running-your-app-in-simulator-or-on-a-device). Lastly, if you feel up to it, review more of the Swift syntax and functionality at https://docs.swift.org/swift-book/documentation/the-swift-programming-language/.

I hope you're feeling excited because you're about to start creating real applications that utilize the Apple Vision Pro features. This upfront work in this chapter can seem tedious, but soon you'll be able to start using your creativity to build things that no one, including yourself, has seen before.

CHAPTER 2

From Traditional Applications to Spatial Workspaces with SwiftUI

If you've been paying attention the past few years, you've seen popular VR headsets released like the Meta Quest family, Valve Index, and PlayStation VR2. The common thread between all these platforms is *games*. Yes, there are productivity solutions, but none offer an integrated experience with thousands of polished and stress-tested applications that users run on their phones, tablets, or desktops every day.

The Apple Vision Pro and visionOS change that dynamic. The Vision Pro is just as comfortable running productivity applications from iPadOS and sharing the table with Universal applications that run on multiple platforms as it is playing a game. SwiftUI is the interface magic that makes this possible. SwiftUI is used across the Apple ecosystem and can be used to make traditional applications for your desktop, or immersive experiences in three dimensions. In fact, you'll find out firsthand how to build a traditional two-dimensional app and bring it into the new world of spatial computing.

Chapter 1, "Understanding the visionOS Toolkit," gives you a tour of the Xcode development environment and the tools you're going to be using for the rest of the book. In this chapter, you're going find out about application interface building, common interface components, and how to provide interactivity to users. By the end of this chapter, you'll have created an application that runs on the Apple Vision Pro—and it's even going to have 3D visionOS elements. Along the way, I cover topics including

- **SwiftUI:** The language of Apple user interfaces. SwiftUI builds on the Swift programming language to give you the tools you need to write application interfaces that run on all of Apple's platforms, including the Vision Pro.

- **SwiftUI views and modifiers:** In SwiftUI, every interface control is a view and every view can have dozens of modifiers that change its appearance. Learn how to use views and modifiers to create elaborate interfaces with simple code.

- **Actions, events, and bindings:** This trio of terms will be a big part of how your applications interact with users. Learn the mechanisms Apple provides to monitor and react to user actions in your applications.

- **Depth and animation in visionOS:** Everything you see on your screen can have depth in visionOS. Make things pop and animate without even trying (that hard.)

In your first project, you'll create a simple quiz application using SwiftUI, visionOS specifics, and just a tiny sprinkle of Swift code. Will it be a masterpiece that you want to publish to the App Store? Well... maybe not, but it will give you the tools needed to work toward that goal!

> **NOTE** Make sure that you've downloaded the project files from https://visionproforcreators.com/files/ or www.peachpit.com/visionpro before proceeding. You use the Chapter 2 files throughout this lesson.

UNDERSTANDING SWIFTUI

When I started developing on the Mac platform, Apple had just acquired NeXT Computer and released Mac OS X Server based on NeXT's operating system—roughly 1999. Interfaces were built graphically using a tool called Interface Builder. In Interface Builder, you could lay out your interface and connect it directly to your code by clicking and dragging. It was an intuitive process that connected variables to input fields and buttons to actions, and it led to some convoluted and complicated interface code. I loved it.

Interface Builder seemed like a futuristic tool that let me code as I thought. In time, I developed applications for the App Store. It was amazing! Amazing, that is, until Apple started introducing new devices with different screen sizes and aspect ratios, and I started getting calls to port applications to macOS. I ended up with code that was dependent on so many individual devices' interface definitions that development turned from fun to NOPE.

In 2019, Apple released SwiftUI, ending the reign of Interface Builder and ushering in a new code-based declarative interface definition system. This means that you, the developer, use SwiftUI to *declare* what you want, not describe how to do it. For example, to display text, you type

```
Text("Something to display")
```

You don't have to know what device you're displaying text on, what font is appropriate to use, or where it's going to go. Don't worry, you can still customize things to your heart's content, but SwiftUI is going to make sure that the right thing is displayed on your device—whatever it may be!

> **NOTE** How is SwiftUI different from Swift? It isn't. SwiftUI provides a way to build user interfaces using Swift syntax. It's just such a break from the techniques used over the past two decades that Apple decided to give it its own name.

Comparing HTML and SwiftUI Views

You've probably heard of **HTML** (Hypertext Markup Language), the language that powers the World Wide Web (along with CSS and JavaScript). HTML uses tags with attributes to define an interface.

A simple web page with three lines of text reading "Top," "Middle," and "Bottom" might be written as

```
<html>
    <head>
        <title>Content</title>
    </head>
    <body align="center">
        <p>North</p>
        <p><img src="globe.png" alt="a photo of a tiny planet
                                surrounded by clouds"></p>
        <p>South</p>
    </body>
</html>
```

Even if you don't know HTML, you can likely make some sense of it just looking at it. Everything within a set of <> symbols is called a **tag** that describes the structure of the page and what is displayed within it.

In this example, the tags <html> </html> tell us we're about to define a webpage using HTML. The start of the page is within <head> </head>, where the title for the page is set to "Content." The <body> </body> tags tell us that everything between those tags is everything else that will be displayed on the screen.

Finally, the content of the page is contained within three <p> </p> tags. These define three paragraphs (elements displayed on separate lines): one displaying the word "North," another with an image of a tiny planet, and a third with the word "South." Your web browser displays elements as they occur in the HTML file—one on top of the other.

The HTML also includes **attributes** that modify how an HTML tag works or adds additional information to the tag. In the example, three attributes are in use:

- align="center" sets the body of the page to be centered, similar to clicking on the center justification button in your favorite word processor

- src="globe.png" determines from where the image tag <img> is going to retrieve the actual image. Here, it is loading a PNG file named globe.png.

- alt="a photo of a tiny planet surrounded by clouds" includes a text description of the image to assist low-vision users in understanding the content of the page.

The end result can be found at https://visionproforcreators.com/files/chapter2/globehtml/ and looks like **FIGURE 2.1**.

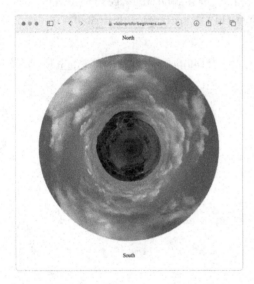

FIGURE 2.1 A simple webpage with text and an image

Not too bad. But certainly it's going to be worse in SwiftUI, right? You may be surprised to find out that it's *easier* to read the SwiftUI code than the HTML.

In SwiftUI, everything that you show on a screen, an iPhone, or your Vision Pro is a **View**. This means that it is a block of some sort of content (text, images, 3D models, and so on) that will be displayed in the application. All of the different views you define are aggregated together by SwiftUI into a single view, called the **body view**, which is stored in a data structure and displayed on the screen of your devices.

Sounds complicated? Sure, but I can put those fears to rest. Here is a SwiftUI view that does the same thing as the earlier HTML webpage:

```
struct ContentView: View {
    var body: some View {
        VStack {
            Text("North")
            Image("Globe")
                .resizable()
                .scaledToFit()
            Text("South")
        }
        .padding()
    }
}
```

Based on the words in the code alone, you can easily surmise that there's going to be some text with the word "North," an image named "Globe," and more text with the word "South." All of this is contained in something called a VStack, which is in turn contained within a body. Both exist inside another structure named ContentView. This code generates something very similar to the web page shown in **FIGURE 2.2**.

To see this yourself, open up Chapter 2's **Globe** project file in Xcode. Make sure that the Navigator is showing and the ContentView Swift file is selected in the Navigator. Select Apple Vision Pro or a platform of your choosing from the Preview Device menu in the bottom corner of the Preview pane.

You can also choose to run the file in the Simulator or, if you have a Vision Pro in hand, on your device. There's no smoke and mirrors here folks!

> **TIP** When using Xcode previews, sometimes the system encounters a bug or another process forces the preview to pause. When this happens, you'll see a Preview Paused message and a refresh arrow (like one from a web browser) to start the preview again. Just click the refresh arrow and you should be back in business.

Before I get to the good stuff, I want to get a few foundational basics out of the way to help you understand what you're seeing when you look at the SwiftUI code and much of the other code in this book.

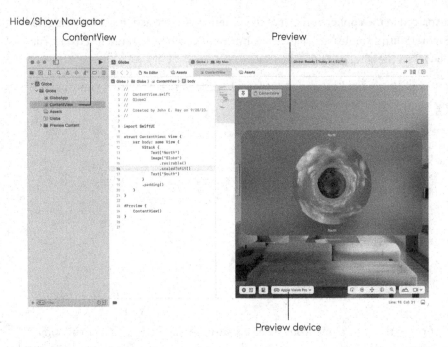

Hide/Show Navigator

ContentView

Preview

Preview device

FIGURE 2.2 Previewing the application in Xcode

Getting to Know Variables and Structures

In Swift (and most programming languages), a **variable** is something that holds a piece of information. For example, I might declare a Swift variable named myName that holds a text string "John"—like this:

```
var myName = "John"
```

Swift automatically knows that "John" is a string of characters and creates a variable named myName holding a string. Sometimes, however, Swift requires that we be more explicit about what a variable is going to hold because it can't infer it automatically. Alternatively, you, as a developer, might want the extra clarity in your own definitions. In these cases, you would add a **variable type** to the definition, such as this:

```
var myName: String = "John"
```

Here, I'm explicitly stating that myName is of the variable type String. Both lines have the same result, but there's no doubt the second declaration is dealing with strings.

There are many different types of information that variables can hold—an infinite amount, in fact. Why? Because you can create your own variable types using structs (and Objects, but it's not time for that).

A `struct`, or **structure**, is a collection of variables of the same or different types and can also include functions (programming logic that performs an action.). For example, let's assume that rather than *just* storing a name, I want to define a something that can store a first name, last name, and an age. I'll call this a Person:

```
struct Person {
    var firstName = ""
    var lastName = ""
    var age = 0
    func printPerson() {
        print("\(firstName) \(lastName) is \(age) years old")
    }
}
```

This structure, named `Person`, defines variables `firstName`, `lastName`, and `age`, which are typically known as **properties** of `Person`. The first and last names are set to an empty string, and the age is set to zero. This essentially gives me a "blank" person, by default, each time I use the structure. Swift can infer that these are strings and a number, so no need to explicitly state what they're storing. To round out the structure, I can define a **function** using the `func` keyword. This is a block of code that I can call repeatedly to perform an action. Here, the `printPerson` function uses the Swift `print` command to output a line of text that displays a person's name and age. The syntax `\(<variable name>)` substitutes the contents of a variable into the line of text being displayed.

To use this data structure, I begin by declaring a new variable:

```
var johnPerson: Person = Person()
```

This creates variable `johnPerson` of type `Person` (our struct), that is assigned to the default person values with `Person()` (the name of the structure and empty parenthesis).

I may then set the individual properties (variables) in the structure like this:

```
johnPerson.firstName="John"
johnPerson.lastName="Ray"
johnPerson.age=90
```

Alternatively, instead of initializing `johnPerson` to empty values with `Person()`, I can use this notation and assign everything all at once:

```
var johnPerson: Person = Person(firstName: "John",lastName: "Ray", age: 90)
```

Finally, I print out a message with my name and age by calling the structure's `printPerson` function:

```
johnPerson.printPerson()
```

As you can see, structures give you the flexibility to store all kinds of variables and even include functions for processing information. As I mentioned in Chapter 1, this is *very* similar to object-oriented programming and the use of **classes**. Object-oriented programming is also supported in Swift, and you'll encounter it in various places throughout the book.

WHAT'S WITH ALL THE BRACES?!

In Swift, braces ({}, also known as curly brackets) are used to define blocks of code. These can be statements in a function that are executed sequentially, conditional logic that is executed when someone performs an action, and so on. Any time you see braces, you're looking at a group of lines of code that are intended to be grouped together as a single block.

And then you have the parentheses, which have a very different role from braces. Parentheses are used when calling functions, defining new structures and classes (see the `johnPerson` variable in this section), and writing logical expressions, which you do throughout the book.

Something to keep in mind about parentheses in Swift is that a single statement is sometimes broken out over multiple lines. For example,

```
var johnPerson: Person = Person(firstName: "John",lastName: "Ray", age: 90)
```

Can also be written as

```
var johnPerson: Person = Person(
                            firstName: "John",
                            lastName: "Ray",
                            age: 90
                        )
```

This can be confusing when you're starting out because although it looks similar to braces, it really is a single line of code. Sometimes code is broken apart like this to improve legibility or keep extremely long lines from wrapping. Just be careful when you're typing examples that you're using braces, not parentheses, for blocks of code.

Laying Out and Populating a SwiftUI Interface

As previously mentioned, everything in your SwiftUI interface—text, images, buttons, and so on—is a View, but how do you get these individual elements onto the screen? The answer is that you define a structure with the `struct` keyword. Each application you build will typically contain at least a single structure for your user interface. By default, Xcode defines an initial interface view called `ContentView`. You can change this name if you want, but unless you *really* object to it, it's easiest to leave it until you're working on larger projects.

```
struct ContentView: View {
}
```

On its own, the structure doesn't do you much good. There's nothing in it. It also looks different than the "Person" structure from earlier. The : View code that occurs after the ContentView name tells Swift that this structure is going to conform to a **Protocol** named View. A protocol isn't anything complicated. Think of it as a template that says, "These are the things that are required to be in your structure." In the case of a structure that conforms to View, you need to have a body variable that contains the views you want to display. For more information on the View protocol, see https://developer.apple.com/documentation/swiftui/view.

To properly conform to the required View protocol, you add the body variable:

```
struct ContentView: View {
    var body: some View {
    }
}
```

This is closer to useful, but it still contains no content. This also looks different from the variable assignments you saw earlier. For one, the Swift keyword some is included before the View type that body will contain. This means that you don't really have to be explicit about what kind of views you're using. Whatever body contains, it's going to be *some* sort of view! The next unusual thing you see is that rather than assigning a value to body, it is defined by a code block {}. The statements within that block of code generate views, and that becomes the content of body.

Do you want to know the best part about this? It *doesn't really matter.* As long as you have the struct and body lines in your code, you can fill them with the good stuff: content!

Back to your SwiftUI code, have a look at the elements that give you something to see:

```
struct ContentView: View {
    var body: some View {
        VStack {
            Text("North")
            Image("Globe")
                .resizable()
                .scaledToFit()
            Text("South")
        }
        .padding()
    }
}
```

The keyword VStack takes a block of code that provides (returns) any number of views and stacks them on top of each other from top to bottom. In addition to VStack, you can also use HStack and ZStack to arrange views horizontally or overlap them on top of one another. For example, assume you have three rectangles you are adding to your interface: A, B, and C. Using a VStack, HStack, and ZStack lays out the rectangles as shown in **FIGURE 2.3**.

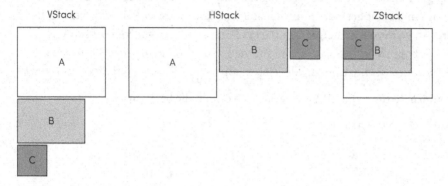

FIGURE 2.3 Using combinations of stacks to create your layout

VStack, HStack, and ZStack can be used within one another to create horizontal stacks inside of vertical stacks inside of layered stacks, and so on. You'll be using these (or at least seeing them) in every single interface you create, so familiarize yourself with them and the layout that each creates.

Understanding SwiftUI Views and Modifiers

Inside the VStack of the example, I first use Text() to add a view displaying the text "North" to the interface, followed by an Image view using a file named Globe and then another text view containing "South." Much like the attributes in HTML, you can add special information, effects, and styles to these views to customize them as needed. In the case of the Image view, I set a modifier .resizable() so that the image can be resized appropriately by the code. I follow that with another modifier .scaleToFit() which resizes the image, keeping the proper proportions so that fits within the interface of whatever device is being used.

> **TIP** Although it might look like .resizable() and .scaleToFit() are just lines of code listed after Image("-Globe"), they aren't. They're part of the same statement, and the order in which they appear is important.
>
> ```
> Image("Globe")
>         .resizable()
>         .scaleToFit()
> ```
>
> Can also be written as
>
> ```
> Image("Globe").resizable().scaleToFit()
> ```
>
> In the single-line format, it may be clearer that the order of these modifiers matters. You need a resizable image, for example, before it can be scaled to fit.

In the sample code, I have one remaining outlier that I haven't explained: the .padding() modifier. This modifier occurs at the end of the VStack block and has a very simple purpose—to add a platform-appropriate amount of padding (a margin) around whatever it is modifying. In this case, it's modifying everything the VStack contains. If I want to add padding to the text or image separately, I could add additional .padding() modifiers after the Text and Image views.

All in all, not too bad! There are some syntax complexities in how code is structured, but following basic patterns is all it takes to get started creating interfaces in 2D and, yes, 3D!

But wait, there's more! Applications do more than just display photos and text to users. They also provide interactivity—all through SwiftUI.

USER INPUT WITH ACTIONS, EVENTS, AND BINDINGS

Most applications allow the user to interact with onscreen controls (or "in your living room controls" on the Apple Vision Pro) through clicks, touches, or gestures. In this section, I review several different mechanisms for retrieving and responding to user input. You can see examples of all the elements by opening the **SwiftUI Playground** Xcode project and selecting the ContentView Swift file. Feel free to play with the example views and modifiers as we dive into adding interactivity to SwiftUI interfaces.

Actions

An **action** occurs when a user interacts with an interface element like a button. When the user activates a button, you probably want to make something happen. Consider the following SwiftUI code that adds a button to the screen:

```
Button(action: {
        //Do Something
    }, label: {
        Text("A Button")
})
```

Here, the Button SwiftUI view does some heavy lifting via action and label **parameters**. The action parameter is used to define a block of Swift code {} that executes when the button is clicked. The label parameter takes a block of views that are then presented as a label on the button, as shown in **FIGURE 2.4**.

If all the braces make you go blurry-eyed, you can also define your action as a function outside of the view you're creating.

FIGURE 2.4 A simple Button view

If you create a function outside of your SwiftUI code like this

```
func doSomething() {
    // We'll write some Swift code here
}
```

The button can then be written as

```
Button(action: doSomething, label: {Text("A Button")})
```

> **TIP** The double forward slashes (//)in Swift code denote a comment. You can type anything you want after adding //, and the system will ignore it. You can use this to document your code or add other information that you might want to reference later.

Unfortunately, Apple hasn't been entirely consistent on how actions are implemented. An interface component in our upcoming project demonstrates this: NavigationStack and NavigationLink. NavigationLink, like a button, can run Swift code when it is activated *and* take the user to a new interface view. You can think of this as being similar to a link on a webpage that takes you to another page. The NavigationLink is always enclosed in a NavigationStack block that groups together all the SwiftUI views you want to be replaced by the new view. Typically, you want the entire interface to be replaced by something new, so NavigationStack wraps around *everything* in the body of your interface view.

For example, here is a simple application that displays a button labeled Go to New View and then displays, well, a new View:

```
struct ContentView: View {
    var body: some View {
        NavigationStack {
            NavigationLink("Go to New View") {
                //Do something here and go to a new screen
                NewView()
            }
        }
    }
}

struct NewView: View {
    var body: some View {
        Text("This is a new View!")
    }
}
```

The "action" performed by interacting with the Go to New View button is whatever Swift code is added to the code block after the `NavigationLink` statement. Also note that the label for the button is just a string. So much for consistency, huh?

The results of this simple `NavigationLink` and action are shown in **FIGURE 2.5**.

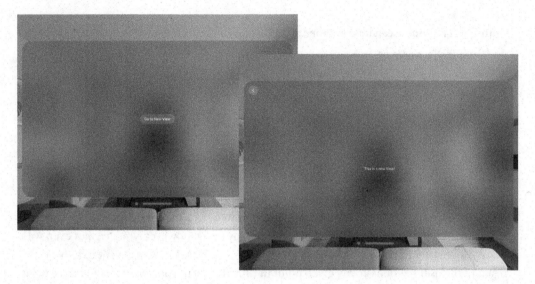

FIGURE 2.5 Navigate from one view…to another

In short, when you interact with something that needs to perform an action, there may be different ways to write the code. I explain how each statement works as we encounter them throughout the book.

Event Modifiers

Another way you can tie interactivity to SwiftUI code is by way of **events**. Events are "things that happen" while a user is interacting with your application. Items appear, disappear, text is added to fields, items are picked from lists, and so on. They are modifiers—like those that I touched on earlier with the Globe image—but with more flexibility. A straightforward example is `.onAppear()` and `.onDisappear()`. These can be added to any SwiftUI view to execute code when something on the screen appears or disappears. For example, if I want to do something when a Text element appears on my screen, I could write:

```
Text("I should do something when I appear...")
    .onAppear() {
        // I'll do this!
    }
```

Similarly, when the text is removed from the screen (such as when navigating to a new view), I might use

```
Text("I should do something when I disappear...")
    .onDisappear() {
        // I'll do this!
    }
```

Both event modifiers can be combined so that code can be executed when the text appears *and* disappears:

```
Text("I should do something when I appear and disappear...")
    .onAppear() {
        // I'll do this!
    }
    .onDisappear() {
        // I'll do this too!
    }
```

There are dozens of event modifiers that you can apply to SwiftUI views. Text fields and toggle buttons might use the `.onChange()` modifier to detect when someone types it into a text field or turns a toggle switch on and off. In many cases, however, you may not even want to pay close attention to when things happen in the interface. You'll just want to know the result of the user's actions at any given point in time. For that, you can use one of the easiest SwiftUI conventions, **Bindings**.

Bindings

Think, for a moment, about text fields, selection lists, toggle switches, and other interface elements that you're accustomed to seeing. How many of these *really* need to do something as soon as the user interacts with them? You can certainly use the `.onChange()` modifier to do this, but most frequently you'll only care about *what* the user has typed or chosen, not *when* they've done it. For this, you can use variable Bindings.

A Binding assigns a variable to a SwiftUI view that collects user input. You can then use that variable, at any time, to access what the user has typed, chosen, and so on.

Let's look at a simple view that defines a variable called `name`, uses a text field to collect the user's name, and then displays the `name`. Sound complicated? It's just three SwiftUI elements (not counting the standard view/body/VStack that accompany almost every interface view):

```
struct ContentView: View {
    @State private var name: String = ""
    var body: some View {
        VStack {
            TextField("Enter your name",text: $name)
```

```
                    .padding(.horizontal,100)
            Text("Your name is \(name)")
        }
        .padding()
    }
}
```

The only lines that should be unfamiliar at this point are the variable definition and the Text-Field. The statement

```
@State private var name: String = ""
```

Creates a new variable called name that is a string and assigned to be empty (""). The @State keyword is required before all variables that are used directly in your SwiftUI interface. This tells SwiftUI that when the variable changes, the interface might need to be updated. The subsequent private keyword limits the **scope** of the variable—where it can be used. Here, it can be accessed by any code within ContentView but nowhere else.

In general, if you're using variables as part of your interface code, you always *need* to add @State and will *want* to add private.

In this example, I bind this variable to the TextField:

```
TextField("Enter your name",text: $name)
    .padding(.horizontal,100)
```

The TextField statement has two parameters: The first sets a message displayed in the background of the field, whereas the second, text:, binds the variable name to whatever the user has typed in the text field. Note that the $ precedes the variable name when creating a binding; you won't need to use it elsewhere when referencing the variable.

In this example, I've added a horizontal padding modifier to the text field to make it appear the way I want on in the interface.

Finally, I can display the name variable to show what the user has typed:

```
Text("Your name is \(name)")
```

Because name is *bound* to the text field, I use it anywhere within the interface, and it will always contain the current contents of TextField—no need to check repeatedly or use complicated code. The results are shown in **FIGURE 2.6**, running in the Vision Pro Simulator.

Bindings are used for many other user interface views, such as Toggle (on/off toggle switches) and Picker (menu) views. Before you can use these views, you need to understand how repetition and conditional statements can be mixed with SwiftUI.

FIGURE 2.6 When `TextField` changes, so does `name`.

Conditionals and Repetition

SwiftUI can react to changes within SwiftUI. Huh?

Simply put, if a user does something in your SwiftUI interface, you can programmatically change your interface to adapt to the changes. You saw this with displaying the contents of a `TextField` while a user was typing. You can also do this with more complex controls. In this section, I go over two specifically: `Toggle` and `Picker`.

A `Toggle` is an on/off switch. You might use a toggle as a setting or perhaps to hide and show a portion of your user interface. Using a variable binding and an `if` statement, it's easy to make a toggle control anything you want! Because you've already seen variable bindings, let's look at the missing piece: the `if` statement:

```
If <condition> {
    //Do something here
}
```

When the code executes, the condition is evaluated, and, if it is `true`, the code block is executed. Conditions frequently compare multiple values for equality or inequality. The `if` statement can also be expanded with `else` to include code that executes if a condition isn't met:

```
If <condition> {
    //Then do something here
} else {
    // Otherwise, do this
}
```

Consider this view that displays a toggle switch and a message when the switch is on:

```
struct ContentView: View {
    @State private var toggleState: Bool = false
    var body: some View {
        VStack {
            Toggle("A Toggle Switch", isOn: $toggleState)
                .padding(.horizontal, 100.0)
            if toggleState {
                Text("Hey, I'm on!")
            }
        }
    }
}
```

First a `toggleState` variable is defined. This a **Boolean** value (`true` or `false`) that tells whether the switch is on or off. It's initially set to false. In other words, the initial state of the toggle is off.

Next the `Toggle` SwiftUI function is used to add a toggle view to the content. The first argument sets a label for the switch, while the second argument `isOn:` is bound to `toggleState`. This means that the variable `toggleState` is `true` when the switch is on and `false` when it isn't.

To react to this change in the interface, an `if` statement is added that evaluates the condition of `toggleState`. Because `toggleState` is true when the switch is on, the text view reading "Hey, I'm on!" is added when the switch is on and removed when the switch is off, as shown in **FIGURE 2.7**. Any number of view elements could be nested in the `if` statement to change the interface dramatically depending on the switch.

FIGURE 2.7 Using the toggle switch to hide or show a view

NOTE In the toggle switch example, I've added horizontal padding to the toggle switch. This is optional and was done purely for aesthetics.

Another technique that you can use to add more functionality to SwiftUI interfaces is repetition via the `ForEach` **loop**. A loop repeats a block of code over and over. When building SwiftUI interfaces, you can use `ForEach` directly in your interface code to repeat elements. Swift supports several different ways to loop, but you're restricted to `ForEach` when interacting with SwiftUI elements.

The two most common forms of the ForEach loops that you'll use are loops over a **range** of numbers and loops that go through a list of data called a **collection**. Let's start with the range.

To loop over a range of numbers, use the format:

```
ForEach(<starting number>..<<ending number+1>) { <count> in
    // Do something with the <counter> here.
}
```

Yes, that is as weird as it looks. You always provide a starting number, two periods, a less-than symbol (<), and a number that is 1 greater than the highest number to which you want to count. The `<count>` in that follows the number range tells SwiftUI that you want each number to be available in whatever variable name you want.

Assume you want to add five copies of a Text view to your interface. You could write `Text ("Here is some text")` five times over, or you could do the same thing with a `ForEach` loop:

```
struct ContentView: View {
    var body: some View {
        VStack {
            ForEach(1..<6) { number in
                Text("Here is some text \(number)");
            }
        }
        .padding()
    }
}
```

In this example, you're counting from 1 to 5 (that is, less than 6), and the variable that holds the current value is `number`. You can get away with not defining a `number` variable in the code because SwiftUI will do that for you in this special case. The end result is five copies of the text, each one also showing a corresponding number from 1 to 5.

The second type of repetition is repetition over a Collection. You use this when you're dealing with different choices that a user must choose among. The `Picker` view, for example, displays a range of different values (words, numbers, and so on) and allows the user to pick one.

The easiest way to use a `Picker` is by defining a collection and using `ForEach` to loop over it. To do that, it might be helpful to know what a Collection *is*. A Collection is a type of variable that holds multiple values. Most commonly, you use an **array** (or "list") variable.

An array is defined like any other variable but is enclosed in square brackets ([])—for example,

```
private var userNames: [String] = ["John","Germain","Simon","Rose"]
```

I first let Swift know that `userNames` is an array of strings by putting the `String` variable type in brackets. You can do this with any variable type to create an array of that type. Next, the array is initialized to four strings—"John", "Germain", "Simon", and "Rose"—all enclosed in the square brackets and separated by commas.

If you want to reference an individual name, you can do so by using its **index**—the number that describes an element's position in the array. (You start with 0 to count the positions.) In this example, John is 0, Germain is 1, Simon is 2, and Rose is 3. To reference the value "Simon", I could type `userNames[2]`, and it would be the same as typing "Simon".

When `ForEach` is used with collections, most commonly it is used with collections that conform to the **Identifiable** protocol. This means that members of the collection each must have a unique ID. This is necessary to ensure that you can identify one choice from among many. It also means that the format for the loop changes. If you have a collection that includes an ID (conforming to the Identifiable protocol), this would just be

```
ForEach(<collection>) { <member> in
    // Do something with each <member> in the <collection>
}
```

You can read more about Identifiable Collections and their use with `ForEach` at https://developer.apple.com/documentation/swiftui/foreach.

For most purposes, I like to try to keep things simple and just provide an ID on the fly for each element in my collections. This approach uses a `ForEach` loop that looks more like this:

```
ForEach(<collection>, id:<unique ID for collection member>) { <member> in
    // Do something with each <member> in the <collection>
}
```

Like the `<counter>` variable used earlier for looping over a range of numbers, looping over a collection provides a variable (`<member>`) that references the current element of the collection that you're looping through.

Suppose you want to present three menu choices to the user:—Yes, No, and Maybe—and enable the user to pick one. You start by creating an array, `pickerChoices`, inside your content view that contains the different options to display:

```
private var pickerChoices: [String] = ["Yes","No","Maybe"]
```

Because these choices are static and don't influence the interface itself, you can get by *without* using `@State`. You do, however, need to provide a binding, `pickerSelection`, that defines the initially selected value and stores any subsequent user updates:

```
@State private var pickerSelection: String = "Maybe"
```

Finally, the `Picker` SwiftUI view is added wherever you want it displayed. It expects an initial label string, followed by a `selection:` parameter that is bound to the variable you chose: `pickerSelection`. A code block follows the `Picker` function. Within the braces, you can manually add your choices or just use a ForEach loop to populate the Picker menu with the content of pickerChoices:

```
Picker("Choose Yes or No", selection: $pickerSelection) {
    ForEach(pickerChoices, id: \.self) { pickerItem in
        Text(pickerItem)
    }
}
```

As previously mentioned, this form of the ForEach loop must conform to a protocol named Identifiable that provides a unique ID for each element in the collection. Instead of dealing with protocols and additional structures, you can just provide the parameter id: with the value \.self. This tells Swift that the unique ID for each choice is the choice itself. The pickerItem in at the start of the loop tells the SwiftUI move through the array and place each item of the array in the pickerItem variable. This can then be used with the SwiftUI Text view to add that view as a selection.

> **TIP** I don't like complexity for the sake of complexity. The preceding ForEach examples have needed some form of <variable> in at the start of the loop code to access what element the loop is currently on. In the numeric Range loop, I used a variable to hold the counter. In this Picker example, the variable held one of the choices in the array. In both cases, however, the <variable> in format can be dropped entirely, and I can simply access the same value as $0.
>
> The loop over the pickerChoices array can be written as
>
> ```
> ForEach(pickerChoices, id: \.self) {
>         Text($0)
> }
> ```
> We'll use this format where possible moving forward.

The value of the Picker can be accessed at any time through the bound variable pickerSelection like this:

```
Text("You've made up your mind and selected \(pickerSelection)!")
```

An example of a Picker is shown in **FIGURE 2.8**.

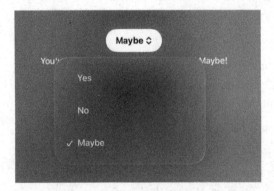

FIGURE 2.8 Pickers provide a means of displaying a list of options to a user.

SIMPLE 3D WITH SWIFTUI

It would be wrong to write an entire chapter about creating for the Apple Vision Pro without anything that's specific for the platform. To that end, let's take a look at how you can add depth to the different SwiftUI views you've already seen. Relax, you've made it through the difficult stuff for the chapter. 3D is gonna be easy!

Changing the Z-Axis Offset (or Making Things Float!)

In Chapter 1, you learned some basics of thinking in 3D for spatial computing. Specifically, you learned that the z-axis controls whether something is closer or further from your viewpoint. The higher the z-value, the closer it is (or it could even be behind you!). The lower the value, the further away.

Would you believe that you can move any element in your SwiftUI interface along the z-axis to make it float in front of your application window or behind it? You should because you can, and it's just a single modifier that makes it happen:

```
.offset(z:<integer>)
```

Adding this modifier to any of your SwiftUI Views makes that element stand out of your application window. In the Globe example, where we started our SwiftUI journey, we displayed two text labels and a photo. Go ahead and reopen the **Globe** project file and add the `offset` modifier to the Globe image. Use an offset of about 20 to 50 points for a nice subtle floating effect.

Oh no, instead of the effect I promised, you see an error message in Xcode, similar to **FIGURE 2.9**. What gives?

```
struct ContentView: View {
    var body: some View {
        VStack {
            Text("North")
            Image("Globe")
                .resizable()
                .scaledToFit()
                .offset(z:50)          ⊘  Incorrect argument label in call (have 'z:', expected 'x:')
            Text("South")
        }
        .padding()
    }
}
```

FIGURE 2.9 When you start using visionOS-specific features, errors may appear based on your other destination platforms.

This delightfully nondescript warning is appearing because we've been working on Xcode projects that support multiple devices, and the Vision Pro is currently the only device that supports real spatial computing. The error occurs because other devices have no idea what an offset on the z-axis even is. To get past this problem, we can use a handy Xcode directive that isolates code that only works on the Vision Pro.

```
#if os(visionOS)
    // Do something special for the Vision Pro
#endif
```

Place the `.offset()` modifier within the `#if` and `#endif` lines like this:

```
struct ContentView: View {
    var body: some View {
        VStack {
            Text("North")
            Image("Globe")
                .resizable()
                .scaledToFit()
            #if os(visionOS)
                .offset(z: 20)
            #endif
            Text("South")
        }
        .padding()
    }
}
```

Now try previewing or running the code. You can get a sense of the depth by looking at it from the sides or top/bottom using the Move Around Content/Orbit Camera control, as shown in **FIGURE 2.10**. Fancy, isn't it? You need to use the special `#if os(visionOS)` statement in applications that work across multiple devices if you intend to add Vision Pro–specific features. For our purposes, we'll be building Vision Pro–*only* apps after this chapter, so you won't be seeing it much later.

Setting an offset on two-dimensional views does give you depth, but different layers of flat objects isn't quite the excitement you've been promised in this book. Full 3D scenes and models are also within your grasp. The SwiftUI view `Model3D` loads and displays a full 3D object in your application, which, in turn, you can navigate around in your Vision Pro headset. just as if it were sitting in your living room (or wherever you happen to be.)

To add models, you first need to tell your project that you're going to be using **RealityKit**. RealityKit, as you might remember, is Apple's augmented reality toolkit for all Apple Devices (https://developer.apple.com/documentation/realitykit/#). To do this, add `import Reality-Kit` to the top of your Swift code file (ContentView.swift):

```
import RealityKit
```

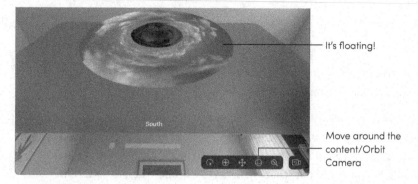

It's floating!

Move around the content/Orbit Camera

FIGURE 2.10 The image now subtly floats above the application interface.

Next, add the `Model3D` SwiftUI view within your interface:

```
Model3D(named: <model name> ) { <model> in
    <model>
        <modifier>
        <modifier>…
} placeholder: {
    ProgressView()
}
```

This SwiftUI view is still in beta and only available on Vision Pro, so you also need to add `#if os(visionOS)` and `#endif` around the Model3D view. Unlike other SwiftUI views, this one is unusual in how you add modifiers. Rather than modifying the Model3D view itself, you must modify the loaded model within the Model3D code block. To access the model, we again provide a variable (this is most frequently seen as `model` in the code you'll encounter but can really be anything you want). Modifiers are then applied to *that* variable within the block. Additionally, the `placeholder:` block defines a view that is presented while the 3D model loads (some complex models may take a few seconds.). The `ProgressView()` function provides a nice spinning wheel, perfect for this purpose. You could substitute other SwiftUI views in place of `ProgressView()`, but why not use the system appropriate view that already exists?

Apple can make some weird looking code. As you experience more of the Swift language, you'll understand that there is reasoning behind some of these unusual looking structures, but rarely is that esoteric knowledge needed to be a successful creator.

As I've said, I like simplification, so, like the `ForEach` example earlier, you can get rid of the `<model>` and just reference the data you want to work with as `$0`:

```
Model3D(named: <model name> ) {
    $0
        <modifier>
        <modifier>…
```

```
} placeholder: {
    ProgressView()
}
```

I'm not going to show you what that looks like just yet because you're about to start working through a project from scratch that includes a 3D object.

Before you begin the hands-on exercise, I'd like to acknowledge an elephant in the room. There are so many different SwiftUI views that you can use in your applications that it's absolutely impossible to describe them all in a chapter. The good news is that there are plenty of resources available to help you figure out what elements to use and when to use them.

SWIFTUI INTERFACE TOOLS AND REFERENCES

Now that you understand more about SwiftUI and how an interface is defined, let's look at how you can explore the different elements that can be used to make your interfaces, what modifiers are available, and what tools you can use to make all of this easier. There are literally dozens of interface elements, dozens of modifiers, and millions of ways that they can be put together. Clearly, I don't have a million pages in this book. Instead, Xcode can provide some assistance, and a few external apps and websites provide even more.

Finding and Setting Modifiers in Xcode

Open the **SwiftUI Playground** project included with this chapter. Make sure that the Project Navigator is showing and the ContentView Swift file is selected in the Navigator. Select Apple Vision Pro or a platform of your choosing from the Preview Device menu in the bottom corner of the Preview pane. Verify that the Inspectors pane is open and the Attributes inspector is selected. Your workspace should look similar to **FIGURE 2.11**.

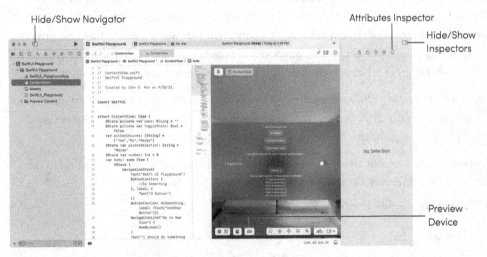

FIGURE 2.11 Xcode can assist in finding the perfect modifier for your views.

The Attributes Inspector will be your best friend as you try to determine what modifiers can be set for a given SwiftUI view. To see how this works, click on a SwiftUI interface view from the code; the line `Text("Swift UI Playground")` is a good choice. The Attributes Inspector refreshes to show common modifiers for the Text view. You can add accessibility information, set the font, set padding around the object, as well as the **frame**. The frame defines the width and height of the view, in case you want to manually set the amount of space something will occupy in your interface.

Using the fields, menus, and buttons in the inspector, you can add and customize modifiers directly in your code. The font selection, for example, gives you the ability to choose from different uses for a Text view—such as Title, Body, Caption, and so on—and automatically sets the right font style for that use. Setting Font to Title, as shown in **FIGURE 2.12**, automatically adds a `.font()` modifier to the view:

```
Text("Swift UI Playground")
    .font(.title)
```

FIGURE 2.12 Using the menus in the Attributes Inspector to add and update modifiers

The available modifiers go far beyond what you initially see in the inspector. Within the code, click on any view that is visible in the preview or just keep working with the Text view. Now, click the Add Modifier field at the bottom of the Attributes Inspector. After a second or two, a huge list of potential modifiers should appear. Scroll down to Effects and choose Blur, as shown in **FIGURE 2.13**.

When you choose Blur, a new modifier is added to your code (`.blur()`) and the Attributes Inspector refreshes to show a new Blur section (see **FIGURE 2.14**) where you can adjust the radius of the blur effect (how much "blurriness" is applied to your SwiftUI view).

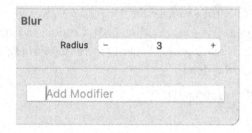

FIGURE 2.13 Adding visual effects to your SwiftUI views

FIGURE 2.14 New modifiers add new controls to the Attributes Inspector.

At the same time, your preview will update to show the effects of the modifier. In this case, as you might expect, one of our interface elements is quite blurry (**FIGURE 2.15**). Although this might not be the effect you'd really want on a piece of text, there are dozens more to explore through the Attributes Inspector.

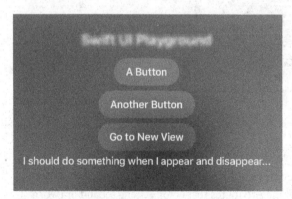

FIGURE 2.15 A Blur modifier may not be the best choice for your Text views.

SwiftUI References

One of the difficulties about writing about SwiftUI is that it is constantly evolving. New views and modifiers are added on an ongoing basis, and existing views and modifiers are updated with new features.

The best resource for up-to-date information on SwiftUI is, of course, Apple. I highly recommend reviewing Apple's four-plus hours of online training for SwiftUI, located at https://developer.apple.com/tutorials/SwiftUI#app-design-and-layout.

If you feel like you have a good handle on the basics, jump directly into the official documentation at https://developer.apple.com/documentation/swiftui/, which will expose you to *all* the views available in SwiftUI and provide code samples to help understand their use.

Another great source for SwiftUI information, albeit not as up to date as Apple's documentation, is Gosh Darn SwiftUI at https://goshdarnswiftui.com. This is the work-friendly version of the site title and URL, I'll leave it as an exercise to the reader to discover the official site and URL, although the work-friendly version has the exact same information.

For those wishing for a great reference app to use alongside Xcode, A Companion for SwiftUI (https://apps.apple.com/us/app/a-companion-for-swiftui/id1485436674?mt=12), which is shown in **FIGURE 2.16**, is a top-notch application that includes references for *all* SwiftUI in a well-designed and searchable Mac application. It's updated almost immediately when Apple introduces changes to SwiftUI.

At the time of this writing, the app does not yet have visionOS-specific SwiftUI information, but it is still invaluable for learning SwiftUI. I have no doubt it will be expanded to cover the new OS. There is a cost associated with the application, but for such a complete and growing reference, it's worth it.

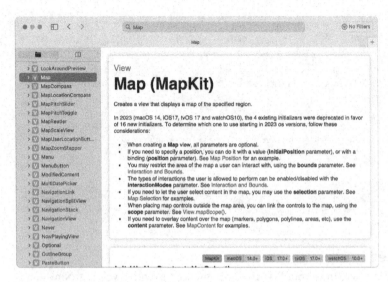

FIGURE 2.16 A Companion for SwiftUI can help you quickly find the views you want.

SwiftUI Interface Tools

At the start of this chapter, I mentioned that developers (including me) used to use Xcode Storyboards to build interfaces visually. Unfortunately, Apple has not made such a tool available for SwiftUI, but enterprising developers *have*.

If pointing and clicking is more appealing than typing, a great place to start is DetailsPro, which is shown in **FIGURE 2.17**. It enables you to build your interfaces visually and then simply export the SwiftUI view code directly for use in Xcode. It's an excellent playground for learning SwiftUI and the code that makes it work. You can download a free version to get your feet wet at https://apps.apple.com/us/app/detailspro/id1524366536.

You may also want to consider Judo: Design and Build Apps, another no-code interface-building solution for SwiftUI interfaces that can export SwiftUI code into Xcode. Judo, shown in **FIGURE 2.18**, focuses on designers who want to create as much functionality as possible without writing code. This is a great app for getting an interface polished and ready without touching Xcode. As with DetailsPro, there is no visionOS support at present, but this should change shortly. Download a free version of Judo from the Mac App Store at https://apps.apple.com/us/app/detailspro/id1524366536.

At this point, you should have the knowledge and tools to build a simple application from scratch. Let's round out this introduction to SwiftUI with your first project!

FIGURE 2.17 DetailsPro is an excellent tool for learning SwiftUI and building application interfaces.

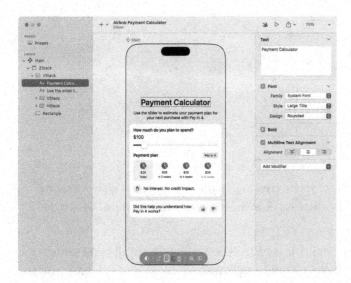

FIGURE 2.18 Judo focuses on providing a codeless app design experience for creatives.

HANDS ON: EARTH DAY QUIZ

Typical programming tutorials start out with "Hello World!" being displayed on a device screen. Apple, however, writes that same code *for* you each time you make a new project! To keep with the "world/planet" theme, I started this chapter with the Globe Xcode project—looking at a simple SwiftUI interface that displayed two Text views and an image of a tiny planet. The hands-on project—Earth Day—continues the trend. Earth Day is a simple application that quizzes the user about which day in April is Earth Day. The project incorporates three-dimensional aspects to create your first true "experience" on the Apple Vision Pro. And, if you're feeling adventurous, you'll even get to add a tad bit of animation!

Creating the Project

To get started, open Xcode. When prompted, click Create New Project, as shown in **FIGURE 2.19**. If you're already in Xcode (good for you!), just choose New, Project from the File menu.

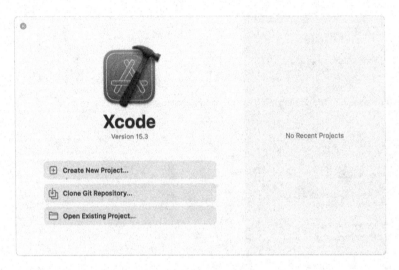

FIGURE 2.19 Creating a new project

Xcode asks you what type of project you're creating. In this lesson, you're going to create something that runs almost everywhere, so choose Multiplatform and App and then click Next, as shown in **FIGURE 2.20**.

Enter **Earth Day** as the Product name. Uncheck Include Tests and leave all other settings with their defaults. **FIGURE 2.21** shows what it looks like for my account. If you don't have any information showing up, be sure to read Chapter 1 to learn more about setting up Xcode. Click Next.

Choose a template for your new project:
Multiplatform
iOS
macOS
watchOS
tvOS
visionOS
DriverKit
Other
Filter
Application
App
Document App
Game
Safari Extension App
Framework & Library
Framework
Cancel
Previous
Next

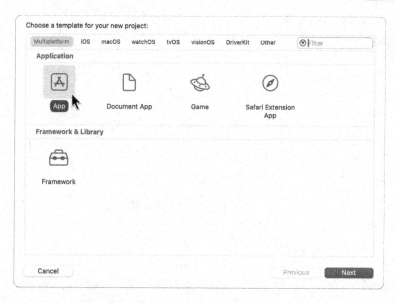

FIGURE 2.20 Setting the type of application you will be building

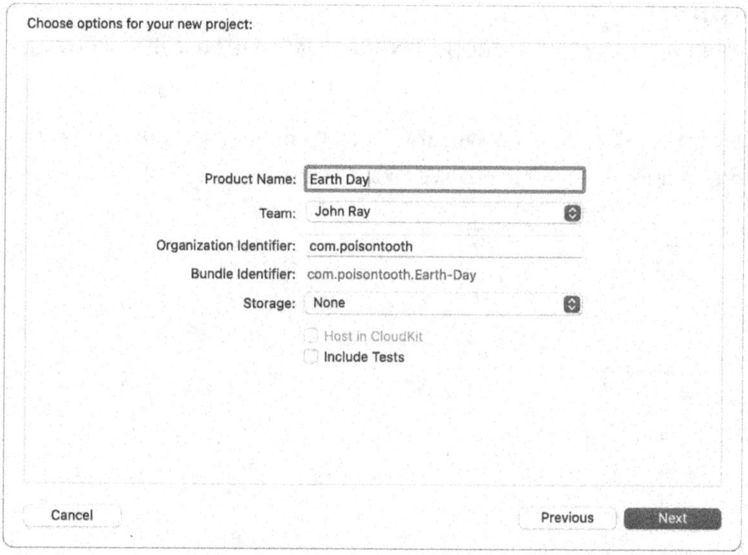

Choose options for your new project:
Product Name: Earth Day
Team: John Ray
Organization Identifier: com.poisontooth
Bundle Identifier: com.poisontooth.Earth-Day
Storage: None
Host in CloudKit
Include Tests
Cancel
Previous
Next

FIGURE 2.21 Entering the product name and turning off Include Tests

Choose where to save the project and uncheck Create Git Repository on My Mac. Finally, Click Create, as shown in **FIGURE 2.22**.

FIGURE 2.22 Choosing a location to save your project and turn off Git support

Adding visionOS Support

Congratulations! You've created your very first Xcode project (that's going to be truly your own). Before you can start building, you need to add visionOS as a supported destination platform.

Click the top level Earth Day line in the Project Navigator. Click General in the tabs that appear to the right. Your screen should resemble **FIGURE 2.23**.

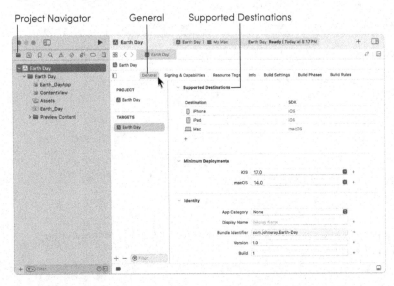

FIGURE 2.23 Navigating to the Supported Destinations settings

Within the Supported Destinations section, click the plus button at the bottom of the list of platforms (note that visionOS is *not* one of the defaults), as shown in **FIGURE 2.24**.

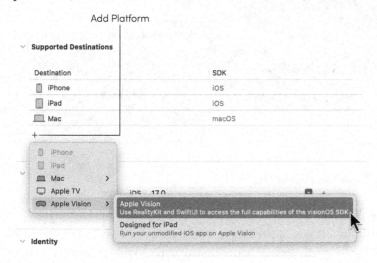

FIGURE 2.24 Adding a new destination platform to your project

Choose Apple Vision Pro to enable full visionOS features in your application. If you find yourself just trying to get an iPad application working on the Vision Pro, you can just click Designed for iPad to be up and running in minutes.

After adding Apple Vision Pro support, you'll be prompted to Enable Destination Support. Click Enable and you're ready to code the project!

In this exercise, you create three separate views. The main ContentView prompts the user to pick the day in April on which Earth Day falls. Once the user selects a day, they click a button to check their answer. If the answer is correct, the congratulatory CorrectView is shown. If not, you let them know that they're not very Earth friendly by displaying IncorrectView. The three views used in the app are shown in **FIGURE 2.25**.

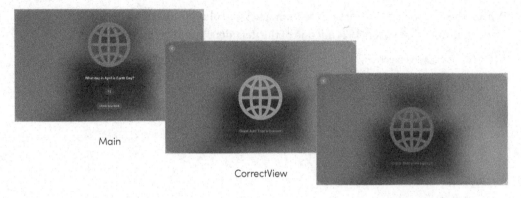

Main

CorrectView

IncorrectView

FIGURE 2.25 Our application consists of three interface views.

Creating the Three Views

The first step in building the project is to create the basis for the three views. You do your coding in the ContentView Swift file, so first you'd better get rid of the sample code Apple adds to each project. Within Xcode, select the ContentView file in the Project Navigator. Wait a few seconds and, when the preview of Apple's "Hello World" template shows up, change the preview device to Apple Vision Pro. Your screen should be similar to **FIGURE 2.26**.

Project Navigator

ContentView

Preview Device

FIGURE 2.26 Your starting workspace should look like this.

TIP I've encountered some issues with the preview never appearing despite no errors being displayed. If this happens, try running the application in the full Simulator, stop the application, and (tada!) the Preview functions again. Annoying, but it works, and the problem isn't an everyday occurrence.

Now remove Apple's default code from the `ContentView` definition. You can remove everything inside the VStack. There's no point in deleting the basic structures that you're going to need!

Next, add two new views below the `ContentView` definition. One should be named **Correct-View** and the other **IncorrectView**. Your entire ContentView Swift file should now look like **LISTING 2.1.**

LISTING 2.1 Three Empty Views, Waiting for Content

```swift
import SwiftUI

struct ContentView: View {
    var body: some View {
        VStack {
        }
        .padding()
    }
}

struct IncorrectView: View {
    var body: some View {
        VStack {
        }
        .padding()
    }
}

struct CorrectView: View {
    var body: some View {
        VStack {
        }
        .padding()
    }
}

#Preview {
    ContentView()
}
```

This is the structure for your entire application. Next, you add some content to your views. Refer to Figure 2.25 to see that each of the three views has a simple globe graphic with some text underneath it. The graphic is a built-in system image named globe, and can be displayed with

```swift
Image(systemName: "globe")
```

Unfortunately, if we use the system image as is, it's going to show up as a tiny symbol in the interface. We need some modifiers to make it visible and to style it. Start by changing its size. To do this, you need three modifiers: .resizeable(), .scaledToFit(), and .frame(). The first two tell SwiftUI that the image should be resizable and that when it resizes, it should keep the same proportions. The .frame() modifier lets you set a size for the image, which you do with the width: parameter. I'm going to use 300 points for my size; you can test other sizes if you'd like.

```
Image(systemName: "globe")
    .resizable()
    .scaledToFit()
    .frame(width: 300.0)
```

Add the Image view as the first element to *each* of the three different views. You should see the preview refresh to show a nicely sized globe illustration, as shown in **FIGURE 2.27**.

TIP At the end of your ContentView Swift file, you'll notice a function labeled #Preview with ContentView() as the only line. This is yet another view that determines what is displayed in the Xcode preview. To show your incorrect or correct views—that is, IncorrectView() or CorrectView()—just substitute them for ContentView. You can even add another SwiftUI element like VStack, place all your views inside the VStack code block and see everything at once!

For some variation, I want to change the color of the globe image so that it is unique in each of the views: gray in the main view, red in the incorrect view, and green in the correct view. To do this, I add another modifier: .foregroundStyle(<color>). Add this to your three Images now. The resulting code for ContentView's Image should look like this:

```
Image(systemName: "globe")
    .resizable()
    .scaledToFit()
    .frame(width: 300.0)
    .foregroundStyle(.gray)
```

Use .red and .green for the Image in IncorrectView and CorrectView, respectively. Alternatively, you can click on the Image in your code and use the Attributes Inspector to set the Style Color modifier, as shown in **FIGURE 2.28**.

The next component in the interface is text. Each of the three views has a line of text underneath the image. In the ContentView, this text is the question What day in April is Earth Day?; in CorrectView, the text states Good Job! That's Correct!; and in IncorrectView, the text is Oops! That's not correct! You can feel free to change these to whatever messages your heart desires. You want the text to stand out, so use the .font() modifier to set the text to an appropriate title font.

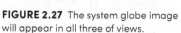

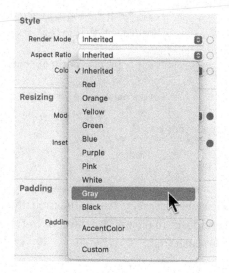

FIGURE 2.27 The system globe image will appear in all three of views.

FIGURE 2.28 Adding a color to each of the three globe images used throughout the interface

Add the Text view after the image in `ContentView`:

```
Text("What day in April is Earth Day?")
    .font(.title)
```

In my project, I've also chosen to set the `.foregroundStyle()` of the text to the same color as the globe in `IncorrectView` and `CorrectView` (red and green, respectively.) Again, you can carry out these actions by typing the `.font()` and `.foregroundStyle()` modifiers directly or using the Attributes Inspector in Xcode.

When you have the image and text in the interface, take another look at the preview. When doing this while writing the project, I decided that the globe and the text are just too close together. To fix this, I *could* add a `.padding()` modifier for each element, or I can provide a `spacing:` parameter to VStack that sets a consistent space between each element. Normally VStack is written alone, but it can also be written as a function with parameters. In this case, use `spacing: 50.0` as a parameter in each view to add 50 points of space between stacked views. For example, my `IncorrectView` code looks like this:

```
struct IncorrectView: View {
    var body: some View {
        VStack(spacing: 50.0) {

            Image(systemName: "globe")
                .resizable()
                .scaledToFit()
```

```
                .frame(width: 300.0)
                .foregroundStyle(.red)

            Text("Oops! That's not correct!")
                .font(.title)
                .foregroundStyle(.red)
        }
        .padding()
    }
}
```

The other views should be very similar, with just a variation in colors and text. Both your CorrectView and IncorrectView are functionally complete and can serve their purpose of providing feedback to the user. At the end, you'll add some tweaks, but first you need to make the app DO something!

User Input Elements

For Earth Day to be a functional application, it needs logic to be added. The user chooses a date in April, clicks a Check Your Work button, and then is sent to either CorrectView or IncorrectView as appropriate. (Earth Day is April 22, by the way.). You provide this interactivity by adding a Picker element with date options between 1 and 30 and a NavigationLink button to ContentView.

Recall that to use a picker, you need to first define an array of choices and a variable that will be bound to the user's selection. Add the following two lines to the top of your ContentView, before the var body line:

```
@State private var selectedDay = "1"
private var dateChoices = ["1","2","3","4","5","6","7","8","9","10","11","12","13","14","15","16","17","18","19","20","21","22","23","24","25","26","27","28","29","30"]
```

Notice that I've dropped the long/explicit form of the variable definitions (no : String or : [String] to explicitly state the variable types of String or an array of Strings). Although it's important to know what is going on when a variable is defined, this isn't rocket science, and we can still tell what's what when using the shorter form of variable definition.

> **NOTE** You might be wondering why all the numbers are in quotes. Doesn't this mean we're using strings instead of numbers? Wouldn't numbers be easier? Yes, we're using strings to store the days of the month, and no, numbers wouldn't be easier. Strings give us more flexibility. We can choose to write the first of the month as "1st" and the code stays the same. If we define the choices as numbers, we also need to convert numbers to strings because the Picker wants Text views to make up its choices. It's not that difficult, and it's certainly doable, but for this exercise, strings are just easier.

Add the `Picker` view after the `Text` view in `ContentView`:

```
Picker("Select a Day",selection: $selectedDay) {
    ForEach(dateChoices, id: \.self) {
        Text($0)
    }
}
```

We provide the picker with a prompt and a binding to `selectedDay`. We then populate the choices with the `ForEach` loop, iterating over the `dateChoices` array and adding each array element ($0) as a `Text` view to the picker. If this syntax looks confusing, remember that $0 is a simplified way of referencing the current item in a `ForEach` loop. Review "Conditionals and Repetition" earlier in this chapter for a refresher. **LISTING 2.2** shows the "almost complete" ContentView code.

LISTING 2.2 Complete User Interface

```
struct ContentView: View {
    @State private var selectedDay = "1"
    private var dateChoices = ["1","2","3","4","5","6","7","8","9",
                               "10","11","12","13","14","15","16",
                               "17","18","19","20","21","22","23",
                               "24","25","26","27","28","29","30"]
    var body: some View {
        NavigationStack {
            VStack(spacing: 50.0) {

                Image(systemName: "globe")
                    .resizable()
                    .scaledToFit()
                    .frame(width: 300.0)
                    .foregroundStyle(.gray)

                Text("What day in April is Earth Day?")
                    .font(.title)

                Picker("Select a Day",selection: $selectedDay) {
                    ForEach(dateChoices, id: \.self) {
                        Text($0)
                    }
                }
            }
            .padding()
        }
    }
}
```

The Preview for the application should now look like **FIGURE 2.29**. You should also be able to interact with the view and display the dates in the picker.

> **TIP** When interacting with the Apple Vision Pro Simulator or the Preview, make sure you select the Interact with Content control rather than a camera control; otherwise, you're going to be clicking and nothing will happen!

FIGURE 2.29 You've added everything you needed for interaction with your users!

One last hurdle, providing the logic that checks the selection made in the picker and, if it is 22, takes the user to the CorrectView, or, if not, displays IncorrectView instead. You accomplish this with a NavigationStack and a NavigationLink. Recall that the NavigationStack wraps around all the views in the interface that you want to "go away" when you navigate to IncorrectView or CorrectView. In other words, the entirety of ContentView. Add a NavigationStack block {} around the VStack block in ContentView.

This change doesn't alter anything in the Preview. It just gives you the ability to add a NavigationLink button (labeled Check Your Work) that does all the remaining processing.

Update ContentView yet again by adding a NavigationLink after the Picker view:

```
NavigationLink("Check Your Work") {
    if (selectedDay=="22") {
        CorrectView()
    } else {
        IncorrectView()
    }
}
```

The first parameter to the NavigationLink defines the label on the button (Check Your Work). Then, within the code block for the NavigationLink, you use the entirety of the Vision Pro's processing power (joking!) to check whether the variable bound to selectedDay is equal (==) to the string value "22". If it is, you load CorrectView(); otherwise, you load IncorrectView().

That's it. You now have a perfectly functional application, ready to run on your Vision Pro, Mac, iPad, or iPhone. The final code listing of ContentView should be similar to mine, shown in **LISTING 2.3.**

LISTING 2.3 The Final Code for ContentView

```swift
struct ContentView: View {
    @State private var selectedDay = "1"
    private var dateChoices = ["1","2","3","4","5","6","7","8","9",
                               "10","11","12","13","14","15","16",
                               "17","18","19","20","21","22","23",
                               "24","25","26","27","28","29","30"]
    var body: some View {
        NavigationStack {
            VStack(spacing: 50.0) {

                Image(systemName: "globe")
                    .resizable()
                    .scaledToFit()
                    .frame(width: 300.0)
                    .foregroundStyle(.gray)

                Text("What day in April is Earth Day?")
                    .font(.title)

                Picker("Select a Day",selection: $selectedDay) {
                    ForEach(dateChoices, id: \.self) {
                        Text($0)
                    }
                }

                NavigationLink("Check Your Work") {
                    if (selectedDay=="22") {
                        CorrectView()
                    } else {
                        IncorrectView()
                    }
                }
            }
            .padding()
```

```
            }
         }
      }
```

Making It Spatial

You have a functional application, but who wants *functional* when they can have *pizzazz*! (We all do, by the way.) Using the `.offset()` modifier and `Model3D` view, we can quickly add some spatial computing elements to the application that bring it to the next level.

As we learned earlier, to use some of the nifty visionOS features, you need to add support to the code for RealityKit, using the statement `import RealityKit`. Add this to the top of the ContentView Swift file, after the line `import SwiftUI`.

Next, view the code for `IncorrectView` and `CorrectView`. Add the modifier `.offset()` to set a z depth of 200 for each Image. This gives the globe images in both views a nice "floating" effect. Remember that this modifier works only on visionOS, so you need to add a check to make sure the platform the user is running it on *is* visionOS.

```
#if os(visionOS)
    .offset(z:200)
#endif
```

Try the application again in the Simulator or the preview pane. When you reach a correct or incorrect answer, use the Move Around the Content tool (or Orbit Camera in the Simulator) to move the camera to the side of the view. You should be able to see the globe illustration lifted off the application window, as shown in **FIGURE 2.30**.

> **TIP** If Xcode doesn't launch the Simulator correctly, review the section "Using the Simulator Directly" in Chapter 1.

You could stop here. You have a legitimate application up and running on your Apple Vision Pro! But wait... there's one more thing (maybe two)! When a user gets a correct answer, you can do something more special, such as display a 3D model that the user can approach, walk around, and look at from any angle.

First, you need a model. I've provided a universal scene description file named Earth_Day.usdz in the Chapter 2 folder for this purpose. This Earth Day image was created by Chaitanya Krishnan and can be previewed at https://skfb.ly/Nvpx (see **FIGURE 2.31**). (This is a shortcut to an ugly URL at sketchfab.com, a reliable source for 3D models—paid and free—for your projects.)

To use the model in Xcode, add it to your project. Drag the icon for Earth Day.usdz from the Finder into the Project Navigator, just under the ContentView file, as shown in **FIGURE 2.32**.

Move Around the
Content/Orbit Camera

FIGURE 2.30 The globe image now floats in front of the main application interface.

FIGURE 2.31 Previewing the project model

FIGURE 2.32 Adding the 3D model to your project

When prompted for options, verify that Copy Items if Needed is selected and then click Finish, as shown in **FIGURE 2.33**.

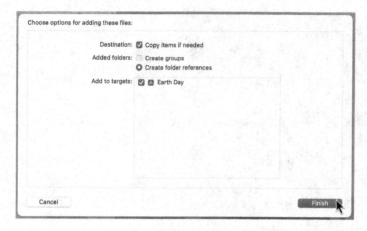

FIGURE 2.33 Make sure Copy Items if Needed is selected.

You now see an Earth_Day file in the Project Navigator. Clicking the file name shows a preview of the model, as shown in **FIGURE 2.34**.

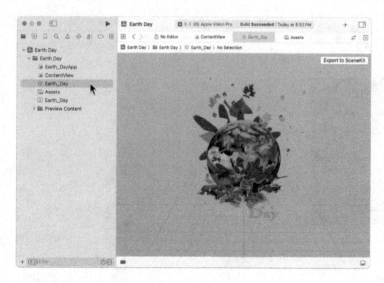

FIGURE 2.34 Previewing the model in Xcode

Now that the model is available to the project, you can use it with the Model3D SwiftUI view. This, however, is gonna be tricky because you want to show the 3D model when you're running on visionOS and the globe image on everything else. You need to lean on the #if os(visionOS) directive to make it work. Update your CorrectView to include the model, as shown in **LISTING 2.4**.

LISTING 2.4 Add Code to CorrectView to Display the 3D Model

```
struct CorrectView: View {
    var body: some View {
        VStack(spacing: 50.0) {

            #if os(visionOS)
                Model3D(named: "Earth_Day") {
                    $0
                        .resizable()
                        .scaledToFit()
                } placeholder: {
                    ProgressView()
                }
            #else
                Image(systemName: "globe")
                    .resizable()
                    .scaledToFit()
                    .frame(width: 300.0)
                    .foregroundStyle(.green)
                #if os(visionOS)
                    .offset(z:200)
                #endif
            #endif

            Text("Good Job! That's Correct!")
                .font(.title)
                .foregroundStyle(.green)
        }
        .padding()
    }
}
```

The Model3D view is added by referencing the file we added to the project ("Earth_Day") in the named: parameter. Note that file extensions aren't necessary when a resource is added directly to your application. Model3D, as discussed in "Adding a 3D Model" earlier in this chapter., requires you to use modifiers differently, so please refer to that section if this seems foreign to you. You want to make sure the model has .resizable() and .scaledToFit() modifiers so that it scales correctly in your interface. You use #if os(visionOS) to make sure that the model is only displayed on visionOS, and all other operations systems show the boring system globe image.

Preview your application one more time, using the Move Around the Content (Orbit Camera) control to look from the side. Load and run it on your Vision Pro, if possible. You now have a very lovely 3D scene floating in your living room, as shown in FIGURE 2.35.

FIGURE 2.35 Oooh! A nifty 3D model in the living room.

We could call it quits here, but I'd like to provide one more piece of code that will make your model even more interesting to the user.

One More Thing... Animation

I'm not going to delve deeply into animation at this time, but I thought I'd give you a little extra credit exercise for the application. SwiftUI provides a modifier for any SwiftUI view named .rotation3DEffect() that, when applied to a model, rotates it a specified number of degrees around X, Y, or Z axes. Unfortunately, it does this once, meaning that to get an animation effect, you need to update this modifier repeatedly to advance the animation step by step. You will do this via a Timer, which executes a block of code in the background a set number of times or continuously.

You need two new variables added to the CorrectView: one to hold the number of degrees of rotation (rotation) and one that holds the Timer (rotationTimer). Add these lines at the very top of CorrectView (before var body):

```
@State private var rotation: Angle = .zero
@State private var rotationTimer: Timer!
```

Angle is a new complex variable type that includes a property called degrees that you use in the .rotation3DEffect() modifier. You initialize rotation to .zero—0 degrees of rotation.

rotationTimer is declared to be a variable of type Timer. The exclamation point at the end signifies that you're aware you haven't yet set an initial value for rotationTimer and that you acknowledge that if you try to use it before it is initialized, there may be problems. (Swift refers to this as **explicitly unwrapping** the variable, giving you the freedom to set up the variable without setting it to any value.)

On to the animation itself. Surprisingly, all the magic is going to happen with two modifiers: `.rotation3DEffect()` and `.onAppear()`. The first provides the rotation effect on the model, whereas the second modifier lets you write Swift code that is executed when the object appears on the screen. Update the `Model3D` code in `CorrectView` to read as

```
Model3D(named: "Earth_Day") { model in
    model
        .resizable()
        .scaledToFit()
        .rotation3DEffect(rotation, axis: .y)
        .onAppear() {
            rotationTimer = Timer.scheduledTimer(withTimeInterval: 0.01,
                            repeats: true) { timer in
                rotation.degrees=rotation.degrees+1
                if (rotation.degrees>=360) {
                    rotationTimer.invalidate()
                }
            }
        }
} placeholder: {
    ProgressView()
}
```

The `.rotation3DEffect()` modifier takes the `rotation` angle variable as the first argument, and the axis around which we're rotating (.y) as the second. In the `.onAppear()` modifier's code block, you start a timer that executes every hundredth of a second (`withTimeInverval: 0.01`) and repeats indefinitely (`repeats: true`). Timer has its own code block that increments `rotation.degrees` by one each time it "fires." The code also checks the current degree property within `rotationTimer` and, if it has rotated a full 360 degrees, you call `<timer variable>.invalidate()` to disable the timer and stop the animation—that is, `rotationTimer.invalidate()`.

Timers are a powerful tool that can come in handy any time you want to do something over and over in the background of your application. You can learn more about timers at https://developer.apple.com/documentation/foundation/timer. There are other ways you'll animate objects in visionOS, but I wanted to give you a taste of how easy it can be to apply a single effect modifier over and over and end up with an animated scene.

Congratulations! You've made it through your first hands-on exercise. Review your app in the Simulator, preview pane, or on your Vision Pro. Now, when you get the correct answer, not only do you see the 3D Earth Day model, but it spins in front of your eyes!

SUMMARY

In this chapter, I introduced you to the structure of SwiftUI interface views, the many component views that make them up, and the modifiers that can be applied to style them in myriad ways. You've also learned about reacting to common user input elements, such as toggle switches, text fields, and pickers. All of this can be daunting, but it's your first attempt at writing in SwiftUI.

It takes time to get used to Apple's new interface paradigm, but with practice it will seem like second nature. Frankly, I'd rather be writing my interfaces in SwiftUI and Swift than dealing with the nightmare that is modern HTML, CSS, and JavaScript. Just think, in one chapter you've (potentially) gone from never having written an application for an Apple system to having one up and running on all of Apple's flagship platforms, including the Apple Vision Pro! That's quite an achievement.

Go Further

We've barely scratched the surface of the different interfaces you can build in SwiftUI. I strongly encourage you to review the resources provided, especially Apple's Swift and SwiftUI documentation at https://docs.swift.org/swift-book/documentation/the-swift-programming-language/ and https://developer.apple.com/documentation/swiftui/.

A great tool for learning SwiftUI views and structures is Swift Playgrounds. This programming "sandbox" walks you through coding tutorials where you can practice your SwiftUI and Swift skills in fun game-like exercises. The software is available for macOS and iPad OS at https://developer.apple.com/swift-playgrounds/. You can even write code from scratch and export your creations into Xcode—a great way to work on interfaces and code on the go.

Above all, you should be playing in Xcode, testing the different SwiftUI views that we've been using, and exploring the many different modifiers that can be applied to each. For fun, go back to the Earth Day example and update it so the globe rotates 360 degrees on all axes. Or change it so the 3D model spins forever. You can even add animation to the original Globe project by slowly increasing the z offset on the image so that it appears to come toward the user.

This is the right time to make mistakes and experiment. I move through material in future chapters more quickly now that the basics are behind us.

CHAPTER 3

Getting Started with Reality Composer Pro

When I think about augmented reality and virtual reality, I think of being able to interact with objects that don't exist within an environment that may or may not exist. There is a sense of wonder with being able to go to new places or see things that you will never see in person. As a creator, you get to build these worlds and objects and share your creativity and vision with others.

Even if you don't consider yourself a "creative type," chances are, you use your phone or camera to record moments in time for yourself or others. We're all creators and consumers—even if we don't want to admit it. In Chapter 2, "From Traditional Applications to Spatial Workspaces with SwiftUI," I talk about the basics of SwiftUI, and you coded your first Apple Vision Pro application, complete with a 3D model. Unfortunately, the exercise didn't give you much opportunity to color outside the lines. What fun is that?

This chapter introduces a new application, Reality Composer Pro, to your development toolkit. Reality Composer Pro gives you a playground for experimenting and compositing 3D objects—even previewing them on the Vision Pro—without writing a single line of code. Of course, I'm not going to let you get away that easily. This chapter also gets into some new code for window management and presentation.

By the end of this chapter, you'll understand

- **Reality Composer Pro:** A tool for creating three-dimensional scenes that can be included in your applications. This tool will become a starting point for many of your future creations.

- **RealityKit, Scenes, and Entities:** I introduce the concept of scenes and entities—alternatives to adding 3D models as you did in Chapter 2—and then show you how to manipulate them in code via RealityKit.

- **Volumes (volumetric windows):** Windows are typically used to display 2D content, but what about a volumetric window? Learn more about window control and how volumetric windows offer similar features to a traditional window—but in 3D space.

- **Managing Multiple Views:** The ol' ContentView is going to get some company. We'll explore how multiple views can be added and used within an application.

- **Data Sharing:** The more complicated the application, the more likely data used in one component will be needed in another. Review approaches for sharing application data across different views.

In writing the samples used in these chapters, I frequently found myself saying, "Well, wouldn't it be cool if it also did *this*?" You should be able to start having those conversations with yourself after this chapter. You still have a long journey ahead of you, but the pieces will start falling into place.

> **NOTE** Make sure that you've downloaded the Chapter 3 project files from https://visionproforcreators.com/files/ or www.peachpit.com/visionpro before continuing.

INTRODUCING REALITY COMPOSER PRO

Reality Composer Pro—what does it do? Despite the name, the application does very little with *reality*. Instead, it lets you compose 3D scenes that you can bring into your Apple Vision Pro reality using RealityKit. (It's almost like the word "virtual" should be thrown in there somewhere, but I digress.

You'll use Reality Composer Pro whenever you want to take a 3D object and make it available to your project. It can be a single primitive shape, like a sphere, or a complicated compilation of dozens of models. You might be saying, "But wait, John! I added a 3D model to my project in the last chapter by dragging it into the Project Manager in Xcode." Although that works, Reality Composer Pro also offers the benefit of taking your assets and compiling them into a format that is quicker to load and more efficient than raw 3D file formats.

Reality Composer Pro even lets you set objects up for animation, alter their materials, design new materials, position sounds in 3D space, and more. I cover these advanced functions in more detail in later chapters, but you'll learn (and use) the core features now.

A COLLISION COURSE IN TERMINOLOGY

Throughout this chapter, I use the words *scene* and *entity* repeatedly. It's important to understand upfront that depending on the context, these words can mean different things.

In Swift, a scene is anything you've displayed on the screen with SwiftUI. That can include a RealityKit scene—which itself is a 3D scene. Two different uses for two different concepts.

Entities, on the other hand, refer to something that can be a part of a 3D scene. In a scene with a car parked in a garage, the car and the garage might be individual entities. The entities themselves might be made of other entities, like the car being made up of a body, wheels, and decorations. If you don't care about the car and garage being independent of one another, you can consider the combination of the two to be an entity that you might add to a house scene.

To me, the difference between a scene and an entity boils down to a scene being "the stuff we're displaying," and an entity is "an item within a scene that we want to manipulate."

Launching Reality Composer Pro

It might seem like a silly place to start, but you might as well figure out how to launch the application, right? You search for it and... nothing? Well, maybe it's just hanging out in the Applications folder? Nope. Like Simulator, Reality Composer Pro is part of Xcode. It can be used independently, but the easiest way to start the application is via Xcode.

When you create a visionOS project in this chapter, the template will include a package file that Reality Composer Pro uses to save your resources. You can use that as a jumping-off point to launch the application—like launching the simulator from an Xcode. In the meantime, you can get used to the tool by using it in a standalone capacity.

To do this, start Xcode and then choose Xcode, Open Developer Tool, Reality Composer Pro from the menu bar, as shown in **FIGURE 3.1**.

FIGURE 3.1 Opening Reality Composer Pro

When Reality Composer launches from outside an active Xcode project, it displays recent projects that you've worked on (including those initiated from Xcode), as well as gives you an opportunity to create a new project or a new scene, as shown in **FIGURE 3.2**. A project is what you'll use with Xcode. It can contain multiple scenes and assets and includes the special package format for quick loading. The alternative, a scene file, is a standalone Universal Scene Description ASCII (.usda) file that can contain a single 3D scene. For our purposes, we'll work through this introduction with a full project file because, frankly, there are few instances where you wouldn't want the flexibility and speed gained with a Reality Composer Pro project.

When asked to save the project, give it the name **Composer Practice** and click Save Project. Within a few seconds, the Reality Composer Pro workspace appears.

FIGURE 3.2 Choose Create New Project when prompted.

Touring the Interface

The Reality Composer Pro workspace is structured differently than Xcode, so I'm going to help you get your bearings. If you've created a new project, your screen should resemble **FIGURE 3.3**.

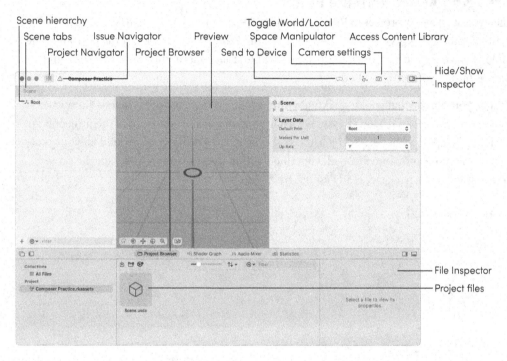

FIGURE 3.3 The Reality Composer Pro workspace

There are plenty of panels that can be hidden or shown throughout the interface, so if your display doesn't quite match the example, use the View menu to access anything that might be hidden.

The toolbar at the top of the interface has controls for hiding and showing the major pieces of the interface. On the left side, the Scene Hierarchy button shows all the objects that make up a scene you're working in. The Issues Navigator shows any problems with your project. (I hope there are none!)

On the right, the Apple Vision Pro icon enables you to send the current scene directly to a connected headset for viewing. The Manipulator Space icon setting determines the coordinates you're working in (I explain this later in this chapter in the "Using the Manipulator" section) while the Camera icon enables you to choose where the camera is positioned and save positions for easy access in the future.

The + button opens a Content Library with objects you can use for free in your projects!

Finally, Hide/Show Inspector icon hides (or shows) the entire right side of the window, which is where you'll be able to view information about selected files, entities, scenes, and more.

Managing Assets with the Editor

When you start a new project in Reality Composer Pro, you're not going to see much of anything—just an empty scene with no entities. The Editor area (located at the bottom of the window) is where you get information about the files that contain the entities, scenes, and other resources your project needs.

Initially, you can see that you're working within a folder named for the project—Composer Practice—with the extension .rkassets (Reality Kit Assets). To the right of the project is an icon for an (empty) scene file, Scene.usda, as shown in **FIGURE 3.4**. As you build up your project, you add more and more files—all contained within the .rkassets folder for the project and compiled into a package, ready for use by Xcode.

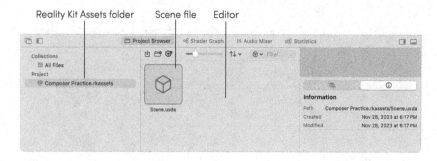

FIGURE 3.4 Viewing the files that make up your Reality Composer Pro project

It's unlikely that you want just an empty scene, so the first step is to add asset files to your project. These can come from multiple sources.

Importing External Files

In Chapter 2, you downloaded an Earth Day asset from SketchFab (https://sketchfab.com), which is my suggestion for thousands of high-quality (both free and paid) models that you can use in your creations. In Chapter 4, "Creating and Customizing Models and Materials," I share ways to create your own objects to add to scenes, but, for now, third-party models will have to do.

> **TIP** You can add any Universal Scene Description (USD) file to Reality Composer Pro. This format is offered by most online asset collections, including SketchFab. Unfortunately, the world is full of alternative formats, so it isn't always going to be "drag and drop." Apple provides a tool (Reality Converter) that can convert many other formats into the USD standard. To learn more about the tool and download it, visit https://developer.apple.com/augmented-reality/tools/.

I've included a lovely Rubber Duck model by the artist Ikki_3d. This model was originally downloaded from SketchFab (https://skfb.ly/6TsSv) and is free for use under the Creative Commons Attribution license (http://creativecommons.org/licenses/by/4.0/). You can find the file Rubber_duck.usdz in your Chapter 3 zip file.

To add a third-party model to your project, simply drag it into the center of the Editor area or click the Import content button, as shown in **FIGURE 3.5**. Do this with the rubber duck model now.

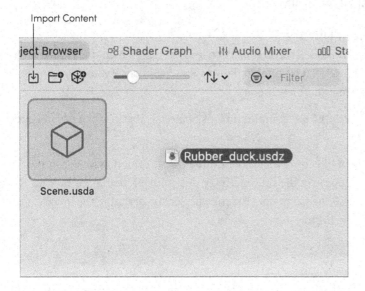

FIGURE 3.5 Dragging the file into the editor to import it

The Editor now shows the scene file and the rubber duck file, as shown in **FIGURE 3.6**.

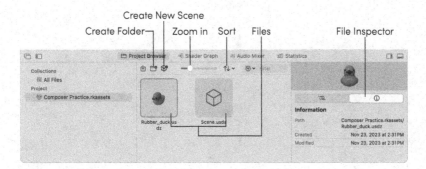

FIGURE 3.6 The rubber duck file is now part of the project.

Think of the Editor as a mini version of the Finder. You can use the controls above the files to arrange your assets into folders, zoom in on the icons, or sort them. With only a few assets, this is unnecessary, but feel free to test the tools. Delete files (or folders) by selecting them and then pressing the Delete key.

To the right of the Editor is the inspector for the selected file. The Information Inspector, active in **FIGURE 3.6**, shows information about when the file was created, as well as showing an interactive view of the contents of the file.

Importing from the Content Library

When you need a high-quality 3D model, the first place to look is Apple's included Content Library. To access the library, click the + symbol in the Reality Composer Pro toolbar or choose Show Content Library from the View menu.

The Content Library, shown in **FIGURE 3.7**, contains dozens of models that you can use in your projects.

When you find a model that you'd like, drag it into the Editor's file area; it downloads into your project. You see a new file appear in the Editor. To try this yourself, search for **Jar** and add the Medical Glass Jar model to the Composer Practice project by dragging the image from the Content Library into the Editor.

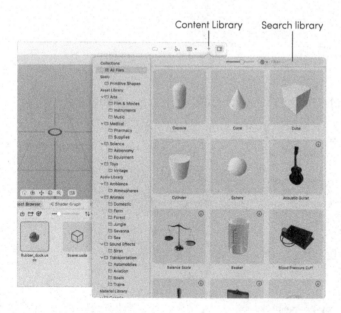

FIGURE 3.7 Accessing Apple's content library in Reality Composer Pro

Your project editor should now resemble **FIGURE 3.8**.

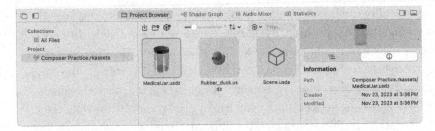

FIGURE 3.8 Your project should now have entity files for a glass jar and a duck.

There's another type of object, called a primitive shape, which is also available in the Content Library but does *not* add an additional file to the project, and it won't be visible in the Editor. Primitives, like cubes and spheres, are special because they don't need an external file to describe them. This means they'll only come in handy in building your scenes, as you do in the next section.

> **NOTE** If you double-click an object in the library, the file is added to your project and inserted into the default scene in the project.

Building a Scene

You're possibly wondering what in the world we're doing with a project that contains a jar and a duck. Well, I happened to think it would be nice to build a scene consisting of a rubber duck sitting on a red ball inside of a glass jar. Doesn't everyone?

Get started on building this scene by clicking to select the Scene.usda file shown in the Editor. You'll be paying attention to the upper part of the workspace, as shown in **FIGURE 3.9**.

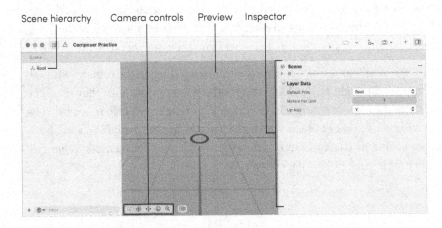

FIGURE 3.9 Using tools in the upper portion of the window to build the scene

On the left side of the Reality Composer Window is the scene hierarchy, which displays all the objects in a scene and their composition. By default, you just see a Root node. This is the top level of the scene, and it doesn't represent any specific visible object. The Preview area in the middle of the screen behaves like the Xcode Canvas Preview or the Simulator. The one big change is that, unlike those other tools, you can *edit* the objects in the preview—something you need to do to create the perfect "ducky and ball in a jar" scene. On the right is the Inspector area. The Inspector enables you to view the different components used to configure an object and set their properties by hand.

> **TIP** Don't think about the fact that you're editing a scene in the Preview, and not the Editor. Just don't.

Adding Objects to the Scene

In the Preview area, note that there is an origin point with a circle in the center and that the preview "floor" is a grid. The grid itself provides some useful information; each major square in the grid is 1 square meter. Having this as a reference is helpful as you start to size and resize objects. Unfortunately, although you can set the size of objects to a particular unit of measure, you can't change the unit used for the grid. I suspect this will change in the future because the original "non-pro" version of Reality Composer has the feature.

To add an object into the scene, drag it from the Editor into the Preview. As you drag into the preview area, you'll notice a circle "target" appear on the grid. This shows you where the object will be placed when you release the mouse/trackpad button. Go ahead and do this with the Jar model. Try to position it as close to the center of the grid as you can.

Once the object is added to the scene, it also appears in the Scene Hierarchy, as shown in **FIGURE 3.10**. You can drag objects "into" other objects within the hierarchy to establish parent and child objects. For example, if you place a sphere object inside the Jar, the jar becomes the parent and the sphere a child. This is meaningful when you want to resize, tilt, or move the jar. Because it's the parent, performing an action on it also performs the same action on the children.

I'm betting your display doesn't look much like the figure. Depending on the dimensions used in the model, objects you add might be sized like their real-life counterparts, or they might be crazy large or small. Use the camera controls in the lower left of the Preview to move the view so that you can see what you're doing! When you're finished moving the camera around, be sure the "interact with content" control is active (the cursor within a partial circle); otherwise, subsequent clicking to manipulate objects isn't going to work.

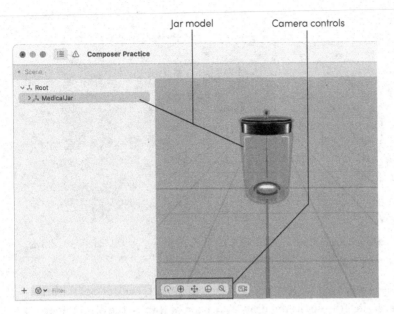

Jar model   Camera controls

FIGURE 3.10 As you add objects to the scene, you see them appear in hierarchy.

Using the Manipulator

Once you're close enough to an object to see it, you can move it around, resize it, and tilt it using the ominous-sounding **Manipulator**. The Manipulator is a series of controls that appear when you select an object. **FIGURE 3.11** shows a detail image of the Manipulator as it appears around the jar.

To move an object along the x-axis (side to side), y-axis (up or down), or z-axis (closer or farther) click one of the three arrows visible in the Manipulator and drag. The red arrow moves along the x-axis, the green arrow along the y-axis, and the blue arrow along the z-axis. As you drag, you see a measurement that displays how far you've moved the object from the origin point, as shown in **FIGURE 3.12**.

> **TIP** You can also move objects freely by clicking and dragging them within the preview. This, however, can sometimes lead to unpredictable results. You think you might be dragging something "up" the y-axis only to find you've been moving it further away on the z-axis (which looks like "up" against the grid).

Notice that when you clicked one of the arrows to drag, a similarly colored circle appeared around the object. This circle is used to rotate along the corresponding axis. Click within the colored circle and drag in a circular manner. The object rotates and displays how many degrees it has rotated as you drag.

Arrows   Rotation/scaling circle

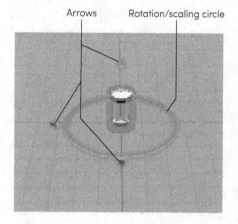

16.58271 cm

FIGURE 3.11 Using the Manipulator to position objects in your scene

FIGURE 3.12 Dragging the object along an axis shows a measurement of how far it has moved.

The Manipulator's circle is *also* used for resizing. To resize an object, click one of the arrows so a circle is visible. Next, click the circle and drag away from or toward the object; it grows or shrinks in size. It doesn't matter which axis the circle belongs to; it only matters that you can click and drag it.

Try this out now by adding the duck to your scene. You should immediately notice a GIANT problem, as demonstrated in **FIGURE 3.13**.

Using the Manipulator for the duck, click *any* circle and drag toward the center of the duck until it is small enough to fit inside the jar. This is *not* a single action; you probably need the camera controls to zoom in and reposition your view several times to resize it properly.

Once the duck is a decent size, drag it *into* the jar. Viewing the scene from the top can help with this step because you can see when the objects are on top of one another rather than in front or behind one another. Your preview should now be similar to **FIGURE 3.14**.

TIP This step is probably going to be frustrating as you get used to the controls. One big problem is clicking on an object and accidentally selecting the wrong one. For more precision, use the Scene Hierarchy on the left to select your objects. That helps ensure you're looking at the right Manipulator for the right object.

You may also just want to consider using the Inspector and Transform Component (discussed next) to make the manipulations using numbers.

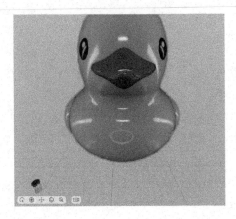

FIGURE 3.13 That's a mighty big duck.

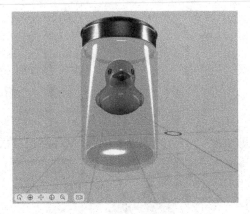

FIGURE 3.14 Placing the duck inside the jar

WHAT ARE LOCAL AND WORLD COORDINATES?

In the Reality Composer Pro toolbar is an icon to toggle between **Local** and **World coordinates**. It can be helpful to understand this feature so you can use the right selection at the right time. When using World coordinates, you move and rotate objects in relation to the overall scene—up is up, down is down, and so on—things move the way you'd expect. With Local coordinates, the Manipulator works relative to the selected object or the parent object. For example, if you rotate an object in world coordinates, you'll see the overall degrees of rotation measured from the "world" perspective. A 90-degree rotation shows as 90 degrees in the Transform component. If you then rotate 5 degrees more, the angle reads as 95 degrees in World coordinates but only 5 degrees in Local coordinates.

When applied to objects in a hierarchy, if you move or rotate an object *inside* another object, the movements are in relation to the parent object. In the jar scene you're building, if you rotate the jar onto its side and then switch to Local coordinates and use the Manipulator to move the duck along the y-axis, it moves side to side. The duck is moving relative to its parent, the jar… which, even though it is lying on the side, still has a local coordinate system where the y-axis runs through the top and bottom of the jar.

Changing Scale, Rotation, and Position with the Transform Component

Reality Composer Pro offers an alternative to the Manipulator that gives you a more precise means of positioning, rotating, and scaling objects. When an object is selected in the hierarchy, look at the Inspector column on the right. The Transform component, shown in **FIGURE 3.15**, provides numerical access to the position, scale, and rotation of the object.

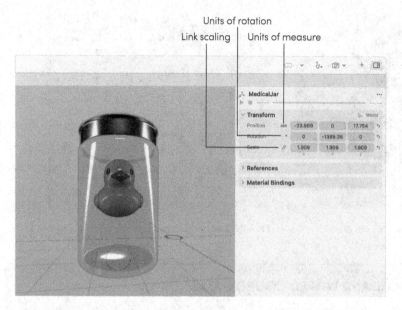

FIGURE 3.15 Manipulating your object with the Transform component

Use the three values in the transform fields to change the object position along the x-axis, y-axis, and z-axis. The symbols in front of the Position and Rotation fields can be used to change the unit of measure or rotation for the object. The icon in front of the scaling fields controls linked scaling. When linked scaling is on (the default), resizing an object resizes it along all axes. If you turn off linked scaling, you can resize independently along axes, meaning you can stretch objects to make them appear very differently from how they were originally intended.

The Inspector, in conjunction with the Transform component, can be helpful in cleaning up the sloppiness of using the Manipulator by correcting values to the sizes and positions you intended rather than what "looked good" in the Preview.

Managing the Scene Hierarchy

As previously mentioned, objects in the scene can have parent/child relationships. In the example, the duck is inside the jar, but there is no relationship between the objects. They're both at the same level of the Scene Hierarchy on the left.

To create a relationship, drag the Rubber_duck line on top of the MedicalJar line, as shown in **FIGURE 3.16.**

The MedicalJar object expands and shows that the duck is now contained within it. This means that if you scale, rotate, or move the jar, the duck scales and moves with it!

If you don't like any of the object names in the hierarchy, click the name to edit it. You'll use the names to refer to the objects in code, so having simple names can be helpful.

> **TIP** When you hover over a line in the hierarchy, a lock icon appears at the end of the line. Click the lock to prevent any further changes from being made to that object.

Working with Primitive Shapes and Customizing Materials

You still need a red ball in the scene, so use the Content Library to add a primitive object—a sphere—to the scene. Unlike other objects, you won't see it anywhere in the Editor; it only appears in the scene.

Use the Manipulator and/or Transform component to position the sphere inside the jar underneath the duck (or on top of it). Once in place, drag the sphere into the Jar within the Scene Hierarchy. Your layout should resemble **FIGURE 3.17**.

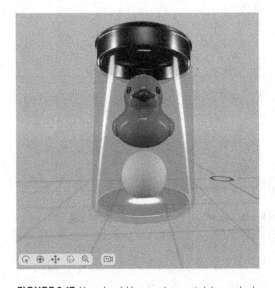

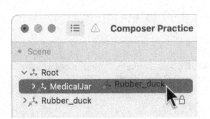

FIGURE 3.16 Creating a relationship in the Scene Hierarchy

FIGURE 3.17 You should have a jar containing a duck and a white sphere.

There's only one thing wrong with this scene: the ball looks like an egg, which is not the goal. You need to adjust the material that covers the sphere so it looks like a red rubber ball.

Click the Sphere in the Scene Hierarchy and then expand it using the disclosure arrow by its name. You see a line labeled DefaultMaterial, as shown in **FIGURE 3.18**.

Click the DefaultMaterial line for the sphere and use the Inspector to expand the Material component on the right side of the window. Your display should be similar to **FIGURE 3.19**.

To change the color of the sphere, click the Diffuse Color well to open a macOS color picker. Pick a nice color for the sphere. It's a black-and-white book, but take my word for it—I chose red.

Congratulations! You've completed building your first scene and even added customization. Test the other material attributes to see their effect on the sphere. This is one of the more amusing places to go nuts, so have at it.

Before I explain how to incorporate Reality Composer Pro creations into visionOS projects, I'd like to show you *one more thing* in Reality Composer Pro—just for fun.

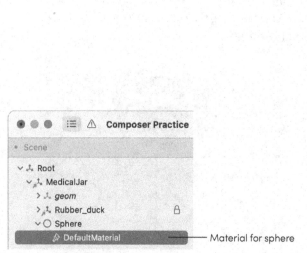

FIGURE 3.18 Expanding the object in the hierarchy to access its materials

FIGURE 3.19 Using the Material component and Inspector to configure the appearance of your sphere

Adding Particle Emitters

Let's take a few moments for some unnecessary excitement and add one last object to the Composer Practice project: a particle emitter. Particle emitters represent an object in space from which "particles" are released and behave in some manner. Examples of particles moving in 3D space include environmental effects like snow, rain, smoke, fire, and even confetti. A particle emitter can provide an infinite number of effects. It's a matter of finding the right parameters for the effect you want.

Before adding the emitter, move your jarred duck-n-ball to the side. You're going to add the emitter to the origin point, and you need some room to play around.

To add a particle emitter, choose Insert, Particle Emitter. You see a spot appear in the center of the Preview that sprays colorful dots upward, as shown in **FIGURE 3.20**. If you don't see the animation, click the Start button in the top of the Inspector area on the right.

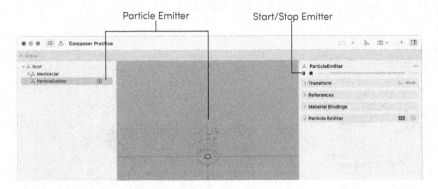

FIGURE 3.20 Adding a particle emitter for some visual flare

What I was thinking for my Composer Practice particle emitter is that I'd like something to show what it would look like if our jarred duck started to get stinky. A particle emitter to emit cartoony green "smell" particles that spiral upward into a green cloud—that would be perfect!

How can you take this starting emitter and turn it into a green cloud creator? By playing with the dozens of settings in the Particle Emitter component. **FIGURE 3.21** shows the Particle Emitter component's Emitter and Particles settings.

For my emitter, I've left the Emitter settings largely the same but increased the speed of the particles to 1 meter/second.

In the Particles settings under Color, I've set the Start Color to a fluorescent green and set the End Color to a dark green. I've also adjusted the Opacity Over Life Mode to Gradual Fade In Out. to make the particles appear and disappear gradually.

Next, in the Properties section, I've updated the size of the particles so that they grow to 10 centimeters while onscreen. This increases the size and "puffiness" of the particles over time. They still shoot off the screen without making a cloud, but they look better.

To force the particles to slow down and "cloud" after they are emitted, I chose a drag of 2 in the Motion settings. This creates the effect I want, but I'd like the cloud to be more turbulent. To make it more dynamic, I've set a vortex strength of 10 with the Force Fields options. The vortex direction is set to 1 on the y-axis, which means the cloud spins like a tornado.

Lastly, in the Rendering section, I've turned on Lighting Enabled to deliver a more realistic effect. The Particle Emitter should now be making pretty green clouds.

When your particle emitter looks the way you want, add it to the jar, located under the lid. Be sure that it is contained within the jar in the Scene Hierarchy. When in motion, the cloud is emitted just under the lid but coalesces above the jar.

The final duck jar scene should look very similar to **FIGURE 3.22**.

FIGURE 3.21 There are more than a few ways to configure your particle emitter.

FIGURE 3.22 Enjoy your bizarre modern art creation.

This is a great place to spend a few minutes experimenting. You can create many different effects by trying different combinations of emitter and particle settings. It's a great way to add visual interest to scenes with realistic environmental effects. There's more Reality Composer Pro to learn later, but if you'd like to get started early, review Apple's documentation at https://developer.apple.com/documentation/visionos/designing-realitykit-content-with-reality-composer-pro.

When you're ready, continue reading. You've spent some time learning how to create scenes from entities, primitives, and particle emitters, but what good is that if you can't use them in your code? I explain how to do that now, starting with how to create multiple windows to display your scenes.

UNDERSTANDING VISIONOS WINDOWS

You used a few windows in your early projects, but there isn't much you've done besides willing them into existence by writing an app. To take things to the next level and prepare for your upcoming project, let's spend some additional time learning more about windows in visionOS.

Setting Up WindowGroups

In the upcoming project, the application presents two different types of windows. This necessitates a quick lesson in the **WindowGroup** function and how it can give you a way to treat your windows as templates—loading up different windows and styles as your applications run.

To start, open the included empty project file WindowTests in Xcode and view the source of the WindowTestsApp.swift file to follow along.

In the file, notice that you have a code block that looks like this:

```
import SwiftUI

@main
struct WindowTestsApp: App {
    var body: some Scene {
        WindowGroup {
            ContentView()
        }
    }
}
```

Here, when this code starts executing, it creates a scene consisting of a WindowGroup that is populated with ContentView. A **WindowGroup** is the container that holds all the subviews that make up your overall interface view, and a **scene** contains the different WindowGroups that your application will use. In Chapter 2, you built out these subviews inside the ContentView.swift file. You could have added the SwiftUI directly into the WindowGroup code block, but that would get messy. Instead, the code was kept in ContentView.swift and loaded in the WindowGroup with ContentView().

Adding a New WindowGroup

What if you want another type of window? To create a new window that you can use in your project, add another WindowGroup. For example, if you want a second window—InstructionView—to be available in your app, you might update <ProjectName>App.swift with a block like **LISTING 3.1.**

LISTING 3.1 An App File That Defines Two Different Windows, Populated by `ContentView` and `InstructionView`

```
import SwiftUI

@main
struct WindowTestsApp: App {
    var body: some Scene {
        WindowGroup {
            ContentView()
        }
        WindowGroup(id: "InstructionView") {
            InstructionView()
        }
    }
}
```

Note that the second window group has an `id` parameter of `InstructionView`. This can be any unique string that you want to use to reference the windows created from a window group.

Where in the world is this window's content going to be defined? It's a valid question. ContentView.swift provides the content for your main window, but what if you want the new `InstructionView` window group to load its content from a file called InstructionView.swift?

Adding a New SwiftUI View Template

To add a new file to your project that contains the SwiftUI view for InstructionView, choose File, New, File from the menu. When prompted, as shown in **FIGURE 3.23**, choose visionOS and SwiftUI View; then click Next.

When saving the file, set **InstructionView** as the name, and verify that Where is set to the name of your name project code folder, and that the target (also named after your project) has a check mark in front of it, as shown in **FIGURE 3.24**. Click Create. In this example, I'm creating a new InstructionView file in an application called WindowTests.

The new file, complete with the structure you'd expect (almost identical to `ContentView`) is added to your project.

> **TIP** Despite what it might seem, the name of the SwiftUI view file is irrelevant. I named the file after the view it creates for clarity. If you want to name the file "smiggledeedoo," Xcode would still be able to find everything it needs because the file is part of the project.

FIGURE 3.23 Creating a new SwiftUI view file

FIGURE 3.24 Adding the new SwiftUI View file to your project

Opening (and Closing) Windows

You've now seen how to create a new `WindowGroup` and a corresponding code file to use while designing the content, but how does that window get displayed? It's quite easy, but with a "what the ?!?@*" catch. There are two functions—`openWindow` and `dismissWindow`—you can use, but, before you can do that, you must retrieve these features from your application's active environment.

Do this by placing the following lines at the top of any View definition (before the var body: some View { line). If you want to open and close windows within your ContentView, you'd update the ContentView struct like this:

```
…
struct ContentView: View {
    @Environment(\.openWindow) private var openWindow
    @Environment(\.dismissWindow) private var dismissWindow
…
```

Now, you can use openWindow(id: <WindowGroup ID>) and dismissWindow(id: <WindowGroup ID>) to open and close windows. For example, you might have open and close buttons that open and close the InstructionView window like this:

```
Button("Open Instructions") {
        openWindow(id: "InstructionView")
 }

Button("Close Instructions") {
        dismissWindow(id: "InstructionView")
 }
```

You need to add the @Environment lines to any view that can open and close other windows. (Yes, this is weird, but it works, and that's the tool we currently have.)

> **TIP** You can dismiss a window without its ID by adding the following line to the top of any view, just like open-Window and dismissWindow declarations:
>
> `@Environment(\.dismiss) private var dismiss`
>
> Now, within that view, all you need to do is call the function *dismiss()*, and the view dismisses itself.

WHAT'S AN ENVIRONMENT?

When your application runs, it establishes an environment that holds information about the application state and system-wide settings the app is operating within. Information about accessibility, display, controls, and so on are available throughout the environment.

The keyword @Environment is called a **property wrapper** and is used to set up access to these internal features—which is what we're doing with the openWindow, dismissWindow, and dismiss functions. You can see the full list of environment values at https://developer.apple.com/documentation/swiftui/environmentvalues.

The environment of your application can do much more than give access to pre-defined properties. It can also store information that we want to share throughout our application. I explain how this works via the `@EnvironmentObject` wrapper (and you implement it in your hands-on project) shortly.

Setting Window Styles

In the first two chapters, you've grown accustomed to seeing **plain** windows, which are the visionOS default. These are useful for providing 2D controls and feedback to your users, but they aren't immersive. As you've learned, you can update the Z level offset or add a 3D Model to your windows, but they're still not going to deliver the best experience. For that, you need a new type of window—a **volumetric** window. Volumetric windows have width, height, *and* depth and like a plain window can be moved and positioned in 3D space.

A big difference between volumetric windows and plain windows, however, is that plain windows are sized for readability wherever you place them in your space. A volumetric window maintains the same virtual "physical" size within your environment, making it perfect for representing real-world objects.

NOTE Apple refers to the three types of 3D components that you can view in your headset as Windows (plain windows), Volumes (volumetric windows), and Spaces (immersive areas). With the introduction of Volumes in this chapter, two of the three experience types are covered!

To set the different types of windows, we turn again to the <Project Name>App.swift file. You execute the function `windowStyle(<style>)` on a `WindowGroup` to set the window to a particular style.

Consider the two window groups you created earlier: `ContentView` and `InstructionView`. If `ContentView` is a plain window, and you want the `InstructionView` to be a Volume, you'd update the `WindowGroups` in the <Project Name>App.swift file like this:

```
WindowGroup {
        ContentView()
}
WindowGroup(id: "InstructionView") {
        InstructionView()
}
.windowStyle(.volumetric)
```

With the *single* `.windowStyle` addition, the `InstructionView` is defined as a volumetric window rather than plain. Speaking of which, you *could* add `.windowStyle(.plain)` to the first WindowGroup, but because plain is the default, there's no real need.

Setting Window Dimensions

In the previous chapters, you've run a few applications in the Simulator (and hopefully on your physical headset), but you've left the application to present its windows however it wants. This has led to some user interfaces that are quite small yet are located within giant (or at least not aesthetically pleasing) windows. It's time to find out how to size windows.

2D Sizing

The easiest way to size a 2D window is to set a default size on the `WindowGroup` using the `defaultSize(width:<width in points>, height:<height in points>)` function.

For example, to set a default size of 200 x 200 points, you might use

```
WindowGroup {
        ContentView()
}
.defaultSize(width: 200, height: 200)
```

> **TIP** Don't worry too much about using "points" in visionOS sizing. On iOS devices, a point is an abstract value that represents a single unit of measure on the device screen. A device may have Apple's super-duper latest Liquid Retina Platinum XL display with 4 billion pixels, but that number is abstracted to a (relatively) small number of points. The 11-inch iPad Pro, for example, uses 2 pixels for every point horizontally and vertically, for a total of 4 pixels per point. On the Apple Vision Pro, this is a teensy bit more difficult to calculate because you can position windows in your space and move around them, effectively making the point-to-pixel comparison useless. When sizing with points in visionOS, it's best to test and make corrections until onscreen objects appear the size you want.

Another approach to setting the size of a 2D window is to use the function `windowResizability(.contentSize)`. This sizes the window to hold the content being displayed within. Applied to a WindowGroup, in theory, this makes the most efficient use of your space:

```
WindowGroup {
        ContentView()
}
.windowResizability(.contentSize)
```

The window also gained a resize handle, shown in **FIGURE 3.25**, that can be used to manually change the size of the window within the Vision Pro interface.

> **TIP** The *.windowResizability(.contentSize)* approach is used heavily throughout the book to create nicely sized windows. If you can memorize only one thing about window sizing, this is it.

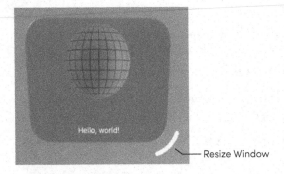

Resize Window

FIGURE 3.25 Setting `windowResizability` to enable resizing the WindowGroup

In other situations, you may want to have more control over the window size, and you can do so by setting a dimension on the content itself within your WindowGroup. For example, if the ContentView size was best displayed in a window between 100 and 400 points wide and 200 to 500 points high, you can add a modifier to the *view* (*not* the WindowGroup) that sets the **frame** size. The frame is an imaginary rectangle that encompasses the content of the window.

```
WindowGroup {
        ContentView()
                .frame(
                    minWidth: 100, maxWidth: 400,
                    minHeight: 200, maxHeight: 500)
}
```

The frame can be modified on *any* view—including the views that build up your interface— such as buttons, images, text, and so on to give a very precise means of controlling size.

You can also combine resizability with the `.frame(minWidth: <width in points>, maxWidth: <width in points>, minHeight: <height in points>, maxHeight: <height in points>)` modifier to set the smallest and largest dimensions of a resizable window. Here, for example, I'm creating a window that can be resized from 100x100 to 200x200:

```
WindowGroup {
        ContentView()
                .frame(
                    minWidth: 100, maxWidth: 200,
                    minHeight: 100, maxHeight: 200)
}
.windowResizability(.contentSize)
```

3D Sizing

When you work in three dimensions, your projects start to understand how the "real world" relates to what you're seeing in your headset. This means that while sizing 2D plain windows can be hit or miss, resizing volumetric windows is *easier*!

To size a Volume, you can refer to its dimensions in real-world units. To do this, use the same defaultSize function used with a 2D window, but this time include a depth and a unit of measure:

```
defaultSize(width: <width>, height: <height>, depth: <depth>, in: <units of measure>)
```

The recognized units of measure include .feet, .yards, .inches, .meters—way more relatable terms for setting the size of a 3D object. To see the full list of units supported, visit https://developer.apple.com/documentation/foundation/unitlength.

For example, to set the size of a Volume (volumetric window) to 2 feet wide, 3 feet high, and 1.5 feet deep, I might use something like this:

```
WindowGroup(id: "InstructionView") {
        InstructionView()
}
.windowStyle(.volumetric)
.defaultSize(width: 2.0, height: 3.0, depth: 1.5, in: .feet)
```

The content within the Volume needs to *fit* in the available space. This function doesn't scale the content. This sets a limit on the size of the space allocated for displaying your 3D scene.

In general, I use the default metric units of measurement (meters and centimeters) throughout the book. The use of "feet" here is to give you an idea of the flexibility you have in sizing.

DISPLAYING AND MANIPULATING 3D SCENES AND ENTITIES WITH REALITYVIEW

Earlier in this chapter, I talk about building scenes in Reality Composer Pro. Each scene that you build is comprised of entities, which can be anything from 3D models to primitive shapes, and, as you'll learn later, even *sounds*.

In the upcoming project, you build a simple scene made from several entities. You want to be able to access these entities in code directly, so the "load a 3D model" approach from Chapter 1 isn't going to work here. When you fully embrace RealityKit, you gain access to all sorts of interactive features, such as gestures, that you wouldn't have otherwise.

Loading Scenes

To get started using RealityKit, you can add it as a view, like a button or text, to our SwiftUI view code, using this syntax:

```
RealityView { content in
    // Load entities/scenes here
} update: { content in
    // Update entities/scenes in here
}
```

In this structure, the variable content is provided to the two code blocks for loading and updating the view. This variable contains a collection of all the entities that make up the scene. You can add and remove entities or alter the appearance of individual items from this collection to change what is displayed to the user.

For example, to load a scene called Boxes that you've built in Reality Composer Pro, you'd write this:

```
RealityView { content in
    // Add the initial RealityKit content
    if let scene = try? await Entity(named: "Boxes", in:
                                     realityKitContentBundle) {
        content.add(scene)
    }
} update: { content in
    // Update content if needed
}
```

The line that begins if let scene = try? is syntax that you haven't seen before. What this does is search the package that Reality Composer Pro creates (realityKitContentBundle) for an entity that is named Boxes. If found, the entity is loaded into a constant, scene.

This statement syntax was created to deal with the fact that the loading process might fail—if the entity doesn't exist or you haven't used Reality Composer Pro for adding your models, for example. If it succeeds, it adds the entity (contained in scene) to the content of the Reality-View (content.add(scene)), displaying it on your device.

If you follow this format

```
if let <scene> = try? await Entity(named: <scene name> in:
                                   realityKitContentBundle) {
        content.add(<scene>)
}
```

you'll be properly handling any errors that your code might encounter. Of course, this code does *nothing* if it doesn't succeed, so you might want to add an else statement to deal with a failure to load the entity.

Accessing and Hiding Entities

Once a scene is loaded, you can access any of the entities that it contains using the handy findEntity function. This function, which is executed on the constant you've used to load your scene, takes an entity name, and returns a constant you can use to access the entity. Because this can also fail, you need to use a similar if let <constant> syntax.

```
if let <entity> = <scene constant>.findEntity(named:
                                        <entity name>) {
        // Do something with <entity>
}
```

Once you have a way to reference an individual entity in the scene, you can modify it with functions and properties. A property you'll be using today is .isEnabled, which, when set to false, prevents the entity from being displayed.

Putting this all together, if you load a scene called Boxes and then search within it for an entity named "Amazon", you can hide the "Amazon" entity with this code:

```
RealityView { content in
    // Add the initial RealityKit content
    if let scene = try? await Entity(named: "Boxes", in:
                                realityKitContentBundle) {
        content.add(scene)
        if let amazon = scene.findEntity(named: "Amazon") {
            amazon.isEnabled = false
        }
    }
} update: { content in
    // Update content if needed
}
```

Using this technique, you can start customizing scenes as they're loaded and in response to user actions!

> **TIP** Sometimes you need to load scenes/entities into a variable rather than a constant. No worries; just replace *let* with *var*, and the code works just fine.

SHARING INFORMATION WITHIN YOUR APP

The last topic that I cover in this chapter will be very useful in your future creations—be they traditional 2D applications or spatial computing masterpieces. This section covers how to share information throughout your application. You've already seen that you can create functions that take information and provide results and access properties in your application's environment using the @Environment property wrapper, but that's very different from being able to set variables in one window and access them in another. This is a critical function of applications that can lead to many hair-pulling moments when it *doesn't* work.

Global Variables

One way to make information available throughout your application is by way of **global** variables—variables that can be used *globally* in your code. To define a global variable (or global, for short) use the public keyword with the variable declaration. These declarations should happen after the import statements in any of your code files, like this:

```
import SwiftUI
...
public var globalHello = "Hello Everywhere!"
public var globalScore = 0
```

Here, the variables globalHello and globalScore are defined. These can now be used *anywhere* in your code, not just within a code block where they were declared or within a single code file. Globals can be complex data structures like structs or objects or simple types (as shown here). After being declared, they can be treated like any other variable.

If you're a getting-things-done person like me, you probably see this and think, "Well, heck, this is simple! Let's use globals and make life easy!" You're welcome to do this and, in many cases, it is more straightforward than any other solution.

Unfortunately, that's not the end of the story, and not the solution that I should be (in good conscience) teaching you about. Most developers decry the use of global variables and won't even mention (or consider) their existence, let alone their use.

Global variables can be declared anywhere and modified anywhere, which means that *any* code can change its value across the *entire* application. This is *not* good for code reuse or for sprawling projects with hundreds or thousands of objects and variables. Imagine trying to debug a calculation when variables in the expression may be changing simultaneously all over the application. You also only encounter the definition of the variables in the code that declares them, which can lead to the accidental reuse of the same name (with unpredictable results) elsewhere in your development.

With all that in mind, like I said, feel free to use globals when you want. They're not going to affect your ability to create mind-blowing applications nor prevent your apps from being accepted on the App Store. What they do, however, is generate scorn from peer developers waiting for a "Tsk! Tsk! Tsk!" moment.

Environment Objects

To avoid global variables but still have information that can be shared throughout your application, you can take advantage of the environment. Specifically, you can add an object to the application environment and then make it available in any of your views.

Going Object-Oriented

We're going to head into new territory with some *very* minor **object-oriented programming**. Much like structures, **objects** can contain properties and methods that can be reused throughout your code. You define what an object does and holds within a **class** code block. Classes can be created within your existing code files, or you can add a new source file to your project and create a class within it.

You've been using both structures and classes in your code, and in most cases, there's no need to differentiate between which is which. In the case of adding information to the environment, however, you can only store an object, so structures are out of the question.

To define a class, you create a block of code using this syntax:

```
class <Class name> [: Superclass or Protocol] {
    // Class code goes here
}
```

The class name is whatever you want to call the data structure—it's up to you. Class names should be contextually significant (so you can tell what they provide) and formatted such that each word in the name is capitalized—like a struct. The **superclass**, if provided, is the name of a class from which your class should **inherit** properties and functions. If you're building stand-alone functionality, you can skip the superclass. If you're developing a class for a specific purpose (such as sharing information between different views in your application), you may want or be *required* to include a superclass.

In some cases, rather than a superclass, you need to provide a protocol. A protocol, as I discussed in Chapter 2's "Getting to Know Variables and Structures", is a template that tells Xcode that a class needs to implement certain features in order to meet the requirements of the protocol.

A common use for environment objects is sharing application settings. For example, to define a class Settings that contains a few generic properties (attribute1, attribute2, attribute3), you might write this code:

```
class Settings: ObservableObject {
    @Published var attribute1: Bool = false
    @Published var attribute2: String = "John"
    @Published var attribute3: Int = 35
}
```

In this example, `ObservableObject` is a protocol—one that requires us to use a new property wrapper to share information across the application: `@Published`.

Applied to the properties in the class, this wrapper states that their definitions can be shared and updated. Note that I can't use the keyword `private`; doing so would do the disservice of making the properties shared but inaccessible.

Once the class is defined, you create a new **instance** of the class. Creating an instance means that you define a variable to reference the object and populate it with default values. In the `Settings` class, you already set defaults for the properties, so you can create your object with only this:

```
private var mySettings = Settings()
```

Now `mySettings` is an instance (or an object) of the `Settings` class.

Adding the Object to the Environment

After you create an object from a class, you're ready to add the object to the environment. I find it simplest (and providing the most flexibility) to create this object and add it to the environment from within the App Swift file (<Project Name>App.swift).

Begin by creating an instance of the class just after the `struct` line in your App file:

```
struct WindowTests: App {
    @StateObject private var mySettings = Settings()
    …
```

Yet another property wrapper is required here. The `@StateObject` wrapper tells Xcode that this variable will be shared and is required when instantiating an observable object.

Next, use the modifier `.environmentObject(<Object Name>)` on each view to make that object available within any of your windows (including Volumes). To add the object to `ContentView`, update the App Swift file to include the modifier within the `WindowGroup` block:

```
WindowGroup {
    ContentView()
        .environmentObject(mySettings)
}
```

You can use the same modifier to add the object to any other windows you create, making the values effectively available throughout the user interface.

Accessing the Environment Object in Other Views

After the object is added to the environment and shared with the different views, you still need a way to access the different properties within the object. You add a reference to the object with a single line, added after the `struct` line of any view:

`@EnvironmentObject` **`private var`** `<Variable name>: <Class name>`

To access the `mySettings` object within the `ContentView`, you add

```
struct ContentView: View {
    @EnvironmentObject private var mySettings: Settings
```

Although the line looks as though it might be defining a new variable for a new instance of Settings, the `@EnvironmentObject` wrapper changes everything. This keyword instructs the application that it should search for an object of the type `Settings` within the environment. If it finds a matching object, it attaches the object to the variable name provided (`mySettings`).

> **NOTE** You can use any variable name to create your reference to the *Settings* environment object; it doesn't have to match the object you instantiated in the App file. I find it convenient to use the same name as the initial object for consistency.

At long last, you can now access any of the properties within the object (`attribute1`, `attribute2`, and `attribute3`) by providing the object name, a period, and the property:

```
mySettings.attribute1 = true
mySettings.attribute2 = "Ray"
mySettings.attribute3 = 25
```

You can learn more about structures and classes by reading Apple's helpful comparison guide at

https://docs.swift.org/swift-book/documentation/the-swift-programming-language/classesandstructures/

I continue to introduce recipe code throughout the book, so there's no big need for you to memorize what is an object versus a structure in Apple's visionOS development.

You've learned the basics of Reality Composer Pro, window types and controls, data sharing, and more. It's time to use this knowledge with a hands-on project.

> **TIP** In the "Singletons" section of Chapter 10, "Components, Systems, and the Kitchen Sink," you'll see another (easy) way to share data across an application that draws on what you've learned here.

HANDS-ON: A CONFIGURABLE SNOW GLOBE

In this chapter, you've learned a new application for building 3D scenes and several new coding tricks. You're going to put these skills together into an application that enables users to build and position virtual snow globes around their room. This is also the first time that you're using the stand-alone visionOS application project template, so there will be some differences in the setup process.

This project requires you to develop two different views for two different types of windows. The main ContentView acts as a control panel where the user can create snow globes with a snowperson, a tree, and a snow generator—or any combination of these decorations. The display of the snow globes (users can create as many as they want!) makes use of a Volume (volumetric window) named Globe. You design the scene in Reality Composer Pro, and then it's loaded by a GlobeView SwiftUI file you add to the project. **FIGURE 3.26** shows the design of my interface and snow globe.

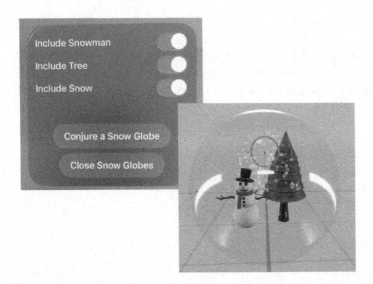

FIGURE 3.26 When finished, we'll be in snow globe heaven.

> **TIP** I recommend that you follow along with your own project, but if you get stuck along the way, the full project files are included in the Chapter 3 archive.

Creating the Project

Begin by creating a new visionOS app project in Xcode. Name the project **Snow Globe** with the initial scene set to a Window, as shown in the setup screen in **FIGURE 3.27**.

Choose options for your new project:

Product Name: Snow Globe

Team: John Ray

Organization Identifier: com.poisontooth

Bundle Identifier: com.poisontooth.Snow-Globe

Initial Scene: Window

Immersive Space Renderer: None

Immersive Space: None

☐ Include Tests

Cancel   Previous   Next

FIGURE 3.27 Setting up the new visionOS application project

When the template opens, take a glance at the Project Navigator. You see a RealityKitContent folder in the Packages folder, as shown in **FIGURE 3.28**. This is a Reality Composer Pro project that was created as part of the new application template. You use it to create a snow globe scene shortly.

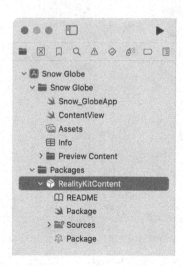

FIGURE 3.28 The visionOS template adds a Reality Composer Pro project to your Xcode project.

Creating the Snow Globe

The most difficult process of the entire project is putting together the globe, so let's start there.

Included in the project folder are files Snowman_-_Low_Poly by Bharad and Pine_Tree by samlee.fms. These 3D models are downloaded from SketchFab (https://skfb.ly/6Fp6C and https://skfb.ly/oB9z6, respectively) and shared under the Creative Commons Attribution license (http://creativecommons.org/licenses/by/4.0/). The globe itself is a primitive sphere with some adjustments to its material.

Open Reality Composer Pro by expanding the `Packages` and `RealityKitContent` folders in the Project Navigator. Select `Package` at the bottom of the Project Navigator. You should see a scene with a white globe, as shown in **FIGURE 3.29**. This is a default scene added automatically by the project template. Click Open Reality Composer Pro to start editing.

> **NOTE** Depending on where you're storing your files, you may be prompted to provide permission for Reality Composer Pro to access certain folders. This is part of the standard macOS security protections; granting access does not pose a threat to your system.

When Reality Composer Pro launches, click to select Scene.usda in the Editor and then clean the scene by deleting the white sphere and the sphere material (GridMaterial) within the Scene Hierarchy. You should have an empty scene file with a Root node and nothing else.

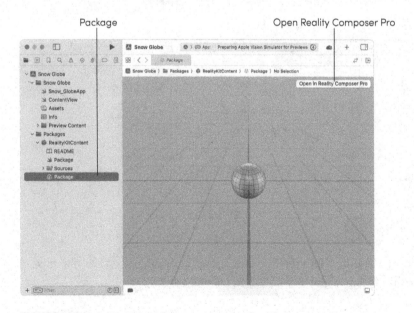

FIGURE 3.29 Selecting the package and opening Reality Composer Pro

Adding the Globe, Snowperson, and Tree

You need four different entities for this project—a snowperson, a tree, a particle emitter for snow, and a globe. Drag the snowperson and tree USDA files from the Chapter 3 folder into the Reality Composer Pro Editor to import the files. You're going to add a globe to the scene first and then the snowperson and tree.

Select the Scene.usda file in the Editor and then add a new sphere to the scene using the Content Library. Resize the sphere in the Preview (or zoom in) so that it is large enough to work with. During my design phase, I worked with a sphere that was about a meter in diameter.

A white sphere is a perfect frozen-solid snow globe, but that's not really what I think most people want. To change the sphere material, use the Scene Hierarchy and expand the sphere line; then select the default material. To create something like glass, update the Diffuse Color and Emissive Color to a deep bright blue. Set the Roughness to 0.0 and Opacity to 0.1. Finally, set the Clearcoat to 1.0.

You should now have a project workspace much like **FIGURE 3.30.**

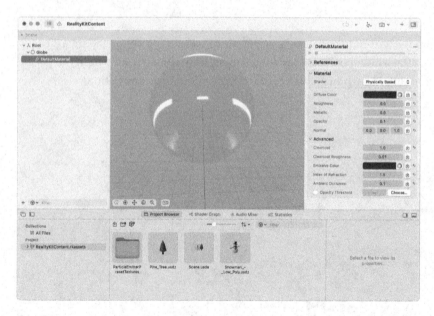

FIGURE 3.30 A scene with a shiny globe

Now drag the tree file from the Editor into the Preview. Using the Manipulator, size and position the tree so it fits within the glass globe, as shown in **FIGURE 3.31.**

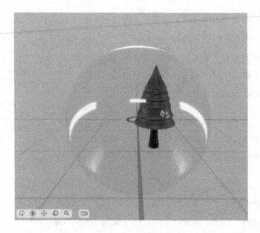

FIGURE 3.31 Adding and sizing the tree to fit nicely in the globe

Repeat this process for the snowperson. Position and size are your decision. The only requirement is that the decorations fit within the body of the globe. My final layout is shown in **FIGURE 3.32**.

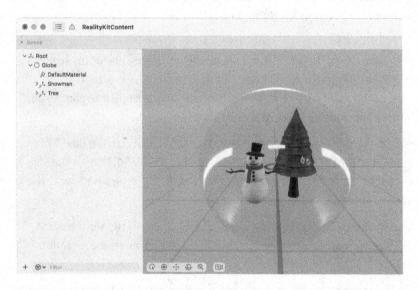

FIGURE 3.32 Positioning the snowperson within the globe to finish the basic scene

Once things are arranged in a way you like, add the tree and snowperson entities into the scene hierarchy *under* the globe. This ensures that if you resize or move the globe, the tree and snowperson move/resize accordingly.

Also use the Hierarchy Navigator to set names for the globe (Globe), snowperson (Snowman), and tree (Tree), respectively. You use these names later to access those entities in your windows. The names and an appropriate hierarchy are also visible in Figure 3.32.

Adding the Snow

The last entity to be added to your scene is a particle emitter that makes it look like snow is falling within the snow globe. I recommend sizing your globe (and its contents) down to the size you want available to be placed in your application. Mine, at about 40cm in diameter, is oversized, but you're not confined by any real-world norms, so do as you'd like.

The reason for setting the size of your globe ahead of time is that a particle emitter creates particles of a certain size and quantity. This does not "scale" with the globe as you resize it. An emitter releasing 500 1-centimeter-sized particles looks very different in a space of a meter versus a few centimeters.

Use the Insert menu to add a Particle Emitter to your scene. Using the Scene Hierarchy, name the emitter Snow so you can easily reference it in your code. Within the Particle Emitter component in the Inspector, click the icon with six squares in the upper-right corner of the panel. This displays a few preset emitter options, including snow, as shown in **FIGURE 3.33**.

Choose Snow to get a quick start on the snow globe emitter. This is a point where things can get tricky. As I said earlier, the best way to get familiarized with emitter settings is to use them. The snow in the default emitter wasn't "fluffy" enough for me, nor did it spread enough when positioned inside the globe.

I used the Inspector to update the Particle Emitter to make a few adjustments for my scene. Specifically, I changed the Emitter Shape to a Sphere and the Emitter Shape Size to 0.5, 0.5, and 0.5 in all three fields, as shown in **FIGURE 3.34**. This makes the snow appear to come from the surface of an invisible sphere located in the globe.

Next, switch to the Particles settings and set the Opacity Over Life settings to Gradual Fade In Out. Set the Size to about a third of a centimeter—fluffy but not too big (0.35). Set the Size Over Life to 1. Mass should be 0.5 and Life Span, 1. The effect of these settings is to make the snowflakes larger and have them fade in and out of existence.

I've set Acceleration in the y-axis to -0.05. This simulates gravity and pulls the snow toward the bottom of the globe. I've increased the Noise Strength to 0.2, which lends some randomness to the falling flakes.

Once you're happy with the effect of the emitter, position it within the globe in an area where the effect surrounds the snowperson and the tree and avoids any spillage outside of the sphere. Make sure that the emitter is also added to the Scene Hierarchy under the Globe.

> **NOTE** The snow in the globe is not confined to the globe! You can adjust the emitter settings to prevent it from expanding beyond the globe, but the particles pass through other objects.

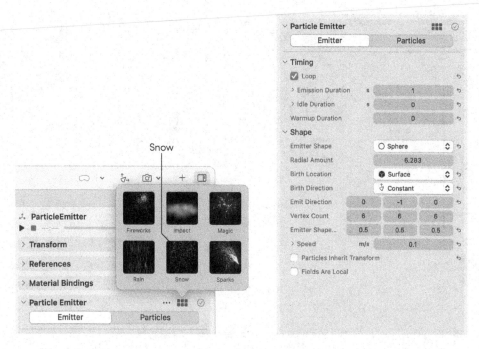

Snow

FIGURE 3.33 Choosing from a few emitter presets   **FIGURE 3.34** Adjusting the Emitter

You've nailed the scene, but now you need to put some logic around it. Recall that your goal is to create a ContentView for configuring a snow globe and a GlobeView that displays the globe.

Adding a WindowGroup

This application requires two window groups to be defined. The first, ContentView, already exists, but you still need the window for your Volume. Open the Snow_GlobeApp.swift file in Xcode. Under the existing WindowGroup code block, add the following WindowGroup to create a new volumetric window referred to as "Globe":

```
WindowGroup(id: "Globe") {
    GlobeView()
}
.windowStyle(.volumetric)
```

You need to add a new SwiftUI View—GlobeView—to hold the code for presenting the volumetric window. To do this, select the Snow Globe folder in the Project Navigator in Xcode and then choose File, New, File from the menu. When prompted, choose to create a new visionOS SwiftUI View file, as shown in **FIGURE 3.35**.

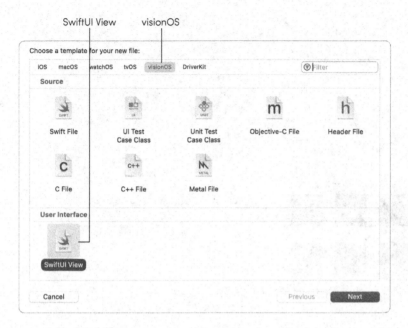

FIGURE 3.35 Using the visionOS SwiftUI template to make a new view.

Save the view as GlobeView, as shown in **FIGURE 3.36**.

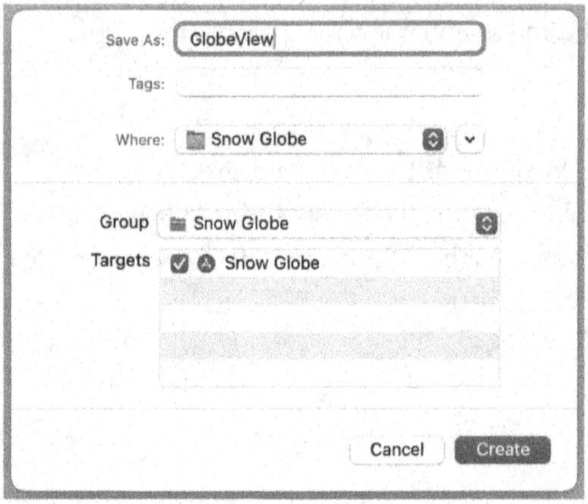

FIGURE 3.36 Saving the new SwiftUI View file as GlobeView within your project

It should now appear in your Project Navigator. Select the new file because you need to make a few changes before it's ready.

You need access to RealityKit features, but the GlobeView file only imports SwiftUI. Add the other necessary RealityKit frameworks by adding two additional import lines:

```
import RealityKit
import RealityKitContent
```

These lines already exist in `ContentView`, so you only need them in the GlobeView.swift file.

Because you're going to be working with more than one window, you need the ability to display and dismiss them. Recall that you gain this by adding in `@Environment` property wrappers to a view. Because you'll be controlling the `GlobeView` from the `ContentView`, add this code to `ContentView` immediately after the `struct ContentView: View` line.

```
@Environment(\.openWindow) private var openWindow
@Environment(\.dismissWindow) private var dismissWindow
```

You now can open and dismiss the `GlobeView` window from within `ContentView`.

Adding an Environment Object for Settings

The application is going to present the user with options for how they want the snow globe to appear. You collect that information in the `ContentView` window, but we'll use it in the `GlobeView`. To do this, you can make use of the global variables or an environment object, as I discuss earlier in this chapter.

Create an environment object to hold the settings. There are three attributes of a snow globe that you want to track and modify:

- Is the snowperson displayed?

- Is the tree visible?

- Is it snowing?

Add a new class to the end of the ContentView.swift file. The class should be named Globe-Features, and it conforms to `ObservableObject`, like what we reviewed earlier. The class should publish three variables—`snowVisible`, `snowmanVisible`, and `treeVisible`—*and* set their defaults. Your final class code should be similar to **LISTING 3.2**.

LISTING 3.2 Create a Class to Hold the Snow Globe Settings

```
class GlobeFeatures: ObservableObject {
    @Published var snowVisible: Bool = false
    @Published var snowmanVisible: Bool = false
    @Published var treeVisible: Bool = false
}
```

Now, you need to instantiate the class and make sure that you have a modifiable object available in the environment of the `ContentView` and `GlobeView`. You do this in the App file,

Snow_GlobeApp.swift. Open the file; immediately following the `struct Snow_GlobeApp:` View line, add the code to create the new object:

```
@StateObject private var globeSettings = GlobeFeatures()
```

This gives you a `globeSettings` object that you now attach to the views that create your window content. Add this modifier

```
.environmentObject(globeSettings)
```

to the window group code blocks, modifying `ContentView` and `GlobeView` respectively. Your `WindowGroup` code in Snow_GlobeApp.swift should now resemble this:

```
WindowGroup {
    ContentView()
        .environmentObject(globeSettings)
}
WindowGroup(id: "Globe") {
    GlobeView()
        .environmentObject(globeSettings)
}
.windowStyle(.volumetric)
```

You need to declare a variable in `ContentView` and `GlobeView` that you'll use to refer to the object. I'm using the name `globeSettings`, the same as the original object. Add this line to *both* view files, immediately after the `struct <View Name>` line:

```
@EnvironmentObject private var globeSettings: GlobeFeatures
```

Both views now have access to the object `globalSettings` by way of the identically named variable `globeSettings`. This means that the core foundation for the application is set. You now need to code your interface and write some logic.

Creating the ContentView

The `ContentView` for the application is a traditional window and displays a few toggles and buttons, as shown in **FIGURE 3.37**.

You can create this view in whatever manner you'd like. You need to collect Boolean values for whether the different Snow Globe entities are displayed, and you need to store those values in the environment object (`globalSettings`) already created.

In my implementation, I started by adding three `@State` variables to the `ContentView` after the `@Environment` lines:

```
@State private var snowmanSetting = true
@State private var treeSetting = true
@State private var snowSetting = true
```

FIGURE 3.37 A few toggles and buttons to control the Snow Globe.

Once you have these variables set through the user interface, you copy them into the environment object and have access to them in `GlobeView`. How will you set them? Using toggle Bindings, which I cover in Chapter 2.

Clear out whatever cruft the default visionOS template has added to your view. Leave the `VStack` block and associated padding but no other content. Within the Stack, add three toggle switches:

```
Toggle("Include Snowman", isOn: $snowmanSetting)
Toggle("Include Tree", isOn: $treeSetting)
Toggle("Include Snow", isOn: $snowSetting)
```

These switches are bound to the Boolean variables. When a switch is changed, so is the value of the variable.

The view now needs two buttons. One copies these settings to the environment object and then open the volumetric window with a snow globe. The other dismisses any snow globes that you might be displaying.

```
Button("Conjure a Snow Globe") {
        globeSettings.snowVisible=snowSetting
        globeSettings.treeVisible=treeSetting
        globeSettings.snowmanVisible=snowmanSetting
        openWindow(id: "Globe")
}
Button("Close Snow Globes") {
        dismissWindow(id: "Globe")
}
```

NOTE When using *dismissWindow* with an *id*, you close all windows with that id.

The final code listing for the ContentView.swift file is available in **LISTING 3.3**.

LISTING 3.3 ContentView.swift

```swift
import SwiftUI
import RealityKit
import RealityKitContent

struct ContentView: View {
    @EnvironmentObject private var globeSettings: GlobeFeatures
    @Environment(\.openWindow) private var openWindow
    @Environment(\.dismissWindow) private var dismissWindow

    @State private var snowmanSetting = true
    @State private var treeSetting = true
    @State private var snowSetting = true

    var body: some View {
        VStack {
            Toggle("Include Snowman", isOn: $snowmanSetting)
            Toggle("Include Tree", isOn: $treeSetting)
            Toggle("Include Snow", isOn: $snowSetting)
            Spacer()
            Button("Conjure a Snow Globe") {
                globeSettings.snowVisible=snowSetting
                globeSettings.treeVisible=treeSetting
                globeSettings.snowmanVisible=snowmanSetting
                openWindow(id: "Globe")
            }
            Button("Close Snow Globes") {
                dismissWindow(id: "Globe")
            }
        }
        .padding()
    }
}

#Preview(windowStyle: .automatic) {
    ContentView()
}

class GlobeFeatures: ObservableObject {
    @Published var snowVisible: Bool = true
    @Published var snowmanVisible: Bool = true
    @Published var treeVisible: Bool = true
}
```

Creating the GlobeView Content

The content for GlobeView is already done; the scene we built in Reality Composer Pro becomes the content for the "Globe" WindowGroup. You need to load the scene and display it. You'll add a tad of if-then logic to hide the Snow, Snowman, and Tree entities, but otherwise, you only need to display the scene, and you're finished.

As you did with the ContentView, open the GlobeView.swift file and edit the view to remove any unnecessary template content added to the view. To display the scene, add a RealityView that loads the Scene.usda file from the Reality Kit assets:

```
RealityView { content in
        // Add the initial RealityKit content
        if let scene = try? await Entity(named: "Scene", in:
                                    realityKitContentBundle) {
                content.add(scene)
        }
} update: { content in
        // Update the content
}
```

This is *almost* all the code you need, and your app should now run and let you create snow globes around your room, but it isn't going to react to the settings that were made in ContentView. To turn on and off the different entities (Snow, Snowman, and Tree), you first find the entity in the scene and then use the isEnabled property to hide (or show) it based on the globalSettings object properties.

For the snow entity, this looks like this:

```
if let snow = scene.findEntity(named: "Snow") {
        snow.isEnabled=globeSettings.snowVisible
}
```

Adding in the other entity controls results in three statements, like this:

```
if let snow = scene.findEntity(named: "Snow") {
    snow.isEnabled=globeSettings.snowVisible
}
if let snowman = scene.findEntity(named: "Snowman") {
    snowman.isEnabled=globeSettings.snowmanVisible
}
if let tree = scene.findEntity(named: "Tree") {
    tree.isEnabled=globeSettings.treeVisible
}
```

These lines should be located *before* the Scene is added to the view with the line content.add(scene). You can hide the entities *after* the content is displayed, but there may be a visual glitch where it is displayed and immediately hidden.

The final listing for GlobeView.swift is in **LISTING 3.4**.

LISTING 3.4 GlobeView.swift

```
import SwiftUI
import RealityKit
import RealityKitContent

struct GlobeView: View {
    @EnvironmentObject private var globeSettings: GlobeFeatures
    var body: some View {
        VStack {
            RealityView { content in
                // Add the initial RealityKit content
                if let scene = try? await Entity(named: "Scene", in:
                                                realityKitContentBundle) {
                    if let snow = scene.findEntity(named: "Snow") {
                        snow.isEnabled=globeSettings.snowVisible
                    }
                    if let snowman = scene.findEntity(named: "Snowman") {
                        snowman.isEnabled=globeSettings.snowmanVisible
                    }
                    if let tree = scene.findEntity(named: "Tree") {
                        tree.isEnabled=globeSettings.treeVisible
                    }
                    content.add(scene)
                }
            } update: { content in
                // Update the content
            }
        }
    }
}

#Preview {
    GlobeView()
}
```

Fixing the Previews

You may have noticed while working on your project that one or both of the Previews for your views are no longer functioning. The reason for this is that the views now rely on the existence of an environment `GlobeFeatures` object that won't be available unless the application is running normally. To fix the problem, update the `Preview` block to include a newly initialized environment object. For the `GlobeView` preview, this is

```
#Preview {
    GlobeView()
        .environmentObject(GlobeFeatures())
}
```

Add the environment object to both previews, and Xcode should be happy.

Cleaning Up

As a last step, set defaults on the sizes of the windows being created in the window groups. Recall that you can use the `defaultSize` function on the `WindowGroup` to set a size in points for the 2D window or in common units of measure for volumetric windows. You make these changes in Snow_GlobeApp.swift.

I'm sizing my `ContentView` window to 400x275 points, while my Globe fits nicely in a 0.45 cubic meter volume. The final code for Snow_GlobeApp.swift is available in **LISTING 3.5**.

LISTING 3.5 Snow_GlobeApp.swift

```
import SwiftUI

@main
struct Snow_GlobeApp: App {
    @StateObject private var globeSettings = GlobeFeatures()
    var body: some Scene {
        WindowGroup {
            ContentView()
                .environmentObject(globeSettings)
        }
        .defaultSize(width: 400.0, height: 275.0)

        WindowGroup(id: "Globe") {
            GlobeView()
                .environmentObject(globeSettings)
        }
        .windowStyle(.volumetric)
        .defaultSize(width: 0.45, height: 0.45, depth: 0.45, in: .meters)
    }
}
```

Launch the finished Snow Globe application and give it a whirl. Configure snow globes and position them around your space. **FIGURE 3.38** shows the final creation at work.

FIGURE 3.38 Enjoy a world filled with virtual snow globes.

SUMMARY

Chapter 3 continued to introduce new features for existing concepts (such as WindowGroups) as well as new coding and application features. Using Reality Composer Pro in conjunction with RealityKit provides a smooth workflow for prepping, compositing, and displaying 3D content in applications—and that's barely scratching the surface.

You should be getting accustomed to how SwiftUI and Swift code work to join interfaces with logic and content. Interactivity is one of the focuses for the later chapters of this book, so the next chapters continue with a few more basics, and then I move on to showing you how the Apple Vision Pro is more than an expensive way to look at scenes and entities.

Go Further

Think about the snow globe application you created and work to improve it. You may want, for example, to provide control over colors, increase the number of configurable entities, add a fire effect, and so on. You can also update the code so that changes can be applied to snow globes in real time. The project you completed sets up the globe when it's first displayed, but you can easily expand that to update it dynamically as the settings change.

As I've already mentioned, be sure to spend some time with Apple's Reality Composer Pro documentation and tutorials at https://developer.apple.com/augmented-reality/tools/ and https://developer.apple.com/videos/play/wwdc2023/10083/. You may also want to establish a full user account on the SketchFab site (https://sketchfab.com/) to simplify buying and downloading new models.

CHAPTER 4

Creating and Customizing Models and Materials

The first few chapters of this book have immersed you in the tools you need to be a successful Vision Pro developer. In the last two chapters, you've even built functional bare-bones applications. Something you haven't done, however, is make applications your own. Sure, you can use prebuilt objects and download content from SketchFab (and others), but using and reusing publicly available content is a quick way to find your development efforts labeled as "cookie cutter" apps. To be successful, you want to stand out. Even as a hobbyist, you have to ask yourself whether composing scenes using the same objects over and over and over is fun or gets monotonous.

This chapter takes a break from coding to spend some time explaining how to create your own models and materials to use in applications. No, you're not going to need to become an expert at 3D design or CAD drawings. Everything is going to be point and click!

By the end of this chapter, you'll understand several new technologies, including

- **Photogrammetry:** The process of gaining information about objects by analyzing the changes between a series of images. A version of Reality Composer that runs on your iPhone or iPad makes this a breeze.

- **MaterialX:** An Open-source standard for the definition of object materials. Reality Composer Pro (and the Apple development platform) support the use of MaterialX to define the appearance of objects for the Vision Pro. This can be used to add high-quality visual effects (and even animations) to your objects.

- **Node graphs:** A means of visually designing and implementing materials using a series of interconnected nodes that each contribute to the overall appearance of a material. Traditionally, material definition has required specialized hands-on coding, but using Reality Composer Pro's visual tools, you can create new materials in minutes.

- **Surface shaders:** A surface shader is the generic name for the materials you will build to customize the surface appearance of your objects. Using different MaterialX components and functions, surface shaders can dramatically alter how your creations look in the Vision Pro.

- **Geometry modifiers:** Much as a surface shader modifies the appearance of the outside of an object, a geometry modifier can change the appearance of the entire object by changing its shape. Using a geometry modifier, you can create objects that morph over time or because of user interactions. These changes occur during each frame of the rendering process, making your creations more than mere static objects to be displayed.

Despite the friendly interfaces, there's quite a bit of science and math behind these tools and processes. There are ample opportunities to test ideas and make mistakes. Should you be inclined to dive deeper into these tools, I suggest additional resources as we go.

WORKING WITH PHOTOGRAMMETRY AND REALITY COMPOSER

One of the first classes I took in college was computer-aided design (CAD) for engineers. I loved it. I found it fascinating that creating a precise model of real-world objects suddenly gave me access to more information than just a drawing alone. I could see the interactions between different components, design objects that enhanced or altered existing systems, and solve problems that previously would have been guesses. That, however, was a long time ago, when rendering a 3D scene took hours or days, and an entire semester's coursework—including the CAD software itself—could fit on a single-sided 3.5-inch floppy.

Today, although I remain proficient enough to create models of objects if I must, I do not have the time or patience to spend hours making the perfect objects to include in my applications (nor am I remotely as talented as a professional 3D artist.) My options for high-quality 3D assets are either to buy models or commission others. Unfortunately, project budgets (especially personal projects) rarely take asset costs into consideration, so I'm left scratching my head looking for the best way to represent my grandfather's ancient alien artifacts in a scene on the Vision Pro.

> **NOTE** No, I do not have ancient alien artifacts. That's an attempt at humor. All my alien artifacts are relatively modern.

In 2023, Apple introduced a new "guided photogrammetry" feature to Reality Composer. Reality Composer is a lightweight version of Reality Composer Pro that runs on modern iPhones and iPads. Despite the lack of a "Pro" suffix, Reality Composer has features that aren't available in the Pro variant, including photogrammetry.

Earlier I mentioned that photogrammetry uses a series of images to generate data about objects in the photos. While the science and tech needed to generate that data is beyond the scope of this book, the concept is easy to understand. Our bodies use it every day.

Neither of your eyes "knows" anything about an object's size and distance. Each eye "captures" an image that is two-dimensional. Your brain combines these two images into a view that allows you to perceive distances and relative sizes. This is possible because your eyes are offset from one another by an inch or so. The slight change in perspective of each captured image gives your brain the information it needs to extract data about size and distance. Are you conscious that this is taking place? Nope. With photogrammetry, developers have recreated this process on your device. Thanks to the LiDAR sensor in modern iPad Pros and iPhones, the entire process is guided and easy to follow. The whole capture process will take you 5-10 minutes.

Hands-on: Capturing an Object with Photogrammetry

Because you're not going to be coding in this chapter, the hands-on exercises involve Reality Composer on your iPhone/iPad and Reality Composer Pro on your Mac. First, get your devices ready!

Downloading Reality Composer

To begin capturing your own models, you need to download Reality Composer for your iOS/iPadOS device from the App Store (see **FIGURE 4.1**): https://apps.apple.com/app/reality-composer/id1462358802/.

TIP The Reality Composer photogrammetry process involves walking (or crawling) in circles around the object you want to capture, so I highly recommend using an iPhone for comfort's sake.

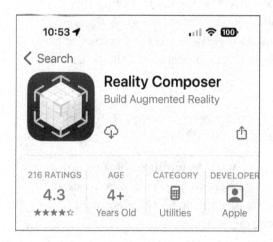

FIGURE 4.1 Getting Reality Composer for your iPhone or iPad from the App Store

Once the app is installed, you'll want to put down your device for a few minutes to prep your capture area. The better the setup, the better the result.

If your device includes a LiDAR sensor but isn't compatible with the object capture feature of Reality Composer, download 3D Scanner App from the App Store (https://apps.apple.com/us/app/3d-scanner-app/id1419913995). This free app offers similar features but works on a larger range of devices.

Picking the Object and Setting Up for Capture

Object Capture works best with nontransparent and matte objects. In my experience, it is surprisingly forgiving, so even if you have something that may be problematic, give it a try. Fine details are a challenge; don't expect to see the individual hairs on a doll. Despite these caveats, the results can be nothing short of amazing.

Everything you need for object capture is readily available in most homes. I find that a waist-height table or stool makes the perfect stand for the object. A white sheet or towel draped across the surface helps isolate the object from its background and also helps you focus during the capture process. Most importantly, you must have the ability to comfortably move around the object at a constant distance. I had great difficulty getting a clean capture when I tried to pass my phone around the back of an object by hand. Only once I was able to walk around the stand was I able to start getting the results I wanted.

Lastly, make sure the environment is lit with even diffuse lighting. Harsh shadows are your enemy during the process. **FIGURE 4.2** shows my chosen object and its evenly lit stand. Yes, that's a creepy antique mannequin hat model (or "Creepy Head" as I will refer to it throughout the chapter).

FIGURE 4.2 In a well-lit area, place your object on a white stand with plenty of room to walk around.

Take a few minutes to select an object and create a capture area in your home, classroom, or workplace. If there isn't enough room, head outside and commandeer a picnic table or the top of a trashcan. Natural diffuse lighting is great for captures.

Using Guided Capture

To use guided capture, you need the ability to follow simple onscreen instructions. If I can do it, so can you. Open the Reality Composer app on your device and tap the + button in the upper right, as shown in **FIGURE 4.3**.

Next, choose the Object Capture by touching the large gray picture button at the bottom of the screen, as shown in **FIGURE 4.4**.

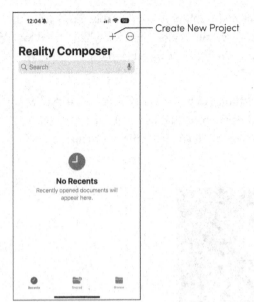

Create New Project

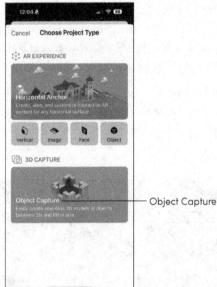

Object Capture

FIGURE 4.3 Tapping + to create a new object capture project

FIGURE 4.4 No, that's not a header graphic, it's a button. Tap Object Capture to begin.

Reality Composer asks you to place the white dot on the center of your object. You don't need to place it perfectly—just in the vicinity of what looks like the vertical and horizontal center of the object, as shown in **FIGURE 4.5**. Tap Continue when you're satisfied with the positioning.

Using the LiDAR sensor in your device, Reality Composer analyzes what it can see and draws a **bounding box** around the object that it detects. A bounding box is intended to encompass all parts of a 3D model. You need to walk around your object to see if the box fully contains your object. If it doesn't, you need to resize the box.

Along each edge of the bounding box is a glowing white handle. Touch and drag on a handle to expand or shrink that side of the box, as shown in **FIGURE 4.6**.

When ready, touch Start Capture to begin the capture process. As I've already mentioned, this is *guided* capture and requires a bit of direction-following. So that's exactly what you're going to do—follow the onscreen instructions!

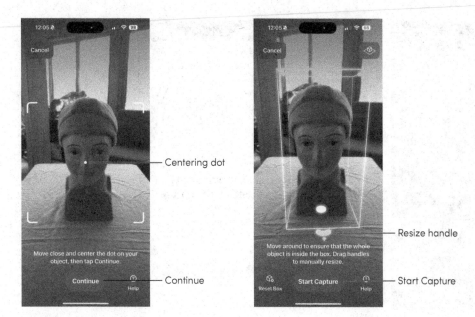

FIGURE 4.5 Center your object in the preview and tap Continue.

FIGURE 4.6 Using the handles on the box to size it to fit your object

Keeping the dot on your object and maintaining a steady distance from it, move around the object, filling in the segmented completion graph in Reality Composer. If segments are missing, you need to revisit those areas, as shown in **FIGURE 4.7**. Errors about distance, speed, and lighting will appear, directing you to correct your approach mid-flight.

As you fill in the circle, you see points start to appear that represent the shape of your object. This is called a **point cloud**. Don't pay too much attention to this. It is a *very* rough approximation of the object.

> **TIP** There is no need to use the additional buttons in the UI. Feel free to explore, but be assured that the guided capture process moves from step to step automatically.

At points during the capture, you may be prompted to lay the object on its side and continue capturing, as shown in **FIGURE 4.8**. This ensures you're getting *all* sides and textures. This doesn't work with all objects, however, so Reality Composer informs you if you need to skip this step.

Error

Point cloud

Completion graph

FIGURE 4.7 Moving around the object and filling in the segments around the base

FIGURE 4.8 If prompted, lay your object on its side, and continue capturing.

You need to make at least three passes around your object—from low, medium, and high angles. With the completion of each pass, Reality Composer prompts you to start another.

Once you've finished the capture process, tap Finish, as shown in **FIGURE 4.9**. This is the longest step because the computation is happening. Prepare to wait 5 to 10 minutes.

> **NOTE** During the guided process, you're asked whether to include the surroundings of the object. You can try this, but in my experience, it creates too much "noise" to be useful. If you initially don't include surroundings, you still have a toggle switch to reprocess and include surroundings after the initial module is generated. This is visible in **FIGURE 4.10**.

After a few minutes, the model appears. As you can see in **FIGURE 4.10**, the creepy mannequin head looks almost photorealistic. Drag and pinch with your fingers to move and resize the model. Use the AR button to view the object in augmented reality mode and see how well it blends with your space.

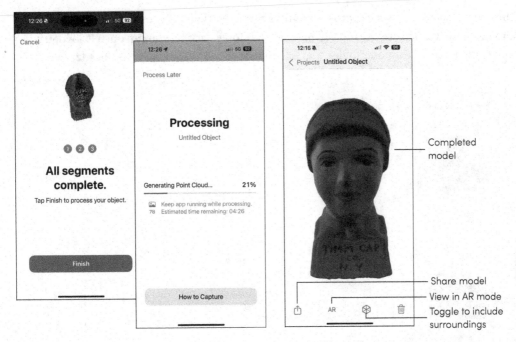

Completed model

Share model
View in AR mode
Toggle to include surroundings

FIGURE 4.9 Tap Finish when prompted. Wait patiently while your device creates the model.

FIGURE 4.10 The completed model can be manipulated in three dimensions.

Sharing with Reality Composer Pro

Once your model is ready, you can share it with Reality Composer Pro through a few different means. The first (and fastest) is through the Share button. After taping Share, you'll be prompted to choose between two different formats for the model, as shown in **FIGURE 4.11**.

The first format, 3D Model Only, creates a .usdz file that can be sent via AirDrop, Messages, email, and so on. As you learned in the last chapter, a universal scene description file can be opened directly in Reality Composer Pro and immediately used in your projects.

The second option, 3D Model and Photos, is a bit different, and the result is much larger in size. When you share using this option, you're sending an object capture (.objcap) file rather than the finished model. This is a special folder structure that includes all the photos taken to generate your model. Your Mac can use the capture data to generate models at different levels of detail rather than the default level of your iPhone or iPad. I talk more about this in a bit.

> **NOTE** If you use the Reality Composer interface to rename your object capture project, it disappears and is replaced by a folder. For some reason, Reality Composer strips the file extension when renaming and makes your capture session inaccessible. To fix this issue, just rename the folder, adding **.objcap** to the end, and it turns back into a file that you can work with.

The *easiest* way to access the captured model is through iCloud. If your devices are all logged into the same iCloud account and you have iCloud storage active, you can open iCloud, navigate to the Reality Composer folder, and find the file there, as shown in **FIGURE 4.12**.

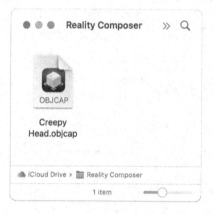

FIGURE 4.11 Choosing how you want to share the model

FIGURE 4.12 If you use iCloud storage on your devices, the files are accessible across all your devices.

Reprocessing the Model in Reality Composer Pro

If you'd like to eke out an extra level of detail in your model, make sure that you've transferred the .objcap file to your Mac and then double-click to open it. Reality Composer Pro opens, displaying the captured images and presenting a few options for generating a model, as shown in **FIGURE 4.13**.

The Quality settings change the "resolution" of the mesh that will make up your model. A mesh made of tiny polygons can capture more detail but requires many more system resources to render than a large polygon mesh.

The model you created on your handheld device is equivalent to the "reduced quality" setting. Choose from the quality popup menu and decide whether to include the environment with your object. Click Create Model, visible in Figure 4.13, to begin processing the images.

After a few minutes, the window updates to show the new model, as shown in **FIGURE 4.14**. If you want to try something else, use the popup menus to choose new settings and click Reprocess. Otherwise, click Export and save your final .usdz file, which is ready for use.

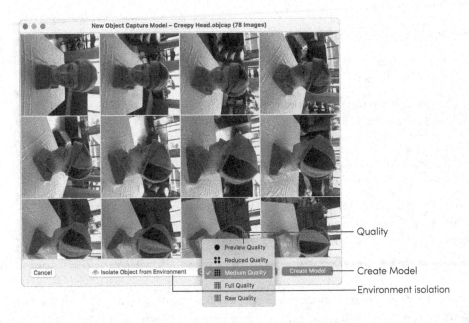

Quality

Create Model

Environment isolation

FIGURE 4.13 Using the Mac to create a model at several different quality settings

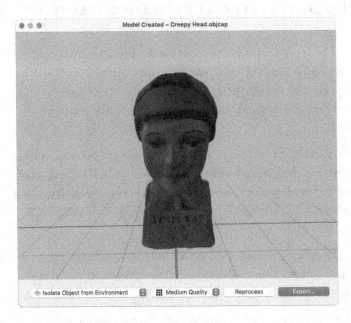

FIGURE 4.14 Export or reprocess your model.

Now that you can create your own models, let's take a look at creating *materials*. You can retire your iPhone or iPad; you'll spend the rest of the chapter in Reality Composer Pro.

CUSTOMIZING SCENES WITH MATERIALX, SHADERS, AND NODE GRAPHS

In the last chapter, we learned the basics of constructing scenes in Reality Composer Pro, and you even customized a material by setting colors, opacity, and other attributes. You used a "physically based" material. The built-in shader offers the ability to quickly generate some lovely materials, but it barely scratches the surface (unintentional pun!) of what you can accomplish with a custom shader.

MaterialX was developed by Industrial Light and Magic in 2012, released as open source in 2017, and adopted by industry giants such as Sony, Adobe, Pixar, and now Apple. The goal of the project is to build an open format for defining object appearance that can be used without royalties and shared among production companies and applications. (You can learn more about MaterialX at https://materialx.org.)

You will build custom surface shaders that use MaterialX as the underlying technology, and that's all you really need to know about MaterialX. The creation of the shader is what's important, not what is hidden on the backend.

Surface shaders are built in a node graph —also called a shader graph in some Apple documentation—within Reality Composer Pro. Using a term like node graph, in my opinion, is a convenient way to "gate" the process of creating effects by making it seem overly technical. A node graph is a series of boxes, connected by lines, where the output of one box is connected to the input of another (think "flowchart"). You might define a custom wood shader by connecting an "image" node that references a wood grain texture image to the surface color attribute of a material node. I give you an example shortly.

If this all sounds like technobabble to you, just know that you're going to be creating materials (surface shaders) by connecting different components that help describe the surface (a node graph). Making it all work behind the scenes is MaterialX.

I SEE THERE ARE SOME NICE HIGH-QUALITY MATERIALS THAT I CAN DOWNLOAD FOR FREE. CAN I USE THE TEXTURES I DOWNLOAD?

Open-source formats frequently result in a wealth of public content being made available, and MaterialX is no different. Unfortunately, in its current state there is no way to import MaterialX (.mtlx) materials into Reality Composer Pro. Apple supports importing materials that are part of USD files, but standalone textures are a no-show.

That being said, MaterialX *is* an open-source and text-based XML format. If you download a MaterialX material, it comes as a zipped folder structure. Within the folder are any resources required to build the material, along with a .mtlx file that describes each node and value that goes into the shader. After you've had a bit of experience creating your own custom shaders, you'll find it pretty easy to recreate the shader just by reading the text file and configuring the building blocks (nodes) within Reality Composer Pro.

I've included a car paint material ("Car_Paint_2k_16b") that you can use as a practice project at the end of this chapter. You can find other examples at the free online library here: https://matlib.gpuopen.com/main/materials/all

Hopefully Apple adds support for directly importing these materials soon!

Node Graphs

It isn't very easy to describe a node graph while showing you how to build one, so let's start with a graph that already exists, and I'll talk you through how it was created. Within the Chapter 4 download, open the Wooden Material folder and then double-click the Package. realitycomposerpro file to launch Reality Composer Pro.

When the workspace opens, you probably won't see much of anything except a wooden sphere, a bit like **FIGURE 4.15**.

By default, Scene.usda *should* be open, if not, switch to the Project Browser to open it (see Chapter 3, "Getting Started with Reality Composer Pro," for more details on working in the Project Browser). Make sure that the scene hierarchy is expanded so you can see Sphere and Wood Grain.

Now click Wood_Grain in the scene hierarchy and click the Shader Graph tab directly above the editor. You are now looking at the material definition for the wood appearance of the sphere, as shown in **FIGURE 4.16**.

Scene Hierarchy

Scene   Project Browser   Shader Graph

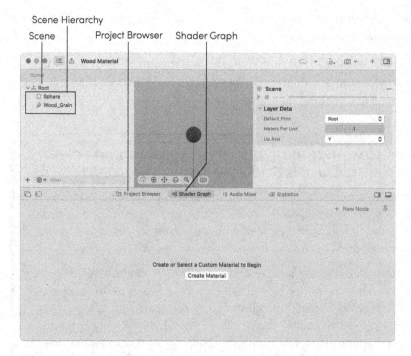

FIGURE 4.15 Open the project and expand the scene hierarchy.

Set the object color to the tiled image

Load image file   Tile image   Send the new material to the Custom Surface" input

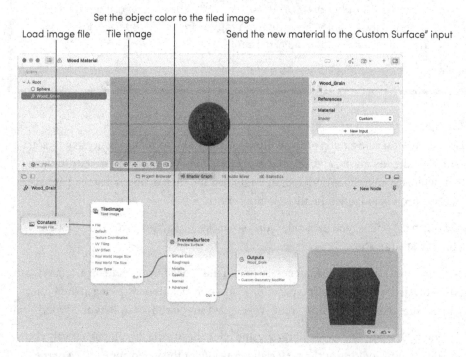

FIGURE 4.16 The scene contains a woodgrain sphere. Zoom in if you don't believe me.

Dissecting the Shader Graph

There are four nodes that make up the node graph (also known as the custom surface shader), and each performs a simple function along the way.

On the far left, the initial node opens an image file. What image file? Let's find out! Select the Constant Image File node and look at the Inputs panel in the inspector. Any values that can be configured manually are displayed here. As shown in **FIGURE 4.17**, the image file is set to woodgrain.jpg, an image file I've already added to the project. Clicking to the right of the filename in the inspector allows me to pick from any image in the project.

> **NOTE** To be clear, you can pick only images you've added via the Project Browser in Reality Composer Pro, not images located elsewhere on your Mac.

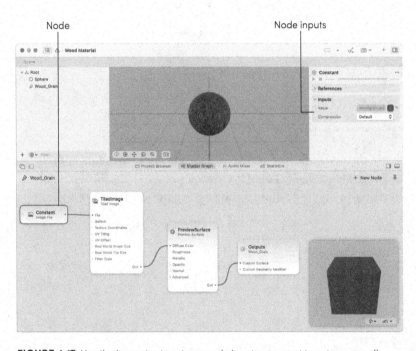

FIGURE 4.17 Use the inspector to set any node inputs you want to enter manually.

In the shader graph, I've added a Tiled Image node. This node can take an image and tile it so that a single image isn't stretched over huge objects. If you remember when you used to have to apply repeating desktop patterns on your Mac versus having a giant background, this is the same concept.

I create a tiled image from the single woodgrain image—three tiles horizontally and three vertically. I do this by selecting the Tiled Image node and using the inspector to edit the inputs beside UV Tiling; I enter 3 in the first field (horizontal) and 3 in the second field (vertical), as shown in **FIGURE 4.18**.

Node connection
File input   Tiling node   Tiling inputs

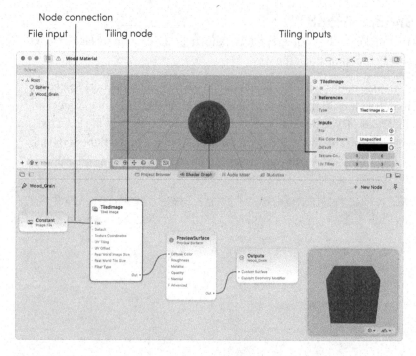

FIGURE 4.18 Tiling the image gives more texture to work with.

Initially, the image loaded in the first node isn't available to the tile node, so there's nothing for it to tile. To make the image file available, I drag from its output dot to the file input dot on the second image. This is visible in Figure 4.18 and is shown in a close-up in **FIGURE 4.19.**

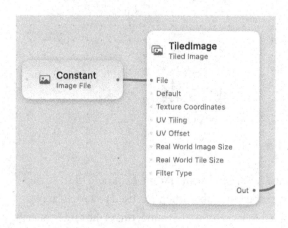

FIGURE 4.19 The output of the image node feeds the input of the tile node.

Now, I'm left with two nodes: Preview Surface and Outputs. These nodes are added automatically to shaders. The first, Preview Surface, is a configurable physical surface node identical to the physical surface attributes that you used last chapter. Using the inputs of the Preview Surface node, you can manually configure any of the physical surface properties you'd like. You can feed others, such as the Diffuse Color (the base color), via the output of one of your nodes. For the tiled woodgrain texture, I choose to use the output of the Tiled Image to feed the Diffuse Color input, as shown in **FIGURE 4.20**. I've also set the Roughness input of the Preview Surface node to 1.0. This wood isn't intended to be shiny.

Finally, the Preview Surface node's output contains the finished surface. To make it apply to an object, it feeds the Custom Surface input of the Output node. This connection is added by default; breaking it causes your objects to show a dismal gray color as the surface.

That's it! That's all there is to this shader. It's now available to use on any object I add to my Reality Composer Pro project.

FIGURE 4.20 The Tiled Image node subsequently outputs an image that provides the Diffuse Color input for the Preview Surface node.

COMPLEXITY FOR LEARNING'S SAKE

I'm going to come clean. This surface shader is largely unnecessary and was just a means of providing an easy-to-understand example. If you were reading closely, you might have noticed that the node graph takes an image file and feeds it to the File input of Tile Image. Rather than bother with the node that loads the image, it could just be set in the inspector when viewing the Tile Image node, resulting in a shader graph with only one real node.

Furthermore, if I wasn't concerned about the tiling, I could have just set the image file directly as the diffuse color of a physically based material and never bothered with a graph at all.

Surface Shaders Versus Geometry Modifiers

The graph that we've just reviewed is an example of a surface shader. In looking at the nodes, you may have noticed that the Outputs node has another input: Custom Geometry Modifier.

As previously mentioned, a surface shader changes the outside appearance of an object. The shader graph is run once for every single pixel that is displayed for the object *per frame*. A geometry modifier (or geometry shader) is built in an identical fashion but alters the geometry of the object. In other words, a geometry modifier can change the attributes that define the shape, location, and size of an object.

Geometry modifiers work by altering the vertices of a model, once per frame. A **vertex** is a corner or edge where two faces of a 3D object come together. If you increase the X value of all the vertices in an object, the object moves to the right. Add to the Y value, and the object moves up, and so on.

Not all objects have vertices. Spheres, for example, do not have any edges that come together. However, you can still apply geometry modifiers to these objects, and MaterialX makes sure they do what you want.

> **TIP** For a vertex-less sphere, you can imagine that the vertices are three lines that run perpendicularly to one another: side to side, front to back, and top to bottom. The same can be assumed for a cylinder—another shape with no vertices. In other words, just because a shape doesn't technically have vertices doesn't mean it can't be modified. These special cases will be taken care of for you.

Later in this chapter, you create a geometry modifier and see how a material has more power than just slapping a coat of paint on a shape.

CREATING A CUSTOM SHADER GRAPH

Now that you've seen what to expect from a node graph (and a shader graph, specifically), it's time to find out how to build one from scratch. To do this, start with a blank slate in Reality Composer Pro. Name the new project **Mottled Colors**. You're going to create a surface that looks a bit like an abstract watercolor painting or a tie-dye shirt. Although you could create a new material without an object, it's easier to work with a basic scene so that you can get a good look at your creation.

To that end, add a sphere to the default scene in the new project. Within the scene hierarchy, expand the Sphere object. Your scene should resemble **FIGURE 4.21**.

Now, select DefaultMaterial and press Delete. DefaultMaterial is the white/grayish default material that is attached to the sphere when you add it, and you don't need it. The sphere takes on a swirly candy-cane appearance (see **FIGURE 4.22**) to show it doesn't have a material attached.

You now have a scene with a sphere and zero materials. Time to add one!

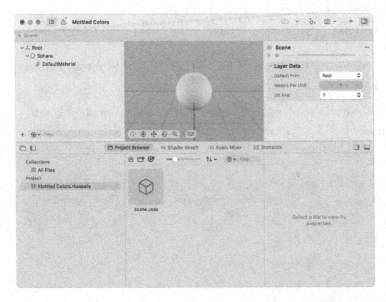

FIGURE 4.21 Add a sphere to the scene and then expand the sphere within the scene hierarchy.

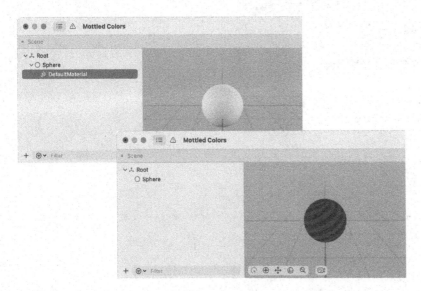

FIGURE 4.22 Select and delete the default material. Objects without a material have a pinkish candy-cane surface.

Adding a Material

To add a new material, make sure you select the Shader Graph tab above the editor area. Click the Create Material button in the center of the editor or click the + below the scene hierarchy and choose Material, Custom, as shown in **FIGURE 4.23**.

Once the new material is added, you see the shader graph refresh to show the Preview Surface and Outputs nodes, as in **FIGURE 4.24**.

You build the rest of the (small) shader graph off the Preview Surface node. You can use your trackpad or mouse (and typical macOS gestures) to zoom in and out in the graph editor. You effectively have an infinite canvas for the graph.

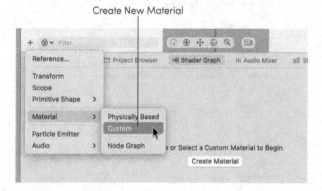

FIGURE 4.23 Creating a new material

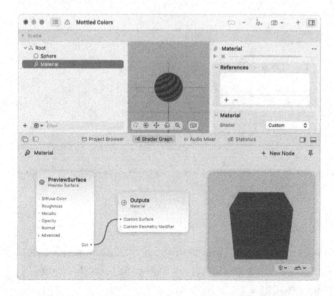

FIGURE 4.24 The shader graph for the new material has two nodes added by default.

Adding Nodes

To add a new node to the graph, you can either click + New Node in the upper-right corner of the editor or click and drag from an existing node input that you want connected to the new node.

I prefer (and encourage you) to drag from the input dot when possible because doing so restricts the node choices to only those that are compatible with the input. For this surface, I want to change the color of the surface, so I click and drag from the Diffuse Color input in the Preview Surface to an empty spot in the graph, as shown in **FIGURE 4.25**.

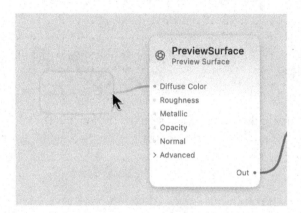

FIGURE 4.25 Adding new nodes by dragging from existing inputs

When you release your mouse or trackpad button, you're prompted for the type of node to add, as shown in **FIGURE 4.26**.

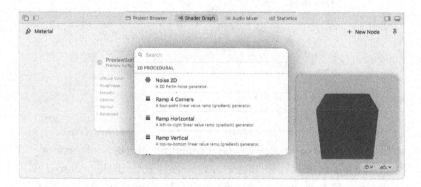

FIGURE 4.26 Choosing the type of node to add

Use the Search field to find a node type based on description or name; alternatively, scroll through the list and click the node you want. I'm adding a Fractal3D node, which uses a fractal algorithm to generate organized patterns. As soon as the node is added, you can see the effect in the preview square in the lower right of the editor, as shown in **FIGURE 4.27**.

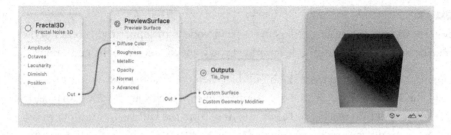

FIGURE 4.27 The new node immediately starts feeding the Diffuse Color input of the surface with the result displayed in the preview area.

NOTE If you choose to add a node using the + New Node button, the only difference is that you can choose from a much longer list of nodes (some of which might not be compatible with what you're trying to do), and you need to click and drag from the Out of the node you added to the input dot of the node you want to feed.

I didn't particularly like the initial appearance of this material, so I selected the Fractal3D node and used the inspector to alter the inputs as shown in **FIGURE 4.28**. I've set the Amplitudes to 3, Octaves to 5, and Lacunarity to 3.

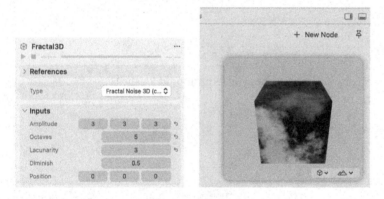

FIGURE 4.28 Altering node inputs to achieve the desired effect

Let's address the elephant in the room. How in the world do you know what any of these values *do*? Describing all the node inputs and outputs and the mathematics behind them would be a wonderful book, but it isn't *this* book. Thankfully, you can refer to the MaterialX specification found on the MaterialX website for a description of all the available nodes; visit https://materialx.org/Specification.html.

In this case, I simply played with the values until I found an effect I liked, and I encourage you to do the same. If you add a node that doesn't do what you want, just select it and press Delete. No harm done.

Naming the Material

By default, the materials you create have the very descriptive name of *Material*. To change this, click the name in the scene hierarchy and then slightly wiggle the cursor or press Return. The text becomes editable, and you can change it to anything you want. In **FIGURE 4.29**, I've changed the material to be named "Tie_Dye."

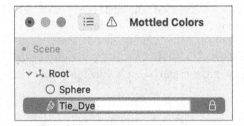

FIGURE 4.29 Setting the names of the material to something descriptive

Assigning the Material to an Object

After you've created a material, you can apply it to a scene's objects. To do this, select an object within the scene hierarchy and then turn your attention to the Material Bindings in the inspector.

In my sample scene, I select the sphere I've added and choose Tie_Dye from the Material Bindings inspector (see **FIGURE 4.30**).

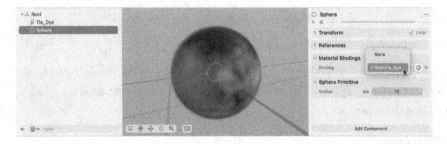

FIGURE 4.30 Using the inspector and the Material Bindings panel to bind your custom material to an object

> **NOTE** If you try to name a material with spaces or dashes (or other special characters), Reality Composer Pro will "fix" the name for you. Tie-Dye, for example, becomes Tie_Dye.

Using Inputs for Reusable Materials

Once you've created a new material, you can assign it to any object within your scene. What you *can't* do, however, is make any changes to the material without it affecting all the objects that use it. You can, of course, make as many copies of the material as you want, but if you decide to make a change in one, you have to make the change in all your copies.

To create something more reusable, you can use **Inputs**. An input is a special node type that you add through the inspector. It appears slightly differently from other nodes.

For example, let's suppose I want to reuse my Tie_Dye material on multiple objects, but I also want to alter the Lacunarity value for each to change how "mottled" the surface appears (very smooth at 0 to a very dotty dithered appearance at 100).

By adding an Input to the material, I can connect it to the Lacunarity (or any other input) on Fractal3D node and be able to change the appearance of the material each time it is used.

Adding Inputs

To add an input, I select the Tie_Dye material in the object hierarchy and then click New Input from the Material panel of the inspector, as shown in **FIGURE 4.31**.

FIGURE 4.31 Adding inputs to enable customization of finished materials

When prompted, choose what value the input should provide and a name. I'm going to name the Input node "Mottledness" and set it to be a floating-point value (see **FIGURE 4.32**). Click Add to finish adding the input.

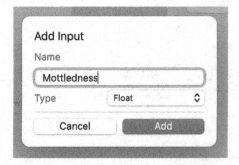

FIGURE 4.32 Configuring the input with a name and value type

A new Input node (designated by a blue color) is now available in the shader graph. I can connect this node to the Lacunarity value of the Fractal3D node. **FIGURE 4.33** shows my completed (and now reusable) shader.

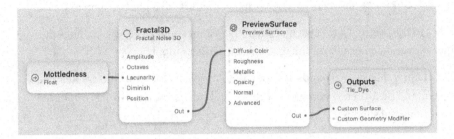

FIGURE 4.33 Connecting the Input nodes to the appropriate inputs of your other nodes

Adding a Material Instance

To use the newly improved material on another object, you must create an **instance** of material. An instance is a reference to the original material that enables you to change the input value (Mottledness for my example) but nothing else. To create a new material instance, right-click the Tie_Dye material in the hierarchy and choose Create Instance, as shown in **FIGURE 4.34**.

The new instance will have the suffix _1 added (or a number that represents how many instances you've created), but you can rename it as if it were any other material. In **FIGURE 4.35**, I've renamed the new instance to "Spotty_Tie_Dye." If you attempt to view the shader graph, you find out it's an instance and can't be edited.

FIGURE 4.34 Creating a new instance of the material

FIGURE 4.35 Renaming the instances to keep track of what they are

Using the inspector, I can change the Mottledness input of the material instance. I'm choosing to set it to 50.

Now you can add a new object to the scene (I've picked a Capsule) and apply the updated material instance. **FIGURE 4.36** shows my scene with one material driving two appearances.

If I make changes to the original Tie_Dye material, my instance inherits those changes but keeps its unique appearance because of the unique Mottledness input.

To close out the chapter, I have two hands-on node graph projects for you. One creates a custom surface shader and the other a geometry modifier. In both cases, the result is *animated* materials, not just colorful shapes!

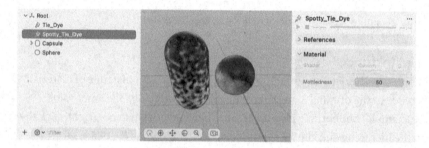

FIGURE 4.36 A single material can provide multiple variations through instances.

HANDS-ON: ANIMATED VISIBILITY

The shader graphs you've seen are fine, but they are small examples created with the intention of introducing you to different nodes and how they interact. What I haven't covered is how you make shader graphs "do" something without requiring some manual configuration of parameters. Even the Mottledness attribute in the reusable graph in the last section is a manual input.

How can a graph generate its own input? The answer is a very useful node called Time that provides the current time in seconds. During this project, you'll see how a simple counting Time node can be used in interesting ways.

In this project, you create a custom material that fades in and out of existence. To do this, you need to adjust the opacity of the surface from 0 to 1 and back again. You also need some way to adjust the speed so that you can get a fast urgent effect or a slow calm fade.

FIGURE 4.37 shows the two states: visible and invisible, with a fading transition. Be kind, it's difficult to show animation in a printed image.

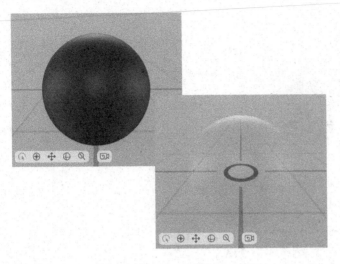

FIGURE 4.37 Now you see it. Now you don't!

Setting Up the Project and Scene

We're at a point now where you should have many basics under control. I still guide you through this exercise, but I don't describe steps that you've been through several times (such as setting up Reality Composer Pro or Xcode Projects) in detail.

To get ready for the new animated material, you'll need a new Reality Composer Pro project and a scene populated by an object with no materials. Follow these steps to prepare:

1. Create a new Reality Composer Pro project named **Now You See Me**.

2. Prepare the default scene by adding a sphere or another object of your choice.

3. Delete the default material from the object.

Your project workspace should resemble **FIGURE 4.38**.

Great! You're ready to start creating your animated material. Rather than just adding nodes willy-nilly, it makes sense to think through the shader logic and decide what you need ahead of time. Plan then implement.

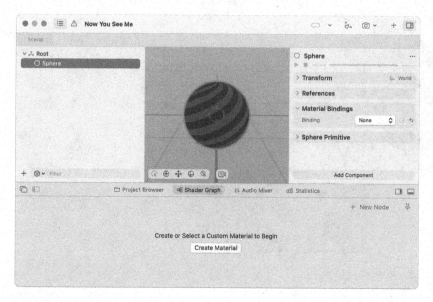

FIGURE 4.38 Creating a new project with a single object containing no material

Planning Shader Graph Logic

To build a material that animates, you know that you need a value that changes. Animations happen over time, so a Time node is the obvious starting point for any animated graph.

Time

Time is a representation of the current time in seconds and is constantly increasing. The goal of this project is to vary the opacity of the surface between 1 and 0. If you use Time to feed opacity directly, the object would be permanently opaque because it is *never* going to be zero. Nevertheless, Time will be the primary driver of this surface shader.

Sin

How do you modify the time so that it becomes a nice smooth count from 1.0 to 0.0 and then back again? The answer is found in the sine wave function: Sin, for short. Sin is a periodic function that varies from –1 to 1 and then 1 to –1 over time, as shown in **FIGURE 4.39**.

With that knowledge, you should be able to feed a Time node to a Sin node and get back a value that varies from –1 to 1 over time.

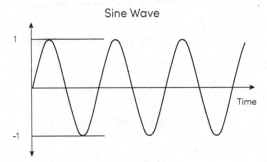

FIGURE 4.39 A sine wave is a great way to get something to count up and then back down again.

Remap

For this project (and many others), you're looking for a value that isn't in the range of –1 to 1. For opacity, we need 1 to 0. Other projects may have different requirements; you just need a way to turn one range into another. The key to this is a node named Remap. Remap takes one range and turns it into another. You can feed it with the output of Sin and have it produce values from 1 to 0 (or any other range) without having to do anything but configure and connect the nodes.

The output of the Remap node can directly feed the opacity, giving the desired result.

Division

One of the requirements of this new material is that we have an easy way to set the speed of the fade-in and fade-out. Because you can't "slow down" the real-world time value produced by the Time node (unless you are a superhero or villain), you need some way to make time appear to be slower or faster before it enters the Sin node.

You don't really care what the time *is,* just that it is an increasing number. This means you can effectively slow it down through simple division. If you want the effect to take twice as long to run, you can divide the time by 2. If you want it to run twice as fast, you divide by 0.5. And you do this with... you guessed it... a Divide node.

Inputs

To make this material reusable with different speeds, you add a single input—a floating point Speed Input that will be the divisor in our Divide node.

The Solution

Putting all these pieces together results in a planned shader graph that looks a bit like **FIGURE 4.40.**

In plain English, you start with a Time node, Divide it by an arbitrary Speed node (a floating-point number). That result feeds a Sin node, and then you use the Remap node to change the output of Sin from 0 to 1. The result drives the Opacity input in the default Preview Surface node.

If that sounds pretty simple, it is. Let's get to building!

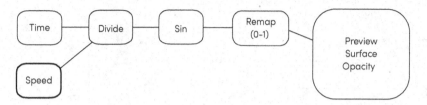

FIGURE 4.40 The plan for the shader graph that creates a speed-controlled fade-out/in effect for an object.

Creating the Shader Graph

Begin by creating a new material within the scene. Rename the generic Material to something more meaningful, such as **Pulsing_Opacity**. You should now have a simple shader graph consisting of the Preview Surface node and the Outputs node. Select Preview Surface and use the inspector to set a Diffuse Color input that you like. If you don't do this, you'll just have a gross gray default color to stare at.

I also find it useful to set the scene's object(s) to the new material before it is even fully built. This enables you to preview the scene in real time as the material is created. Select the object in your scene and use the Material Binding settings in the inspector to assign Pulsing_Opacity. Your workspace should now resemble **FIGURE 4.41**.

> **NOTE** If you're wondering why I bother adding a new object rather than just using the preview in the lower right of the graph, it's for the sake of flexibility. The preview offers almost zero control over what you're seeing, which is fine for a quick peek. However, it isn't nearly as effective as using any object you want and seeing a material's effect directly within a scene.

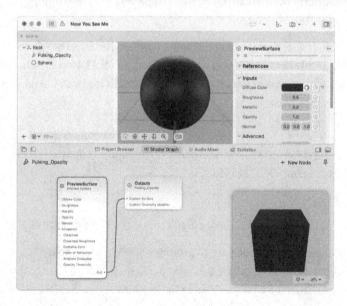

FIGURE 4.41 Your workplace should contain an object and a new material (Pulsing_Opacity) with a diffuse color assigned.

Adding the Nodes

Start the graph by adding a new Time node. Click the + New Material button, type **Time** in the node type search field (see **FIGURE 4.42**), and then click the Time entry to add it to the graph.

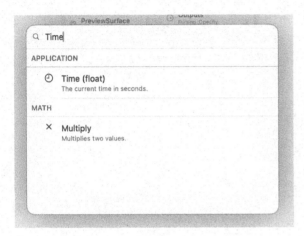

FIGURE 4.42 Adding a Time node

Click and drag the Time node so it is on the far left of the graph, just like the node plan we reviewed earlier. Because you want to control the "speed" of time through division, you need a Float input for the speed and a Divide node to handle the division.

Drag from the output of the Time node to a blank space beside it. When prompted to choose a node type, either scroll or search for Divide and add it to the graph. **FIGURE 4.43** shows the current graph.

To add the second value (the divisor), click New Input within the Materials panel of the inspector. (Remember, Input nodes are *not* added with the + New Node button.) Name the new input **Speed** and set it to a Float value. Drag from the output of the new Speed Input node bottom input dot of the Divide node.

Once the connection is added, use the inspector to change the Speed value to 2.0. If you forget to set a speed, nothing happens once all the parts are connected. Your graph should now look like **FIGURE 4.44**.

Turning back to the plan, you want to use the results of the division to feed the Sin function. Drag from the output of the Divide node to a blank spot on the canvas and choose Sin when prompted. **FIGURE 4.45** shows the updated graph.

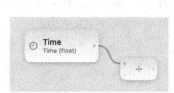

FIGURE 4.43 Time needs to be divided.

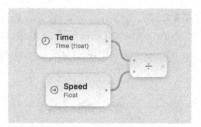

FIGURE 4.44 You now have an adjustable time value available at the output of the Divide node.

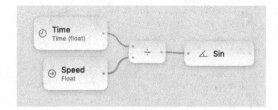

FIGURE 4.45 You now have a value that varies from 1 to –1 at an adjustable speed.

There's only one more step to go! You need the values that you hand off to the Opacity input to be between 1 and 0. Drag from the output of the Sin node into an empty space beside it. When prompted to add a node, choose Remap. Notice that Remap has quite a few more inputs than the other nodes, as shown in **FIGURE 4.46**.

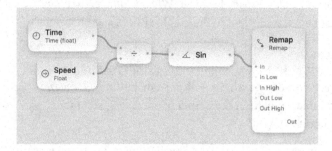

FIGURE 4.46 The Remap node requires a teensy bit of configuration.

You provide the inputs that Remap needs by selecting the Remap node and using the Inputs panel in the inspector. The Sin function provides the main input, but you still need to config-ure In Low, In High, Out Low, and Out High. These inputs are largely self-explanatory. For the In Low and High values, provide –1 and 1 (the values produced by the Sin node). For the Out values, you want Low to be 0 and the High to be 1, as shown in **FIGURE 4.47**.

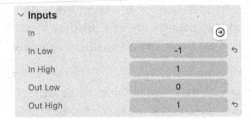

FIGURE 4.47 Remapping the Sin output into proper Opacity values

Lastly, drag from the output of the Remap node to the Opacity input node on Preview Surface. Your time-based animated surface shader is now complete, and your scene object should begin pulsing in the workspace. **FIGURE 4.48** shows the final shader graph for the Pulsing_Opacity material.

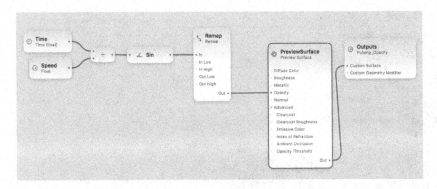

FIGURE 4.48 The finished shader graph

More Exploring

This is just a starting point for time-based materials. Try driving other inputs using time-based values. Revisit the Mottled Colors project (provided in your Chapter 4 downloads) and use the time (remapped to a larger range of values, of course) to drive Lacunarity. Or just play around; altering the **normal** (the direction in which light reflects from a surface) is a fun way to get some interesting effects. You can use the provided Animated Shine example to see some additional effects that you might want to incorporate into your materials.

HANDS-ON: ANIMATED SIZE WITH A GEOMETRY MODIFIER

Earlier I mentioned that in addition to creating animated surface appearances, you can alter the geometry of objects through a Geometry Modifier. This is constructed in an *identical* manner to custom surface shaders; you just make use of a Geometry Modifier node rather than the Preview Surface node you've used so far.

These shaders are more math-centric because they aren't just about coloring and texturing a surface; instead, you're modifying the points in 3D space that make up the object. If this topic seems interesting, it might be worth dusting off an old geometry book to see what formulas you might use.

In this project, you use a Geometry Modifier to make another pulsing object. This time, instead of the surface changing, the object grows and shrinks with time. You use many of the same approaches as the previous hands-on exercise. In this case, however, you're going to be setting a Model Position Offset input on a Geometry Modifier node. The position offset can be used to change the coordinates of an object's vertices in 3D space and consists of three values: X, Y, and Z. Multiplying an object's existing vertices by 2.0, for example, makes the object twice as big. Using 0.5 makes it half as big as the original static object.

By combining this with the handy Time, Sin, and Remap nodes, you'll end up with an object that grows and shrinks repeatedly, as demonstrated in **FIGURE 4.49**.

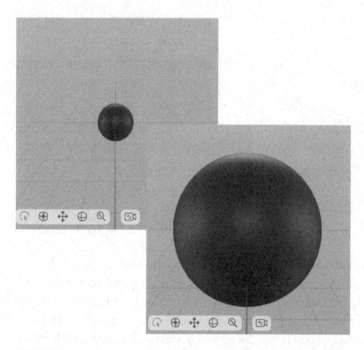

FIGURE 4.49 The finished object transitions from small to large over time.

Setting Up the Project and Scene

Once again, begin by setting up a new Reality Composer Pro project and adding a new material:

1. Create a new Reality Composer Pro project named "Pulsing Sphere".

2. Prepare the default scene by adding a sphere or another object of your choice.

3. Delete the default material from the object.

4. Create a new material named **Pulse_Modifier**.

5. Modify the Diffuse Color of the Preview Surface node so that it isn't an ugly gray color.

6. Assign the Pulse_Modifier material to the object in the scene.

Now you can jump straight into defining the geometry modifier.

Planning the Geometry Shader Graph Logic

You build this shader graph with many of the same components as the first. In fact, the initial four nodes are *identical* to the previous graph. An initial Time node output will be divided by a Speed Input, fed to a Sin node, and then delivered to a Remap node. From there, things change a bit.

Remap

Instead of mapping the output of Sin (1 to –1) to 1 to 0, you use the Remap node to provide an output that varies from its default size in the scene to a maximum size. You use a floating-point Input (just like Speed) as the input to Remap's Out High value. This sets the upper limit on the expansion of the object.

Combine 3

To expand (or contract) the object, you need to multiply the coordinates (X, Y, Z) of each vertex by a scaling (size) value. If you only multiply by X, Y, or Z, the object stretches into an oval in that dimension. This isn't necessarily a bad effect, but in this case, the goal is for the object to keep its proportions and expand.

You need to provide X, Y, and Z multipliers, all the same, to the rest of the graph. Because Remap only gives a single value, what will you do? You can feed three copies of the single multiplier value into a special node called Combine 3 that puts them into the proper three-value (X, Y, Z) format you need. To do this, you connect the output of the Remap node to X, Y, and Z inputs in the Combine 3 node.

Position

With the Combine 3 output feeding the multiplier for the multiplication, you need to determine the object's position as the multiplicand (it's just the "other number"). You can add a node called Position that does nothing but return the X, Y, and Z coordinates for wherever the object is located in the scene.

> **TIP** Although it's easiest to think of this as applying these operations to an object, in reality they're working with all the vertices that make up the object. This may be thousands of calculations a frame, not just a simple one-time multiplication, division, or other operation.

Multiply

The final step in the graph is to take the current position of the object and multiply it by the output of the Combine 3 node. We'll add a Multiply node to handle this function.

Geometry Modifier

The output of the multiply node needs to go somewhere; it contains the expanded (or shrunk) coordinates that make up each part of your object. For a surface shader, you already have the Preview Surface node, but because Geometry Modifiers are a bit less common, Apple leaves out the Geometry Modifier node you need for your final connections. You add this as a last step in creating the graph.

Inputs

Like the preceding exercise, you want this material to be reusable, so you add a Speed Input (Float) and a MaximumSize Input (Float) and connect them to the graph.

The Solution

FIGURE 4.50 shows how these different nodes combine to create the growing/shrinking geometry modifier.

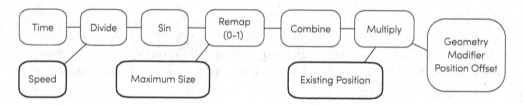

FIGURE 4.50 This geometry modifier shader graph plan uses many of the same functions as the previous project but introduces a few new nodes.

Once again, you start with a Time node and divide it by an arbitrary Speed node (a floating-point number). The result again feeds a Sin node and then uses a Remap node to change the output of Sin from 0 to a Maximum Size constant. The single Remap output value is provided to all three (X, Y, and Z) inputs in a Combine 3 node. The result of Combine 3 and the current Position of the object is multiplied, and that output is used to set the Model Position Offset input of a Geometry Modifier node.

Creating the Shader Graph

Select your Pulse_Modifier material and open the Shader graph. Using the previous project for reference, recreate the portion of the graph beginning with Time and ending with the Remap node, as shown in **FIGURE 4.51**. Remember to use the inspector to set the Speed Input to something other than zero. I'm using 0.5 for a quick cycle.

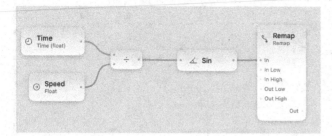

FIGURE 4.51 Building out the same time-based nodes that drive the shader logic

REUSING PIECES OF GRAPHS

You've seen how materials can be made more useful by adding inputs and using instances. In this exercise, you're rebuilding a portion of the previous project and will likely be using similar logic again in the future. You *can* copy and paste between shader graphs, but you can also package portions of a shader graph into a stand-alone node graph. For example, if I want to create a node graph out of everything up to the Remap node in the previous hands-on exercise ("Animated Visibility"), I could select it in the shader graph, right-click, and choose Compose Node Graph from the menu, as shown in **Figure 4.52**.

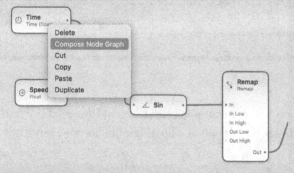

FIGURE 4.52 Creating stand-alone "pieces" of your shader graph by creating new node graphs

The selected portion of the graph collapses into a single node, and a new entry is added to the scene hierarchy *within* your material. **Figure 4.53** shows a collapsed section of the graph, now represented by a single node that I've named Time_based_Output. Double-clicking the node (or choosing it in the hierarchy) enables you to edit the graph it contains.

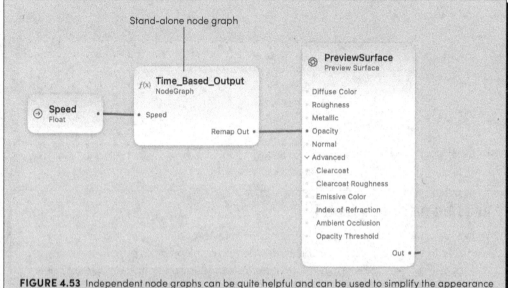

FIGURE 4.53 Independent node graphs can be quite helpful and can be used to simplify the appearance of your graph.

Like materials themselves, you can add inputs to these graphs, create instances, and drag them into your other shaders.

If you'd like to see some interesting reusable node graphs, take a look at https://github.com/JamieScanlon/RCPMaterials. This repository provides a number of reusable node graphs for generating textures made of geometry shapes.

Adding the New Nodes

You need a new Input node to constrain how big your objects can be. Add a second Input to the graph using the inspector. Like Speed, this should be a floating-point number but with the name **MaximumSize**.

Drag from the MaximumSize Input to the Out High input of the Remap function. This will set the upper limit on how big the object can grow. Before you forget, use the Inspector to set the MaximumSize to 3; otherwise, the geometry modifier isn't going to modify any geometry.

Next, you need to tweak the Remap node. Use the same –1 and 1 values for In Low and In High, but Out Low should be set to 0, as shown in **FIGURE 4.54**.

FIGURE 4.55 shows the current version of the shader graph. You have a bit more to go, but this is a good start.

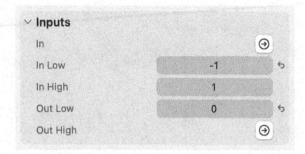

FIGURE 4.54 The Remap node has the same values as before, except for Out Low (0) and Out High, which is driven by the MaximumSize input.

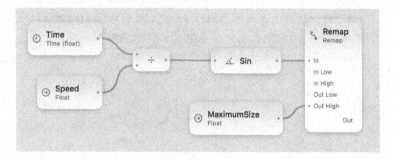

FIGURE 4.55 Your shader graph should look very similar to this.

Now, some new nodes. Create the three value (X, Y, Z) multiplier that is applied against the object's position; drag from the Out of the Remap node to a blank space and choose Combine 3 when prompted. Notice that when the node is added, only the first input dot (X) is connected. Drag from the Remap Out to the other two dots (Y and Z) so that your resizing object does so symmetrically. Your graph should now look like the example in **FIGURE 4.56**.

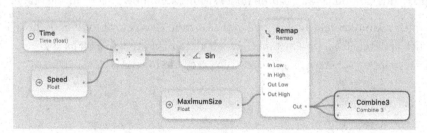

FIGURE 4.56 Use the Combine3 node to create a three-value multiplier that can be used with coordinates in 3D space.

Before you go any further, select the Combine3 node and, using the inspector, change the type to vector3f, as demonstrated in **FIGURE 4.57**. This ensures that you're dealing with floating point numbers that are in the same format as the vertex positions they'll be multiplied with.

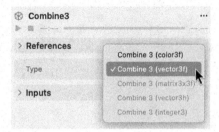

FIGURE 4.57 Changing the Combine3 type to vector3f

Now that you have the multiplier value, drag from the output of Combine3 to another blank spot and add a Multiply node. I've shifted the Combine3 output to feed the lower input in multiply, just to keep the graph neat. You don't *need* to do this because it's multiplication and the order is meaningless; I'm doing it to be neat. My graph is getting close to done (see **FIGURE 4.58**).

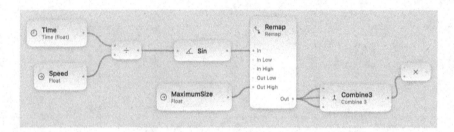

FIGURE 4.58 Adding the Multiply node, fed by Combine3, into the graph

The other value you need as part of the multiplication is the current position of the object. If you *don't* consider where the object is in the scene before you change its size, the object moves back to the origin point (0,0,0). Drag from the empty input on the Multiply node to another blank space, this time adding a Position node. **FIGURE 4.59** shows the resulting graph.

Lastly, add a Geometry Modifier node connected to the Custom Geometry Modifier of the Outputs node. Click and drag from the Custom Geometry Modifier input to a blank space in the canvas. When prompted, you have one choice: Geometry Modifier. Add it.

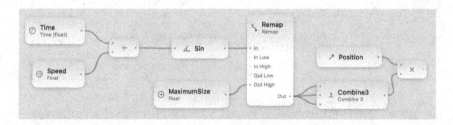

FIGURE 4.59 Adding a position node to the multiplication

Drag from the output of the Multiply Node to the Model Position Offset input node of Geometry Modifier. Your object starts changing size immediately! The final shader graph is shown in **FIGURE 4.60**.

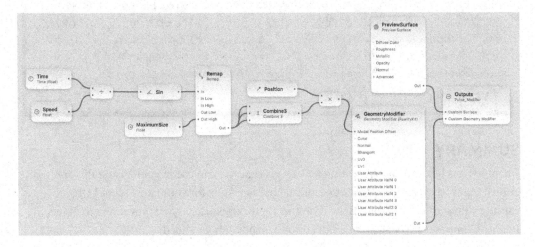

FIGURE 4.60 The final Pulse_Modifier geometry modifier graph

Exploring More

Oh, there is so much more here to explore that I encourage you to pause after this chapter to play around with the different inputs and possibilities of geometry modifiers. For example, try swapping out the Multiply node with an Add node. Your object will start flying in a diagonal line from the origin. Use the equation of a circle (x=Radius*cos(Time), y=Radius*sin(Time)) to feed a Combine3 node and make your objects orbit in space. You can look at the included Orbits project to see what this might look like in practice (or just steal the graph and use it!)

Introduce "noise" into the position of your objects, causing them to move in unpredictable ways. The sky (or at least the positive Y axis) is the limit!

TIP Apple has provided a few nice textures in the Reality Composer Pro Content Library. To access these textures, open the content library and use the table of contents to choose Material Library. Double-click any material to add it to an open scene; then assign it to your objects as you would any other texture.

SUMMARY

Chapter 4 has been all about creating new assets that you can use in your Vision Pro creations. Don't have a model of a stuffed animal but need one for your latest scene? Object capture (iPhone/iPad) to the rescue. Want to apply new surfaces and movement to objects? Reality Composer Pro's Shader Graph editor has the tools you need.

Surface Shaders, Geometry Modifiers, and time-based animations open a new realm of possibilities without using a line of code. Yes, it will take some time to get to know all the graph nodes you can use and what they do, but experimenting with node graphs is a low-stakes, high-reward, and rather entertaining way to pass an afternoon.

In the next chapter, you find out how the materials you create in Reality Composer Pro can *also* be used directly in code, giving you the ability to generate complex appearances on the fly.

Go Further

Take some time to familiarize yourself with the MaterialX specification (https://materialx.org/Specification.html) and the nodes available to you. The specification isn't the most user-friendly documentation, but it is the only "official" documentation you'll find. You may also be interested in watching Apple's WWDC presentation on Material creation at https://developer.apple.com/videos/play/wwdc2023/10202/.

Something to keep in mind when working with shaders is that there may be dozens of solutions for creating material that looks or performs in a certain way. Some graphs may use 100 nodes, whereas others use 3 or 4. The quantity of nodes doesn't determine the quality of the shader. If you like it and it looks great on your Apple Vision Pro, *that's* the outcome that matters.

There are quite a few samples included in this chapter, and I encourage you to test, tweak, and try rebuilding them all.

CHAPTER 5

Object Interaction and Transformation

So far in this book, I've talked about shaders, windows, and volumes, and if you've been working in order, you've created some basic interactivity with a customizable snow globe. A virtual environment where you just flip switches and push buttons in a window isn't much fun, though. You invested in this ecosystem to be able to interact *directly* with virtual objects.

visionOS offers the tools to provide control over objects—such as changing their size, location, or other attributes—but how do you turn them into completely dynamic scenes? With very little development effort, you can use intuitive gestures like tapping, dragging, and pinching to control your volumetric windows. Soon your 3D scenes will be more than just a static display.

This chapter ties together several key concepts: loading scenes and objects, attaching gestures to entities, and controlling shaders and object transformations from those gestures. There's some logic needed to make gestures useful, but nothing you can't handle.

After completing this reading, you'll understand

- **Indirect gestures:** A type of gesture that uses your gaze and simple hand movements to manipulate controls and objects. You use these now to navigate the operating system and other applications on the Apple Vision Pro.

- **Object transformations:** An object in a view is more than just its outward appearance. It's also defined by size, location, and rotation. Changing these attributes after an object is added to a view is called a *transformation* and is necessary if you want your objects to do more than just sit around.

- **Material inputs:** A means of quickly customizing an instance of a material without duplicating its logic. In addition to Reality Composer Pro, this can also be done programmatically—dramatically and dynamically changing the appearance of an object already in a scene.

- **Programmatic primitives:** In addition to Reality Composer Pro assets, RealityKit gives you access to several simple shapes (and materials) that you can add to your scenes programmatically.

I don't stray too far from the code you've seen in previously, but I do make some tweaks to demonstrate new capabilities. I found myself asking, "Why?!" more than a few times as I wrote the chapter, So I've included several cautions to help you avoid some potential head-scratchers.

> **NOTE** Remember to go to https://visionproforcreators.com/files/ or www.peachpit.com/visionpro to grab the Chapter 5 project files.

UNDERSTANDING INDIRECT GESTURES

You've been using indirect gestures for your entire development journey. In fact, you were probably using them before you even picked up this book. Every button you tap, every application you launch, and every piece of user interface code you've written uses an **indirect gesture**. If you have an Apple Vision Pro, much of your user experience is based on this type of gesture.

An indirect gesture uses the viewer's gaze to identify a target and hand or finger motions to act on the target. You might, for example, look at a button and then tap your index finger and thumb to activate it. This provides a way for users to interact with objects regardless of where they are located within a room. Because indirect gestures are accessible from seated positions and by those with limited mobility, Apple recommends providing them for all actions in your apps.

> **TIP** Indirect gestures are available on many of Apple's platforms, although they're activated differently on the Vision Pro,. In addition to improving accessibility, using indirect gestures helps keep your application code portable if you plan to offer them elsewhere in the Apple ecosystem.

When you've built projects with buttons, switches, and other elements, you implicitly defined indirect gestures. Standard SwiftUI controls are automatically activated with the appropriate gestures; no additional development is needed. When it comes to custom volumes, however, you're on your own. VisionOS has no idea what it means to tap or drag on a creepy mannequin head, so you'll have to put in some elbow grease if you want your users to be able to interact intuitively with 3D scenes.

Common Gesture Types

To understand what gestures you have at your disposal, let's review the common gesture types:

- **Tap:** Effectively the "mouse click" of visionOS or iPad/iOS applications. A tap gesture can be configured to look for one or more taps, enabling the creation of single, double, and triple tap gestures from a single gesture type.

- **Drag:** The drag gesture is activated by tapping and holding and then moving your hand in the desired direction of the drag. Drag gestures are frequently used for moving content or as a swipe to move between different views.

- **Long Press:** A tap gesture that is held for a minimum length of time (usually 0.5 seconds). Long press gestures can be used for showing contextual menus or activating features that you don't want to be accidentally triggered with a stray tap.

- **Magnify:** Magnify is performed by tapping and holding with both hands, and then moving your hands closer or further apart. This specialized gesture is frequently used for zooming in or out of content or making an object larger or smaller.

- **Rotate:** The rotate gesture requires both hands to perform a tap and move in a clockwise or counter-clockwise motion. The rotate gesture is used to rotate content in the user's view.

INDIRECT GESTURES IMPLY THE EXISTENCE...

Yes, of **direct gestures**. Direct gestures enable users to approach objects and interact with them directly via touch. Of course, you can't *really* touch virtual creations, but through the hand-tracking capabilities of the Vision Pro, you'll be able to try *really* hard. Direct gestures will come into play once we introduce immersive spaces, which, as luck would have it, will be the next chapter.

Apple encourages developers to include indirect gestures wherever possible, so even if you want your users to "touch" objects directly, you'll still want to include the indirect approach introduced in this chapter.

Gesture Modifiers

To attach gestures to objects, you use **gesture modifiers**, which are similar to other modifiers you've applied to UI elements.

A gesture modifier is attached to a SwiftUI view. In the case of a volumetric window that includes a RealityView, you attach one or more gesture modifiers to the view, and, if desired, target the gesture on a specific object within the RealityView. You can extend this to multiple RealityViews for complex interactive layouts.

The basic syntax for a gesture modifier added to a RealityView looks like **LISTING 5.1**.

LISTING 5.1 Adding a Gesture to a RealityView

```
RealityView { content in
    // Add the initial RealityKit content
} update: { content in
    // Update the RealityKit content
}
.gesture (
    <Gesture Type>(<Gesture Parameters>)
    .targetedToEntity(<Entity>)
    .onEnded { value in
        // React to the completed gesture
    }
)
```

The setup code for the RealityView is in Chapter 3, "Getting Started with Reality Composer Pro," so that should be familiar. The `.gesture` modifier handles the work of detecting a specific indirect gesture and reacting to it.

The next section gets into different gesture types, parameters, and events.

Gesture Events

For a gesture to be useful, it needs to provide your code with information, such as *when* a gesture is complete or perhaps *where* the gesture took place.

In Listing 5.1, I included the event `.onEnded`, which is typically used for the code you want executed after the gesture is completed. I also included the `.targetedToEntity` gesture modifier, which applies the gesture recognizer to the named entity within the RealityView.

The events and modifiers you'll add to the gestures are typically one of the following:

- **`.onChanged`**: Performed after the gesture is recognized and has generated data. Once a user has started a drag gesture, for example, you can use this event to determine how far something has been dragged.

- **`.onEnded`**: Executed after a gesture has been completed, such as a Tap having taken place.

- **`.updating`:** A special event that occurs after the gesture is running and as its data has been changed. This can be used (in many instances) like the `.onChanged` event, but it can also bind a variable to the gesture's state. In other words, you can have a variable that changes along with the gesture and reverts to its default value once the gesture ends. I show you an example of this soon, so it'll make more sense.

- **`.targetedToEntity`**: While not an event, this important modifier sets which entity (if any) within the RealityView should be the focus for the gesture. If unset, *any* object reacts to the gesture.

Each gesture can be different, and the modifiers won't be the same each time, but to give you an idea of the setup and capabilities of each, let's review the code required for each primary gesture type.

Tap

The tap gesture is the easiest gesture to implement: Either the user taps a specific number of times, or they don't. It would be rather difficult to partially tap something, don't you think?

The format for implementing a tap gesture is

```
TapGesture(count: <Number of taps to detect>)
    .onEnded { _ in
        // The required number of taps has occurred.
        print("You have completed the right number of taps.")
    }
```

Provide a count, react to the `.onEnded` event, and poof! Your objects are interactive! Remember that if you want your tap to register with a specific entity within the RealityKit view, you also need the `.targetedToEntity` modifier. This is the same for *all* gestures and something you'll see frequently in the upcoming hands-on exercise.

Long Press

A long press is similar to a tap but occurs over a period of time—a trait that is shared with other gesture types and something that makes these gestures just a tad more complex to implement.

For starters, the long press gesture can accept more parameters than a tap:

```
LongPressGesture(minimumDuration: <Duration of press in seconds>,
                 maximumDistance: <maximum cursor movement allowed>)
    .onEnded() { _ in
        // The Long Press has ended.
        print("The Long Press is complete.")
    }
    .onChanged() { _ in
        // Long Press is taking place.
    }
```

When `minimumDuration` is provided, it represents the minimum time in seconds that the long press must be held before it is considered a complete gesture. Likewise, `maximumDistance` is the largest distance the cursor can move before the gesture is considered invalid. For example, if you're looking at an object on the left side of your view while executing a long press, and then look to the right, you won't expect the long press to be valid.

Long press gestures can be used for contextual menus or to provide additional selection control when more than a tap is needed.

> **TIP** If you're wondering what happens when a gesture becomes "invalid," it's quite straightforward. Gesture recognition is canceled, and the .onEnded event is never called.

Drag

Assuming you've used any operating system created within the last 30 years, it's very likely you understand what a drag gesture is. In visionOS, the user focuses on an object, pinches their fingers, and moves their hand in the direction of the drag. The drag is used to move objects within a space, rotate entities, and anything else that makes sense within the context of your application.

A drag gesture frequently requires a minimum distance (minimumDistance) before it is considered complete. This helps prevent inadvertent drags that might be recognized if you tap and happen to move your hand.

```
DragGesture(minimumDistance: <minimum distance for the drag
                             to be considered valid>)
    .onEnded { value in
        // value.location.x and value.location.y contain the drag
        // coordinates
        print("I've been dragged!")
    }
    .onChanged { value in
        // value.location.x and value.location.y contain the drag
        // coordinates
        print("I'm in the process of being dragged.")
    }
```

Within the drag events, you can use the value passed to the event to access the coordinates of the drag—for example, value.location.x and value.location.y.

Drag gestures can be initialized with a coordinateSpace parameter set to .local for the local coordinate system of the entity or .global for the coordinate space of the volume. This alters the location coordinates provided to the events. You make use of this later in the chapter.

Magnify

The magnify gesture is more complex than other gestures but surprisingly easy to implement. To magnify, you perform the tap gesture (thumb to index finger) with both hands and then pull your hands apart, like stretching a rubber band.

If desired, you can set a mimumScaleDelta parameter to ensure that the gesture is intended. There isn't much point in bothering to react to the gesture if the scale has only changed by a tiny fraction.

While the magnify gesture is taking place, you are provided with a simple floating-point value, value.magnification, as in the following code fragment.

```
MagnifyGesture(minimumScaleDelta: <minimum scale to be a valid gesture>)
    .onEnded { value in
        // Magnify has finished
        print("The magnify gesture has ended.")
        print("I've been magnified \(value.magnification)X.")
    }
    .onChanged { value in
        // Magnify is taking place
        print("I'm being magnified \(value.magnification)X.")
    }
```

You can use magnification directly in the rest of your code to magnify or shrink objects by the value provided. No need to worry about coordinate systems or interpreting the results further.

Rotate

The last gesture is rotate. As the name implies, rotate is primarily used for rotating objects. Think of the controls for rotating an image on your iPhone or iPad. You place two fingers down and then move them as if tracing a circle. Using this in a 3D environment primarily makes sense for rotating around the Z-axis from your point of view. The gesture is invoked by pinching with both hands and moving your hands in a circular motion.

```
RotateGesture(minimumAngleDelta: <minimum angle change
                                 to be valid rotation> )
    .onEnded { value in
        // Rotate has finished.
        print("The rotate gesture has ended.")
        print("I'm being rotated \(value.rotation.degrees) degrees.")
    }
    .onChanged { value in
        // Rotate is currently taking place.
        print("I'm being rotated \(value.rotation.degrees) degrees.")
    }
```

As with the magnify gesture, the rotate gesture gives you a rotation value that you can use directly in your code.

COULD YOU CLARIFY WHAT A "ROTATION VALUE" IS?

Certainly! The rotation is a structure called an Angle. Angles are handy because, once initialized, they can provide an angle in degrees or radians depending on your needs. For example, consider the following code:

```
var myAngle : Angle = .zero
myAngle.degrees = 45.0
print("\(myAngle.degrees) = \(myAngle.radians)")
```

Here I declare a new variable—myAngle of the type Angle set to .zero—a special value that is effectively the same as setting it to zero degrees or zero radians. I then set myAngle in degrees to 45.0. Finally, I use the built-in conversion of this structure to print the angle in degrees and radians.

You can learn more about Angles and how they can be initialized directly with degree or radian values in the Apple Developer Documentation at **https://developer.apple.com/documentation/swiftui/angle**.

If you're struggling to remember what radians are (which is quite reasonable if you haven't been in a geometry class in the last six months), you can get a quick introduction at **https://www.mathsisfun.com/geometry/radians.html**.

The Updating Event

I saved the updating event for last because it is a rather strange beast. The updating event, like onChange, is executed while the gesture is taking place. It differs in that it can bind a variable to the current state of the gesture. This variable, denoted with an @GestureState wrapper, can be accessed in other functions and code that might be running concurrently. You can use it, for example, to provide updates to objects or trigger the addition of new objects in the RealityView update: code block. When the gesture is finished, the variable automatically reverts to the original value you assigned it.

To implement the updating event, first create a variable to hold the status of the gesture, placing the definition inside the struct of your view. Depending on the gesture type, the state is represented with different corresponding data types:

- **Long press:** A long press is either happening or not happening, so the state is a Boolean value: true or false.

- **Drag:** When dragging, the gesture state is represented by a location value of the type CGPoint (an X,Y point value). For those who are wondering, the CG in CGPoint stands for Core Graphics, a foundational technology in Apple's operating systems.

- **Magnify:** With magnify, the state is simply the `magnification`, a floating-point number. Initially, `magnification` should be 1.0 to indicate the object is 100% of its original size.

- **Rotate:** When using the rotate gesture, the state is the current angle of rotation, of the type `Angle`.

For example, if I want to use the `updating` event with the Magnify gesture, I first define a variable to bind to the state of the gesture:

```
…
struct ContentView: View {
    @GestureState private var magnifyScale = 1.0
…
```

Then within the magnify gesture, I'd add the `updating` event:

```
MagnifyGesture()
    .updating($magnifyScale) { currentState, gestureState,
        transaction in
        gestureState = currentState.magnification
    }
```

The code here can look "unusual" because there are several different values made available to the event. The first value (`value`) is always the instantaneous current state, followed by the state that is currently being reported in the bound variable (`gestureState`). Finally, a variable, `transaction`, holds additional information about the gesture, but it's rarely used.

Once set up, whenever a magnify gesture is taking place, the variable `magnifyScale` is updated continuously with a floating-point number representing how much the object should be scaled. When the gesture ends, `magnifyScale` automatically resets to the initial value declared. In this case, 1.0.

You can access the `@GestureState` variable anywhere within your view's code, giving you access to gesture data wherever you need it, as it happens.

Reusable Gestures

Later in this chapter, you build an example application that uses quite a few gestures to perform, well, quite a few different actions. As you're working through the code, you might start to wonder if there is a way to break up the code to make it easier to use or to be reusable by entities that should react identically to gestures. Yes, there is. You can define a variable that holds the code block for the gesture actions. For example, take the simple tap gesture—you might implement it within a view in a form similar to **LISTING 5.2**.

LISTING 5.2 The Basic Form for a Tap Gesture on a RealityView

```
struct ContentView: View {
    var body: some View {
        RealityView { content in
            // Add the initial RealityKit content
        } update: { content in
                // Update the RealityKit content
        }
        .gesture (
            TapGesture(count: 1)
                .onEnded { _ in
                    print("I've been tapped!")
                }
        )
    }
}
```

This is perfectly fine. You add a RealityView to the content and attach a .gesture modifier that uses the tap gesture. No problem. Now imagine this with a dozen gesture modifiers strung together, one after the other. It's not a particularly pretty picture, is it?

Alternatively, you can define a variable of the type **some** Gesture that holds the TapGesture code, as shown in **LISTING 5.3**.

LISTING 5.3 Gesture Recognizers Outside the Gesture Modifier

```
struct ContentView: View {
    var body: some View {
        RealityView { content in
            // Add the initial RealityKit content
            }
        } update: { content in
                // Update the RealityKit content
        }
        .gesture(myTap)
    }

    var myTap: some Gesture {
        TapGesture(count: 1)
            .onEnded { _ in
                print("I've been tapped!")
        }

    }
}
```

Here, the `myTap` variable has been defined with the same `TapGesture` code you saw in Listing 5.2. This means that `myTap` can now be added as a parameter directly in the gesture modifier—that is, `.gesture(myTap)`. The resulting code can be easier to read, *and* `myTap` could be added to any other gesture modifier where you want the same actions to take place. Using this form is up to you; it's a handy optional approach to keep up your sleeve.

EXAMPLES APLENTY

It really isn't fair to throw a ton of code at you and expect you to retype everything. If you check your Chapter 5 project files, you'll find projects for each of the gesture types that I've discussed, along with examples of the `updating` event and a reusable tap gesture. When running these samples, you can see the output of the gesture events in the Debug area. The gestures *do not* affect the onscreen volumetric window; it's provided as an attachment point for the different gesture modifiers. Make sure the Debug panel is open, as shown in **Figure 5.1**.

Gesture   Gesture results

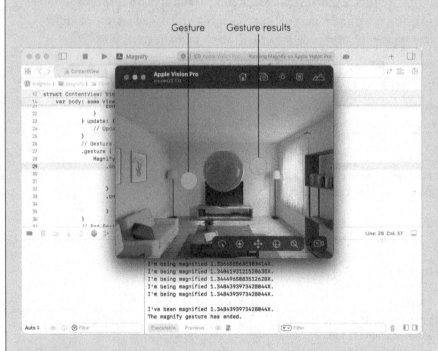

FIGURE 5.1 Monitor the Debug area to see feedback from the different gestures.

A few notes for clarity's sake: First, you *can* use the Xcode Canvas to test the gesture, but the Simulator works much better. In its current state, using the preview in Xcode results in an unwanted window behind a volumetric window. This is not a problem when using the Simulator. Second, the next part of the chapter is dedicated to making the gestures trigger changes in the `RealityView` and associated entities, so you won't be stuck with boring text for much longer.

PREPARING ENTITY INTERACTIONS

Gestures are a core feature of visionOS and the Apple Vision Pro experience. They are intended to be simple and easy to remember, and they should feel intuitive without requiring strenuous movements. Aside from the plain 2D windows that we've used previously, nothing in our volumetric windows can even *use* a gesture—yet.

Gestures assume that you are interacting with something you could touch. The scenes and entities from past chapters are clearly visible but are nothing more than digital phantoms floating in space. To interact with these objects, you need to make them more "real" from the perspective of your headset.

When writing a book, I tend to try to be conversationally clever—perhaps eye-rollingly so. My original idea for this section's title was "Do Me a Solid" or "Touching Something of Nothing." Thankfully, I went with a heading that at least makes *some* modicum sense. The next few chapters look at how you can interact with entities and have entities interact with the environment. Before something in a scene can be manipulated, it must have defined **collision components**. Collision components determine what portion of an entity can interact with other objects or, in this case, gestures. Without these components, the object exists only as a hologram within your application—something that can be seen but not touched by you or any other virtual entities.

> **NOTE** Recall that entities and scenes are treated the same way in your development. A scene can have multiple entities yet can be treated like an individual entity. Basically, if you load something and display it, you're displaying an entity, regardless of how many other entities make it up. I tend to refer to entities with the generic term **object** because (in most cases) that's how we see and think about them.

Thankfully, you need to do very little to generate collision components for the objects you display. In each of the examples provided with the chapter, you'll notice that when a `RealityView` is created, there are two additional lines that you haven't encountered before:

```
RealityView { content in
    // Add the initial RealityKit content
```

```
            if let scene = try? await Entity(named: "Scene", in:
                                    realityKitContentBundle) {
                scene.generateCollisionShapes(recursive: true)
                scene.components.set(InputTargetComponent())
                content.add(scene)
            }
    } update: { content in
        // Update the RealityKit content
    }
```

To generate the collision components for the entity that has loaded (in this case scene), you use the function

```
<entity>.generateCollisionShapes(recursive: <true or false>)
```

This creates the shape you need to detect collisions and for the operating system to detect gestures interacting with the object. The recursive parameter should usually be set to true, enabling shapes to be generated for any other objects that make up the scene. You can get away with this being false for simple objects, but if you find yourself in a situation where something just doesn't seem "touchable" the way it should, try switching to true.

Next, you need to configure the object needs so that it can receive input from visionOS by setting an input target component:

```
<entity>.components.set(InputTargetComponent())
```

Until this final function is used, the object is ready for interaction, but the system does not consider it a valid source for detecting input. With the addition of these two lines, you make the object "real" and tell visionOS to start monitoring it for interactions.

> **NOTE** I do a deeper dive into components (including collision and input components) and how they can be added via Reality Composer Pro in Chapter 6, "Spaces, Direct Gestures, and a Touch of Physics." Later, in Chapter 10, "Components, Systems, and the Kitchen Sink," I talk about writing your own components!

TRANSFORMING OBJECTS

Interactivity, at least from my perspective, requires two things: an action (your gestures) and a reaction. Right now, you can detect a gesture, but what are you going to do when it happens? Apple strongly suggests that gestures perform actions that seem natural. For example, if you detect a magnify gesture on an entity, it makes sense to change the size of the entity appropriately. The same goes for the other gestures—when they are detected on an object, you should do something to the object to demonstrate a change.

You can do this through **transformations**—the process of altering the location, size, or rotation of an object. Transformations are defined in a **transformation matrix**.

Matrices

You may or may not remember matrix math from school; for many, it's a distant memory that never felt particularly useful. A **matrix** is a table of numbers where the values in the rows and columns represent a mathematical expression. In the case of entities, you're interested specifically in a **transformation matrix**. Transformation matrices can be applied to an object to change its appearance, and, thankfully, they're generated automatically for most things you'll want to do. While this can be a complicated topic that is usually taught in linear algebra, you just need to understand that if you want to alter the location, size, or rotation of something, you define a corresponding transformation and apply its `matrix` property to an entity's transformation matrix property. You've previously modified these values directly in Reality Composer Pro through the Transform attributes, shown in **FIGURE 5.2**. Now you need to do the same thing in code. This is much easier done than said.

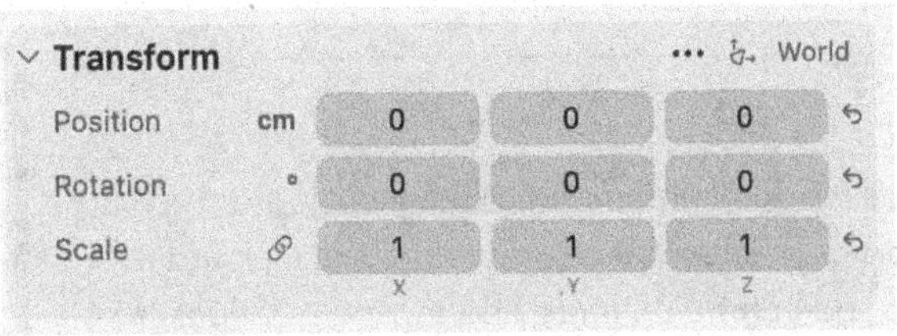

∨ **Transform**				••• 🜚 World	
Position	cm	0	0	0	↺
Rotation	°	0	0	0	↺
Scale	🔗	1	1	1	↺
		X	Y	Z	

FIGURE 5.2 Using Reality Composer Pro to assign an initial transformation with the Transform attributes.

> **TIP** For a straightforward introduction to matrices and transformation matrices, read www.mathsisfun.com/algebra/matrix-introduction.html and www.mathsisfun.com/algebra/matrix-transform.html. This is optional, so if you aren't particularly interested, no worries.

Let's look at the three types of transformations you use in this chapter and how the matrices are defined.

Translation (Position)

Changing the position of an object is a transformation called a **translation**. An entity is "translated" from one location to another. (Hey—I don't make the terms; I'm just telling you what they are!)

To apply a translation to an object, you first create a translation transformation structure with a syntax like this:

```
let <my translation>: Transform = Transform(translation:
                                     SIMD3<Float>(<x>,<y>,<z>))
```

Then you apply the translation transformation's matrix to the transformation matrix of the entity you want to move:

```
<entity>.transform.matrix = <my translation>.matrix
```

For example, if I want to position an entity called "earth" one unit (by default meters) right, up, and away from the origin point of a volumetric window, I write:

```
let positionTransform: Transform = Transform(translation:
                                   SIMD3<Float>(1.0,1.0,1.0))
earth.transform.matrix = positionTransform.matrix
```

The earth entity within my view would now be displayed at one unit to the right (positive X), one unit up (positive y), and one unit back (positive z). As you can see, I'm using matrices, but the behind-the-scenes details aren't really a concern.

SIMD3<FLOAT>WHAT?!

Yes, this is a variable type, and yes, you'll be using it quite frequently when dealing with object transformations. The <Float> portion is to be typed as is; it doesn't designate a parameter. Using SIM3<Float>() creates a **vector** with three floating-point values. A vector is a number that has both magnitude and direction. We can infer the direction depending on whether the number is positive or negative. A +1.0 X value is one meter to the right, +1.0 Y is a meter up, and +1.0 Z is a meter back.

The SIMD3<Float> type is required when creating transformations and other object manipulations in 3D. Just concentrate on the X, Y, Z values, and don't worry about the rather strange declarations in your code.

Scale

Scaling an object changes its size relative to its original size. If you have a one-meter sphere in a scene and you scale it by 2.0, you end up with a two-meter sphere. Scaling requires a scale transformation to be created and applied, like this:

```
let <my scale>: Transform = Transform(scale:
                            SIMD3<Float>(<x>,<y>,<z>))
<entity>.transform.matrix = <my scale>.matrix
```

the x, y, and z values are the scaling factor along the corresponding axes rather than indicators of position. If you want an object to be the same size wide and deep but twice as tall, you use x, y, and z values of 1.0, 2.0, and 1.0, respectively. Typically, however, most scaling is performed uniformly, so most frequently all three values are identical.

Scaling the hypothetical earth entity so that it is twice as large is simple:

```
let scaleTransform: Transform = Transform(scale:
                                        SIMD3<Float>(2.0,2.0,2.0))
earth.transform.matrix = scaleTransform.matrix
```

Rotation (Orientation)

The last type of transformation is rotation, also *occasionally* referred to in the Xcode as the *orientation* of an object. Creating this transformation is uglier than the others because it requires the definition of a **quaternion**, a mathematical description of the rotation of an object. It also requires you to use radians rather than degrees to define the rotation.

The syntax for setting and applying a rotation transformation is

```
let <my rotation>: Transform = Transform(rotation:
      simd_quatf(angle: Float(Angle(degrees:<angle in degrees>).radians),
                axis: SIMD3<Float>(<x>,<y>,<z>)))
<entity>.transform.matrix = <my rotation>.matrix
```

The big difference here is that rather than providing the `rotation` parameter as a `SIMD3<Float>`, it must be a quaternion of the type `simd_quatf`. To initialize this structure, you provide an angle parameter (in radians) and an `axis` parameter (as our friend `SIMD3<Float>`). The angle can be given by initializing a new `Angle`, providing it the degrees of rotation, and then accessing its radians property. The angle must also be converted to a Float value, so it is wrapped in `Float()` for the conversion:

```
angle: Float(Angle(degrees:<angle in degrees>).radians)
```

The axis as a parameter is cleaner. This is another `SIMD3<Float>` type where the x, y, and z values are 0 or 1. If set to 1, the rotation takes place around that axis. If multiple axes are set, the rotation takes place around them all. Using a negative value changes the direction of the rotation.

```
axis: SIMD3<Float>(<x>,<y>,<z>)
```

To rotate the earth entity to a point 45 degrees around its y-axis, I might use the following code fragment:

```
let rotationTransform: Transform = Transform(rotation:
                simd_quatf(angle: Float(Angle(degrees:45.0).radians),
                        axis: SIMD3<Float>(0,1,0)))
earth.transform.matrix = rotationTransform.matrix
```

It isn't exactly pretty, but if you have the supporting code in place, it really only requires the rotation in degrees and a 1 or 0 for each axis depending on whether it should rotate around that axis.

Multiple Transformations

As much as I'd like to say, "That's it!" for matrices and transformations, I'm not quite done yet because there's a *gotcha* that I haven't quite mentioned. Hold your curses for now because in a few minutes, I know my ears are going to be burning.

When you create a transformation and apply it to the transform matrix of an entity, it is the *only* transformation that is applied. In other words, if you set a translation (position) transformation and subsequently apply a scale transformation, only the last transformation applies—that is, the object is scaled but reverts to its original position. Any transformation matrix undoes anything that came before it.

I can hear the screams starting.

Thankfully, there is a way to combine all your transformation matrices into a single matrix that carries *all* the changes you want to make by multiplying the matrices and then setting the entity's transformation matrix to the result.

Multiply two matrices as you would any other numbers:

```
let <new matrix> = <matrix 1> * <matrix 2>
<entity>.transform.matrix = <new matrix>
```

Using the previous scale and rotation transformation examples, you can combine and assign them to the earth entity like this:

```
let finalTransformMatrix = scaleTransform.matrix *
                           rotationTransform.matrix
earth.transform.matrix = finalTransformMatrix
```

That's not so bad now, is it!? Are you ready for the part that's going to make you scream or curse? Here it is: There's a way to do *all* of this that requires a lot less effort, code, and is far easier to implement.

The reason I included transformation matrices in this chapter is because you're going to encounter them in code, and it's good to know how they work. You can certainly use the techniques discussed here with your objects, but in many cases, you'll just want to assign values to transformation properties that are available for the entities in your scenes.

Simple Property-Based Transformations

As it turns out, much of what you can do with the transformation matrices can also be done just by setting properties on any entity. What makes this an even more attractive solution is that when you set the properties, the *other* properties don't reset to their original values.

You still need the SIMD3<Float> and simd_quatf data types, but now that you've seen them used with matrices, you'll have no problem understanding them here.

Translation

To set the location of an entity, update the value of the position property on an entity to a SIMD3<Float> value containing the new position:

```
<entity>.position = SIMD3<Float>(<x>,<y>,<z>)
```

To recreate the effect of moving the earth object to x=1.0, y=1.0, and z=1.0, you might use:

```
earth.position = SIMD3<Float>(1.0,1.0,1.0)
```

If you want to change only x, y, or z, you can access the x, y, and z properties of the position directly and assign a value:

```
earth.position.x = 1.0
```

It doesn't get much easier than that!

Scale

Scaling works the same but uses the scale property of the entity:

```
<entity>.scale = SIMD3<Float>(<x>,<y>,<z>)
```

The values x, y, and z are floating point numbers that determine a multiplication factor applied to the entity's size across all three axes. Scaling the earth entity by two times is accomplished with this:

```
earth.scale = SIMD3<Float>(2.0,2.0,2.0)
```

As with position, you can set the individual x, y, and z properties of scale to apply scaling only along a single axis:

```
earth.scale.y = 2.0
```

Rotation

Lastly, rotation. You must still work with a simd_quatf value, but overall the code is much easier to write and understand. This is also where Apple's terminology gets slightly mushy. Rather than setting a rotation property, you set orientation instead:

```
<entity>.orientation = simd_quatf(angle:
                    Float(Angle(degrees:<angle in degrees>).radians),
                    axis: SIMD3<Float>(<x>,<y>,<z>)))
```

Rotating earth 45 degrees around the y-axis becomes:

```
earth.orientation = simd_quatf(angle: Float(Angle(degrees:45.0).radians),
                    axis: SIMD3<Float>(0,1,0)))
```

You're done with transformations. You use them heavily in the upcoming exercise, so make sure you've given this section a thorough study before continuing.

CONTROLLING SHADERS

Once you've uncovered the ability to change an object's location, size, and rotation, you should have quite a few tools for reacting to gestures or just making your scenes more dynamic. But wait, there's more!

Remember creating shaders that animated objects in Chapter 4, "Creating and Customizing Models and Materials"? You might also recall defining inputs on those shaders to give an easy way to configure them without touching the shader graphs. As luck would have it, you can access, modify, and change object shaders directly in your code, giving access to even more ways to react to user input and spice up your experiences.

Loading the Shader

To load a shader, you first want it added to a scene within your project's RealityKitContent Package. In Chapter 4, you developed a Pulsing Sphere geometry modifier within Reality Composer Pro. You can refer to either the Chapter 4 or 5 project files to find a copy of this modifier.

As you can see from the window in **FIGURE 5.3**, you have a scene named Scene.usda, and within the scene a shader called Pulse_Modifier. Pay close attention to the project hierarchy in the upper-left corner. You need to know the path of the material. Typically, this would just be /Root/<Material Name>—or, in this case, /Root/Pulse_Modifier.

Once you have your material located, the next step is to set up a variable of the type ShaderGraphMaterial and load the shader from RealityKitContent. Note that you cannot use a constant because you will be modifying the shader once it is loaded.

```
var <my shader> : ShaderGraphMaterial = try! Await
        ShaderGraphMaterial(named: "<Path to shader>",
                from: "<Scene file name>", in: realityKitContentBundle)
```

For the Pulse_Modifier material, this would be

```
var pulseShader = try! await
        ShaderGraphMaterial(named: "/Root/Pulse_Modifier",
                from: "Scene.usda", in: realityKitContentBundle)
```

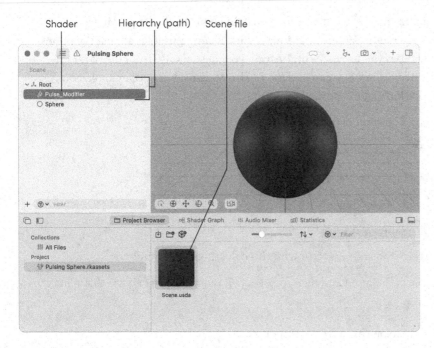

Shader **Hierarchy (path)** **Scene file**

FIGURE 5.3 Make sure the shader is available within a scene and take note of the path of the material you want to use.

Setting Shader Parameters

After loading the shader, you can set its parameters using the input names that were established while creating the shader graph. In Pulsing Sphere, for example, you added `Maximum-Size` and `Speed` inputs, as shown in **FIGURE 5.4**.

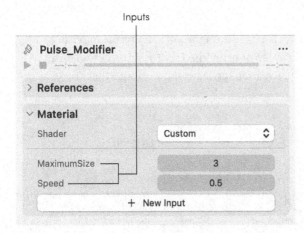

Inputs

FIGURE 5.4 Accessing the defined inputs from the Swift code

You reference the inputs using the same names you defined in the shader graph. Unfortunately, setting the value requires some additional effort. Shader variables are *not* the same types as the variable types you use in Swift. Instead, you must choose from the `Material-Parameters` enumerated values. You can find the full list at https://developer.apple.com/documentation/realitykit/materialparameters/value.

Here a few of the most common of these types:

- `bool(<Bool value>)`: A Boolean value

- `float(<Float value>)`: A floating-point number

- `int(<Int value>)`: An integer

- `color(<CGColor value>)`: A Core Graphics color

- `simd3Float(SIMD3<Float>)`: A vector with three floating-point numbers

Armed with the name of the input and the type of data it requires, you can use this syntax to set a shader parameter:

```
try <my shader>.setParameter(name: "<Input name>",
                        value: .<Data type>(<Input value>))
```

Applying this to the `pulseShader` example with the inputs `MaximumSize` and `Speed` set to 5.0 and 1.0, respectively, looks like this:

```
try pulseShader.setParameter(name: "MaximumSize", value: .float(5.0))
try pulseShader.setParameter(name: "Speed", value: .float(1.0))
```

Once the shader is loaded and configured, the last step is assigning it to an entity.

Applying the Shader

To set a shader as an entity's material, you need a handle on the entity. This means either tracking entities as you add them to a `RealityView` or using the `findEntity` function on a scene containing multiple objects. Reference Chapter 3 to learn more about `findEntity`, or just follow the syntax here:

```
let <my entity> : ModelEntity = <scene>.findEntity(named:
                            "<Entity name>") as! ModelEntity
```

> **NOTE** We need to explicitly force the located entity to be the specific type of entity—`ModelEntity`, to set the shader—thus, the `as! ModelEntity` portion. In a few chapters, we'll look at entities that have no shape or size - like sounds - so not all entities can have a material applied. By stating that the entity you're working with is a `ModelEntity`, you acknowledge that you're applying the shader to something that does support materials.

Creating New Entities

Beyond loading models that are part of your project, RealityKit offers several predefined objects that can be created with no effort and no existing files via the `ModelEntity` function and a mesh generation function. I'll let the names of these functions speak for themselves:

- `.generateSphere(radius: <Radius of sphere>)`

- `.generateCylinder(height: <Height of cylinder>,`
  `radius: <Radius of cylinder>)`

- `.generateCone(height: <Height of cone>, radius: <Radius of cone>)`

- `.generateBox(size: <Length, width, and height of box as SIMD3<Float>>,`
  `cornerRadius: <Curvature value to smooth corners>)`

- `.generateText(<String of text>, extrusionDepth: <Depth of text>,`
  `font: UIFont.systemFont(ofSize: <font size>))`

Yep, this means you can generate three-dimensional text (and the other objects) and add them directly to your views!

> **TIP** For generateText, I've included just a few of the possible parameters and set the font to the system font. You can explore more options by reading the full developer documentation at https://developer.apple.com/documentation/realitykit/meshresource/ and clicking the `static func generateText` entry in the right navigation. To learn more about fonts, visit https://developer.apple.com/documentation/uikit/uifont.

To create a new entity using one of these functions, use the format

```
let <New entity> = ModelEntity(mesh: <Mesh generation function>)
```

For example, to create a new sphere with a radius of 1.0, you could type

```
let mySphere = ModelEntity(mesh: .generateSphere(radius: 1.0))
```

Or, to generate 3D text that says "Hi!" with a depth of 0.02 and a font size of 0.1, use this:

```
let myText = ModelEntity(mesh: .generateText("Hi!",
                    extrusionDepth: 0.02,
                    font: UIFont.systemFont(ofSize: 0.2)))
```

Any entity created in code needs to have a shader or simple material attached and be added to the content of the `RealityView`. **LISTING 5.5** shows how you might generate 3D text and add it during the setup of a RealityView.

LISTING 5.5 Adding a Text Entity to the Content

```
RealityView { content in
    let myText = ModelEntity(mesh: .generateText("Hi!",
                                extrusionDepth: 0.02,
                                font: UIFont.systemFont(ofSize: 0.2)))
    let textMaterial = SimpleMaterial(color: .red,
                                      roughness: 0.1,
                                      isMetallic: false)
     myText.model?.materials = [textMaterial]
     content.add(myText)
} update: { content in
    // Update the RealityKit content
}
```

FIGURE 5.5 demonstrates the result. Keep in mind that any entities you create in this manner can be manipulated just like those you load from the RealityKitContent package.

FIGURE 5.5 Three-dimensional text can be generated and manipulated like any other object.

In this chapter, you've seen more than a few different code examples for adding interactivity, and the time has come to put them into practice. This chapter concludes with a project that is one part interactivity sandbox and one part experiential art.

HANDS-ON: TOUCHY VOLUMES

With so many different topics in this chapter, I struggled to find a project that could adequately demonstrate the different skills covered, and then I started playing. What if you could display a tiny solar system? What if you could rotate it? What if you could rotate planets individually? What if you could make the sun go supernova? What if you could generate *more* planets? Thankfully, for all our sakes, I eventually stopped asking questions and created a project that does all of this. Within about an hour, so will you!

Based on the series of questions I just described, I think you probably already have a good idea of what to expect in this exercise. You start by setting up a RealityView with the sun, earth, and moon and a customized version of the Pulse_Modifier shader. Next, you apply gestures and transformations to the different entities. Finally, you enable a gesture to create a limitless amount of randomly styled planets and place them in the RealityView. One of the nice things about this project is that you can do as much or as little as you want. Because the gestures are all self-contained, if you don't feel like implementing one, don't!

In **FIGURE 5.6**, you can see a few of the many appearances that the running application can produce.

FIGURE 5.6 Once your users can start interacting with your objects, the fun starts.

There are a few "different" facets to this project that you haven't seen yet, so I encourage you to not skip this, even if you have better ideas for something to build.

Setting Up the Project

To start, open Xcode and create a new project for a visionOS application. Don't click through the setup screens just yet because you'll be making a minor tweak this time.

Name the project **Touchy Volumes** and make sure that the Initial Scene is set to Volume, as shown in **FIGURE 5.7**. By setting the initial scene to a volume, you won't present *any* 2D interface; you jump straight into an interactive volumetric view.

All the coding work takes place within the ContentView.swift file. Open the file in the Xcode editor and replace *everything* within the body with a simple empty RealityView definition.

Yes, this includes the gesture and all the demo content that Apple conveniently provides. **LISTING 5.6** shows the bare-bones ContentView.swift file after cleanup.

FIGURE 5.7 Configuring the Touchy Volumes project with an Initial Scene of Volume

LISTING 5.6 A Clean Version of the ContentView

```swift
import SwiftUI
import RealityKit
import RealityKitContent

struct ContentView: View {
    var body: some View {
        RealityView { content in
            // Initial content goes here.
        } update: { content in
            // Additional content can be added here.
        }
    }
}

#Preview(windowStyle: .volumetric) {
    ContentView()
}
```

With that out of the way, you have a nice clean slate to build upon. Let's go ahead and set up the resources you're going to need using Reality Composer Pro.

Adding the RealityKit Content Resources

Within the project hierarchy, drill down to the package file inside Packages, RealityKitContent. Select Package, and click the Open in Reality Composer Pro button in the upper-right corner of the window.

By default, you're going to have a single sphere with a grid material applied, as shown in **FIGURE 5.8**.

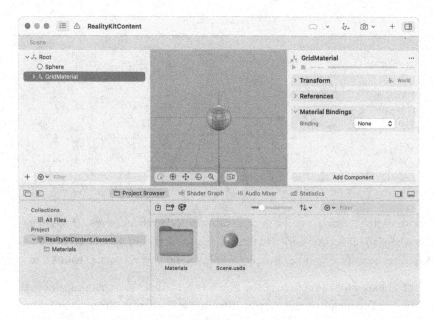

FIGURE 5.8 You need to do additional cleanup of the predefined content.

Select the GridMaterial line in the scene hierarchy and press Delete to remove it. You can do the same for the Materials folder in the Project Browser at the bottom of the window. When prompted, choose Move to Trash.

Finally, using the Project Browser again, edit the name of Scene.usda to be **Sun.usda**. The cleaned Reality Composer Pro project should now resemble **FIGURE 5.9**.

Now that you've stripped things down, you can start building them up again.

Open your Reality Composer Pro window so that it takes up a decent amount of space on your screen. Click the + in the upper-right corner to open the Content Library. Within the library, search for **Earth**. When you see the Earth model appear, drag it from the library into the Project Browser portion of the Reality Composer Pro window. This keeps it from being added to the scene and just adds the model as an available file within your project.

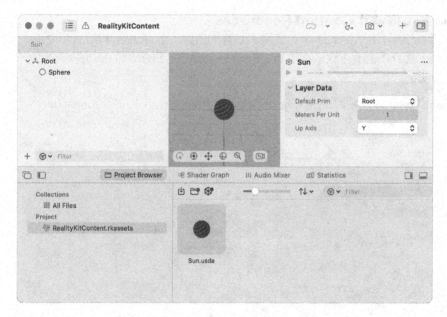

FIGURE 5.9 You should have a single scene named Sun with a single sphere and no materials applied.

Do the same for Moon, adding it directly to the Project Browser rather than a scene. If you happen to have an issue where an object gets added to the Sun scene, just select it in the scene hierarchy and press Delete. Your Reality Composer Pro project file should now resemble **FIGURE 5.10**.

The last step is adding a shader for the sphere in the Sun scene. Rather than spending another 10 pages making a shader, I've included one for you. This shader is an evolved version of the `Pulse_Modifier` shader that adds a dynamic surface appearance that, in my opinion, seemed just about perfect for a sun-like object.

Open the Example Touchy Volumes Content folder that's included with this chapter's content. Double-click Package.realitycomposerpro to open it in Reality Composer Pro. In the project that opens, select the Sun.usda scene, highlight the `Pulse_Modifier` line in the hierarchy (see **FIGURE 5.11**), and choose Edit, Copy from the menu bar.

Switch back to the Reality Composer Pro window for *your* project, select the Sun.usda scene, and paste. Ta-da! You have my shader material ready to use in your exercise. The first use is, of course, applying it to the sphere in the Sun.usda scene. Incidentally, you should feel free to edit, change, or completely scrap this shader if you don't like it. It's just intended as another example to build from.

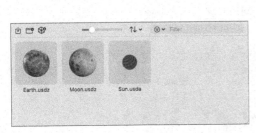

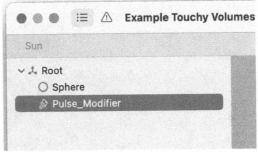

FIGURE 5.10 You should now have a Sun scene and Earth and Moon models in your project.

FIGURE 5.11 Highlight and copy the material to the clipboard.

Select the Sphere line in the scene hierarchy. Use the Material Bindings panel in the Attributes inspector to set the material to the `Pulse_Modifier` shader, as shown in **FIGURE 5.12**.

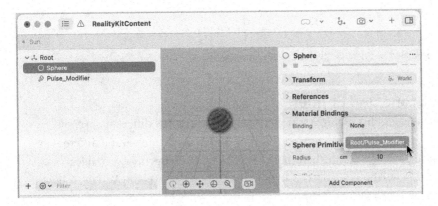

FIGURE 5.12 Assign the material to the sphere. We now have a sun.

FIGURE 5.13 shows the final setup of the RealityKitContent package. You need everything named as it is here before proceeding.

With that, the coding can begin. Close Reality Composer Pro, open ContentView.swift in the Xcode editor, and put your programmer hat on. Some logic in this project can be confounding at first glance.

> **NOTE** If you're wondering why you have a scene with only the sun in it versus the models for the earth and moon, you're doing great. You could have easily built this as a single scene, but I'm hoping this example drives home the point that anything can be an entity, and not everything has to be in a scene for it to be added to an experience. Bear with me.

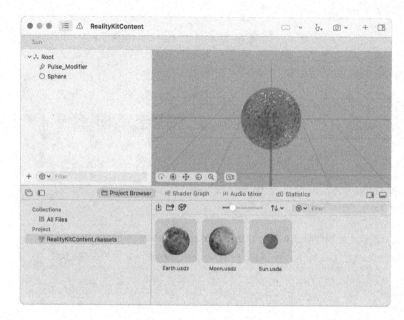

FIGURE 5.13 The completed RealityKitContent resources for the exercise.

Loading the Scene and Entities

Unlike previous exercises, this requires that you be able to access the different onscreen objects throughout the code to set their size, position, and so on within several different gestures. Before you add anything to the bare-bones RealityView, define three variables—sun, earth, and moon—that will be available throughout the ContentView code. Add the following declarations after the initial struct ContentView line:

```
@State private var earth : Entity = Entity()
@State private var moon : Entity = Entity()
@State private var sun : Entity = Entity()
```

This initializes the three celestial variables to be empty entities. You assign them to real entities as you load them in the RealityView setup code. Speaking of which, do that now. Edit the RealityView code block so that it reads as in **LISTING 5.7**.

LISTING 5.7 Loading the Initial Content in RealityView

```
RealityView { content in
    // Initial content goes here.
    if let sunEntity = try? await Entity(named: "Sun",
                                in: realityKitContentBundle) {
        sun = sunEntity
```

```
            sun.generateCollisionShapes(recursive: true)
            sun.components.set(InputTargetComponent())
            content.add(sun)
        }

        if let earthEntity = try? await Entity(named: "Earth",
                                            in: realityKitContentBundle) {
            earth = earthEntity
            earth.generateCollisionShapes(recursive: true)
            earth.components.set(InputTargetComponent())
            earth.position.x = -0.3
            content.add(earth)
        }

        if let moonEntity = try? await Entity(named: "Moon",
                                            in: realityKitContentBundle) {
            moon = moonEntity
            moon.generateCollisionShapes(recursive: true)
            moon.components.set(InputTargetComponent())
            moon.position.x = 0.3
            content.add(moon)
        }
    } update: { content in
        // Additional content can be added here.
    }
}
```

This code should look *very* familiar but with a few additions that come in handy later. First, upon successfully loading an entity, it is assigned to one of the empty entity variables sun, earth, or moon so that it can be used throughout your code.

Second, the setup is used to prepare the entities for interaction by generating collision shapes and setting them as possible input targets.

Lastly, the position.x values of earth and moon are adjusted to -0.3 and 0.3, respectively. This puts the earth to the right of the sun and the moon to the left of the sun. The sun sits squarely at x = 0 because you never moved the sphere within the Sun.usda scene.

This results in an application that presents three objects—the sun, the earth, and the moon— as shown in **FIGURE 5.14**. As you can see, there's nothing "magical" about loading a scene versus loading a model. They're all just entities (cough, objects, cough) within the RealityView.

FIGURE 5.14 The application now has three different objects set up for interactivity.

Adding the Gestures

So many gestures, so little time! You've seen how to write gesture code; now it's time to implement a few. You'll work through each gesture on an entity-by-entity basis, starting with the center of your bizarre little system: the sun.

> ### ORDER MATTERS WITH GESTURES
>
> Something to note that can be a "gotcha" is that the order of the gestures, as they are attached to the `RealityView`, matters. The reason order matters is that some gestures can be considered part of other gestures. If you add a drag gesture for an entity followed by a tap gesture for the same entity, for example, it probably won't work the way you expect. The drag gesture will capture the tap as part of recognizing the drag, meaning that the tap actions will go unexecuted or be executed at weird times. This is just something to keep in mind as you go off on your own. Think about the gestures and apply them mindfully in an order that makes sense.

Sun Shader Tap Gesture

When I first viewed the project after adding the sun and "planets" (yes, I know the moon isn't a planet), I thought, "The sun is waaay too small or the earth and moon are waaay too big." Rather than correcting that problem by resizing things in Reality Composer Pro, I chose to use the (new) `Pulse_Modifier` shader to make the sun grow really large— so large it consumes the rest of the celestial objects in its path.

Of course, I don't want this destructive action to take place constantly, so I figured just a nice single tap toggle targeted to the sphere (the sun) in the Sun scene would be a good trigger. After tapping, the code would update the `Pulse_Shader` to set a `MaximumSize` and `Speed` different from the default values of 0.0 (no scaling) and 1.0.

To implement this, another variable, `sunAnimated`, needs to be added to the growing list of ContentView variables to track whether the sun is currently animated. Add this variable, with a default value of `false`:

```
@State private var sunAnimated : Bool = false
```

Now the gesture itself. This loads the shader and sets it to scale larger, if `sunAnimated` is true, or return to its defaults, if `false`. After updating the shader, `sunAnimated` makes use of the Boolean function `toggle()` to set its value to the *opposite* of what it current holds.

LISTING 5.8 is my version of this logic. This should be placed in ContentView immediately following the `RealityView` update code block.

LISTING 5.8 Generating a Supernova with a Single Tap

```
.gesture(
    TapGesture(count:1)
        .targetedToEntity(sun)
      .onEnded { _ in
          Task {
              var sunShader = try! await ShaderGraphMaterial(named:
                                     "/Root/Pulse_Modifier",
                                     from: "Sun.usda",
                                     in: realityKitContentBundle)
              if (!sunAnimated) {
                  sunAnimated.toggle()
                  try sunShader.setParameter(name: "MaximumSize",
                                                value: .float(5.0))
                  try sunShader.setParameter(name: "Speed",
                                                value: .float(2.0))
              } else {
                  sunAnimated.toggle()
                  try sunShader.setParameter(name: "MaximumSize",
                                                value: .float(0.0))
                  try sunShader.setParameter(name: "Speed",
                                                value: .float(1.0))
              }
              let sunModel : ModelEntity = sun.findEntity(
                                     named: "Sphere") as! ModelEntity

              sunModel.model?.materials=[sunShader]
```

```
        }
    }
)
```

The gesture begins with a TapGesture, set to detect a count of 1 tap. I use the .onEnded event to identify when the tap has completed. Once the tap is detected, I load the Pulse_Modifier shader into a new variable sunShader. Next, I set up an if-then-else statement to check to see if sunAnimated is true (or false).

For the condition where the sun is *not* animated (!sunAnimated), I complete three actions: I use sunAnimated.toggle() to change sunAnimated to true, and then set the MaximumSize input to 5.0 and Speed to 2.0. This results in a very large sun, and a much slower animation speed (the higher the speed value, the slower the animation.)

For the else block, the process is virtually the same, but MaximumSize is set to 0.0 and Speed to 1.0.

After setting the shader parameters (either animated or not), the shader needs to be applied to the sphere in the scene. Recall the *scene*, not the object, is named Sun. The object is just called Sphere. To get a handle on Sphere, I use findEntity on the sun scene and store it in the sunModel constant.

Lastly, sunModel material is set to a single value array made up of the shader [sunShader].

Run your application and try tapping the sun. You should see it quickly consume everything, as in **FIGURE 5.15**.

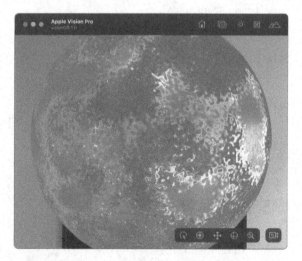

FIGURE 5.15 The Sphere model within the Sun scene can now "reach out and touch" your other objects.

That might seem like a lot, but we're just getting started.

Earth Scaling with Double Tap

The second gesture I've chosen to implement is a double-tap, this time targeted to the earth entity. When a double-tap is detected, I resize earth from a scale of 1.0 to 1.5, 1.75, and back to the original 1.0. This demonstrates the use of a scale transformation to alter the scene. Add the code in **LISTING 5.9** immediately after the first gesture.

LISTING 5.9 Toggling the Earth's Scale

```
.gesture(
    TapGesture(count:2)
        .targetedToEntity(earth)
        .onEnded { _ in
            switch earth.scale {
            case SIMD3<Float>(1.0,1.0,1.0):
                earth.scale = SIMD3<Float>(1.5,1.5,1.5)
            case SIMD3<Float>(1.5,1.5,1.5):
                earth.scale = SIMD3<Float>(1.75,1.75,1.75)
            default:
                earth.scale = SIMD3<Float>(1.0,1.0,1.0)
            }
        }
)
```

The gesture starts by setting up a TapGesture recognizer with a count of 2 (double-tap!). Again, the onEnded event identifies when the gesture has completed and performs the scaling. I've used a switch statement to evaluate the current earth.scale value. If the current earth.scale matches a scaling vector (SIMD3<Float>) of 1.0 in all dimensions, it is the original size, and it should be bumped up to the next size by setting the scale to 1.5. If the scaling is 1.5, earth should be scaled to 1.75. Finally, if earth.scale is anything but 1.0 or 1.5 (aka 1.75), it should be reset to the original 1.0 scale.

Run the project and try double-clicking the earth a few times to see it cycle through three different sizes. **FIGURE 5.16** shows the earth at its largest size.

Next up, rotating the earth with a drag gesture.

FIGURE 5.16 Not so big now are ya, sun??

Earth Rotation with Drag

In this gesture, dragging left or right on the earth causes it to spin around the Y-axis. Unfortunately, you need to do some math (just a teensy bit) in this implementation to know whether you're dragging left or right. To do this, you must keep track of where you *were* and where you *are* while dragging.

Add two new variables to the growing list of variables at the top of the ContentView:

```
@State private var earthRotationY: Angle = .degrees(0)
@State private var earthLastLocation: CGPoint = .zero
```

The variable earthRotation tracks the current number of degrees the earth entity is rotated and is initialized to 0 degrees. With earthLastLocation, you store a point (x,y) where the drag gesture ended.

Enter **LISTING 5.10** after the previous gesture. I talk through the details once you're ready.

LISTING 5.10 Detecting Left and Right Drags

```
.gesture(
    DragGesture()
        .targetedToEntity(earth)
        .onChanged { value in
```

```
        var xChange = value.location.x - earthLastLocation.x
        if (earth.position(relativeTo: nil).x > 0) {
            xChange = -xChange
        }
        if (xChange>0) {
            earthRotationY.degrees = earthRotationY.degrees + 5.0;
        }
        if (xChange<0) {
            earthRotationY.degrees = earthRotationY.degrees - 5.0;
        }
        earthLastLocation = value.location
        earth.orientation = simd_quatf(angle:
                        Float(earthRotationY.radians),
                        axis: SIMD3<Float>(0,1,0))
    }
)
```

So what is going on here? First, the gesture is targeted to the earth entity. Unlike the other gestures, you're going to do your work in the onChanged event. This gives you the ability to animate and change directions before the gesture has even finished.

Start by calculating a variable xChange—the amount of change in the x coordinate from the current drag location to the previous location (initialized to 0). The current location is accessed via the value provided to the action. If you drag to the right, xChange is always positive (a larger number minus a smaller number). When dragging to the left, xChange is negative (a smaller number minus a larger number). These values are relative to the earth entity itself.

You use two if statements to check to see if xChange is positive, and, if so, you increment earthRotationY.degrees by 5.0. If xChange is negative, you subtract 5.0 degrees.

Once completed, update earthLastLocation to the current location (value.location) and then use the earth.orientation property to rotate earthRotationY.radians around the Y-axis. Refer to the earlier "Rotation" section if you don't remember the syntax.

All in all, it's not *too* bad, but I've conveniently skipped a few lines:

```
if (earth.position(relativeTo: nil).x > 0) {
    xChange = -xChange
}
```

If you left these lines out, chances are you might not even notice a problem. This if statement uses earth.position(relativeTo: nil).x to check the earth's x position relative to the entire RealityView.

Why do this? Because if you spin the entire view around, the earth will suddenly be on the *right* side of the sun. In this case, you need to negate the xChange (xChange = -xChange) so that the comparison still works even with the entire view reversed.

The earth can now be dragged to rotate around the Y-axis. Start the application again and drag left or right on the earth entity. It reacts to the drag, even shifting direction mid-drag. This also works when the earth is scaled; using the transform properties doesn't reset any other properties you've set.

Moon Rotation with Drag

You're in the home stretch now. The drag gesture is the worst gesture implementation, and now that you understand how it's done, it's easy to reproduce. It's time to add the same functionality to the moon, starting with yet more variables added to track location and rotation:

```
@State private var moonRotationY: Angle = .degrees(0)
@State private var moonLastLocation: CGPoint = .zero
```

Implement the gesture code in **LISTING 5.11**, immediately following the last gesture. This is virtually identical to the earth rotation with one minor change.

LISTING 5.11 Enabling Rotation on the Moon Entity

```
.gesture(
    DragGesture()
        .targetedToEntity(moon)
        .onChanged { value in
            var xChange = value.location.x - moonLastLocation.x
            if (moon.position(relativeTo: nil).x < 0) {
                xChange = -xChange
            }
            if (xChange>0) {
                moonRotationY.degrees = moonRotationY.degrees + 5.0;
            }
            if (xChange<0) {
                moonRotationY.degrees = moonRotationY.degrees - 5.0;
            }
            moonLastLocation = value.location
            moon.orientation = simd_quatf(angle:
                                    Float(moonRotationY.radians),
                                    axis: SIMD3<Float>(0,1,0))
        }
)
```

The implementation is the same apart from checking to see whether the view is reversed. The moon starts on the right side of the view, where the `moon.position(relativeTo: nil).x` is positive. If the view is rotated until it is reversed, the moon's x position relative to the view is negative (the opposite of `earth`), and `xChange` is inverted.

Give the moon a spin. Start the application again and try rotating the moon by dragging left or right. I'd show a figure, but I'm pretty sure you can visualize what a rotating sphere looks like.

RealityView Rotation with Drag

The final drag gesture occurs when dragging the sun. Unlike the earth and moon, dragging the sun isn't going to rotate the Sphere in the sun scene directly (it will rotate, but that's incidental). It's going to spin the *entire* RealityView around *its* X-axis. This means *everything* you can see is going to spin as if it is rotating around the sun.

> **NOTE** The sun entity is positioned at the center of the RealityView, so everything appears to rotate around the sun. In reality, it's rotating around the origin point—where the sun happens to be placed.

Add two *more* variables to the list. These track the location and rotation of the entire view.

```
@State private var viewRotationY: Angle = .degrees(0)
@State private var viewLastLocation: CGPoint = .zero
```

This time, the listing is different. There's no need to check for whether the sun's position is reversed because it's located at the center of the view, so those lines are gone. `DragGesture` is initialized to require a `minimumDistance` parameter of 1.0 to help avoid accidental drag recognitions. Additionally, a `coordinateSpace` parameter is set to `.global` (the default is `.local`). This forces the gesture to be considered over the entire coordinates of the `RealityView`, not just the coordinates of the sun scene. Implement the final drag gesture, as shown in **LISTING 5.12**.

LISTING 5.12 Dragging the Sun to Rotate the RealityView

```
.gesture(
    DragGesture(minimumDistance: 1.0, coordinateSpace: .global)
        .targetedToEntity(sun)
        .onChanged { value in
            let xChange = value.location.x - viewLastLocation.x
            if (xChange>0) {
                viewRotationY.degrees = viewRotationY.degrees + 5.0;
            }
            if (xChange<0) {
                viewRotationY.degrees = viewRotationY.degrees - 5.0;
            }
            viewLastLocation = value.location
        }
)
```

You can try leaving out the coordinateSpace parameter in your implementation. Notice that the application sort of works, but as soon as the view rotates, you stop being able to drag. This is because the sun scene's coordinate system is changing and interrupting the drag. By using global coordinates, you avoid this problem.

Run the application again and try dragging the sphere at the center of the view. Isn't it magnificent?

If you agree, go back and double-check your code because it *shouldn't* be working! You aren't setting the orientation of just a single entity. Instead, you need to use a different approach that can operate on the entire RealityView. You must apply the rotation modifier to RealityView. Scroll to the bottom of the gestures and add this:

```
.rotation3DEffect(viewRotationY, axis: .y)
```

You first encountered this modifier in Chapter 2, "From Traditional Applications to Spatial Workspaces with SwiftUI," but the effect here is much more interesting. Try running the application again. You should now be able to drag on the sun sphere and watch your worlds spin, as shown in **FIGURE 5.17**.

FIGURE 5.17 Rotating the entire scene around the origin point

Moon Magnification

You're down to the final two gestures for the exercise. The first is detecting a magnify gesture on the moon entity and scaling the moon appropriately in real time. Most surprisingly, this is one of the simplest gestures to implement, and it mirrors the sample code you saw earlier in the chapter.

Add the code in **LISTING 5.13** so that it follows the last gesture but precedes the .rotation-3DEffect modifier.

LISTING 5.13 Magnifying the Moon with the Magnify Gesture

```
.gesture(
    MagnifyGesture()
        .targetedToEntity(moon)
        .onChanged { value in
            let moonSize = Float(value.magnification)
            moon.scale = SIMD3<Float>(moonSize,moonSize,moonSize)
        }
)
```

The gesture is targeted to the moon entity. Within the .onChanged action, a constant moonSize is set to value.magnification and converted to a Float value. You can then use this value, repeated three times in a SIMD3<Float> vector, to uniformly set moon.scale and dynamically resize the moon while the gesture is taking place.

Check the results. Target the moon with your gaze (on a physical device) or your mouse cursor in the Simulator. To perform the gesture in the Simulator, hold down the Option key and drag the points further apart or closer together. **FIGURE 5.18** shows the result.

FIGURE 5.18 Using the Magnify gesture to change the scale of the moon

Long Press to Add Planets

The final task in this exercise enables a user to add new planets to the view. You make this more interesting by generating random locations, materials, and sizes for the planets, and you activate the process using the `updating` event of a long press gesture.

You add the new planet entities from the `update` portion of the `RealityView` code. Yes, you're finally using it for something!

> **NOTE** Why a long press? Because I've basically run out of gestures that I can attach. Taps and drags can conflict with a long press, so this isn't ideal, but it will work.

Recall that if you're using an updating event with a gesture that occurs over time, it can be bound to an `@GestureState` variable that, once the gesture is over, reverts to its original value. For a long press, the state is simply `true` or `false` for whether the gesture is taking place. Add a final variable to your sizable list:

`@GestureState` **private var** `addPlanet : Bool =` **false**

This tracks the state of the long press. When the gesture is taking place, `addPlanet` is `true`. When it isn't, `addPlanet` reverts to `false`.

Add the final gesture code in **LISTING 5.14** after the double-tap gesture for the earth. *Placing it elsewhere will produce unexpected results.*

LISTING 5.14 Adding Planets with Long Press

```
.gesture(
    LongPressGesture(minimumDuration: 1.0)
        .updating($addPlanet) { currentState, gestureState,
            transaction in
            gestureState = currentState
        }
)
```

This binds `addPlanet` to the current state of `LongPressGesture`. The `gestureState = currentState` line ensures that as the gesture updates, the `gestureState` is updated to the current value. This, in turn, is reflected in the bound variable `addPlanet`. Refer to the earlier section, "The Updating Event," for more details.

It's important to note that you have *not* targeted an entity here. This means that *any* entity that can receive the gesture will process the action. *Based on your placement of the gesture in the code, only the moon is capable of receiving the long press...for now.*

getRandomColor

Before we can add a new entity to the view, you need to configure it, including building a simple material. You do this by writing two functions: getRandomColor and addPlanet.

Start with getRandomColor. It's used to generate and return a random UIColor object. This object contains the color information needed when creating a new material, as well as many other places where colors are defined throughout Swift development.

Implement **LISTING 5.15** after the gestures and the rotation3DEffect modifier in the Content-View.swift file.

LISTING 5.15 Generating a Random Color

```
func getRandomColor() -> UIColor {
    let red = CGFloat.random(in: 0...1)
    let green = CGFloat.random(in: 0...1)
    let blue = CGFloat.random(in: 0...1)
    let color = UIColor(red: red, green: green, blue: blue, alpha: 1.0)
    return color
}
```

The logic is straightforward: generate random CGFloat values between 0 and 1 for constants red, green, and blue. These values are used to initialize a UIColor object, color, which is subsequently returned to whatever code calls the function.

The need to use CGFloat values versus just Float is another "inconsistency" in Apple development related to dependencies in older frameworks. To learn more about UIColor objects and how they are created, read Apple's documentation at https://developer.apple.com/documentation/uikit/uicolor.

> **TIP** Notice that you can generate a random value of a given data type by adding the function .random(in: <starting of range>...<end of range>) after the data type name. This works for many numeric data types, including Boolean values, which don't need a range to be provided.

addPlanet

The addPlanet function handles much of the heavy lifting of adding new planet-like sphere entities to the RealityView. You call it from the RealityView update code, so you can pass in the content value and add new entities directly from the function.

Add the function in **LISTING 5.16** directly after the addColor function.

LISTING 5.16 Generating a Random Planet

```
func addRandomPlanet(content: RealityViewContent) {
    let sphere = ModelEntity(mesh: .generateSphere(radius:
                            Float.random(in: 0.007...0.04)))
    let material : SimpleMaterial = SimpleMaterial(color:
                        getRandomColor(),
                        roughness: MaterialScalarParameter(floatLiteral:
                        Float.random(in: 0.0...1.0)),
                        isMetallic: Bool.random())
    sphere.model?.materials = [material]
    sphere.position.x = Float.random(in: -0.4...0.4)
    sphere.position.z = Float.random(in: -0.4...0.4)
    sphere.position.y = Float.random(in: 0.1...0.4)
    sphere.generateCollisionShapes(recursive: true)
    sphere.components.set(InputTargetComponent())
    content.add(sphere)
}
```

The code first generates a new sphere entity with a random floating-point radius between 0.007 and 0.04. These are tiny little planets that don't make the sun, moon, and earth look bad. How did I come up with the range? Trial and error. Change the numbers and see what happens.

Next, a new simple material (material) is created with a random color parameter, generated by the getRandomColor function. The roughness is set to another floating-point number between 0.0 and 1.0. The typical Float.random value needs to be converted to a MaterialScalarParameter using the function MaterialScalarParameter(floatLiteral: Float.random(in: 0.0...1.0)). How do I know this? Because trying to use a Float value directly results in an error, with the option to fix the parameter with the conversion syntax used here.

The final parameter of the material, isMetallic, is set to a random Boolean value—either true or false, flip a coin.

The finished material is assigned to the model.material array of the sphere entity. The appearance of the sphere is now complete. The next task is to set a translation (position) for the sphere by altering its position.x, position.y, and position.z values.

Use random floating-point values between –0.4 to 0.4 for the x and z axes, and 0.1 to 0.4 for y. The slightly larger lower value for the y range ensures that the new sphere entities (the planets) are located above the earth, moon, and sun entities.

For good measure, include the lines to generate collision shapes and set the spheres as a valid input source. This means that after a sphere (or multiple spheres) is added, it will be capable of receiving the nontargeted long press gesture and can be used to add even *more* spheres.

Updating the RealityView

The very last step (I swear) is using the update code within `RealityView` to call the addRandomPlanet function when the variable addPlanet is `true`.

Add the following code to `RealityView` update. The beginning of the `RealityView` is provided for context and should not be changed:

```
RealityView { content in
    // Add the initial RealityKit content
    ...
    ...
} update: { content in
    if (addPlanet) {
        addRandomPlanet(content: content)
    }
}
```

Whew! Open the application one last time and give everything a whirl. Spin the objects, spin the view, resize the sun and moon, and try performing multiple long press gestures on the moon. The new randomly generated sphere entities start to appear and collect on your screen. Dragging the sun rotates *everything* for a nice interactive effect, as shown in **FIGURE 5.19**.

FIGURE 5.19 With the addition of gestures, transformations, and materials, our tiny sandbox becomes quite interactive.

This chapter has pulled together many concepts you've been learning in the first half of the book. The next few chapters continue to accelerate as we begin exploring *truly* immersive spaces.

SUMMARY

User engagement in an application depends highly on how enjoyable it is to use. If you set up a view with beautiful 3D objects, it won't make any difference if you can't *do* anything with them. This chapter has addressed the problem from two perspectives. First, how do you detect and react to interactions with your entities, and second, what can you do to show interaction?

You've learned the common visionOS gesture types, how they are attached to entities, and how transformations and shaders can be applied to move, spin, and scale entities. You've even seen how a gesture's action can be used to create new entities and add them to a view—long after the view's initial content has been loaded. Using this knowledge, you can begin to build applications that are more dynamic and truly offer an *experience* to the user.

Go Further

Armed with the knowledge of gestures and object interactivity, I recommend that you return to the Snow Globe project in Chapter 3, "Getting Started with Reality Composer Pro," and update the project so that the snow globes *work*. Use a drag gesture that goes up and down or left and right to simulate a "shake" and turn the snow particle emitter on or off. Let the user resize the globe with a magnify gesture or use your newfound ability to load or create new entities on the fly to create randomized scenes in the globe.

Something I haven't mentioned that you may want to take advantage of is the ability to present traditional 2D windows alongside your `RealityView`. To do this, add your typical window content before or after the `RealityView` block. It appears in a window, just like when you've worked with nonvolumetric windows. Just keep in mind that it is part of the same view presented with your 3D objects and doesn't have independent window controls.

Chapter 6 introduces brand-new capabilities, so perhaps it's best to just rest up for the adventure ahead.

Spaces, Direct Gestures, and a Touch of Physics

We are now at a turning point in the book. Up until this point, we've been working in very confined windows (plain and volumetric). That's fun and all, but Apple likes to talk about the "infinite canvas" that the Vision Pro can create. It's time that we start exploiting the Vision Pro fully and giving users more than bite-sized bits of content. This will take us to the heart of augmented reality and the skills needed to create true immersion.

In this chapter, we're going to be working with entirely new, but familiar, techniques. These will help you build more complex environments and experiences. You'll also be learning more visionOS fundamentals that you've used but that I haven't explained in detail.

After working through these topics, you'll understand

- **Immersive spaces:** An immersive space is an area—real or virtual—where your users can interact directly with the objects around them. No windows from other applications to get in the way and a much more expansive canvas upon which to create.

- **Creating immersive projects:** There are three types of immersive spaces you can present to your users, each offering a different experience. I walk you through creating an immersive space project and how to properly prepare it for whatever you have in mind.

- **Entity component system (ECS):** The ECS is Apple's paradigm for describing and programming entities in RealityKit. Using ECS, you can attach reusable components to different entities to influence interaction handling, properties like gravity, and even animation logic.

- **Direct gestures:** Direct gestures, like the Indirect gestures you learned about in the last chapter, require a user to be close to an object and physically "touch" it in order to interact.

- **Physics:** Simulate real-world physics with object collisions and interactions.

This is the last chapter that works with the visionOS Simulator, but I strongly encourage you to try the project on your Apple Vision Pro. It may even illicit a few "this is cool" moments.

Keep in mind that if you do want to practice on the Vision Pro, you can always don your headset, look at your Mac screen to transfer control, and then do the development directly through your Vision Pro. It's wild!

> **NOTE** As always, go to https://visionproforcreators.com/files/ or www.peachpit.com/visionpro and grab the Chapter 6 project files.

IMMERSIVE SPACES

We've worked with Windows and Volumes, and now it's time to introduce Apple's third application environment for visionOS: Spaces. A Space is very different from what we've experienced to date. In Spaces, visionOS can detect real-world objects and mix your creations with them. The entire world we perceive through the Apple Vision Pro becomes our playground. Spaces are frequently called immersive spaces because that is their function—to immerse the user in a new world or a modified version of their own world.

Types of Immersive Spaces

Apple provides three types of spaces for developers to use. I review the setup for immersive space projects shortly. First, it's important to understand what is offered in each type:

- **Mixed:** A mixed immersive space is what would traditionally be called augmented reality. In this space, the user can still see everything around them with virtual objects mixed into the view.

- **Progressive:** In a progressive immersive space, the user controls the amount of "real" versus "virtual" they are seeing with the digital crown. Depending on the application, the user might choose to block everything out with a virtual background, or they may let everything show through—like a Mixed space.

- **Full:** A full immersive space is just virtual reality. A user cannot see any of the real world. Everything visible must be loaded and presented to them.

FIGURE 6.1 shows the three different immersion styles—ranging from mixed on the left to full on the right—using an Apple White Sands environment and application launcher.

FIGURE 6.1 Mix reality with the virtual, go fully virtual, or anywhere in between.

You might surmise that this really just breaks down to *two* experience types. You have to account for the portions of the real world that are obscured by both progressive and full spaces, so there's not a huge amount of difference between the two. In fact, there isn't really *that* much difference between all three. In each case, you're going to have to define the environment around the user and what they may interact with. It's just a question of whether any of the real world is visible.

Development Differences

Developing for immersive spaces offers you much more area (like the whole world) for your experiences, but everything you've learned so far still applies. One big change that you'll come to appreciate is that you aren't mixing multiple application windows together (only one immersive space can be open at a time), and the coordinate system makes more sense.

When entering an immersive space, the coordinate system starts at your feet and extends in front of you. **FIGURE 6.2** shows the viewer and the coordinates you'll work with based on the viewer's position.

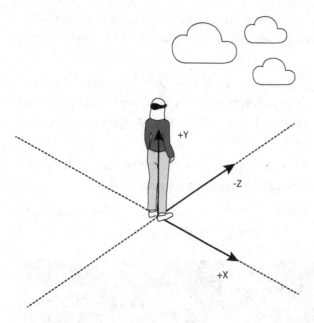

FIGURE 6.2 The x- and z-axes start at the viewer's position and extend to the front, back, and sides.

The y-axis starts with 0.0 at your feet (the floor). Negative y values place objects below the floor, whereas positive numbers move the position upward from the floor.

There are other differences you need to consider, such as asking for the appropriate application permissions to generate data from a user's surroundings, but I cover these as we encounter them.

> **TIP** In immersive spaces, a scene is positioned based on the user's position when they enter the space. That's great for an initial scene, but what happens when you want to move around? In Chapter 7, "Anchors and Planes," I explain how to anchor entities to real-world surfaces, making it possible to position objects in more abstract ways than just x, y, and z coordinates.

Now let's look at the Apple template for immersive spaces and how to create an immersive project.

Creating Immersive Projects

To start an immersive project, you follow the same initial process as any other project: open Xcode, create a new visionOS application, and then, when configuring the project, you want to pick some new options, as shown in **FIGURE 6.3**.

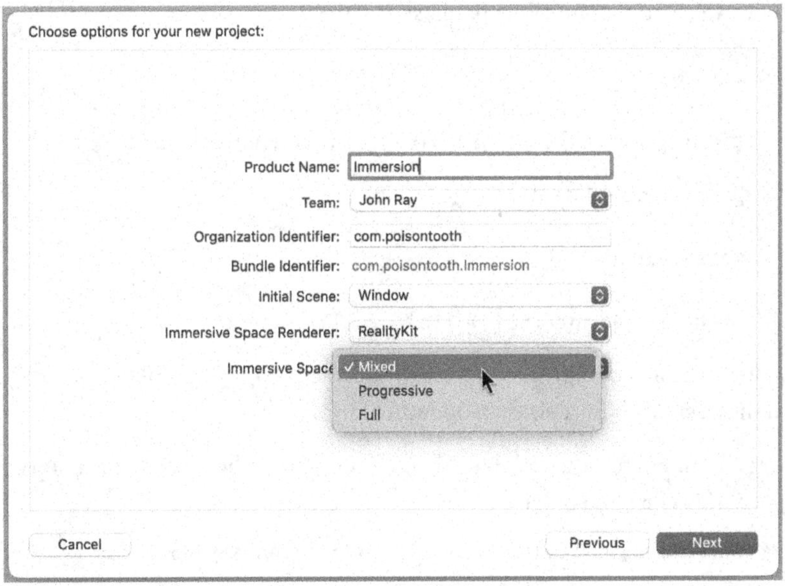

FIGURE 6.3 Configuring an immersive project requires a few new options to be selected.

First, be sure you start out in a Window. Windows are especially important with immersive projects because the user is potentially about to be placed in a location they may find disorienting. You should give them a heads-up before they have to turn their heads....up.

Next, an immersive space renderer must be set. This book only uses RealityKit, so be sure it is selected.

Finally, choose the type of immersive space you plan to build. In reality, this is changing *very* little, as I show you in a few seconds.

Aside from those small changes, the process should be well ingrained in your memory.

Defining the Immersive Space Type

Apple's immersive space template comes in three styles for the three types of spaces. The most important change between each type is the definition of the immersive space in the <App Name>App.swift file.

For mixed spaces, this code is about as simple as it gets:

```
ImmersiveSpace(id: "ImmersiveSpace") {
    ImmersiveView()
}
```

In a progressive immersive space, the definition changes:

```
ImmersiveSpace(id: "ImmersiveSpace") {
    ImmersiveView()
}.immersionStyle(selection: .constant(.progressive), in: .progressive)
```

Finally, a full immersive space is defined with

```
ImmersiveSpace(id: "ImmersiveSpace") {
    ImmersiveView()
}.immersionStyle(selection: .constant(.full), in: .full)
```

This may seem "wordy" for what it accomplishes, and that's because Apple's templates don't quite follow the pattern they establish in their own documentation.

The selection parameter is intended to be a variable. The variable should be placed at the start of the <App Name>App.swift's App code block:

```
@State private var style: ImmersionStyle = <initial immersion style>
```

With that in place, the .immersionStyle call becomes

```
.immersionStyle(selection: $style, in: <initial immersion style>)
```

The value of the style can be .mixed, .progressive, or .full —corresponding to the type of immersion desired.

There's no reason that you need to adopt this approach versus what the templates provide, but it does offer one unique benefit. When using the variable to set the style, you can change the active immersion type while your application is running by reassigning the variable to a new style.

As with windows or volumes, immersive spaces can be opened or dismissed using their id. This will require the addition of two statements inside the main struct of your code files:

```
@Environment(\.openImmersiveSpace) var openImmersiveSpace
@Environment(\.dismissImmersiveSpace) var dismissImmersiveSpace
```

Once defined, you can open and dismiss immersive spaces as needed using the syntax open-ImmersiveSpace(id: <immersive space name>) and dismissImmersiveSpace()—very similar to openWindow and dismissWindow. Note that there is no need for an id to be provided when dismissing a space because you can only have one open at a time.

The default templates include these definitions. Unless you're adding your own files, this is already taken care of for you.

Now let's move on to the content views.

Understanding Content and Immersive Views

The immersive project templates provide two files for developing your content. (You can always add more by adding new Swift files, as discussed earlier in the book). The Content-View.swift file is the same old file you've worked with all along but with some fancy new additions. The ImmersiveView.swift file contains the code for an immersive space.

The lifecycle of all three immersive project templates breaks down to the following:

The application loads an initial window defined in the ContentView.swift file.

This window presents a switch, Show ImmersiveSpace. Activating the switch loads the immersive space defined in ImmersiveView.swift. Depending on the version of the visionOS template you're using, you may see a different style button for entering/exiting the immersive space. No worries—they all work the same way. **FIGURE 6.4** shows this initial window.

FIGURE 6.4 A window is displayed before the immersive space is loaded.

1. If an error occurs, ContentView.swift handles the error (ignoring it).

2. ContentView manages two Boolean variables, showImmersiveSpace and immersiveSpaceIsShown. These are set when the immersive space is about to be shown and when it is visible, respectively.

3. If entering into a Progressive or Full space, visionOS automatically displays a warning telling the user to be aware of their surroundings,

4. The immersive space is loaded.

5. Within the immersive space, the ContentView window remains visible. A Reality Composer Pro scene named immersive.usda is loaded and added to a RealityView. It displays two spheres in front of the user.

6. In the case of the Progressive and Full spaces, the template also includes a light source (light sources are introduced in Chapter 9, "Lights, Sounds, and Skyboxes").

7. Turning off the Show ImmersiveSpace toggle in the ContentView window dismisses the immersive space.

In visionOS 2.0+ templates, you'll notice two new files: AppModel.swift for variables you want to share throughout your application and ToggleImmersiveViewButton.swift that removes the button definition and logic from ContentView.swift and places it in a standalone Swift file.

In all honesty, it's probably taken me longer to describe this flow than it would take you to open the files and see it for yourself. It's quite explanatory, and there isn't any logic you haven't seen before.

NOTE Over the next few chapters, you work exclusively with the Mixed immersive space. In Chapter 9, however, you have the opportunity to create a Progressive or Full space from scratch.

Cleaning Up the Template

All future projects begin by updating the initial welcome screen in ContentView.swift, updating the <App Name>App.swift file to better size the content, and emptying out the ImmersiveView.swift file. Let's look at what you need to change in these files so that you're ready to tackle the future hands-on exercises in the book.

Updating the Content View File

When starting any project, you first update the ContentView.swift file to include a description of what you're going to be creating as well as restyle the toggle switch. This consists of replacing the existing VStack in ContentView.swift with something similar to this:

```
VStack {
    Text("Welcome <Application Name>")
        .font(.largeTitle)
        .padding(40)

    Text("<Do something in the application>")
    Text("<Do something else in the application>")
```

```
Toggle("<Enter The Immersive Space>", isOn: $showImmersiveSpace)
    .toggleStyle(.button)
    .padding(.top, 50)
//In upcoming versions of visionOS templates, the preceding 3 lines
//will be replaced with ToggleImmersiveSpaceButton()
}
```

Throughout the evolution of the visionOS application templates, Apple has switched back and forth between multiple styles of buttons for entering and exiting immersive spaces. They started with a toggle switch styled as a button, moved to a plain toggle switch, and in future visionOS 2.0+ templates, they're moving back to a button—that is, unless they change things yet again. My examples include code like this to create a Toggle element styled as a button.

```
Toggle("<Enter The Immersive Space>", isOn: $showImmersiveSpace)
    .toggleStyle(.button)
    .padding(.top, 50)
```

In visionOS 2.0+ templates, this is replaced with a single line:

```
ToggleImmersiveSpaceButton()
```

To change the button text in these future templates, you edit the ToggleImmersiveSpaceButton.swift file. Near the bottom of the file, you see two strings—Hide Immersive Space and Show Immersive Space; you can change these to whatever you'd like. My examples use the current (at the time of printing) approach of generating and styling the toggle button in the ContentView.swift file.

Updating the Content View Sizing

Once a helpful welcome screen has been defined, I usually update the code in <App Name>App.swift to resize the ContentView window to an appropriate size to fit the content. Add the .windowResizability(.contentSize) modifier to the WindowGroup containing ContentView:

```
WindowGroup {
        ContentView()
}.windowResizability(.contentSize)
```

> **NOTE** VisionOS 2.0+ templates include a new file called AppModel.swift containing variables that your application can use anywhere. Although you don't need to update this file, you will see small changes in the <AppName>App.swift , ContentView.swift, and ImmersiveView.swift files to include these variables when a preview is being generated or a WindowGroup is being defined. Specifically, a modifier is added to the view that gives access to the variables defined in AppModel.swift: .environment(AppModel()).

Cleaning Up the Immersive View File

The ImmersiveView.swift file requires a bit more work . The ultimate goal is to edit the file until it resembles **LISTING 6.1**—with the #Preview function changing depending on the immersionStyle being used.

LISTING 6.1 Editing ImmersiveView.swift to the Bare Essentials

```
import SwiftUI
import RealityKit
import RealityKitContent

struct ImmersiveView: View {
    var body: some View {
        RealityView { content in
            // Immersive Content Goes Here
        }
    }
}

#Preview(immersionStyle: .mixed) {
    ImmersiveView()
}
```

Notice that these templates drop the update block you used in RealityView volumes previously, making your new starting template even simpler than other project types. You can add it back, but there really isn't much use for it, as you'll soon see.

Before we get into real coding, I'd like to introduce you to something you've been using without having a full understanding of how they fit together with Apple's RealityKit framework: Components and ECS.

THE ECS PARADIGM

The entity component system (ECS) paradigm is a modular approach used frequently in 3D frameworks, and RealityKit is no exception. ECS is used to describe how objects are created and behave. Rather than requiring heavy amounts of object-oriented programming, building with ECS is straightforward. You use components and systems that can be created and reused throughout your applications.

It's important to note that I'm not talking about an "entity component system"; each of the letters in ECS is a unique concept. In other words, when working with ECS, you're dealing with entities, components, and systems. Let's avoid any further confusion by defining each of these pieces and reviewing what you've done to date; then we can explore a few new (cool) things that add to your toolkit.

Entities

We've made plenty of use of entities over the past few chapters. As you've learned, these are the core building blocks of the worlds you create. They can be fancy models and scenes managed in a Reality Composer Pro package or single objects generated in code. Entities don't even have to be visible objects; they can be lights or sounds—anything you might want to be a part of the three-dimensional environment you're creating for your users.

NOTE Chapter 9 covers light and sound placement. They're the icing on our immersive space cake, so to speak.

You've used code to find and reference entities added in your Reality Composer Pro scenes, such as the snowman in the Chapter 4 project:

```
let snowman = scene.findEntity(named: "Snowman")
```

In Chapter 5, "Object Interaction and Transformation," you started creating new entities outside of Reality Composer, such as spheres:

```
let sphere : ModelEntity = ModelEntity(mesh: .generateSphere(radius: 0.1))
```

Entities can be hierarchical in nature. A "room" entity might hold child entities of a chair, a lamp, or a table. The snow globe in Chapter 4, "Creating and Customizing Models and Materials," for example, contained multiple different entities within a globe. By using this hierarchy of entities, you were able to position the snow globe anywhere just by setting the position of the globe itself, not the individual objects.

You can do the same thing in code, enabling you to work with multiple entities all at once.

For example, in the following code snippet, I create two entities (a sphere and a box) and add them to a third entity (entityCollection) that groups them together:

```
var entityCollection : Entity = Entity()
let sphere : ModelEntity = ModelEntity(mesh: .generateSphere(radius: 0.1))
let box : ModelEntity = ModelEntity(mesh: .generateBox(size: 0.2))
entityCollection.addChild(sphere)
entityCollection.addChild(box)
```

entityCollection can now be treated like any other entity. When I reference entityCollection, however, I also implicitly reference its children: sphere and box. You make use of this feature in the hands-on exercise at the end of this chapter to avoid having to reference many different entities individually.

Components

Components are the second part of ECS and are used to apply configuration details to an entity. These are parameters that affect how an object appears, the properties it possesses (such as mass), and how it reacts under different circumstances. Each entity can have only one of each type of component defined at a time, which makes sense when you consider how they're used.

For example, consider setting a material for a sphere entity using a line like this:

```
sphere.model.materials = [material]
```

You're modifying the `ModelComponent` of `sphere`, which contains all the different visual effects that can be applied to an entity (https://developer.apple.com/documentation/realitykit/modelcomponent).

In Chapter 5, "Object Interaction and Transformation," when you attached gestures to different entities, the entities became interactive only after you added collision shapes to the entity:

```
sphere.generateCollisionShapes(recursive: true)
```

This affected the `CollisionComponent` of the entity, which determines when the system detects collisions between entities (https://developer.apple.com/documentation/realitykit/collisioncomponent). You make even greater use of this component in your upcoming project.

When you've adjusted the location, size, or rotation of an entity through either a matrix transformation or property,

```
sphere.position.y = 1.75
```

this is, behind the scenes, adjusting the `Transform` component of the entity (https://developer.apple.com/documentation/realitykit/transform).

Some components may even slip under the radar, such as setting an entity to receive input, which is required for gestures to be processed:

```
sphere.components.set(InputTargetComponent())
```

In short, all the configuration of the entities you've used (and will use) takes place through the use of components. You can learn more about the available components in visionOS by reading https://developer.apple.com/documentation/realitykit/component. Many of which you use in future chapters.

This chapter introduces new components that deliver some truly magical results—but not on their own. Notice that I've repeatedly used the word *configuration* in this section? This is because a component itself doesn't perform the work of altering an object's behavior or appearance; they just hold the configuration details. To implement the real functionality, you turn to Systems.

Systems

The final piece of ECS is systems. Systems are pieces of code that work with a component to provide the appropriate behavior depending on how the component is configured. While you may set up a material component with a few clicks in Reality Composer Pro, it is a *system* that is taking that component information and applying it to an object's appearance.

A system can update an entity each time a frame is rendered on your Vision Pro headset. This update might include checking for interactions between objects or applying transformations (size/location/orientation) to an entity.
Systems provide the reusable brains for your entities, and their behavior is configured through components..

In Chapter 10, "Components, Systems, and the Kitchen Sink," you put this concept to practice by writing several custom components and systems.

ECS and Reality Composer Pro

Reality Composer Pro works with ECS, enabling you to add many components and systems to your predefined scenes and objects without writing code. You've been doing this all along by including materials in your projects because materials are a part of the `ModelComponent`. But there's more than just materials that can be set up in your scenes.

Here's a quick example: Open up Xcode and then launch Reality Composer Pro by choosing it from the Xcode, Open Developer Tool menu. Create a new project with whatever name you'd like or open the Components Reality Composer Pro project included with your Chapter 6 files.

If building your own example, use the Content Library to add an object to the scene in the project. It doesn't matter what you add. We just need an entity in the project, as shown in **FIGURE 6.5.**

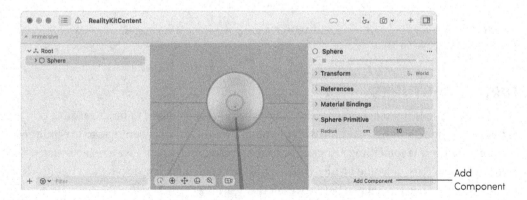

FIGURE 6.5 Create a scene with an entity, select it, and open the Inspector.

Make sure the Inspector is visible on the right. As you can see, the `Transform` component is already represented, along with the Material settings from the `ModelComponent`.

To add a new component, click the Add Component button at the bottom of the inspector. Reality Composer Pro displays a list of the available components, as shown in **FIGURE 6.6**.

Scroll through the list (or search) and find the Collision component; then double-click to add it to the entity. The new component, visible in the inspector of **FIGURE 6.7**, provides the same functionality as the `generateCollisionShapes` function you previously called manually.

Once a component is added, you can configure it using the attributes inspector. For the collision component, you might want to alter the shape used to determine collisions (by default, an imaginary box drawn around the object).

Remember, these components apply only to entities you've added via Reality Composer Pro, so if you plan on generating new entities in code, the components must also be added via code. You see both these approaches later in this chapter.

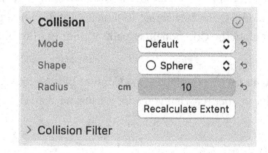

FIGURE 6.6 Scroll through or search the list of components.

FIGURE 6.7 Adding and editing components directly in Reality Composer Pro to save some typing

DIRECT GESTURES

In Chapter 5, you learned how to implement just about every standard indirect gesture available in visionOS. When working with immersive spaces, you can continue to use indirect gestures, but there is something just plain *fun* about interacting directly with objects that aren't even real. Sure, it would be nice if you could *feel* them, but a few dozen more iterations of the Vision Pro need to happen before we get that feature.

By default, when you implement a gesture, it works as an indirect gesture. This is Apple's preferred approach for interaction because it enables everyone to engage in an experience regardless of their mobility. That doesn't mean, however, that you can't *also* provide direct gestures as an additional input type.

Making your objects respond to a direct gesture is *identical* to indirect—with one minor change, courtesy of a component. To set an entity to receive both direct *and* indirect input, use this:

```
<entity>.components.set(InputTargetComponent(
                    allowedInputTypes: [.direct, .indirect]))
```

In the `allowedInputTypes` parameter, you can specify `.direct`, `.indirect`, or both to allow the corresponding input types.

This component can also be set on Reality Composer Pro entities by selecting the entity, clicking Add Component, and then double-clicking the Input Target component, as shown in **FIGURE 6.8**.

Once you've added the Input Component attributes, you can modify them in the inspector, including choosing whether to allow indirect, direct, or both gesture types. **FIGURE 6.9** shows the component and available options.

FIGURE 6.8 Adding the Input Component to entities in Reality Composer Pro

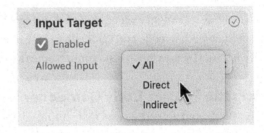

FIGURE 6.9 Select the type of gesture that the entity can receive.

HIGHLIGHT INTERACTION WITH THE HOVER EFFECT COMPONENT

Regardless of the type of gesture you're using, consider adding the hover component to your entities. For indirect gestures, hover adds a soft glow around the entity that the user is focused upon. Direct gestures will highlight the surface of the relevant entity when an interaction is taking place.

To add the hover component to an entity, add this line:

```
<entity>.components.set(HoverEffectComponent())
```

PHYSICS

For many people, the mention of physics may elicit a groan. You took some classes in high school or college and, yeah, you remember a smidge, but you probably don't want to think about all the math involved in getting entities to behave like real-life objects in your projects.

What if I told you that for the low price of $9.99, you could have utterly simple physics implemented in your applications? Sounds too good to be true, right? Now, what if I told you that the price was more along the lines of completely free and can be easily added to any entity within your volumes and immersive spaces?

There are three prerequisites to enabling an entity to act like a real-world object with mass and friction that's subject to the laws of gravity:

- The entity exists.
- Collision shapes have been defined or generated.
- The `PhysicsBody` component has been set on the entity.

The first two requirements shouldn't be a problem for you; you know how to add/create entities, and you've seen how to add collision shapes through code *or* graphically in Reality Composer Pro.

`PhysicsBody`, as you might expect, is the heavy lifter here. Much like collision shapes, physics can be defined both in code and via Reality Composer Pro. Let's start with code because it (believe it or not) seems much less cumbersome than Reality Composer.

Adding the Physics Body Component in Code

Full disclosure up front – there are many things that can be done with physics and animation outside of the built-in components. That said, this will cover much of what most people want to do in applications and games – and will not cause premature graying.

For example, the easiest possible way to add a Physics Body to an entity is to use the syntax:

```
<entity>.physicsBody = PhysicsBodyComponent()
```

What? Surely something is missing! Nope. If you've created or loaded an entity and added collision shapes (`generateCollisionShapes`), this single line adds the necessary behaviors for your entity to fall, tumble, and even bounce.

What's the catch? Simple—a single entity with physics defined has nothing to interact with. You need to add other entities, each with a `PhysicsBody` component, and *then* things will start to get interesting.

For more accurate and complex physics simulations, you can add additional parameters when generating the physics body component by defining PhysicsMassProperties, a PhysicsMaterialResource, and a PhysicsBodyMode:

```
PhysicsBodyComponent(massProperties: <PhysicsMassProperties>,
                     material: <PhysicsMaterialResource>,
                     mode: <PhysicsBodyMode>)
```

Ack! Well, that seems way more complicated, doesn't it? It does, but let's look at what these different parameters really are.

Physics Mass Properties

PhysicsMassProperties provides information about the mass of the object. You can use .default to represent a sphere with 1 kilogram of mass without needing to do anything else. Unfortunately, objects tend to vary in their shape and mass (at least I do), so, for an accurate simulation, you can create a new instance of PhysicsMassProperites like this:

```
PhysicsMassProperties(shape: <entity>.collision?.shapes, mass: <kg>)
```

This approach enables you to specify a mass in kilograms and a use the collision shapes already defined for the entity to calculate the center of gravity. Note that you *must* have already calculated the collision shapes (generateCollisionShapes) for this to work—thus the ? after collision—an acknowledgment that you know the collision component is optional and might not be defined.

Physics Material Resource

Using the PhysicsMaterialResource, you can define the **coefficient of friction** for an entity, along with its **restitution**—or, as Apple puts it, the "bounciness" of a material.

The coefficient of friction determines how readily objects will "slide" against each other. This is typically a value between 0 and 1, with 0 being "slides without any effort" and 1 being "doesn't slide."

Restitution is always between 0 and 1 and, if you don't like the bounciness definition, you can think of it as the amount of energy transferred back into an object after it collides with another. Makes bounciness sound better, doesn't it?

These are values you can play with to get the desired effect, so don't worry about trying to get it exactly right.

To generate the necessary `PhysicsMaterialResource`, use

```
.generate(friction: <friction value>, restitution: <restitution value>)
```

Not too bad, right?

Physics Body Mode

The final parameter is the `PhysicsBodyMode`, which defines how an entity moves when subjected to physical forces (such as gravity). It consists of one of three values:

- **.static:** The entity doesn't move.

- **.dynamic:** The entity responds to external forces and collisions.

- **.kinematic:** The motion of the entity is controlled by the user (in this case, the developer.)

In most cases, you want to use a combination of `.static` and `.dynamic` elements to build realistic environments.

Putting It All Together

Putting all of that preceding information together, here is how you might create an entity, calculate its collision shapes, and then create a customized `PhysicsBody` component for it. I'm using a simple sphere as the entity, but any entity, whether loaded from a Reality Composer Pro package or created in code, works the same way:

```
let sphere : ModelEntity = ModelEntity(mesh: .generateSphere(radius: 0.5))
sphere.generateCollisionShapes(recursive: true)
sphere.physicsBody = PhysicsBodyComponent(
                    massProperties: PhysicsMassProperties(
                        shape: sphere.collision?.shapes, mass: 2.0),
                    material: .generate(
                        friction: 0.1, restitution: 0.9),
                    mode: .dynamic)
```

The line limits of the book make this look more foreboding than it is. I promise it will be less intimidating once you're working with it in Xcode.

You can learn more about the `PhysicsBodyComponent` and its features at https://developer.apple.com/documentation/realitykit/physicsbodycomponent.

Adding the Physics Body Component in Reality Composer Pro

Before moving on to the real hands-on project for the chapter, I want to take you through a short example of how you can use Reality Composer Pro to set up a scene with entities that react to physics—no code needed. I'm choosing to build a scene where two objects fall and bounce on the floor.

You do not have to make your project as basic as I've done. Feel free to use your own models to make it more interesting.

Creating the Project

Begin by opening Xcode and creating a new mixed, immersive space project named Falling Objects. **FIGURE 6.10** shows my configuration for the project.

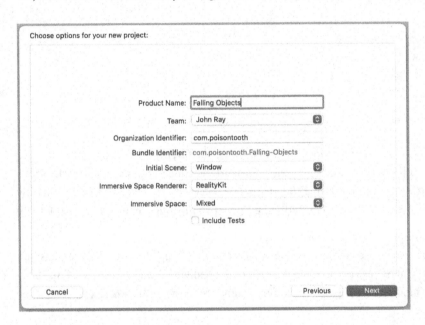

Choose options for your new project:

Product Name: Falling Objects
Team: John Ray
Organization Identifier: com.poisontooth
Bundle Identifier: com.poisontooth.Falling-Objects
Initial Scene: Window
Immersive Space Renderer: RealityKit
Immersive Space: Mixed
☐ Include Tests

Cancel   Previous   Next

FIGURE 6.10 Create a new Xcode project.

Don't bother updating ContentView.swift or the `ContentView WindowGroup`; this is just a quick and dirty example.

After the project workspace has opened, open the RealityKitContent Package in Reality Composer Pro by using the Xcode Project Navigator (select Packages, RealityKitContent, Package and then click Open In Reality Composer Pro).

Editing the Immersive Scene

In Reality Composer Pro, open the Immersive scene by clicking Immersive.usda in the Project Browser. The scene contains two spheres with a grid material attached. You can delete these spheres (Sphere_Left and Sphere_Right) or replace them with objects of your own; it's up to you. In my example, I'm keeping the spheres.

Regardless of the objects you've chosen to add to the scene, adjust them to be larger and closer to the origin point using the Transform component properties in the Inspector area. Feel free to use my settings, shown in **FIGURE 6.11**, for the left and right spheres.

These are the objects that are going to fall and bounce on the floor. What's missing? The floor! Using the Content Library, add a new cube to the scene.

FIGURE 6.11 Use these settings for the left and right objects (or position objects similarly as you see fit).

You need to stretch this out and reposition it to become the floor for the scene, but first, make it more "visible" than a bland gray block. Expand the cube in the scene hierarchy and select the DefaultMaterial entry. Using the Material attribute on the right side of the window, change the cube as you see fit. I've colored mine a purplish hue but otherwise left the defaults.

Now, turn the cube into a shape more floor-shaped. Start at the origin point, spanning about 1.5 meters to the right and left (x-axis), and extend it back (z-axis) about 3 meters. The y dimension can be reduced to almost zero because the floor shouldn't really be rising above your actual floor. My Transform component settings for the standard cube are shown in **FIGURE 6.12**.

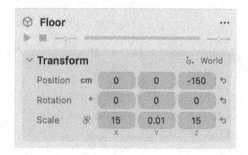

FIGURE 6.12 Placing the floor cube along the actual floor of the scene

FIGURE 6.13 shows the final scene. I know you're excited, but please save your ooohhhhs and aaaahhhhs for later!

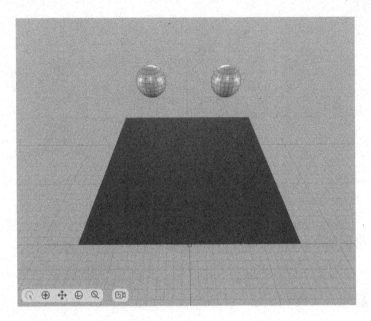

FIGURE 6.13 My final scene: two objects suspended above a floor

Adding the Components

As it stands, this scene isn't going to do much of anything. It shows two suspended spheres and makes a nice-sized patch of your floor appear in a solid color. To make something *happen*, you need to add two components: a Collision component and a Physics Body component.

Select the floor (the smushed cube). At the bottom of the Inspector area on the right, click the button Add Component, as shown in **FIGURE 6.14.**

When prompted, search or scroll through the component list and add the Collision component by double-clicking. The new component should be visible in the Inspector area, as shown in **FIGURE 6.15.**

You can leave these settings at their defaults. The floor is now able to detect and react to collisions.

Next, add the Physics Body component to the floor by following the same steps, except choose Physics Body instead of Collision when prompted for the component type.

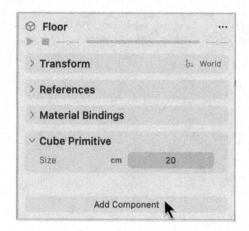

FIGURE 6.14 Adding a new component

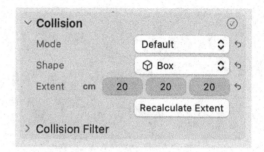

FIGURE 6.15 Configuring the Collision component attributes in the Inspector

Once added, expand the Physics Body component settings in the Inspector. You're going to want to change a few things. First, change the mode to Static and uncheck Affected by Gravity, as shown in **FIGURE 6.16**.

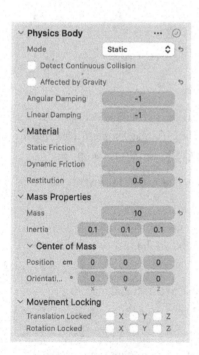

FIGURE 6.16 Updating the Physics Body attributes as appropriate for a floor

You may also want to think about changing the Friction and Restitution values from the defaults—or just play with the values once the project is complete. I've set my Restitution value to 0.5, for example. This makes the floor bouncy, which can cause some interesting interactions with the spheres.

The floor object is now configured to act like a floor. You just need to add the same two components to the spheres so that they can interact with the floor.

Following the same steps, add the Collision Component and the Physics Body Component to both of the spheres.

For the Collision Component, you can leave the defaults or set the collision shape to a sphere (if your entity is a sphere) for a more realistic collision, as shown in **FIGURE 6.17**.

The Physics Body component is where you can have some fun. Alter the mass of the object, set friction and restitution values, and just play around. Be sure to set the Mode to Dynamic, as shown in **FIGURE 6.18**, and allow the entity to be affected by gravity.

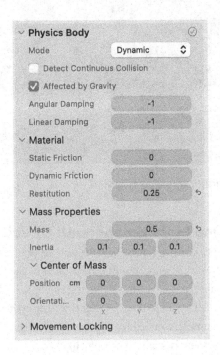

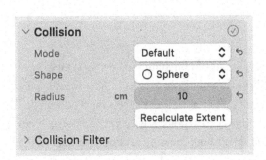

FIGURE 6.17 For spherical shapes, set the collision shape to a sphere.

FIGURE 6.18 Play around with the Physics Body component attributes

Try setting different attributes for each of the spheres so you can test the effects in relation to one another.

Running the Example

When satisfied with your work, close Reality Composer Pro and then run the application in the Xcode Simulator or on your device. When the application starts, you're prompted to enter the immersive space. (This is part of the default template.) Toggle the switch to see what happens. If everything has gone according to plan, you should see a floor right in front of you, and two spheres that appear and fall to the floor—and maybe even bounce around a little—as shown in **FIGURE 6.19**.

FIGURE 6.19 A working floor and some bouncing spheres

One More Component: Opacity

Let's consider one final component before moving on to our big hands-on project: Opacity. Opacity is a component that can vary the visibility of an object from 0 to 1. Why would you want to do this versus altering the opacity of an entity's material? Because a material can be invisible but still have reflective properties. This gives you a quick way to vary an entity from completely invisible (0.0) to completely visible (1.0) without messing around with material settings. In code, this looks like:

```
<entity>.components[OpacityComponent.self] =
                    OpacityComponent.init(opacity: <opacity value>)
```

The same feature is available in Reality Composer Pro via the Opacity component. This component has a single attribute, shown in **FIGURE 6.20**, that can be set to a value between 0 and 100%.

Opacity	✓
Opacity	100%

FIGURE 6.20 Setting the opacity of an entity through the Opacity component

I'm bringing up this component now because in the last example the floor was set to a color and obscured your actual floor. If you wanted the spheres to appear to bounce on your actual floor, you can set the opacity to 0. The floor will still be there, in the same position as your actual floor, but it won't be visible in the scene.

HANDS-ON: IMMERSIVE BUBBLES

In this chapter's project, you use almost everything you've learned to generate a direct touchable physics-enabled scene. The point that I'm hoping to drive home with this exercise is that you can create relatively complex interactive experiences with very little code. In fact, this is one of the easiest projects in the book and uses some of the same code as Chapter 5.

Project Description

This Immersive Bubbles project skips the use of Reality Composer Pro entirely. Instead, you programmatically create everything contained within an immersive space. You use two loops to create a grid of randomly generated spheres directly above your head. Each sphere is added to a parent entity so you can quickly add direct gestures to them all. As you walk around under the spheres, you can reach up and touch the spheres, which briefly highlight and then fall to the floor, bounce, and even interact with other spheres that get in their way.

Setting up the Project

Open Xcode and create a new mixed, immersive space project named **Bubble Immersion**. You follow the steps established earlier in "Cleaning Up The Template" to set up the project.

Updating the Content View Interface

Open the ContentView.swift file in Xcode. Within the default View block, remove the initial VStack block and replace it with code that describes the application and what the user will be doing once they enter the immersive space. Also update the Toggle with the .toggleStyle(.button) modifier, or, if you're using a visionOS 2.0+ template, edit the ToggleImmersiveSpaceButton.swift file to set a label for your button.

```
VStack {
    Text("Welcome to Bubble Immersion")
        .font(.largeTitle)
        .padding(40)
```

```
            Text("Move around your space and touch each
                  bubble to cause it to fall.")
            Text("Be sure to start in a large open space.")
    Toggle("Enter Bubble Immersion", isOn: $showImmersiveSpace)
        .toggleStyle(.button)
        .padding(.top, 50)
    //In upcoming versions of visionOS templates, the preceding 3 lines
    //will be replaced with ToggleImmersiveSpaceButton()
    }
```

Update the Bubble_ImmersionApp.swift file to properly resize the ContentView WindowGroup by adding the .windowResizability modifier:

```
WindowGroup {
        ContentView()
}.windowResizability(.contentSize)
```

This provides a nice title screen and some simple instructions for the user as to what to expect when they enter the space, as shown in **FIGURE 6.21**.

FIGURE 6.21 The application's tidy little intro screen

Cleaning Up the Immersive View Swift File

Now, remove the code that loads the default scene in the ImmersiveView.swift file. The ImmersiveView code block should look like this when you are done:

```
struct ImmersiveView: View {
    var body: some View {
```

```
        RealityView { content in
            // Add the initial RealityKit content
        }
    }
}
```

Your template updates are now complete, and you're ready to start the project!

Setting Up the Immersive Space and Entities

In Chapter 5, you used a mix of a Reality Composer Pro imported scene and programmatically generated entities. In this chapter, you generate everything in code. Test the application frequently as you move through the different steps of setting up the entities to make sure that your coding is in sync.

Adding the Supporting Variables

Bubble Immersion does something that you haven't seen before. It defines an entity (sphereCollection) that will contain all the sphere model entities that make up the scene. When a sphere (a bubble) is created, it is added as a child to sphereCollection.

Return to the ImmersiveView.swift file and add the following line directly after the var body line:

```
let sphereCollection = Entity()
```

Next, you add the functions that help generate the bubbles and fill the sphereCollection.

Defining the Supporting Functions

No surprises here. You want to generate bubble-like spheres in a range of different sizes, colors, textures, and translucency. Sounds familiar to the planets from Chapter 5, doesn't it? Start by entering the *very* slightly modified code for generating unique colors, as shown in **LISTING 6.2**, directly before the end of the ImmersiveView code block.

LISTING 6.2 The getRandomColor function

```
func getRandomColor() -> UIColor {
    let red = CGFloat.random(in: 0...1)
    let green = CGFloat.random(in: 0...1)
    let blue = CGFloat.random(in: 0...1)
    let alpha = CGFloat.random(in: 0.6...1)
    let color = UIColor(red: red, green: green, blue: blue, alpha: alpha)
    return color
}
```

The sole difference in this version of the function is that the alpha channel is now set to a random value between 0.6 and 1. To review the logic, revisit the hands-on project in Chapter 5.

Next, you add the function to generate the spheres themselves. This logic is also very similar to the planet generation in Chapter 5, with some additions. Enter the `generateRandomSphere` function, shown in **LISTING 6.3**, directly before getRandomColor.

LISTING 6.3 The generateRandomSphere function

```
func generateRandomSphere() -> ModelEntity {
    let sphere = ModelEntity(mesh: .generateSphere(radius:
                            Float.random(in: 0.05...0.09)))
    let material : SimpleMaterial = SimpleMaterial(
                color: getRandomColor(),
                roughness: MaterialScalarParameter(floatLiteral:
                            Float.random(in: 0.0...1.0)),
                            isMetallic: Bool.random())
    sphere.model?.materials = [material]
    sphere.generateCollisionShapes(recursive: true)
    sphere.components.set(HoverEffectComponent())
    sphere.components.set(
            InputTargetComponent(allowedInputTypes: [.direct, .indirect]))
    return sphere
}
```

The function starts off the same, generating a sphere `ModelEntity` with a randomized radius between 0.05 and 0.09. A simple material is created and assigned to the model component of the sphere.

The function finishes off by generating Collision Shapes, adding a Hover Effect component, and setting the Input Target component to allow both direct and indirect input.

The finished sphere entity is returned from the function and can be used immediately to help build out a scene in the immersive space.

Generating the Bubble Sky

The sky of bubbles that you're creating is a grid of 7 bubbles across and 6 bubbles deep. To create the grid, you run a loop nested in another loop. The inner loop generates the x coordinates, whereas the outer loop varies the z coordinate. The y coordinate stays the same, meaning that the bubbles are at a constant height.

Drop the following code fragment into the RealityView content block:

```
for z in stride(from: -2.5, through: -1.25, by: 0.25) {
    for x in stride(from: -0.75, through: 0.75, by: 0.25) {
        let sphere : ModelEntity = generateRandomSphere()
```

```
        sphere.position.y = 1.75
        sphere.position.x = Float(x)
        sphere.position.z = Float(z)
        sphereCollection.addChild(sphere)
    }
}
```

The block begins with two loops. The first loop changes z from –2.5 to –1.25 in increments of 0.25. For each step in the z loop, A second loop executes, incrementing x from –0.75 to 0.75 in increments of 0.25.

These values serve as the x and z coordinates for positioning a sphere. How did I come up with values? Trial and error. The numbers are in meters. the x coordinates start 0.75 meters to the left of the viewer and end at 0.75 meters to the right. The z coordinates begin at 2.5 meters in front of the viewer and end at 1.25 meters in front of the viewer. The spacing between the spheres is the same as the increment value: 0.25 meters.

Inside the inner loop, you generate a sphere (`ModelEntity`) and assign its position to the generated x and z coordinates, and a y coordinate of 1.75 meters above the floor. You might want to increase this value if the bubbles appear too low to you.

Lastly, `sphere` is added as a child to the `sphereCollection` entity. Notice that it hasn't yet been added to the RealityKit content. You do that shortly.

Adding an Invisible Floor

The next step in our project is adding the floor. Unlike the floor in the Reality Composer Pro example earlier, this floor is going to be invisible—that is, the *real* floor is going to be showing through the object you define to act as the floor. As you did with Reality Composer Pro, you use a very slim box as the floor entity.

Enter the following code after the loops that create the grid of spheres:

```
let floorEntity = ModelEntity(mesh: .generateBox(size: [5,0.0001,5]))
floorEntity.position.z = -3
floorEntity.position.y = 0
floorEntity.position.x = 0
floorEntity.components[OpacityComponent.self] =
                            OpacityComponent.init(opacity: 0.0)
floorEntity.physicsBody = PhysicsBodyComponent(
                    massProperties: .default,
                    material: .generate(friction: 0.1,
                                        restitution: 1.0),
                                    mode: .static)
floorEntity.generateCollisionShapes(recursive: true)
```

The floorEntity is created as a box that is 5 meters wide (x-axis), 5 meters deep (z-axis), and 0.0001 meters thick (y-axis). The floor is positioned 3 meters back from the viewer (z-axis) and is centered on the x-axis. Why is it centered at x=0 instead of positioning it at x=-2.5? Because it is a large individual entity, and by default, it centers itself at the supplied position. You had to use negative x values for the spheres because they're small, and you needed to center them at points to the right of x=0.

Next, the code sets the Opacity Component for the floorEntity to 0.0, making it invisible.

You also add a Physics Body component with the default mass and a material with a small amount of friction but a very bouncy surface. The mode is set to static because the floor will not be moving (I hope!)

Lastly, collision shapes are generated for the floorEntity so that the spheres can collide with it.

You might be wondering why you didn't add a Physics Body component for the spheres themselves. This is because you won't add that until a gesture detects a touch. Adding the Physics Body at that time causes the sphere to fall and interact with the floor.

> **NOTE** If you remember your geometry, you might recall that a 2D plane would be a better representation of a floor than a smashed 3D box. You're correct. I didn't use a plane because I haven't gotten to the topics of planes yet. If you glance ahead to Chapter 7's title, you may get a hint as to when I discussed that.

Adding the Spheres and Floor to RealityView Content

So far, you've done some development and have nothing to show for it. Not anymore! Go ahead and add the spheres (via sphereCollection) and the floor (via floor) to the RealityKit content, immediately after the floorEntity is defined:

```
content.add(floorEntity)
content.add(sphereCollection)
```

You should now be able to run the application, enter the immersive scene, and see the ceiling of bubbles appear above you. They just won't *do* anything. The application is almost done, so I'll hold off on a screenshot until you add the icing on the cake.

Adding the Gestures

The very last piece of this exercise is adding the gesture that will, in turn, add a Physics Body component to each sphere as it is touched. For this, you use a LongPressGesture with a *very* short minimum duration. This effectively gives you a way to directly touch the spheres without having to pinch.

Find the bottom of the RealityView definition and add a `LongPressGesture`, like this:

```
.gesture (
    LongPressGesture(minimumDuration: 0.001)
        .targetedToEntity(sphereCollection)
        .onEnded { event in
            if let touchedSphere = event.entity as? ModelEntity {
                touchedSphere.physicsBody = PhysicsBodyComponent(
                    massProperties: .default,
                    material: .generate(friction: 0.1, restitution: 0.5),
                    mode: .dynamic)
            }
        }
    )
```

The `LongPressGesture` is defined with a `minimumDuration` of 0.001 seconds. It is targeted to the `sphereCollection` entity. Recall that this is an entity that contains all of the spheres as children. By targeting the parent, the children *all* become targets as well.

Next, you use the `onEnded` event to add the Physics Body Component to the sphere. The event returns the entity involved in the long press gesture in `event.entity`. If a valid entity is identified, the `if` block assigns it to `touchedSphere` and then applies the physics component.

You can now start the application, enter the immersive space, and then run around touching the bubbles and watching them fall and bounce around the floor as you go, as shown in **FIGURE 6.22**.

FIGURE 6.22 Enter the immersive space and touch the bubbles to watch them fall.

SUMMARY

In this chapter, you've hit a few milestones. First, you've turned the corner on making 3D applications into more robust experiences. Second, you've hit the halfway point of the book! If you've made it this far, you're doing great!

You should now understand what an immersive space *is*, the types of immersion, and how spaces are presented through the visionOS immersive templates. You should also have a better understanding of the ECS paradigm and the capabilities that components (and their systems) can give you—especially in terms of adding physics properties to entities. Lastly, now that you've had a chance to implement a direct gesture, you have new ways in which you can create applications that truly immerse your users in a new interactive world.

Moving forward, chapters build on these skills by starting to use some of the world-sensing capabilities of the Apple Vision Pro. There's much more fun to come, so keep reading.

Go Further

As always, read up on the Apple documentation. These links are all good starting points for learning more about immersive spaces and the ECS architecture.

- https://developer.apple.com/documentation/visionos/creating-fully-immersive-experiences

- https://developer.apple.com/design/human-interface-guidelines/immersive-experiences

- https://developer.apple.com/documentation/visionos/understanding-the-realitykit-modular-architecture

This WWDC video is also worth a watch and walks through the basics of implementing immersive spaces with code examples: https://developer.apple.com/wwdc23/10203.

Aside from reading and watching, try *doing*. The bubbles project should give you some ideas that, if space permitted, I would have added myself. For example, rather than only allowing a preset height for the bubbles, give the user the option of raising or lowering the grid of spheres as needed (hint: just update the y position of the `sphereCollection`). Instead of just randomizing spheres, randomize a range of objects:—boxes, cylinders, entities loaded from the Reality Composer Pro package—whatever you want. Try introducing some gamification to the application, such as counting how many bubbles have been touched in a certain amount of time. You should have all the skills to make this happen, so start extending yourself outside the confines of these chapters. Make the experience your own!

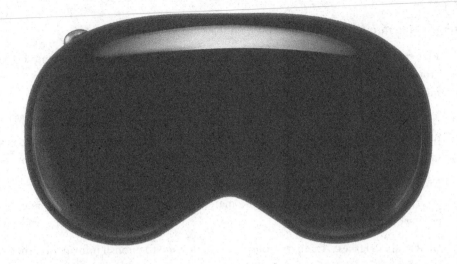

CHAPTER 7

Anchors and Planes

Throughout the book, you've relied on either Reality Composer Pro, manual programming logic, or physics to determine where objects are placed in your scenes. What you haven't done is take advantage of the real-world sensing capabilities of the Apple Vision Pro. When I write an application, I don't want to have to manually define where physical objects are located. It sure would be nice if the fancy cameras, sensors, and processor could do the work for me.

I think you can guess where I'm going with this.

Although the name of the chapter may sound a bit like a children's book, the concepts it covers enable you to start using the Apple Vision Pro to map the area around you, introduce objects that can interact with that area, and connect the virtual world to the physical world in a way that you previously couldn't.

After working through this chapter, you'll understand the following:

- **Planes:** As you move through a space, your Vision Pro is using Lidar to map the objects around you. It recognizes horizontal and vertical planes—or surfaces—where objects might be placed, as well as descriptive features of those planes.

- **Anchors:** Anchors give us the ability to attach virtual objects to physical surfaces. Want to put a vase on a table? Detect the table surface and anchor a vase to it. You can even anchor objects to the user themselves, essentially making things "stick" to them as they move about.

- **Video materials:** I typically try to slip something "different" into each chapter. This time you're going to find out how to make a material out of a video clip for a tremendously creepy effect.

- **Observable classes:** An observable class can be used to publish information that influences a view. As the information changes, the views are updated automatically.

- **Gaze:** For privacy reasons, Apple doesn't provide a means of directly capturing raw data about where a person is looking. Instead, we'll explore a technique that will effectively give us precise information about the user's gaze with very little difficulty.

Unfortunately, at the time of this writing, the visionOS Simulator does not support most of what you do in this chapter—specifically, recognizing planes and adding anchors in environments. If you attempt to run most anything beyond the basic immersive apps in the Simulator, it crashes and leaves you wondering if you made a mistake or if the Simulator did. (It was the simulator, not you!)

> **NOTE** Visit https://visionproforcreators.com/files/ or www.peachpit.com/visionpro and grab the Chapter 7 project files before reading on.

ANCHORS

When you've placed objects in previous chapters, they've always been at a location in space, and you've chosen their locations relative to one another. That's fine for limited experiences or even fully immersive spaces, but for mixed immersion it doesn't make sense. If I place an object two meters in front of me, it stays there until I walk away. What if you want it to come with you? What if you want to track the surfaces in your room, regardless of where you're standing? What if you want to track your fingers? It's hard to imagine how this can be accomplished when you only know how to set the .position attributes for an object.

The magical tool you're looking for is the **anchor**. Think of an anchor as a piece of Velcro that you can place somewhere in the physical world and where it will remain. You can either "attach" other objects to that anchor by manually aligning them with the anchor, or, depending on the type of anchor, add objects to the it and they will inherit the orientation and position of the anchor.

Best of all, an anchor can be attached "logically" rather than simply based on coordinates. For example, you might say, "Give me an anchor on a wall," or "Attach an anchor to my fingertips," and visionOS will give you an appropriate anchor as soon as one appears in the environment.

Getting to Know Targets and Types of Anchors

visionOS supports many different anchor **targets**—anchors for your head, hands, planes, and the "world" in general. These are different from the multiple **types** of anchors that also exist.

When reading the Apple documentation, you're going to find references to RealityKit anchors and ARKit anchors—with lots of crossover and very little consistency. The RealityKit anchors are just repackaged versions of ARKit anchors that make them easier to use. We'll experiment with both, focusing on `AnchorEntity` from RealityKit and `PlaneAnchor` from ARKit. It is necessary to delve into the ARKit anchors because they provide more direct access to data and give us more control over what happens with an anchor in real time.

The easiest anchor to use, RealityKit's `AnchorEntity`, acts as just another type of `Entity` that you can add to your scene—like a 3D model. You can add anchor entities to entities, entities to anchor entities, and so on. In the last chapter, for example, you created an entity that held the touchable spheres and then added *that* to your scene. You do the same with the `AnchorEntity`, using the same methods you've seen time and again.

The anchors for ARKit are rather different. They do *not* behave as entities; they're points and objects tracked by visionOS. When you use ARKit anchors directly, you monitor them for changes and update objects to align with them if and when the anchors change position.

Creating an Anchor

OK, time for the big scary reveal of all the code you're going to have to type to create an anchor. Brace yourself. Creating an anchor entity requires you to include a line like this in your application:

```
let anchor = AnchorEntity(<Anchor Target>)
```

Tongue-in-cheek melodramatics aside, this line of code hides a few complexities based on the target that you choose to use, but not *that* much. Let's go through the common anchor targets that you'll be using.

> **NOTE** As you read through these code fragments, you might notice something missing. I've stopped explicitly listing the type along with every variable or constant definition. By now, you should be getting familiar with Swift code and don't need to be reminded that variables have types. Just let Xcode figure out those types for you!

Head Target Anchor

A head anchor targets the head of the Apple Vision Pro user. It follows the user around and remains attached to them at all times. You might be asking yourself, "How in the world is this useful? I already know where my head is!"

First of all, objects added to anchors can be offset from the position of the anchor. Although it might not be helpful to anchor an object directly on the user's head, you might want to use the anchor to position something like a score display or informational view a few centimeters below or in front of the user that moves with them around a scene.

Secondly, think interaction! An anchor that follows a user's head could anchor an object that participates in a physics simulation or just collisions. Think of the bubble exercise in Chapter 6, "Spaces, Direct Gestures, and a Touch of Physics"—by adding a head anchor and collision detection, you might create a room-scale breakout game that requires the user to jump up and down and hit the bubbles with their head.

To create a head anchor, you use this:

```
let headAnchor = AnchorEntity(.head)
```

That's it. With a single line, you have an anchor entity that follows the user throughout their experience.

Hand Target Anchors

Hand anchors are similarly easy to create but offer more configurability. A hand anchor allows the developer (you) to track left or right hands—or both—as well as a specific location on the hand.

> **TIP** The choice of hands, by the way, is called *chirality* in Apple's ecosystem.

The syntax for a hand anchor starts like this:

```
let handAnchor = AnchorEntity(.hand(<Chirality>,
                        location: <Hand Location>))
```

The value for chirality is one of .left, .right, or .either, corresponding to the left hand, right hand, or, if you don't care which hand is used, either hand.

The hand location argument describes the location *on* the hand that should be used for tracking. There are five different hand locations you can choose to track:

- **.aboveHand:** A position located above the center of the user's palm. The anchor's positive y-axis points through the user's head, whereas the positive z-axis points at the ground.

- **.indexFingerTip:** This anchor is positioned directly at the tip of the user's index finger. In this case, the positive y-axis of the anchor exits directly from the top of the fingernail while the z-axis points toward the thumb.

- **.palm:** A palm anchor is located directly on the user's palm, with the positive y-axis pointing directly "out" of the palm, and the positive z-axis pointing away from the palm.

- **.thumbTip:** Like the index finger location, the thumb tip anchor rests at the tip of the user's thumb. The positive y-axis exits directly up from the thumbnail, and the positive z-axis points away from the rest of the fingers.

- **.wrist:** Lastly, the wrist location is on the back of the wrist, with the positive y-axis pointing out of the wrist, and the positive z-axis pointing in the direction of the thumb.

The names of the locations, in general, give you a pretty good idea of what to expect. The location of the axes is provided because if you anchor an object to a portion of your hand, it's helpful to know the coordinate system you're working in. If you use a hand anchor with a nonsymmetrical object, you likely need to adjust its orientation so that it properly "fits" in or on a hand.

If you want to create an anchor for the user's left hand, specifically their index fingertip, you would use this:

```
let leftHandAnchor = AnchorEntity(.hand(.left, location: .indexFingerTip))
```

Unlike the head anchor, which tracks a user's head continuously, a hand anchor only tracks the location of the hand the instant it's created, which isn't very helpful. To activate continuous tracking, you need to set the anchor's anchoring.trackingmode property to .continuous. For the example leftHandAnchor, this is just

```
leftHandAnchor.anchoring.trackingMode = .continuous
```

Plane Target Anchors

The third anchor target we'll be using in this chapter is a plane. A plane is just a flat surface in the environment. Walls, ceilings, and windows are all examples of planes that can be targeted.

This anchor target is more cumbersome than the others because it ties into the surface recognition features of the Vision Pro, which means *more options*. It is also, arguably, one of the most important targets you'll use. The simple form I discuss here comes with some caveats (which is why I have a complete section dedicated to planes and plane detection later in the chapter).

Unlike head and hand anchors, which track *known* objects moving in the environment, a plane anchor simply identifies a plane and attaches something to it. As a developer, you have very little say in where the planes are detected, but you can describe the characteristics of the plane you want through three different parameters: alignment, classification, and size:

```
let planeAnchor = AnchorEntity(.plane(<Alignment>,
                        classification: <Classification>,
                        minimumBounds: <Width, Height/Length>))
```

The alignment of a plane can be one of three values: `.vertical`, `.horizontal`, or `.any`. You might use `.vertical` to detect walls and windows, `.horizontal` for tables, or `.any` to recognize both horizontal and vertical planes.

Classification is where things get fun. The Apple Vision Pro is capable of identifying multiple types of horizontal and vertical planes and will classify them in one of six different ways:

- **.wall:** A vertical surface that looks like a wall

- **.floor:** A horizontal surface located at foot level

- **.ceiling:** An overhead horizontal surface

- **.table:** A tabletop or similarly positioned horizontal surface

- **.seat:** The horizontal surface of a chair, sofa, ottoman, and so on

- **.any:** Any plane with the chosen alignment

Later, the "Plane Detection via ARKit" section looks at some additional plane classifications that you can access when handling plane anchors via ARKit. For now, these are the types supported by RealityKit's `AnchorEntity`.

Lastly, the `minimumBounds` parameter gives you the ability to set the minimum size for a detected plane. You wouldn't, for example, want to anchor a model that is 1 × 1 meters on a plane that is 0.5 × .05 meters. Using `minimumBounds`, you can set the size you need to be detected to a minimum width and length/height. (I'm saying length/height here because it changes depending on whether it is a horizontal (length) or vertical (height) plane.)

It's best to see this typed out in an example. Assume I want to create an anchor for a 20 × 20 centimeter pillow model that I will place on a plane detected as a seat. I can write this:

```
let seatAnchor = AnchorEntity(.plane(.horizontal,
                         classification: .seat,
                         minimumBounds: [0.25, 0.25]))
```

When the application runs this code, visionOS starts searching for a 25 × 25 centimeter plane that appears to be a seat. Note that I chose to search for a 25 × 25 centimeter plane rather than just 20 × 20. You'll quickly find you want to choose values slightly larger than needed; otherwise, you end up with objects hanging off the edges of planes and other visual weirdness.

World Anchors

World anchors are another useful anchor that you'll want to keep in your toolbox. World anchors can be used to anchor an object to a place somewhere within the "world" your Apple Vision Pro perceives.

Go back and run the Immersive Bubbles example from Chapter 6. When the bubbles appear, walk to another room; the bubbles will stay put. Doesn't that mean they're already anchored to the world? No, they're anchored according to the orientation of your current RealityKit view. Press and hold the digital crown on your device for a few sections. Poof, the bubbles are transported right in front of you as the scene reorients to your new location.

A world anchor doesn't change when you reset your location. Objects attached to the anchor stay put wherever you place them in the world.

You can create a world-targeted anchor entity using this syntax:

```
let worldAnchor = AnchorEntity(world: SIMD3<Float>(<x>, <y>, <z>))
```

or

```
let worldAnchor = AnchorEntity(world: <Transform matrix>)
```

With the first syntax, the anchor is created with just x, y, and z coordinate positions. In the second, the anchor includes orientation (rotation) information in addition to position.

In either case, the coordinates or the transform matrix can be pulled from gesture results or attributes of other objects placed in your scenes. The final project of the chapter includes an example of this.

All you've done so far is create the anchors. You could start adding these examples to your code and they would run, but they wouldn't do anything—at least not anything you can see.

For an AnchorEntity to be beneficial, it needs to have an associated entity, and it must be added to your content. Let's see how that works now.

NOTE While hand and head anchor targets are processed (or can be processed) continuously while an application runs, a plane target is going to return one anchor attached to one plane – and you don't get to choose the plane. This can be limiting unless your goal is simply to add arbitrary decorations around an environment while the application is running. You find out how to make planes more interactive later in the chapter in the "Plane Detection via ARKit" section.

Adding and Using Anchor Entities

To use an anchor, you need to first decide what you're going to "stick" to it. This can be any other entity you want—a 3D model, a collection of models, an object from Reality Composer Pro, and so on. You add it to the anchor using the .addChild function. Next, the anchor itself needs to be added to the RealityKit scene, like any other object.

For example, **LISTING 7.1** is a complete working RealityView structure that you can drop into an immersive project. This will create a 20-centimeter (diameter) metallic red ball anchored to the index finger on the user's left hand.

LISTING 7.1 Creating an Object That Floats at Your Fingertips

```
RealityView { content in
    let fingerSphere = ModelEntity(mesh: .generateSphere(radius: 0.10))
    let material = SimpleMaterial(color: .red, isMetallic: true)
    fingerSphere.model?.materials = [material]

    let fingerAnchor = AnchorEntity(.hand(.right,
                                    location: .indexFingerTip))
    fingerAnchor.addChild(fingerSphere)
    fingerAnchor.anchoring.trackingMode = .continuous

    content.add(fingerAnchor)
}
```

Working with Anchors and Reality Composer Pro

It may come as no surprise that the anchor targets and type (AnchorEntity) that we've reviewed are available in Reality Composer Pro. Within Reality Composer Pro, you can add an Anchor component to an entity that anchors that entity to the very same targets that I've just discussed.

For example, create a new Reality Composer Pro project with a single object or simply open the Components project included with this chapter. Select the object (here, a drum) within the project's scene, as shown in FIGURE 7.1.

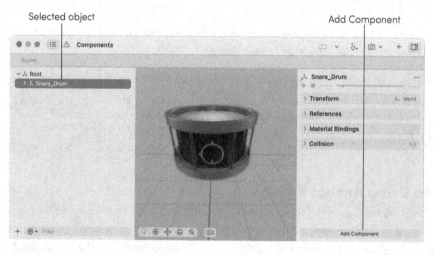

FIGURE 7.1 Add a component to the object in the scene.

When prompted for the type of component to add, choose Anchoring. A new Anchoring component becomes visible in the Inspector on the right. To configure the anchor, use the Target dropdown menu to choose the general type of target, such as Plane, as shown in FIGURE 7.2

After setting the target, the attributes I've previously discussed appear, and you can configure them as you did in code. For example, if you want to place this particular object on a horizontal plane, specifically a table that is at least 30 centimeters square, your configuration would resemble **FIGURE 7.3**.

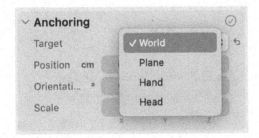

FIGURE 7.2 Choosing the anchor's target and setting other attributes

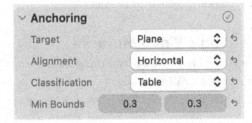

FIGURE 7.3 Configuring the target as you would in code

If you have difficulties adding the component, refer to "The ECS Paradigm" topic in Chapter 6.

> **NOTE** I honestly have no idea if the plane detector could identify a table with vertical alignment. It seems like the alignment could be inferred from the classification, but it is not—and I have no desire to nail a table to my wall to see if classification is as clever as it pretends to be.

Now that you've seen how to create an AnchorEntity in code as well as in Reality Composer Pro, I'll follow up with two simple projects that demonstrate anchors in use. These projects are virtually identical, but one has zero code—just some pointing and clicking.

Before that, however, I'm going to have you tackle something fun that you can include in future projects, including the upcoming hands-on.

VIDEO MATERIALS

In Chapter 6, you reused the sphere generation code that you'd already used in two other chapters. I then defended my decision to use spheres heavily throughout the book. Well, in the forthcoming project, I'm going to use a sphere with a brand-new type of material: video-based material.

Yes, that means that video can be used as the surface of the objects: spheres, planes, boxes, and so on. Using a video material requires adding a new framework, as well as defining variables for the video file location, and a new "player" object that controls the playback of the video.

Importing AVKit

AVKit provides numerous methods to your code that you can use to load and play video and manipulate the playback. You need to add this framework to the Swift file that is implementing a video material before you start coding; otherwise, autocompletion won't work, and you'll start seeing errors before you even try to run the application.

To add AVKit, add the following line after the other `import` lines in the Swift file:

```
import AVKit
```

Now, you can create the material.

Creating a Video Material

A video material requires two things: a reference to the location of the video file and an instance of an AVPlayer object, which controls the playback. Rather than showing these separately, here's a code block that you can use as a pattern:

```
if let <Video File Location> = Bundle.main.url(
                                forResource: <Movie Filename>,
                           withExtension: <Movie Filename Extension>) {
    let <Player Instance> = AVPlayer(url: <Video File Location>)
    let <Material> = VideoMaterial(avPlayer: <Player Instance>)
}
…
<Player Instance>.play
```

This defines a material based on a movie file that is copied into an Xcode project, loads it into a new AVPlayer, and creates a material based on the player. The material can then be used with any object. Playback is initiated using the name of the AVPlayer instance variable and the `.play` function.

If I'm working within a RealityView and I want to add a 20cm sphere to my scene that would display a project movie file named movie.mov on its surface, I could do this with this:

```
let sphereEntity = ModelEntity(mesh: .generateSphere(radius: 0.10))
if let sphereVideo = Bundle.main.url(forResource: "movie",
                                  withExtension: "mov") {
    let player = AVPlayer(url: sphereVideo)
    let material = VideoMaterial(avPlayer: player)
    content.add(sphereEntity)
    player.play()
}
```

This is less code than many of the Simple Material–based materials and can lead to some really neat effects, as you'll soon see.

> **TIP** Video Materials aren't just about the video. They also include audio! In fact, the audio seems to emanate from the object. You can control the audio options of the player using the material's `.controller.audioInputMode` attribute. Learn more about Video Materials and advanced AVPlayer functions at https://developer.apple.com/documentation/realitykit/videomaterial and https://developer.apple.com/documentation/avfoundation/avplayer.

HANDS-ON: ANCHOR PLAYGROUND

This chapter has three full hands-on projects because you have several different ways to accomplish similar functions. Each has benefits and drawbacks. Anchors can play a big part in your future creations, so the time practicing is well spent. You may even be able to create a fun experience or two without writing a stitch of code. Because you've been through this *many* times, I'm going to breeze through the project setup. You can always refer to "Creating Immersive Projects" in Chapter 6 if you get stuck.

In this first project, Anchor Playground, you create a testbed for the different anchor targets. You anchor some cotton balls to fingertips, a creepy video–playing sphere to a head, my good ol' antique head model to a table, and a decorative (in my opinion) movie clapper to the wall. The result, in action, should generate a scene like **FIGURE 7.4**, but, hopefully, within your environment (not my home).

FIGURE 7.4 Anchor Playground places objects on the user and other detected anchors in their environment.

NOTE Due to the way the Apple Vision Pro takes screenshots, you can't quite see all the anchored entities. You need to try this on your own for the full effect.

Setting Up the Project

Create a new Mixed Immersive project in Xcode named **Anchor Playground**. Once open in Xcode, complete the usual steps to get the project ready for your code:

1. Update the ContentView file to include a small introduction to the application. I've chosen to change the VStack in the body to read

```
VStack {
    Text("Welcome to Anchor Playground")
        .font(.largeTitle)
        .padding(40)

    Text("This demo will anchor models to a wall, a seat, and you.")

    Toggle("Show Immersive Space", isOn: $showImmersiveSpace)
        .toggleStyle(.button)
        .padding(.top, 50)
    //In upcoming versions of visionOS templates, the preceding 3 lines
    //will be replaced with ToggleImmersiveSpaceButton()
}
```

2. [Optional] Update the <App Name>App.swift file so that the content view automatically opens to the size of the content. I do this by adding .windowResizability(.contentSize) to the WindowGroup for ContentView:

```
WindowGroup {
    ContentView()
}.windowResizability(.contentSize)
```

3. Remove the extraneous Apple cruft from the ImmersiveView.swift file. Specifically, take out everything from the RealityView definition, leaving only the following:

```
RealityView { content in
    // Immersive Content Goes Here
}
```

I continue to abbreviate the project setup throughout the rest of the book, which gives me more time and space to focus on the unique pieces of each exercise.

Adding Model Resources

This project makes use of two Apple-included models and the Creepy Head.usdz file that I lovingly created many chapters ago. To add these resources to your project, open Reality Composer Pro by drilling down into the Packages folder and then RealityKitContent within the Project Navigator. Select the Package icon and click the Open in Reality Composer Pro button near the upper right of the Xcode window.

You're not going to be using either of the scenes in the file, so don't worry about them or delete them after you add your resources.

Start by adding the Creepy Head.usdz file located in your projects folder. Click the Import button (see **FIGURE 7.5**) and then choose the file and click Import.

Import File

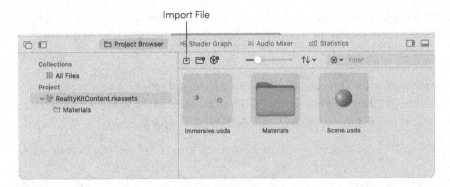

FIGURE 7.5 Using the Import function to add Creepy Head.usdz to the Reality Kit Content

Next, open the Reality Composer Pro Content Library by clicking the + button at the top of the window. Drag the cotton ball model (CottonBall.usdz) into the Project Browser, followed by the movie clapper model (MovieClapperboard.usdz). You can also add these by double-clicking them in the Content Library, but that has the side effect of adding the model to one of the scenes. Because you aren't going to use these scenes, it doesn't matter; it's just something to be aware of.

FIGURE 7.6 shows the Project Browser of the properly configured Reality Composer Pro project.

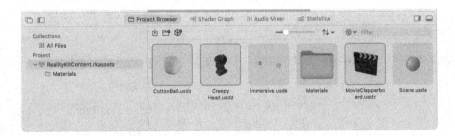

FIGURE 7.6 All the necessary resources added to Reality Composer Pro

You're almost finished getting the content in order, but you have one more piece you need to add: a video for the Video Material you're going to be using.

You can go ahead and close Reality Composer Pro. Your work here is done.

Adding a Video File and AVKit

The last resource you need is a video file to try out your new knowledge of video materials. Included in your project files is the innocuously named eyeball.mov file. This contains a short video click of an eyeball moving around. You're going to map this onto a sphere for an unsettling effect.

To work with the video, we need the AVKit framework added to the project, so begin by adding a new import line immediately after the existing import statements in ImmersiveView.swift:

```
import AVKit
```

Next, drag the eyeball.mov file from the Finder into a convenient spot in the Xcode Project Navigator, or choose File, Add Files to Anchor Playground from the menu bar. When prompted, choose to copy the files, create groups, and add to the project target.

The video is now visible in the Project Navigator and can be referenced directly in your code.

> **TIP** If you don't like individual files showing up in the Navigator, you can place them in a group by choosing File, New, Group. This creates a virtual folder within your project structure that you can use to organize your files. Dragging files into the folder won't affect how you reference them in code; it just adds some organization.

Coding the Anchor Entities

The time spent setting up the project likely will take longer than coding the anchors. So good job! You're almost done! You're going to add a total of five anchors and objects within the RealityView in ImmersiveView.swift:

- **Anchor 1:** A wall anchor with a minimum size of 20 × 20cm. The movie clapper model will be attached to this anchor.

- **Anchor 2:** A seat anchor with a minimum size of 15 × 15cm. The Creepy Head model will haunt this anchor.

- **Anchors 3 and 4:** Left-hand and right-hand index finger anchors with attached cotton ball models.

- **Anchor 5:** A head anchor that places a sphere styled with an eyeball.mov–based video material.

To start, define the anchors within the RealityView code block using what you've learned in this chapter. The anchor definitions should look like this:

```
let wallAnchor = AnchorEntity(.plane(.vertical,
                              classification: .wall,
                              minimumBounds: [0.2, 0.2]))
let seatAnchor = AnchorEntity(.plane(.horizontal,
                              classification: .seat,
                              minimumBounds: [0.15, 0.15]))
let leftHandAnchor = AnchorEntity(.hand(.left,
                                  location: .indexFingerTip))
let rightHandAnchor = AnchorEntity(.hand(.right,
                                   location: .indexFingerTip))
let headAnchor = AnchorEntity(.head)
```

This code handles all the heavy lifting of managing the world and body-sensing capabilities of the Apple Vision Pro. Now all that is needed is the code to attach the various objects and subsequently add the anchors to the `RealityView`.

Adding Entities to Anchor Entities

Start with the wall anchor and add code to load and attach the appropriate model entities. You can use whatever variable names you want for the entities. I've chosen to use `wallObject`, `seatObject`, `rightObject`, and `leftObject` for the MovieClapperboard.usdz, Creepy Head. usdz, and CottonBall.usdz (twice) model files:

```
if let wallObject = try? await Entity(named: "MovieClapperboard.usdz",
                                       in: realityKitContentBundle) {
    wallAnchor.addChild(wallObject)
}
```

Make sure you pair the right entities with the right anchors as you add them. In other words, don't just type the preceding code over and over; you're gonna have to work a little and adjust it appropriately.

Although the preceding code pattern works for the first four anchors (`wallAnchor`, `seatAnchor`, `leftHandAnchor`, `righthandAnchor`), it isn't going to accomplish what you need for the sphere that has a Video Material.

To generate the sphere and the Video Material, add this block following the other anchor/ entity attachments:

```
let watchfulSphere = ModelEntity(mesh: .generateSphere(radius: 0.20))
if let sphereVideo = Bundle.main.url(forResource: "eyeball",
                                     withExtension: "mov") {
    let player = AVPlayer(url: sphereVideo)
    let material = VideoMaterial(avPlayer: player)
    watchfulSphere.model?.materials = [material]
    headAnchor.addChild(watchfulSphere)
    player.play()
}
```

This creates a sphere, `watchfulSphere`, with a radius of 20cm. The code then loads the eyeball. mov movie file you added to the project, initializes an `AVPlayer` with the movie, and generates a video material that is applied to `watchfulSphere`. Lastly, the `watchfulSphere` is added to the `headAnchor` and the `AVPlayer` is told to start playing.

Seems like it should all work, right? Nope, not yet. You still need to add the anchors to the RealityView content.

Adding Anchor Entities to the RealityView

After the code that attaches all the entities to the anchors, add five new lines that add the anchors to the content—just like adding any other model:

```
content.add(leftHandAnchor)
content.add(rightHandAnchor)
content.add(headAnchor)
content.add(wallAnchor)
content.add(seatAnchor)
```

Now you should be able to run your application, look around the room, wave your hands, and see a variety of objects attached throughout your space. Unfortunately, they aren't going to look particularly great. The video won't be positioned properly on the sphere, which may or may not be visible since it is covering your head; the movie clapper will attach to the wall but will stick out sideways and not lie flat; and the video material will finish playing in about five seconds—hardly enough time to get the full effect.

Let's fix those issues now.

Rotating the Movie Clapper

The movie clapper model is oriented so that it stands vertically if placed into a scene. This is fine for placing on horizontal surfaces, but when placed on a vertical plane anchor, it assumes the "correct" orientation for that plane, which is at odds with what you want.

To fix the issue, you can rotate the clapper –90 degrees along the x-axis so that it lies flat against vertical planes. Update the code block that loads the model and adds it to the anchor so that it includes a change in rotation, like this:

```
if let wallObject = try? await Entity(named: "MovieClapperboard.usdz",
                                      in: realityKitContentBundle) {
    wallObject.orientation = simd_quatf(angle:
                            Float(Angle(degrees: -90.0).radians),
                            axis: SIMD3<Float>(1,0,0))
    wallAnchor.addChild(wallObject)
}
```

Note that I've used a –90-degree angle. If I rotated 90 degrees, the back of the movie clapper would be visible instead, and it would be upside down. Play with the numbers and see for yourself.

> **TIP** If you're finding this confusing, just look at a wall and tilt your head sideways so that it becomes the floor. This is how the plane is treated when it is detected. The movie clapper sits on the wall as if the wall was the floor. To make it lie flat, you have to knock it over—or rotate it 90 degrees—the same as you would need to do if it was anchored to the floor.

Rotating and Offsetting the Sphere

Something similar needs to happen for the sphere. With it anchored directly to the head it can't be seen, and the video is also mapped to the sphere in a way that it faces away from the viewer. To fix both of these problems, you need to set the position of the sphere so that it is about a meter away from your head and about 25cm lower. The sphere itself needs to be rotated 90 degrees around the y-axis before the video appears in a pleasing(?!) way.

Update the code block that generates the sphere and video material to include an offset and a rotation:

```
let watchfulSphere = ModelEntity(mesh: .generateSphere(radius: 0.20))
if let sphereVideo = Bundle.main.url(forResource: "eyeball",
                                     withExtension: "mov") {
    let player = AVPlayer(url: sphereVideo)
    let material = VideoMaterial(avPlayer: player)
    watchfulSphere.model?.materials = [material]
    watchfulSphere.position.z = -1.0
    watchfulSphere.position.y = -0.25
    watchfulSphere.orientation = simd_quatf(angle:
                        Float(Angle(degrees: 90.0).radians),
                        axis: SIMD3<Float>(0,1,0))
    headAnchor.addChild(watchfulSphere)
    player.play()
}
```

Using the same position attribute you've used previously, the code positions the sphere 1 meter away (–1 meters on the z-axis) and lowers it a quarter of a meter on the y-axis. A 90-degree rotation around the y-axis is applied to roughly center the sphere so that the eyeball video is facing the user.

I'd love to say "done" and take a nap, but unfortunately there is one other problem (you may think differently) that needs to be fixed: The video plays once and does not loop.

Looping the Video Material

When you start playing the video with the line player.play(), you'll quickly learn that the video is quite short and ends quickly. (Again, you may think of this as a feature.) To loop the video, you can turn to a tried-and-true approach that works for any Video Material you want to use.

Insert the following code before you instruct the AVPlayer to play:

```
NotificationCenter.default.addObserver(
                        forName: .AVPlayerItemDidPlayToEndTime,
                        object: player.currentItem,
                        queue: nil) { (_) in
```

```
            player.seek(to: CMTime.zero)
            player.play()
    }
```

This code uses a feature called `NotificationCenter` that enables code in one part of your application to broadcast a message that can observed and acted upon by another part. As luck would have it, AVPlayer broadcasts a notice named `.AVPlayerItemDidPlayToEndTime` each time it has finished playing a video. This code block watches for that notification and, when it is received, tells the player to seek back to the 0 position in its timeline (`CMTime.zero`) and then start playing again. Learn more about Notification Center, which can be quite handy in monitoring things happening throughout your applications, at https://developer.apple.com/documentation/foundation/notificationcenter.

> **NOTE** Apple provides a feature specifically for managing looping playback called AVPlayerLooper (https://developer.apple.com/documentation/avfoundation/avplayerlooper). Unfortunately, using the looper requires far more setup overhead, making it cumbersome for situations like this. Using Notification Center, you can drop in a few lines of code every time you need it. You don't have to plan your whole project around providing looping capabilities.

Now you can run the project and see the full effect: a creepy floating eyeball that follows you around and an equally creepy mannequin head that will sit beside you. Cotton ball fingertips and a wall-mounted movie clapper round out the surreal experience.

CODE-FREE ANCHORS

If you're code-averse, you can accomplish (almost) the same thing as our preceding exercise entirely in Reality Composer Pro. For a quick tutorial that does exactly that, download Appendix D from www.peachpit.com/visionpro or https://visionproforcreators.com/.

PLANE DETECTION VIA ARKIT

Hold on a second. You just completed an example where you detected planes and used anchors to place objects on them. Why are we heading into *another* section on plane detection?

The answer lies in something I said earlier: RealityKit's `AnchorEntity` is just a simplified fron-tend for ARKit anchors. While that simplification is great, it also masks functionality (and complexity) that can be gained by using ARKit.

When you established plane anchors with `AnchorEntity`, all you could do was specify characteristics of the anchor and hope you get something back. You couldn't choose what you wanted. This can be helpful if you don't care where something ends up in your immersive scene, but frequently you need more control over the process.

ARKit

ARKit is Apple's augmented reality framework for its entire device family and development ecosystem. It provides environment detection, motion detection, and anchor support—many features you've already used. It can provide direct real-time data about what a device is "seeing" as it occurs. The reason you haven't heard of this sooner is because many of the features you can access in ARKit are also available in the much easier-to-use `AnchorEntity` wrapper in RealityKit. The Apple Vision Pro is built for augmented reality, so *everything* you've been doing has underpinnings in ARKit, it's just not something you've explicitly needed to use.

At its core, ARKit has a pretty simple and easy-to-understand lifecycle—one that you'll implement shortly:

1. An `ARKitSession` is initialized. It manages the polling and presenting of data from ARKit. It will be inactive until a `run` command is issued.

2. One or more data providers are defined. A data provider tells visionOS what tracking is needed and provides an interface for you, the developer, to access the data. There are multiple data providers available—`PlaneDetectionProvider`, `HandTrackingProvider`, `SceneReconstructionProvider`, and more. In this chapter, you focus on the `PlaneDetectionProvider`.

3. When the application is ready to receive data, the `ARKitSession` is run with the chosen data providers. It provides a continuous stream of anchor additions, removals, and updates that can be processed however we, the developers, see fit.

Unlike RealityKit's `AnchorEntity`, the anchors you receive via ARKit are standalone data structures. You can use them to align other entities, but it's not quite as simple as adding objects to an `AnchorEntity`. That's the tradeoff for greater functionality.

You can learn more about the different data providers by reading the documentation at https://developer.apple.com/documentation/arkit/dataprovider. Note that there is also a hand-tracking provider, which may seem unnecessary given how easy it already is to set up basic tracking. The difference is that you can get real-time information about the *individual joints* on a user's hand through ARKit. You'll write code in Chapter 8 to perform this detailed hand-tracking.

Requesting Permissions

Advanced tracking in ARKit requires permissions. If you've used an iPhone (or even one of those other lesser devices), you've almost certainly had an app ask for permission to use information, such as location, when it first opens. When using ARKit with the Vision Pro, the user is also prompted for permission—and for good reason. If visionOS is using ARKit, it's seeing and processing your environment, including watching your hands. This isn't data that many people want to share with others, and you shouldn't expect users to accept this behavior without first giving them a heads-up.

To implicitly ask for permission, all you need to do is modify the Info.plist file in any project using enhanced sensing capabilities. In this chapter, you use World Sensing and Hand Track capabilities, which require two keys to be set in the file: `NSWorldSensingUsageDescription` and `NSHandsTrackingUsageDescription`.

The first enables tracking of planes and other real-world sensing capabilities (you use this pretty heavily from now on), and the latter enables hand tracking and is needed only when using features (such as hand anchors) that require precise tracking of the user's hands – which we'll be doing tomorrow.

To set these values within an Xcode project, you first select Info from the Project Navigator, as shown in **FIGURE 7.7**.

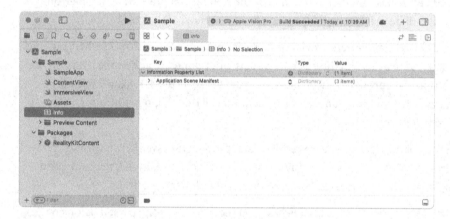

FIGURE 7.7 Opening an Xcode project and selecting the Info file from the Project Navigator

Within the editor on the right, expand the Information Property List entry and click the + button that appears when your cursor is near the line. This adds a new entry within the list. Even though you are prompted with a list of selections, you need to type `NSWorldSensin-gUsageDescription` as shown in **FIGURE 7.8** because it's not included in the dropdown.

The Type should be left as String, and the Value set to an appropriate prompt that the user will see when accessing the application.

If using hand-tracking, you'll also need to repeat these steps with the `NSHandsTrackingUsage-Description` key. **FIGURE 7.9** shows the Info.plist file configured for both of these features.

When an application that has been set up with these keys runs, the user sees a prompt before the application begins to collect data, as shown in **FIGURE 7.10**.

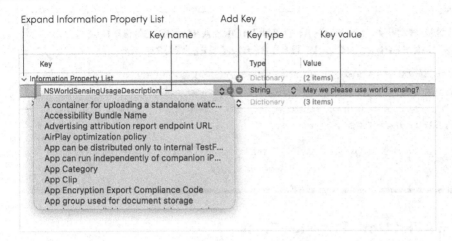

FIGURE 7.8 Create and manually enter a new key.

Key	Type	Value
˅ Information Property List	Dictionary ◇	(3 items)
NSHandsTrackingUsageDescription	◇ String	To use this app, we need to be able to track your hands. Cool?
NSWorldSensingUsageDescription	◇ String	To use this app, we need to be able to track your surroundings. Cool?
› Application Scene Manifest	◇ Dictionary	(3 items)

FIGURE 7.9 File set for both world and hand tracking.

FIGURE 7.10 A prompt when the application attempts to access sensor data.

Creating an ARKit Data Provider Class

Let's look at what an ARKit session looks like in code. Rather than breaking down the individual syntax of each command you would use to establish an ARKit session, it might be helpful to state upfront that you do *not* want to try using ARKit code directly within one of your views. The most straightforward way to use ARKit is to create a class file for the data providers you want to use. Recall that a class, like a struct, is a way to pull together variables and methods that relate to one another and package them in a reusable way.

For ARKit, using a class of the type `ObservableObject` makes the most sense. This type of class allows you to *publish* variables in the class that can then be *observed* elsewhere in your code. Although you could normally just access public variables directly in another class, using the publish/observe model means that your views will automatically be triggered to update when a published variable is updated by its class. **LISTING 7.2** shows a simple definition for a plane detection class, which will give you access to live data about planes that the Vision Pro is detecting within its environment.

LISTING 7.2 A Plane Detector Class

```
import ARKit
@MainActor class PlaneDetector: ObservableObject {

    private let session = ARKitSession()
    private let planeData = PlaneDetectionProvider(alignments: [.any])

    func startDetection() async {
        if PlaneDetectionProvider.isSupported {
            try! await session.run([planeData])
            for await update in planeData.anchorUpdates {
                // Process update.anchor.classification, if desired
                switch update.event {
```

```
                case .added, .updated:
                    updatePlane(update.anchor)
                case .removed:
                    removePlane(update.anchor)
                }
            }
        }
    }

    func updatePlane(_ anchor: PlaneAnchor) {
        // Do something with:
        //     anchor.geometry.extent.anchorFromExtentTransform
        //     anchor.geometry.extent.width
        //     anchor.geometry.extent.height
    }

    func removePlane(_ anchor: PlaneAnchor) {
        // The Plane Anchor is no longer being tracked
    }
}
```

Breaking Down the Code

The code starts by importing ARKit, which you need to use the ARKit-specific functions. Next, the class PlaneDetector is declared of the type ObservableObject.

Two private constants are added: session, holding an instance of an ARKitSession, and planeData, initialized to an instance of PlaneDetectionProvider. Note that the detection provider can be configured to detect .horizontal, .vertical, or .any, just like the AnchorEntity used earlier.

Next, a startDetection asynchronous function is defined. This block of code handles starting and monitoring incoming plane anchor data. Asynchronous (async) is required as this code must run in the background while other application functions continue to operate.

The startDetection code block begins by checking whether PlaneDetectionProvider is supported. This verifies whether the user of the application has agreed to the world-sensing capabilities being turned on in the application (triggered by adding the NSWorldSensingUsageDescription key to the Info.plist file for the application).

Assuming the permission has been granted, the ARKitSession is started with session.run([planeData]), and real-time data from the planeData provider begins to flow into the class.

Data updates arrive in the planeData.anchorUpdates data structure. Using a for loop, you grab each update as it comes in and process it. Despite being a loop that typically stops, this runs indefinitely. There isn't an "end" to the `anchorUpdates` structure as long as the `ARKitSession` (`session`) remains active.

Within this loop, you can examine `update.anchor.classification` to check for the same `.wall`, `.ceiling`, and other surfaces that covered earlier with `AnchorEntity`. There are even two other types—`.door` and `.window`—that can be used to recognize even more real-world structures.

When updates arrive, they are handled by two functions: `updatePlane` and `removePlane`. These functions process plane anchors when they are added or updated (`updatePlane`) and when they are removed (`removePlane`).

The anchors contain both a transform matrix that positions it within world space (`<anchor>.geometry.extent.anchorFromExtentTransform`) and a general size of the plane (`<anchor>.geometry.extent.width` and `<anchor>.geometry.extent.height`). You can use this data to position your objects based on the anchors.

AWAIT, @MAINACTOR, ASYNC: **WHAT'S GOING ON HERE?**

There's quite a bit of complexity in how an `ARKitSession` runs. Some portions must be asynchronous (`async`), but some functions executed asynchronously require that results be returned before the next instruction can be processed (`await`). Furthermore, reading and writing from the data provider must happen on the main thread of the application. This is forced by adding `@MainActor` preceding at the start of the class. If you notice `@MainActor` being mentioned in Apple's documentation, chances are you'll need it when using the associated data or functions being described. It can be placed before the `class` keyword or preceding any function.

It can all be quite a lot, but if you follow the pattern established in this sample class, you'll be fine.

Using the Class

To initialize and use this class in a view (which you do in the upcoming exercise), you create a new instance of the class and then execute the `startDetection()` method:

```
@ObservedObject var planeDetector: PlaneDetector = PlaneDetector()
await planeDetector.startDetection()
```

The `@ObservedObject` property wrapper indicates that you're going to be observing the object (the running `PlaneDetector` class), and any time one of its properties that has been marked with the `@Published` wrapper is updated, it will need to immediately update its views. The sample class doesn't have any published variables, so it isn't very meaningful... yet.

Planes, Spatial Taps, and Gaze

In the next project, you use the Plane Detector class (with more "guts" added so that it does something with detected planes) along with a gesture called the `SpatialTapGesture`. A spatial tap is identical to a normal tap but returns information about where a tap took place in three dimensions. You use it in this form:

```
SpatialTapGesture(count: <number of taps>)
    .targetedToEntity(<targeted entity>)
    .onEnded { event in
        // Do something with event.location3D
        let location3D = event.convert(event.location3D,
                                       from: .local, to: .scene)
    }
```

Two important takeaways from this code snippet are that you can target a spatial tap to an entity (just like any other gesture) and that you can use the information provided when the event ends (in the event variable or whatever you choose to name it) to access a `location3D` property. From that location, you can run a conversion from local to scene coordinates and get back the location you tapped within the scene.

The reason this is both interesting and helpful is that when you apply this to a plane, you get back the *exact* location that the user is looking at on the plane. Because Apple provides no direct access to this "gaze" data, you can't use any straightforward function or data provider. What you can do is place invisible planes throughout an environment and then watch for spatial taps on those planes, which gives you a precise means of "seeing" (yeah, pun intended) where the user is looking.

Now, let's do exactly that.

HANDS-ON: PLANE DETECTION

In this project, you build something fun, but the real goal is to create something useful. You're going to be writing a Plane Detector class that can be reused in your other projects. Some of this code is based on an Apple sample (https://developer.apple.com/documentation/visionos/placing-content-on-detected-planes), but, unlike the sample, it's complete and actually works. I still recommend you read through the Apple documentation for additional insight on data providers and ARKit.

In this project, aptly named Plane Detector, you create a class based on the pattern introduced in Listing 7.1. This class processes incoming plane anchors—doors and windows, specifically. When an appropriate plane anchor is detected, the application creates an invisible plane model (just a flat surface) and positions it using the anchor.

This gives you a surface over your doors and windows, which you can then monitor for spatial tap gestures. You'll use these taps to anchor boards over the doors and windows. In short, you're creating an application where users can protect themselves by boarding up their windows and doors. Please note that this is only effective protection while the Vision Pro is in use.

A secondary feature of the application is a display of a text description of each plane anchor as it is detected and classified.

FIGURE 7.11 shows the expected output from the finished application.

FIGURE 7.11 Plane Detectors show planes as they are detected as well as offer effective home protection from light storms and zombie attacks.

Setting Up the Project

Set up the project as you did for the first hands-on. Name the new project **Plane Detection**, create a simple welcome screen, and clean out the ImmersiveView.swift file so that the immersive RealityView is empty.

This project uses world-sensing capabilities, so your next step is updating the project's Info. plist file (Info within the Project Navigator) to include the keys NSWorldSensingUsageDescription key, along with an appropriate string prompt for the application. Your Info.plist file should look much like **FIGURE 7.12**.

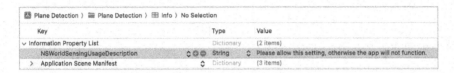

Key	Type	Value
∨ Information Property List	Dictionary	(2 items)
NSWorldSensingUsageDescription	String	Please allow this setting, otherwise the app will not function.
> Application Scene Manifest	Dictionary	(3 items)

FIGURE 7.12 Adding the world-sensing prompt to your project

Now, when you use ARKit plane tracking, the appropriate prompt is displayed to the end user for granting permission.

Creating the Reality Composer Pro Assets

You need a single Reality Composer Pro scene in this project. The scene contains a wooden board that will be used later to board up doors and windows. You can add other objects to this scene if you'd like—nails, pieces of metal, whatever you'd like.

To create the board resource, first open Reality Composer Pro by selecting the RealityKit-Content package in the Xcode project navigator and then clicking Open in Reality Composer Pro in the Xcode editor area.

In Reality Composer Pro, create a new scene named Board, making sure the scene is saved in RealityKitContent.rkassets. Select the scene in the Project Browser to begin editing.

There are two pieces needed for the model that you're adding. The first is the wood material. Open the Content Library and search for Maple Plywood. When it appears, double-click it to add it to the scene. This is *not* adding an object—just a material you can use.

> **TIP** Select the material and use Material settings in the Attributes Inspector to darken the Basecolor Tint. The default color of the Maple is very light and looks much better with a deeper brown (in my opinion).

The second piece is the board itself. You build this out of a cube, so add a cube object to the scene. Using the Attributes Inspector, adjust the Transform component so that it looks like **FIGURE 7.13**. Update the Material Bindings for the cube so it is set to MaplePlywood.

This gives you a reasonable semblance of a wooden board in the proper orientation. Feel free to replace this with whatever you want. In fact, if you'd prefer to place a different object on a different plane entirely (lava potholes on the floor?), you can modify the scene and the detected surfaces (in code) however you'd like. This is a fun project to play with. **FIGURE 7.14** shows the wooden board.

Transform			··· World		
Position	cm	0	0	0	↺
Rotation	°	0	0	0	↺
Scale	✂	5	0.1	1	↺
		X	Y	Z	

FIGURE 7.13 Applying transform settings to a cube

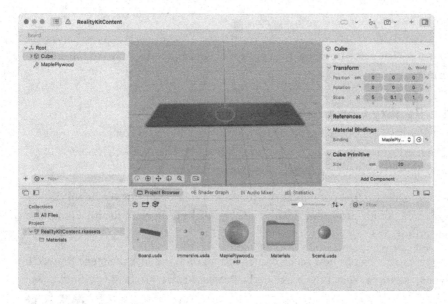

FIGURE 7.14 A transform and a material create our wooden board.

Coding the Plane Detector Class

The workhorse of this project is a new class based on the PlaneDetector code from earlier in this chapter. Unlike the earlier example, this code has logic for tracking plane anchors and adding planes (based on those anchors) to an entity that you can include in ImmersiveView's RealityView.

Create a new file in the project by first selecting the Plane Detection folder in the Xcode Project Navigator and then choosing File, New, File from the menu. When prompted for the template to use, select visionOS, Swift File, and click Next. You're asked what to name the file (**PlaneDetector**) and where to save the file, as shown in **FIGURE 7.15**. Be sure you're adding the new file to the Plane Detection folder *within* the main Xcode folder and that the Group and Target settings are left on the defaults.

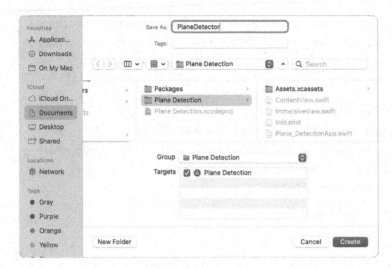

FIGURE 7.15 Adding the new swift file to the Plane Detection project

Adding the Class Structure

The class you're creating needs access to both ARKit and RealityKit, so start by adding two import statements for the frameworks:

```
import ARKit
import RealityKit
```

Next, add the class structure that all the other code will fall within. Remember, this is a class of the type Observable so that you can instantly update your views when something changes:

```
@MainActor class PlaneDetector: ObservableObject {
    // The rest of our code will go in this block
}
```

Defining the Output

This class outputs two things that you use in your ContentView and ImmersiveView. First, the text description of the plane that is being detected ("door", "window", and so on). Call this planeLabel. Secondly, an entity that holds all the different planes that the code detects and creates while it is running. Call this parentEntity.

Add these lines inside the class code block:

```
@Published var planeLabel = "Nothing"
@Published var parentEntity = Entity()
```

The declarations include the @Published property wrapper so that when these two variables are updated, views that are using them properly update. Notice that they are also *not* defined as private; you need to access them in both ContentView (planeLabel) and ImmersiveView (parentEntity).

Defining the Internal Variables

Now, you add code to initialize the ARKitSession and the PlaneDetectionProvider, just as you did in Listing 7.1. You also need a third variable, a collection of key/value pairs, to use throughout the class: entityMap. This keeps track of all the entities attached to the anchors—specifically, the planes you detect and generate.

Add these three lines after the published properties:

```
private let session = ARKitSession()
private let planeData = PlaneDetectionProvider(alignments:
                                        [.vertical,.horizontal])
private var entityMap: [UUID: Entity] = [:]
```

It's time to start building in the logic.

Monitoring for Plane Anchor Updates

To monitor for data that is made available by the PlaneDetectionProvider, you add the function in **LISTING 7.3**. This is very similar to what you saw earlier except it checks for plane anchors that are classified as doors or windows and only processes the incoming data if it detects a match. It also calls a function updateLabel with each detected plane anchor where you will set the planeLabel property so you can use it in your other views. The updateLabel function is called regardless of the anchor classification.

LISTING 7.3 The **startDetection** Function for Monitoring Incoming Plane Anchors

```
func startDetection() async {
    if PlaneDetectionProvider.isSupported {
        try! await session.run([planeData])
        for await update in planeData.anchorUpdates {
            if update.anchor.classification == .door ||
                update.anchor.classification == .window {
                switch update.event {
                case .added, .updated:
                    updatePlane(update.anchor)
                case .removed:
                    removePlane(update.anchor)
                }
            }
```

```
                updateLabel(update.anchor)
            }
        }
    }
}
```

Updating planeLabel

Easy stuff first, right? Updating the `planeLabel` class property is as easy as it gets. Enter the new function `updateLabel`, as shown in **LISTING 7.4**.

LISTING 7.4 Updating the **planeLabel** Property

```
func updateLabel(_ anchor: PlaneAnchor) {
    planeLabel = anchor.classification.description
}
```

This function sets the variable defined earlier (`planeLabel`) to the `.classification.description` attribute of the new anchor. This is a text string such as wall, ceiling, seat, and so on that vaguely describes the plane that the Vision Pro is seeing.

> **NOTE** Notice how this function declaration includes an underscore (_) before the anchor argument? This tells Swift that you're okay with calling the function without writing anchor: first. In other words, you could call this function with both updateLabel(<Plane Anchor>) or updateLabel(anchor: <Plane Anchor>). Whether you include the underscore when defining functions is entirely up to you.

Alright, I've avoided the touch stuff long enough. So, let's get to the meat of this class.

Handling New and Updated Planes

When a plane anchor event is detected in the `startDetection` function, it arrives in one of three states:

- **.added:** A new plane that hasn't been seen previously is available.

- **.updated:** An existing plane has been updated with new data.

- **.removed:** An existing plane is no longer being tracked.

What you do with that information is entirely up to you. For this class, when a new or updated plane is detected, the `updatePlane` function is called, passing in the new plane anchor.

From there, `updatePlane`, for all intents and purposes, builds an anchor entity (from scratch) that holds an invisible plane. This entity is assigned the world coordinates of the plane anchor, turning *it* into something very similar to RealityKit's `AnchorEntity`.

Go ahead and add **LISTING 7.5** to the class, and then I'll walk you through how it works.

LISTING 7.5 updatePlane: The Muscle in Your Plane Detector Class

```
func updatePlane(_ anchor: PlaneAnchor) {
    if entityMap[anchor.id] == nil {
        let entity = Entity()
        let material = UnlitMaterial(color: .clear)
        let planeEntity = ModelEntity(mesh: .generatePlane(width:
                                anchor.geometry.extent.width,
                            height: anchor.geometry.extent.height),
                        materials: [material])
        planeEntity.transform = Transform(matrix:
                    anchor.geometry.extent.anchorFromExtentTransform)
        planeEntity.generateCollisionShapes(recursive: true)
        planeEntity.components.set(InputTargetComponent(
                    allowedInputTypes: [.indirect, .direct]))
        planeEntity.components.set(HoverEffectComponent())
        entity.addChild(planeEntity)
        entityMap[anchor.id] = entity
        parentEntity.addChild(entity)
    } else {
        let entity = entityMap[anchor.id]!
        let planeEntity = entity.children[0] as! ModelEntity
        let newMesh = MeshResource.generatePlane(
                        width: anchor.geometry.extent.width,
                        height: anchor.geometry.extent.height)
        planeEntity.model!.mesh = newMesh
        planeEntity.transform = Transform(matrix:
                    anchor.geometry.extent.anchorFromExtentTransform)
    }
    entityMap[anchor.id]?.transform = Transform(matrix:
                            anchor.originFromAnchorTransform)
}
```

Surprisingly, there's very little code here that you haven't seen before. Some upfront information may help, however. entityMap is going to contain all the entities that are being assigned plane anchor coordinates. You index into entityMap with the id of an anchor and use it to track all the entities you create that are based on the incoming plane anchor.

With that in mind, the code begins by checking entityMap to see if it already holds an entity related to anchor.id (the id of the plane anchor being provided by the startDetection function). If the value is nil, nothing has been stored, meaning that this is a brand-new plane anchor that isn't being tracked.

If the anchor is new, a new empty entity (named entity) is created. Next, an unlit material of the color clear is defined. Why do you need this versus using the opacity component from Chapter

6? Because Apple decided that when the opacity component is 0.0, you can't detect touches on its surface. No worries, by using an unlit and clear material, you get the same effect.

Next, a new `planeEntity` `ModelEntity` is created. This is the same as creating a box, sphere, or other geometric shape. The difference is that it is *just* a plane and has no "thickness" per se. You could use a very thin box, as you did in earlier chapters, but you might as well do it "right" and use the object named for what you're trying to create: planes.

The `planeEntity` is created with the width and height of the detected plane anchor and the clear material.

You then assign the extent transformation matrix for the plane anchor to set the transform component for the `planeEntity`. This ensures you have the right size and position of the plane, relative to the plane anchor. Keep in mind that it does *not* give you the point in world coordinates where it should be located—only the changes *relative* to those coordinates. I explain how to deal with how it gets moved to the right place in a few minutes.

After setting the transform, you do the usual `generateCollisionShapes` (you want to be able to interact with the plane) and assign an `InputTargetComponent` as well as a `HoverEffectComponent`. All code that you've written previously.

Next, you add this model to the empty `entity` you created at the start (`entity.addChild(planeEntity)`), and then the entity to the `entityMap` (`entityMap[anchor.id] = entity`).

Finally, the `entity` is added to the `parentEntity`, which you access in `ImmersiveView`. If you were to display these planes now, they'd still be in the wrong place, so you're not *quite* done with `entity` just yet.

That takes care of the plane *addition* logic, but not the updates. When an update arrives, it is handled by the `else {}` block.

An update means that you've already seen this plane anchor and have generated a plane model to represent it... but visionOS has decided that the plane is now changed somehow (such as opening a closed door or taking a bulldozer to your wall) and needs to be adjusted. Using the `entityMap` and the `anchor.id`, you can grab the `entity` that you generated previously when the plane was new, then use `children[0]` to grab the first child of that entity (the `planeEntity` model you generated).

The shape of a model is determined by its mesh property. If a plane anchor has been updated, the model of the `planeEntity` likely needs to be regenerated. Rather than creating a whole new `planeEntity`, you can use the `MeshResource.generatePlane` function to generate a new mesh and assign it to the `planeEntity.model.mesh` attribute. This keeps the plane models that we're adding to `parentEntity` up-to-date as the Vision Pro continues to track changes and find new planes.

As a last step during the update, the updated `planeEntity` is set to the extent transform of the updated anchor.

Still, the plane models would not appear properly if we added them to ImmersiveView. Something is missing.

Although you set the transform component of `planeEntity` to the extent transform of the anchor, it only provides you with the location/rotation/size of the `planeEntity` relative to the world coordinates of the plane anchor. You still need the `planeEntity` to "know" where the world coordinates of the plane anchor happen to be.

To fix this oversight, the final line of the function sets the transform of the `planeEntity` parent entity (the empty entity you created just to hold `planeEntity`) to anchor.originFromAnchor-Transform—the position of the plane anchor (new or updated) in world coordinates.

The result is a collection of entities in `parentEntity`. Each `entity` is positioned identically to the detected plane anchor. Within each `entity` is a `planeEntity` child that contains a 3D representation of the plane positioned relative to its parent. As long as the code runs, these anchors and entities are kept in sync—the same as an `AnchorEntity`.

> **TIP** Remember that an ARKit anchor is just a description of a location. It doesn't "hold" anything the way that an `AnchorEntity` does. By creating an entity and keeping it synced up with plane data flowing through the system, you can treat that entity just like an `AnchorEntity`.

Removing No Longer Tracked Planes

If the Vision Pro stops seeing a plane, it eventually stops tracking its location. When that happens, a `.removed` update is generated, and the `removePlane` function is called. This function, shown in **LISTING 7.6**, is quite short.

LISTING 7.6 Forgetting Planes That Have Been Removed

```
func removePlane(_ anchor: PlaneAnchor) {
    entityMap[anchor.id]?.removeFromParent()
    entityMap.removeValue(forKey: anchor.id)
}
```

The logic is straightforward. The `entityMap` is referenced using anchor.id to find your pseudo-AnchorEntity. This is then removed from the `parentEntity` with the `removeFromParent` function.

The `entityMap` then removes the entity from itself with the `removeValue` function.

Wow—there's quite a lot going on here. Double-check to make sure you have your code entered properly and you're not seeing any errors in the file. When you're ready, you can implement the rest of the functionality, which will be much easier.

Adding the planeLabel to ContentView

The "easy" function of this application is to display a continuously updating readout of what planes are being detected in the application. This display is located in the ContentView window but is only active when the ImmersiveView is being shown.

Open ContentView.swift now.

Near the top of the view structure, add the following line that creates an instance of the PlaneDetector class:

```
@ObservedObject var planeDetector = PlaneDetector()
```

The @ObservedObject property wrapper effectively "subscribes" to the planeDetector class and tells the view that it needs to update when any of the @Published variables are updated.

You can now access planeDetector.planeLabel to get the text description provided by the PlaneDetector class. Before you do that, however, you need to start processing plane anchor updates by calling planeDetector.startDetection().

Scroll down in the code and look for a switch statement with case .opened. Add **await** planeDetector.startDetection() immediately after the line immersiveSpaceIsShown = **true**. This waits until the immersive space is shown before starting detection.

Now, you can add the planeDetector label wherever you'd like. I've added it with a SwiftUI Text component in the welcome screen's VStack, like this:

```
Text(planeDetector.planeLabel)
    .font(.largeTitle)
    .foregroundStyle(.orange)
    .padding(25)
    .glassBackgroundEffect()
```

You should now be able to start the application for the first time, open the immersive view, and see the welcome window update with different plane descriptions as you look around.

Interesting, but not nearly as fun as putting up boards over windows and doors, don't you think? Let's finish the application now by adding the "boarding" functionality in ImmersiveView.swift.

Implementing Spatial Taps in ImmersiveView

The fun part of this project is enabling the user to look at a detected door or window and tap their fingers (or touch the plane with direct gestures) to make boards begin to appear over the planes in the haphazard way doors and windows are boarded up in your typical illogical horror movie.

Initializing the `PlaneDetector` and `planeObjects`

You need to do a few things here, starting with creating an instance of the `PlaneDetector` class as you did in `ContentView` and then defining an entity `planeObjects` that is a parent to all the board models that get added to the scene.

Add `planeDetector` and `planeObjects` initialization to the top of the `ImmersiveView` struct:

```
@ObservedObject var planeDetector: PlaneDetector = PlaneDetector()
private let planeObjects = Entity()
```

> NOTE If you add the `planeObjects` initialization after the `var` body line, as you did in the Chapter 6 hands-on, the project works, but the boards aren't displayed. When adding to a collection of entities outside of the main `RealityView` setup code, you want to create the collection (here, `planeObjects`) at the top level of the struct.

Adding the RealityView Content

In the ContentView file, all you did was use the published `planeLabel` value. Here, you access all the plane models stored in the `planeDetector` class's published `parentEntity`. You need to add that and the `planeObjects` entity to the `RealityView` content. Add these lines to the RealityView code block:

```
content.add(planeDetector.parentEntity)
content.add(planeObjects)
```

Objects added to both `planeDetector`'s `parentEntity` and `ImmersiveView`'s `planeObjects` will now be displayed in the immersive scene.

Starting the Plane Detector

To start the plane detector running, you use a different approach rather than putting it in an `.onAppear` view modifier. Instead, you use the `.task { }` modifier. This block of code is run asynchronously as the view is loaded. Add these lines immediately following the `RealityView` block:

```
.task {
        await planeDetector.startDetection()
}
```

It's time to define the gesture that will make all the magic happen and let you board things up.

Adding the Spatial Tap Gesture (and Boards!)

To finish things up, you add a spatial tap gesture to the `RealityView`. You target the gesture to the `planeDetector.parentEntity`, which holds all of the detected window and door planes.

As you look at these planes, you see a subtly lit area that corresponds to your gaze. This effect is due to the Hover Effect component that you added to the plane models generated in Plane-Detector.swift.

When you tap your fingers together or tap the plane itself, the board model is loaded and attached to a world anchor that you form from both the detected plane and the tap location. You also add some random rotation to the board so that you get that "I have no planning skills or nailing skills" effect from your favorite movies.

Add the gesture block in **LISTING 7.7** after the preceding Task block.

LISTING 7.7 The Board-Placing Logic

```
.gesture (
    SpatialTapGesture(count: 1)
        .targetedToEntity(planeDetector.parentEntity)
        .onEnded { event in
            let location3D: SIMD3<Float> = event.convert(
                        event.location3D, from: .local, to: .scene)
            Task {
                if let board = try? await Entity(named: "Board.usda",
                                    in: realityKitContentBundle) {

                    let worldAnchor = AnchorEntity(world: location3D)
                    worldAnchor.orientation =
                                event.entity.parent!.orientation

                    let additionalYRotation = simd_quatf(angle:
                            Float(Angle(degrees:
                            Double.random(in: 0.0...360.0)).radians),
                            axis: SIMD3<Float>(0,1,0))
                    let additionalXRotation = simd_quatf(angle:
                            Float(Angle(degrees:
                            Double.random(in: -15.0...15.0)).radians),
                            axis: SIMD3<Float>(1,0,0))

                    board.transform.rotation *= additionalYRotation
                    board.transform.rotation *= additionalXRotation

                    worldAnchor.addChild(board)
                    planeObjects.addChild(worldAnchor)
                }
            }
        }
)
```

The gesture modifier kicks off by creating a `SpatialTapGesture` recognizer that watches for a single tap. When detected, you get the local coordinates for the spatial tap in `event.location3D`. However, you want to create a world `AnchorEntity`, so you need the tap location in world coordinates. You use the `event.convert` function to make the conversion and then store it in `location3D`.

You define the `location3D` constant of the type `SIMD3<Float>`. This is one of the few times you explicitly state the type in this chapter. If you don't, the constant will be of the type `Point3D`, which you wouldn't be able to use elsewhere in your code without additional conversion.

Next, a `Task` (asynchronous) code block is started. The block begins by loading `Board.usda` into the variable `board`. This is the model you need to add to the location of the tap gesture.

A world `AnchorEntity` is initialized with the world location stored in `location3D`. This takes care of the *location* but not the orientation (rotation) of the `AnchorEntity`. When you add boards to windows and doors, you want them to be in the same orientation as the underlying planes. You don't want boards going *through* windows, for example. So, where can you get this information? When the tap gesture takes place, it works because you're targeting the invisible plane models—that is, a `planeEntity` that was created in `PlaneDetector`. Remember that the parent of each `planeEntity` is an entity that was set to the transform of the detected plane anchor. Therefore, by setting the `worldAnchor.orientation` to `event.entity.parent!.orientation`, you're setting it to match the underlying plane anchor, and all will be well!

Whew.

The rest is a breeze.

Two constants, `additionalYRotation` and `additionalXRotation`, are initialized to a quaternion that describes a random amount of rotation around the y and x axes, respectively. The x rotation is limited to –15 to 15 degrees around the x-axis to give the board some "tilt." Y rotation can be anywhere from 0 to 360 degrees around the y-axis.

To add the rotation to the board, you need to multiply the existing rotation of the board (`board.transform.rotation`) by the desired change. Note that you're using a new `*=` operator for the math. This is a shortcut for setting a value to the result of multiplying itself and another value. For example, `x *= 2` is the same as typing out `x = x * 2`.

Finally, the gesture finishes by adding the board as a child of the `worldAnchor`, and `worldAnchor` to the `planeObjects` entity. This results in the new board being displayed and anchored to a door or window of your choosing.

This code could have been made slightly easier without the world anchors. The trouble with *not* using world anchors is that a user would be able to add boards wherever they like, but as soon as they held down the digital crown, the boards would move to a new location relative to the reset view. By attaching them to a properly configured world `AnchorEntity`, they're gonna hold tight no matter how many times you reset your view origin.

Cleaning Up the Boards

As a last cleanup step you should remove the boards when the immersive scene goes away. This is necessary if you have defined an entity container variable at the start of the view's `struct`, as you did with `planeObjects`. If you *don't* take this step, the original objects are still visible if you exit and then reenter the immersive space.

Add this snippet in an `.onDisappear` modifier following the gesture:

```
.onDisappear {
    planeObjects.children.removeAll()
}
```

All instances of `AnchorEntity` and board objects are removed when the immersive view has been dismissed.

The project is complete. Start it up and give it a spin. Something you might notice is that it can take a few seconds before the Vision Pro decides something is a door or window. It depends on the appearance of your doors and windows and the lighting in your room. It isn't quite as instantaneous as one might think or hope.

Imagine what this means for physics simulations. With the ability to add invisible plane objects everywhere, you could build a bouncy house in no time. Before you do, however, I encourage you to read Chapter 8 for an even better way to start integrating everything from your environment—including all those objects cluttered around your room (pillows, chairs, baby elephants). Better start cleaning; your Vision Pro is about to start seeing sooo much more.

> **TIP** If you're having a hard time mentally visualizing the planes that are being detected in `PlaneDetector`, modify the unlit material to have the color `.red` rather than `.clear`. This makes detected windows and doors light up as red rectangles.

SUMMARY

This chapter looked at three different ways of varying complexity to anchor objects within our experiences. The `AnchorEntity` gives you a great deal of power without having to reach into ARKit for data. Reality Composer Pro can even create many different targeted `AnchorEntity` instances for us, without writing a line of code. The last hands-on project, however, introduced some of the real power of the Apple Vision Pro—providing sensing data in real time, identifying and classifying planes, and giving you the ability to use ARKit data to create and anchor objects anywhere in your environment you'd like.

Now, your creations can incorporate real-world surfaces for anchoring their content. Vases can sit on tables, pictures can be attached to walls, and creepy head models can be littered across the floor. What's more, with the ability to automatically detect and create floor and wall planes and hand-anchored objects—all with physical properties—imagine what you could turn the Immersive Bubbles project into!

Go Further

The most important thing you can do is take the code and make it your own. As I mentioned, Immersive Bubbles, coupled with what you learned today, could be the start of a nice break-out game. We're going to learn about collision systems in Chapter 10, "Components, Systems, and the Kitchen Sink," so there are still a few more pieces to go in building out our creator's toolkit, but we're almost to the point where you should close the book and start creating.

In the meantime, review the anchor-related content available from Apple, but keep in mind that RealityKit and ARKit anchors are quite different and require different approaches to use them fully:

- https://developer.apple.com/documentation/realitykit/realitykit-anchors

- https://developer.apple.com/documentation/realitykit/anchorentity

- https://developer.apple.com/documentation/arkit/aranchor

Apple has also published an excellent video on placing objects on detected planes. They use a different approach from the gaze-spatial tap method we implemented, which you may find helpful in your projects. Personally, I think using a user's gaze is more precise and intuitive. Download the example at https://developer.apple.com/documentation/visionos/placing-content-on-detected-planes.

Keep on building and creating.

CHAPTER 8

Reconstructing Reality

When I started this book, I had a plan for where I wanted it to go and what I wanted to cover. There have been some issues that have cropped up (like a Simulator that isn't *quite* capable of fully simulating the Vision Pro), and even some code that just doesn't quite match with the developer documentation. Nonetheless, I have persevered, and you are now in the home stretch! I'm pleased to say that with the technologies covered in this chapter, you'll have a leg up on many of the other visionOS developers I've chatted with.

You're going to be using the data provider pattern established in Chapter 7, "Anchors and Planes," with additional data providers to bring more of the real world into your applications. In the Plane Detection hands-on, you may have noticed that the planes weren't quite as precise as you might hope, and objects placed in your scenes are still visible even if you walk into a different room. This chapter is going to solve those problems using the computing horsepower of the Apple Vision Pro.

This chapter focuses on three useful topics:

- **Hand-tracking:** In Chapter 7, you used a hand `AnchorEntity` to attach objects to your left and right hands. Using the full ARKit hand-tracking provider, however, you can (and will) monitor each finger joint.

- **Scene reconstruction:** See the world around you? When wearing your Vision Pro, you can literally see whatever is in your environment thanks to the high-resolution displays. However, that world is just an image. Yes, you can use a plane detector to find walls and tabletops, but with scene reconstruction, you can represent all the nooks and crannies as well.

- **Occlusion:** Occlusion means to hide or block, and it's something you experience in reality all the time. Walls hide the outdoors, closets hide your clothes, and basements hide unspeakable terrors. With the tools you've used up to this point, *nothing* hides your virtual objects (except other virtual objects). Using occlusion magic, you can make objects in the real world cover virtual objects to deliver much more immersive experiences.

Once again, what you're working on is going to require a real Apple Vision Pro. The simulator just can't provide the sensor access needed.

> **NOTE** Be sure to head to https://visionproforcreators.com/files/ or www.peachpit.com/visionpro and download the Chapter 8 project files.

HAND-TRACKING

Most VR and pseudo-AR headsets require the use of handheld controllers that present themselves as "hands" within your view. This is generally fine for gaming, but it doesn't take long before your brain registers the disconnect between what you're seeing on the screen versus what your hands are really doing. The Apple Vision Pro is designed to use your hands as its controllers, and it does so with almost alarming accuracy.

The hand-tracking you used in the last chapter is fun and can certainly create some interesting effects, but it has very little flexibility in terms of interactions. Wouldn't you like to interact directly with objects with more than just a fingertip and a thumb? A hand-targeted `AnchorEntity` is easy to use, but by employing ARKit with a `HandTrackingProvider` (https://developer.apple.com/documentation/arkit/handtrackingprovider), you can track up to 27 different joints per hand.

Hand-tracking works in the same way as the `PlaneDataDetector`:

1. You create an ARKit session with `ARKitSession()`.

2. A data provider is created. For hand-tracking this is done with `HandTrackingProvider()`.

3. The ARKit session is `run` with the tracking provider.

4. Updates arrive containing a `HandAnchor`.

5. You process the updates however you want!

Hands are different than planes and so is the data that hand anchors provide. Let's take a look at ARKit's `HandAnchor` and what information it contains.

ARKit's HandAnchor

An ARKit hand anchor tracks a hand's position in 3D space and provides three useful properties you'll access in your upcoming code:

- **`.originFromAnchorTransform`:** The location and orientation of the base of the hand in world space.

- **`.chirality`:** The "handedness" of the update. In other words, the `.right` or `.left` hand.

- **`.hand`:** Access to the individual joints in the hand, along with the location of each joint in relation to the base of the hand.

Of these, I'd like to believe that your interest gravitates toward `handSkeleton`—because who doesn't like a skeleton? Read more about HandAnchors at https://developer.apple.com/documentation/arkit/handanchor.

Hand Skeletons and Joints

The `.handSkeleton` property is an instance of a `HandSkeleton` data structure. Within the skeleton is a collection of `joints`, with associated names and transformations.

That, unfortunately, is about all the information Apple makes *easily* available. You can get a list of all the available hand joints at https://developer.apple.com/documentation/arkit/handskeleton/jointname, but the names of the joints don't necessarily make that much sense (what is the intermediate tip of a finger?!).

For a better sense of where the different joints are located, you can turn to a developer video where Apple displays a few frames with a diagram of hand and joint locations: https://developer.apple.com/videos/play/wwdc2023/10082/?time=935.

Assuming you aren't interested in playing a video as reference material, I've provided a screen capture in **FIGURE 8.1**. This figure, however, includes the word "hand" in front of each joint, which has been removed from the actual data structure since the video was created.

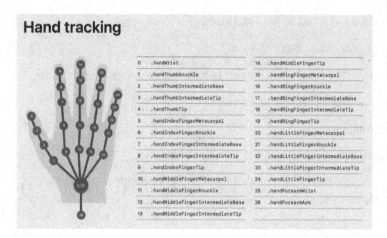

Hand tracking

0	.handWrist		14	.handMiddleFingerTip
1	.handThumbKnuckle		15	.handRingFingerMetacarpal
2	.handThumbIntermediateBase		16	.handRingFingerKnuckle
3	.handThumbIntermediateTip		17	.handRingFingerIntermediateBase
4	.handThumbTip		18	.handRingFingerIntermediateTip
5	.handIndexFingerMetacarpal		19	.handRingFingerTip
6	.handIndexFingerKnuckle		20	.handLittleFingerMetacarpal
7	.handIndexFingerIntermediateBase		21	.handLittleFingerKnuckle
8	.handIndexFingerIntermediateTip		22	.handLittleFingerIntermediateBase
9	.handIndexFingerTip		23	.handLittleFingerIntermediateTip
10	.handMiddleFingerMetacarpal		24	.handLittleFingerTip
11	.handMiddleFingerKnuckle		25	.handForearmWrist
12	.handMiddleFingerIntermediateBase		26	.handForearmArm
13	.handMiddleFingerIntermediateTip			

FIGURE 8.1 The joint locations on a hand— just ignore the "hand" prefix to each joint name

Accessing Individual Joint Locations

To access the current location and orientation (the transform matrix) of an individual joint within a hand anchor, you use this syntax:

```
<joint transform matrix> = <anchor>.handSkeleton?.
                    joint(<joint name>).anchorFromJointTransform
```

The transformation matrix you can get from a joint is relative to the base of the hand, so you can't use it directly. Instead, you must multiply it by the transformation matrix of the base in world space. That value is provided by anchor.originFromAnchorTransform:

```
<world transform matrix of joint> = <joint transform matrix> *
                        <anchor>.anchorFromJointTransform
```

The world transform of the joint can subsequently be used to set the position of an entity. This enables you to create an entity that behaves like an AnchorEntity for every single joint on each hand.

Working with All Joints

When I first started coding the project in this chapter, I began by explicitly referring to individual joints and tracking just a few. After explicitly listing out about a dozen of the joints, I decided that rather than manually coding up a few joints, why not track them all?

To access a collection of all the joints in a HandSkeleton, you use the class property Joint-Name.allCases:

```
HandSkeleton.JointName.allCases
```

From there, you can iterate over each joint with a loop like this:

```
for joint in HandSkeleton.JointName.allCases  {
    if let fingerJoint = anchor.handSkeleton?.joint(joint) {
        // Do something useful with the fingerJoint here.
    }
}
```

That's everything you need to create a tracking class. You'll be doing this as a hands-on project in a way that is slightly different from past projects. Your primary goal in this hands-on is to create a new `HandTracker.swift` class, not to build any fancy interfaces or experiences. Nonetheless, you'll want to create that class within a Mixed Immersive Space project, making it much easier to test the code.

HANDS-ON: CREATING A HAND TRACKER CLASS

One of the difficulties of being this far into the development process is that you're not going to encounter many cases where a line or two of code does something useful. Instead, you need to use established coding patterns that *all* developers use. There are three projects in this chapter, and each fits this category. Don't feel bad about not writing all the code yourself because *no one else did either!*

This project establishes a Hand Tracker class that can be used for tracking all the joints in both hands. The class publishes two variables: `rightHandParts` and `leftHandParts`. Each is a collection using the joint name as the key and an `Entity` as the value. The `Entity` is positioned according to the relevant `HandAnchor` and can be used to hold whatever you want.

To verify that it all works, in ImmersiveView.swift, you attach a `ModelEntity` to each joint in the hand skeleton, as shown in **FIGURE 8.2**. There isn't going to be much hand-holding here (unintentional pun!), because you've been through these processes several times.

FIGURE 8.2 The output: a bunch of clown noses attached to the joints of your hand

Setting Up the Project

Create a new Mixed Immersive project in Xcode named **Hand Skeleton**. Once open in Xcode, complete the usual steps to get the project ready for coding:

1. [Optional] Update the ContentView.swift file to include an introduction and the <App Name>App.swift file to size the content appropriately.

2. Remove the extra sample code from the ImmersiveView.swift file. Make sure the `Reali-tyView` is empty.

3. This project (obviously) uses hand-tracking capabilities, the project's `Info.plist` file ("Info" within the Project Navigator) to include the key `NSHandsTrackingUsageDescrip-tion`, and a string prompt to ask for permission.

> **NOTE** If any of this sounds unfamiliar, please revisit Chapters 6 and 7 to learn more about Immersive Spaces, Data Providers, and the accompanying project setup.

Adding the HandTracker Class

Select the Hand Skeleton folder in the Xcode Project Navigator. Choose File, New, File from the Xcode menu. When prompted for the template to use, select visionOS, Swift File, and click Next. Name the new file **HandTracker** and save it to the folder with your project's other swift files. Also, be sure that the Group and Target settings remain on their default values.

Rather than adding bits and pieces of code to the class file, it makes the most sense to enter the entire contents of the file and then review it. As you already know, this is going to be very similar to the Chapter 7 `PlaneDetector` class. Replace the contents of the HandTracker.swift file with the code in **LISTING 8.1**.

If you don't feel like typing this yourself, use the HandTracker.swift file included with the Chapter 8 project archive. It's much shorter than it looks. The wrapping of the book text makes it appear more unwieldy than it is.

LISTING 8.1 Tracking Each Joint in Each Hand

```
import ARKit
import RealityKit

@MainActor class HandTracker: ObservableObject {

    private let session = ARKitSession()
    private let handData = HandTrackingProvider()
    @Published var leftHandParts: [HandSkeleton.JointName:Entity] = [:]
    @Published var rightHandParts: [HandSkeleton.JointName:Entity] = [:]
```

```
func startHandTracking() async {
    print("Starting Tracking")

    for joint in HandSkeleton.JointName.allCases {
        rightHandParts[joint] = Entity()
        leftHandParts[joint] = Entity()
    }

    try! await session.run([handData])
    if HandTrackingProvider.isSupported {
        for await update in handData.anchorUpdates {
            switch update.event {
            case .added, .updated:
                updateHand(update.anchor)
            case .removed:
                continue
            }
        }
    }
}

func updateHand(_ anchor: HandAnchor) {
    for joint in HandSkeleton.JointName.allCases  {
        if let fingerJointTransform = anchor.handSkeleton?
                    .joint(joint).anchorFromJointTransform {

            let worldspaceFingerTransform =
             anchor.originFromAnchorTransform * fingerJointTransform

            if anchor.chirality == .right { rightHandParts[joint]!.
                    setTransformMatrix(worldspaceFingerTransform,
                    relativeTo: nil)
            } else {
                    leftHandParts[joint]!.
                    setTransformMatrix(worldspaceFingerTransform,
                    relativeTo: nil)
            }
        }
    }
}
```

The class file starts by importing ARKit and RealityKit, the two frameworks needed for this code to work.

An ARKit session is defined (session), as well as an instance of the HandTrackingProvider (handData). Next, the leftHandParts and rightHandParts collections are defined. Each consists of key/value pairs where the key is a joint name (HandSkeleton.JointName) and the value is an Entity. These include the @Published wrapper because they'll be accessed directly in your application views.

The startHandTracking function begins by looping over the full list of joint names:

```
for joint in HandSkeleton.JointName.allCases {
    rightHandParts[joint] = Entity()
    leftHandParts[joint] = Entity()
}
```

With Plane Detector project, you added planes to an Entity as visionOS detected them. It would be impossible to "use" a plane before it was detected. With the joints in a hand, however, you already know all the possible joints. You code could be much simpler if you can access *any* joint at *any* time, regardless of whether it's currently detected by the sensors. To that end, you use this loop to initialize each joint in the rightHandParts and leftHandParts collections to an empty Entity. Now you can access the joints in other code without issue, even if they happen to be momentarily hidden.

> **NOTE** My experience with the HandTrackingProvider has been that it sometimes temporarily loses joints if you move your hands to extreme locations outside the range of the cameras, but they are very quickly reestablished as soon as the Vision Pro can see your hands again.

Finally, the ARKit session is started with the handData data provider. If the application has been granted hand-tracking permission (HandTrackingProvider.isSupported), a loop begins that waits for hand anchor updates (handAnchor.anchorUpdates). When an update with the event type added or updated is received, the switch statement calls handUpdate. If the update is of the type removed, nothing happens. The joint is left as-is until it is redetected.

The updateHand function accepts an incoming HandAnchor in the anchor variable. It loops through all the names of the joints in a hand skeleton (HandSkeleton.JointName.allCases), setting a joint variable to each name as the loop runs. Each joint's location (anchor.handSkeleton?.joint(joint).anchorFromJointTransform) is multiplied by the hand anchor's transform matrix in world space (anchor.originFromAnchorTransform), giving us a final transform matrix worldspaceFingerTransform that can be used to position an entity.

As the final step, the chirality is tested and is used to set either the leftHandParts or rightHandParts collection's entity transform matrix to the worldspaceFingerTransform.

The finished HandTracker class is capable of tracking every single joint available through visionOS and can be used much like an AnchorEntity. You'll do that now.

Adding Model Entities

Open the ImmersiveView.swift file in Xcode. Add an `import` statement for ARKit after the existing imports. This is required to access all the HandSkeleton joint names:

```
import ARKit
```

At the start ImmersiveView struct, add a new @Observed variable for the HandTracker class:

```
@ObservedObject var handTracker = HandTracker()
```

Within the RealityView block, create a new material (I'm using an unlit red material) and an object to anchor on your fingers. My code looks like this:

```
let material = UnlitMaterial(color: .red)

let fingerObject = ModelEntity(
    mesh: .generateSphere(radius: 0.01),
    materials: [material]
)
```

Now, add another loop through all the recognized joints. This time, add a copy of the finger-Object ModelEntity to each joint entity.

```
for joint in HandSkeleton.JointName.allCases {
    handTracker.rightHandParts[joint]!.addChild(
            fingerObject.clone(recursive: true))
    handTracker.leftHandParts[joint]!.addChild(
            fingerObject.clone(recursive: true))
    content.add(handTracker.rightHandParts[joint]!)
    content.add(handTracker.leftHandParts[joint]!)
}
```

> **TIP** You can only add one instance of a given ModelEntity to your content. To use it again, you have to make a copy. You can do this with the clone function. Typing `<model entity>.clone(recursive: true)` creates a brand-new copy of the model entity that can be used elsewhere.

Now the code in ImmersiveView.swift needs to *start* the handTracker. Add a task immediately following the RealityView code block:

```
.task() {
    await handTracker.startHandTracking()
}
```

You may now start the application, enter the immersive scene, and take a look at your sphere-covered hands!

SCENE RECONSTRUCTION

Hand-tracking can enable experiences where interactions with the environment seem very natural. However, the problem is that the environment itself still doesn't seem very natural. Plane detection provides the ability to place virtual objects on real-world surfaces like seats and tables, but it doesn't consider things like pillows on couches and the fact that literally no living human has ever kept a table surface completely clean for more than 47 seconds. As a result, virtual objects added to the planes could exist inside real-world objects that happened to be in the same location on the plane. Let's face it, plane detection is cool, but it just doesn't give us a very "exact" representation of all the different surfaces that virtual objects may encounter.

Scene reconstruction takes plane detection to another level. Think of scene reconstruction as plane detection on steroids. Rather than just looking for flat surfaces, a `SceneReconstructionProvider` (https://developer.apple.com/documentation/arkit/scenereconstructionprovider) considers *all* the incoming data from the Vision Pro to recreate the geometry of all the surroundings where the user is located. It's like taking a giant sheet and covering everything with it, tucking the sheet into all the spaces around all the different objects.

This data is provided by multiple `MeshAnchors`, each with a mesh (shape) that's constantly tracked in the environment. By adding these meshes to your content, you effectively "reconstruct" the real world within a virtual space.

With the right meshes in place, you can have objects interact with the miscellaneous "stuff" you place around yourself. Objects can roll off pillows and under tables and even fall in places that make them difficult to retrieve—making virtual life just as annoying as the real thing.

ARKit MeshAnchors

Yes, a `MeshAnchor` works in a very similar way to the hand anchors and plane anchors, so you're gonna be experiencing more déjà vu. Let's quickly cover the properties you might need when you process mesh anchor updates:

- `.originFromAnchorTransform`: The location and orientation of the detected shape in world space.

- `.geometry`: A collection of the different shapes that make up a mesh anchor.

- `.geometry.classifications`: A classification of each face of the geometry that makes up a mesh. Because a mesh may span multiple objects, one must look at all the different geometry classifications to see everything that has been detected. Review https://developer.apple.com/documentation/arkit/meshanchor/meshclassification if you're interested in what objects can be reported by a `MeshAnchor`.

You can learn more about MeshAnchors at https://developer.apple.com/documentation/arkit/meshanchor, but probably the most important thing to understand is that it takes work to turn a MeshAnchor into something useful. With planes, for example, you need to create a plane ModelEntity and add it to your content. MeshAnchors come to use with geometry information but not in a form you can use.

Generating Collision Shapes

To use a MeshAnchor, you need to turn it into something that can be used in your Reality View content. To do this, you take advantage of a ShapeResource class method that turns a MeshAnchor into a shape that can be used as a collision component.

You might be wondering, "What good does that do? Are you saying it doesn't give a shape I can use to style and present a virtual object?" Yes, that's exactly what I'm saying. You can create an entity and assign a collision component based on the anchor, and then add it to the content. This will have the effect of creating an invisible object that matches the shape and placement of real-world objects, but it only serves the purpose of allowing objects to collide with it realistically.

To generate a collision shape from a mesh anchor, you first generate the shape:

```
let <shape mesh> = try! await ShapeResource.generateStaticMesh(
                                    from: <mesh anchor>)
```

Then, you can create a new ModelEntity, set its collision component to the generated mesh, and add a physicsBody for good measure:

```
let <model entity> = ModelEntity()
<model entity>.collision = CollisionComponent(shapes: [<shape mesh>],
                                    isStatic: true)
meshEntity.physicsBody = PhysicsBodyComponent(mode: .static)
```

Like all the other data providers, this process must be repeated over and over as the headset detects or stops detecting new surfaces, so you need another new class for the implementation (which you make momentarily). But, before you do that, there's "one more thing" I need to discuss because it will truly bring your projects to life.

Occlusion

Apple has built a heck of a device, but the Apple Vision Pro's development tools are still in their early stages. Some tasks that have worked great on the iOS/iPadOS platforms can be painful on the Vision Pro. One of these is **occlusion**, or the process of hiding one object behind another. Your hands, for example, occlude virtual objects, which is necessary for interactions. Virtual objects hide other virtual objects that are behind them. What's missing is for real-world objects to occlude virtual objects.

You may have noticed over the past several exercises that if you place a virtual object somewhere in the environment then walk behind a wall or put a physical object in front of it, you can *still* see the virtual object. It's like having virtual X-ray vision but can also be quite jarring and bring you out of an experience really quickly.

Occlusion Material

Apple provides a special material, called an **occlusion material**, that can be applied to virtual objects. The object becomes invisible to the viewer but still blocks virtual objects behind it:

```
let material = OcclusionMaterial()
```

You *should* be able to take this occlusion material, apply it to the model entities you create during scene reconstruction, and gain the effect of real objects blocking the virtual.

But it's not going to work. The collision shape you add to a model entity isn't a visible surface. You can't apply a material or see a model that only has a collision shape. I suspect Apple will remedy this in the future, but for now, occlusion is not simple.

Or is it?

Occlusion Meshes

As it turns out, the occlusion mesh problem has been solved reasonably well by a GitHub user named XRealityZone. Within their GitHub repository, they maintain a visionOS project called what-vision-os-can-do. This has some useful code snippets that you can use in your creations and is a combination of community contributions and code that Apple has published in its examples.

You can access the repository here:

https://github.com/XRealityZone/what-vision-os-can-do/tree/main

Within the project is a method that translates a `MeshAnchor` into a `MeshResource`, which is exactly what you need to do. You make use of a modified version of this code when you build a scene reconstruction class next. You create entity models with collision shapes and model meshes that can use any material or shader you want—including the occlusion material.

I'm sure Apple will eventually make the process easier, but if you use the `SceneReconstructor` class you're about to code, you'll have that functionality *now*.

HANDS-ON: CREATING A SCENE RECONSTRUCTOR CLASS

Here you are, once again, about to build a class that uses an ARKit session to collect data. This is *yet again* the same code pattern used for plane and hand-tracking. It's also the last time you're going to have to hear me say that. Once you've finished the class, you're going to jump into a third exercise that puts it and the hand-tracking class to good use.

In this project, you create another new class, `SceneReconstructor`, that employs a `SceneReconstructionProvider` to generate `MeshAnchor`s. Each `MeshAnchor` is used to position a `ModelEntity` that is built using the geometry in the anchor. It has both collision shapes and a surface with applied material. You track all of them in an `EntityMap` collection.

In ImmersiveView.swift, you add these model entities to the `RealityView`. Users will see a version of their surroundings covered in any material you choose, as shown in **FIGURE 8.3**.

FIGURE 8.3 You are now living in the Matrix.

Setting Up the Project

Create a new Mixed Immersive project in Xcode named **Room Virtualizer** and then follow these steps:

1. [Optional] Update the ContentView.swift file to include an introduction and the <App Name>App.swift `file to size the content` appropriately.

2. Remove the extra code from the ImmersiveView.swift file. Edit the `RealityView` so that it is empty.

3. The project uses world-sensing capabilities; the project's Info.plist file (Info within the Project Navigator) needs to be updated with the key `NSWorldSensingUsageDescription`, along with a string prompt to ask for permission.

Adding the SceneReconstructor Class

Add a new Swift file named **SceneReconstructor** to your project. Save the file to the same location as the other Room Virtualizer Swift files. Leave the other settings at their defaults.

Open the SceneReconstructor.swift file in the Xcode editor then enter the code in **LISTING 8.2**.

LISTING 8.2 Tracking Shapes Detected by the Vision Pro

```
import ARKit
import RealityKit
import Foundation

@MainActor class SceneReconstructor: ObservableObject {

    private let session = ARKitSession()
    private let sceneData = SceneReconstructionProvider()
    private var entityMap: [UUID: Entity] = [:]
    @Published var parentEntity = Entity()

    func startReconstruction() async {
        try! await session.run([sceneData])
        if SceneReconstructionProvider.isSupported {
            for await update in sceneData.anchorUpdates {
                switch update.event {
                case .added, .updated:
                    let shape = try! await
                            ShapeResource.generateStaticMesh(from:
                            update.anchor)
                    updateMesh(update.anchor, shape: shape)
                case .removed:
                    removeMesh(update.anchor)
                }
            }
        }
    }

    func updateMesh(_ anchor: MeshAnchor, shape: ShapeResource) {
        if entityMap[anchor.id] == nil {
            let entity = Entity()
            let meshEntity = ModelEntity(mesh:
                            anchorToMeshResource(anchor))
            let material = SimpleMaterial(color: .red, isMetallic: true)
            meshEntity.collision = CollisionComponent(shapes:
                            [shape], isStatic: true)
            meshEntity.components.set(InputTargetComponent())
            meshEntity.model?.materials = [material]
            meshEntity.physicsBody =
                            PhysicsBodyComponent(mode: .static)
            entity.addChild(meshEntity)
            entityMap[anchor.id] = entity
```

```
                parentEntity.addChild(entity)
        } else {
            let entity = entityMap[anchor.id]!
            let meshEntity = entity.children[0] as! ModelEntity
            meshEntity.collision?.shapes = [shape]
            meshEntity.model?.mesh = anchorToMeshResource(anchor)
        }
        entityMap[anchor.id]?.transform = Transform(matrix:
                            anchor.originFromAnchorTransform)
    }

    func removeMesh(_ anchor: MeshAnchor) {
        entityMap[anchor.id]?.removeFromParent()
        entityMap.removeValue(forKey: anchor.id)
    }

    func anchorToMeshResource(_ anchor: MeshAnchor) -> MeshResource {
        var desc = MeshDescriptor()
        let posValues = anchor.geometry.vertices.asSIMD3(ofType:
                                            Float.self)
        desc.positions = .init(posValues)
        let normalValues = anchor.geometry.normals.asSIMD3(ofType:
                                            Float.self)
        desc.normals = .init(normalValues)
        do {
            desc.primitives = .polygons(
                (0..<anchor.geometry.faces.count).map { _ in UInt8(3) },
                (0..<anchor.geometry.faces.count * 3).map {
                    anchor.geometry.faces.buffer.contents()
                        .advanced(by: $0 *
                                    anchor.geometry.faces.bytesPerIndex)
                        .assumingMemoryBound(to: UInt32.self).pointee
                }
            )
        }
        let meshResource = try! MeshResource.generate(from: [desc])
        return(meshResource)
    }
}

extension GeometrySource {
    func asArray<T>(ofType: T.Type) -> [T] {
        assert(MemoryLayout<T>.stride == stride,
          "Invalid stride \(MemoryLayout<T>.stride); expected \(stride)")
        return (0..<self.count).map {
            buffer.contents().advanced(by: offset + stride *
```

```
                    Int($0)).assumingMemoryBound(to: T.self).pointee
        }
    }


    func asSIMD3<T>(ofType: T.Type) -> [SIMD3<T>] {
        return asArray(ofType: (T, T, T).self).map
                    { .init($0.0, $0.1, $0.2) }
    }
}
```

> **TIP** No worries if you're not up to typing all of that into Xcode. You can use the SceneReconstructor.swift file included in the Chapter 8 Room Virtualizer project instead.

The logic should be obvious by now: An ARKit session is created along with an instance of SceneReconstructionProvider (sceneData). Supporting data structures parentEntity and entityMap hold all the mesh model entities and a mapping between anchor IDs and model entities, respectively.

The startReconstruction function first verifies you have permission to monitor the environment (SceneReconstructionProvider.isSupported). Assuming there are no issues, it waits for an incoming MeshAnchor and calls updateMesh or removeMesh depending on whether an anchor has been updated/added or removed. For new and updated meshes, a shape is created; this is the collision shape you can *easily* generate from the anchor.

When updateMesh is called, the shape *and* the anchor are provided as arguments. The function checks entityMap to see if the anchor has been seen before. If it hasn't, a new entity is created—our version of an AnchorEntity. A ModelEntity named meshEntity is defined with the generated collision shapes, a metallic red color, a physics body, and an input target component.

> **NOTE** The meshEntity is initialized with a mesh created from the function anchorToMeshResource(<anchor>). This is the utility function that Apple should define for you but doesn't. It takes the MeshAnchor and builds a MeshResource that is used to give meshEntity a visible model.

The meshEntity is then added to entity, which, in turn, is added to the published parentEntity.

If an anchor *has* been seen before and needs an update, the code fetches the entity from entityMap, grabs the meshEntity from that, and changes its collision shapes to the updated shape as well as updating the visible model mesh with anchorToMeshResource.

When a MeshAnchor is no longer being tracked, the removeMesh function removes the entity (and the ModelEntity it contains) as well as any entityMap references to it.

The remainder of the code (anchorToMeshResource, asArray, and asSIMD3 functions) is provided as-is with minor modifications from the community code at https://github.com/XRealityZone/what-vision-os-can-do/blob/ed7adb8c281d68aaf2cdc472986127fc11f44cca/WhatVisionOSCanDo/ShowCase/WorldScening/WorldSceningTrackingModel.swift#L70.

EXTENSIONS

Notice that the asArray and asSIMD3 functions are in a block labeled with extension. An extension enables a developer to add new functionality to an existing class or struct—in this case, an ARKit structure named GeometrySource (https://developer.apple.com/documentation/arkit/geometrysource).

These two data conversion functions aren't part of GeometrySource by default. By adding them as an extension, they behave as if they were features originally provided by Apple.

Visualizing the Results

To view the results of all this work, you need to make some modifications to ImmersiveView.swift. Add a sceneReconstructor variable initialized to the new SceneReconstructor class at the top of the ImmersiveView struct:

```
@ObservedObject var sceneReconstructor = SceneReconstructor()
```

Next, add the parentEntity to the content within RealityView:

```
RealityView { content in
    content.add(sceneReconstructor.parentEntity)
}
```

Finish up by adding a task that starts scene reconstruction immediately after the RealityView block. Apple indicates that any scene reconstruction tasks should be started with *low* priority, which you can indicate with the priority argument:

```
task(priority: .low) {
    await sceneReconstructor.startReconstruction()
}
```

You can now run the application on your Apple Vision Pro and watch as your familiar surroundings are turned into a metallic red nightmare.

Congratulations! You've built hand-tracking and scene reconstructions classes that can be used in future applications. Let's wrap up by building an application that uses these classes to build a fully interactive physics playground that blends virtual and reality seamlessly.

HANDS-ON: RECONSTRUCTION

One of the nice things about creating reusable code is that once it is built, it can just be used without thinking about it again. By reusing the `HandTracker` and `SceneReconstructor` classes in this project, you can focus solely on the functionality you want to provide without getting into the nitty-gritty of data providers and ARKit sessions and all that fun. You just get to build and play.

This exercise is designed to be a playground for you, the developer. You can try different indirect and direct object interactions, mess with gravity, and just practice with all the capabilities you've been learning throughout the book.

In this project, Reconstruction, you use tap gestures to drop random objects from your fingertips. Then you can (carefully) use your hands to scoop up the objects and move them, flick them around, or use an indirect gesture to pick them up and position them throughout the environment. Using scene reconstruction, the application considers the shapes in your space in its physics simulation and virtual objects react to physical objects as you'd expect.

The finished project will likely result in a significant mess around your room, as shown in **FIGURE 8.4**. Thankfully, cleaning up is just a matter of closing the application.

FIGURE 8.4 Place and interact with random objects scattered around your room.

Setting Up the Project

Create a new Mixed Immersive project named **Reconstruction**.

If desired, update the ContentView.swift file to include an introduction and the <App Name>App.swift file to size the content appropriately.

Remove the extra code from the ImmersiveView.swift file. Be sure the `RealityView` code block is empty.

This project needs both world-sensing and hand-tracking; update the project's `Info. plist` file to include keys and string values for `NSWorldSensingUsageDescription` and `NSHandsTrackingUsageDescription`.

Adding the HandTracker and SceneReconstructor Classes

Now add the HandTracker.swift and SceneReconstructor.swift files you created in the previous two projects to the Reconstruction project. The easiest way to do this is to choose File, Add Files to "Reconstruction" from the Xcode menu. When prompted, as shown in **FIGURE 8.5**, drill down into the Hand Skeleton project and select the HandTracker.swift file.

Leave the other settings with their defaults (Copy Items, Create Groups, and Add to Targets are all selected) and then click Add. The file now appears in your Xcode Project navigator. Repeat these steps for SceneReconstructor.swift file found within the Room Virtualizer project.

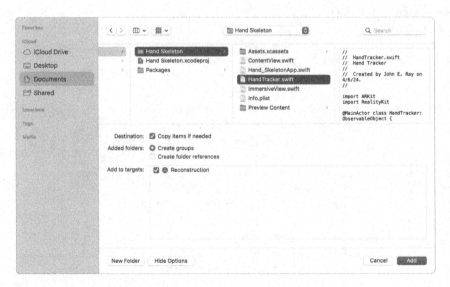

FIGURE 8.5 Importing the class files to the Reconstruction project

Before going any further (and before I forget), open the newly added SceneReconstructor. swift file and comment out the material definition for the red metallic surfaces by adding two forward slashes to the line:

```
// let material = SimpleMaterial(color: .red, isMetallic: true)
```

Add a new line that initializes material to the occlusion material:

```
let material = OcclusionMaterial()
```

This is typically the material you would want in the `SceneReconstructor` class. The red metallic material was only used to help visualize what the reconstruction was doing behind the scenes.

Generating Random Objects

In this project, I'm finally breaking free from the shackles of the lowly sphere and adding in codes, cylinders, and cubes (oh my!). The `generateRandomSphere` function you've used repeatedly is evolving to handle the additional shapes. Let's get this crucial functionality out of the way now. Edit ImmersiveView.swift to include the new `generateRandomObject` function (and the old `getRandomColor` function) in **LISTING 8.3**. These should be placed inside the `ImmersiveView` struct, near the very bottom.

LISTING 8.3 Randomizing Objects and Materials

```
func generateRandomObject() -> ModelEntity {
    var object: ModelEntity
    let randomChoice = Int.random(in: 0...3)
    switch randomChoice {
    case 0:
        object = ModelEntity(mesh: .generateSphere(radius:
                            Float.random(in: 0.005...0.025)))
    case 1:
        object = ModelEntity(mesh: .generateCone(height:
                            Float.random(in: 0.01...0.09),
                            radius: Float.random(in: 0.02...0.03)))
    case 2:
        object = ModelEntity(mesh: .generateCylinder(height:
                            Float.random(in: 0.01...0.09),
                            radius: Float.random(in: 0.02...0.03)))
    default:
        object = ModelEntity(mesh: .generateBox(size:
                            Float.random(in: 0.01...0.05),
                            cornerRadius: Float.random(in: 0.0...0.009)))
    }

    let material : SimpleMaterial = SimpleMaterial(color:
                    getRandomColor(),
```

```
                    roughness: MaterialScalarParameter(
                    floatLiteral: Float.random(in: 0.0...1.0)),
                    isMetallic: Bool.random())
    object.model?.materials = [material]
    object.generateCollisionShapes(recursive: true)
    object.components.set(GroundingShadowComponent(castsShadow: true))
    object.physicsBody = PhysicsBodyComponent(
        massProperties: PhysicsMassProperties(mass: 2.0),
        material: .generate(friction: 1.0, restitution: 0.1),
        mode: .dynamic)
    object.physicsBody?.angularDamping = 0.1
    object.physicsBody?.linearDamping = 0.1
    return object
}

func getRandomColor() -> UIColor {
    let red = CGFloat.random(in: 0...1)
    let green = CGFloat.random(in: 0...1)
    let blue = CGFloat.random(in: 0...1)
    let color = UIColor(red: red, green: green, blue: blue, alpha: 1.0)
    return color
}
```

There are three primary additions to the `generateRandomObject` function versus the sphere-centric version you've been using.

First, you define a generic `ModelEntity` named `object`. To decide what kind of object it will be, a random integer between 0 and 3 is calculated and stored in `randomChoice`. A `switch` statement handles generating models from each of the possibilities of `randomChoice`:

0: Sphere

1: Cone

2: Cylinder

3 (or other): Box

The parameters (radius, height, and so on) of each shape are also randomized so that the appearance changes for each model entity created. The new randomized model is stored in `object`.

> NOTE There is no "logic" to any of the random numbers. I decided to go with relatively small hand-sized objects, but you can increase the size and fill your room with beach balls and traffic cones if you prefer.

The second change is that you use a new component with the object. For the first time, you cast shadows with the `GroundShadowComponent`:

```
object.components.set(GroundingShadowComponent(castsShadow: true))
```

The final change is to define slightly more physics than you have in the past:

```
object.physicsBody = PhysicsBodyComponent(
    massProperties: PhysicsMassProperties(mass: 2.0),
    material: .generate(friction: 1.0, restitution: 0.1),
    mode: .dynamic)
object.physicsBody?.angularDamping = 0.1
object.physicsBody?.linearDamping = 0.1
```

Within the `PhysicsBodyComponent`, I specify a mass of 2.0 kilogram. I found this value helpful for keeping the objects from bouncing everywhere at the slightest touch. Friction is set high (1.0), and restitution (bounciness) is low at 0.1. The physics mode is dynamic, meaning the objects can fully receive and transmit energy through collisions.

You also alter two additional physics body properties: `angularDamping` and `linearDamping`, which are values between 0 and infinity that define how quickly an object slows down when it is spinning or moving, respectively. You can play with all these values to see their effects. I used what I found to offer a pleasing experience after much trial and error.

The rest of the `generateRandomObject` (and `getRandomColor`) code is the same that you've already seen and used many times before.

Initializing the Data Providers

With the supporting functions under control, it's time to initialize and start the two data providers via the `HandTracker` and `SceneReconstructor` classes. At the top of the `ImmersiveView` struct, add these lines:

```
@ObservedObject var sceneReconstructor = SceneReconstructor()
@ObservedObject var handTracker = HandTracker()
```

Use normal (hand-tracking) and low-priority (scene reconstruction) tasks to start each of the detectors running. Add these lines directly following the `RealityView` code block:

```
.task() {
    await handTracker.startHandTracking()
}
.task(priority: .low) {
    await sceneReconstructor.startReconstruction()
}
```

Now, all you need to do is make the application do something interesting. You have two data detectors up and running, so let's make use of them.

Defining the Hand Objects

One of my goals with this project was to try to enable the user to use their hands to interact with the objects added to the Reality View using just the physics simulation. This isn't (currently) a particularly easy thing to do because your hands can't *feel* objects if you try to pick them up. Squeeze too hard and the object "squirts" out of your fingers. For this reason, I've decided to add a plane to the palms of my hands so that I can "scoop" objects into a hand or pick them up and drop them into a hand. In addition to the plane, adding spheres for the joints aids in the interactivity (and provides the ability to flick objects around or pull them toward you).

Importing ARKit

Because you need to access the finger joints by name, you need ARKit imported into the ImmersiveView.swift file. Add the required import line following the other `import` statements:

```
import ARKit
```

Creating Objects and Materials

Within the `RealityView` code, define the material to use for the finger joints as well as a `fingerObject` model entity that can be copied and used at each joint. This is virtually identical to what you did in the Hand Tracker project but with some additional physics properties and a clear material:

```
let material = UnlitMaterial(color: .clear)

let fingerObject = ModelEntity(
    mesh: .generateSphere(radius: 0.005),
    materials: [material]
)
fingerObject.physicsBody = PhysicsBodyComponent(
    massProperties: .default,
    material: .generate(friction: 1.0, restitution: 0.0),
    mode: .kinematic)
fingerObject.generateCollisionShapes(recursive: true)
```

This setup gives you a high-friction sphere you can use with your finger joints. The spheres are clear, so you can't see them, but they'll be able to interact with other objects. Note that the `physicsBody` mode is set to `.kinematic`, which means the object is being controlled by the user.

Next, define a `palmObject` that is used to cover the palm. It's a plane and uses the same clear material and physics properties as the finger joints. Add this code following the `fingerObject` definition:

```
let palmObject = ModelEntity(mesh: .generatePlane(width: 0.09, depth: 0.09),
materials: [material])
palmObject.physicsBody = PhysicsBodyComponent(
```

```
        massProperties: .default,
        material: .generate(friction: 1.0, restitution: 0.0),
        mode: .kinematic)
palmObject.generateCollisionShapes(recursive: true)
```

You now have a finger and a palm object that are configured and can be used for your finger joints and palms.

Adding the Palm Entities

The location of the palm is based on the wrist joint, but it's going to be offset slightly from the wrist so that it roughly covers the average person's palm. Define rightPalmObject and left-PalmObject as clones of the PalmObject and then adjust their positions like this:

```
let rightPalmObject = palmObject.clone(recursive: true)
let leftPalmObject = palmObject.clone(recursive: true)

leftPalmObject.position.x += 0.07
leftPalmObject.position.y += 0.02
rightPalmObject.position.x -= 0.07
rightPalmObject.position.y -= 0.02
```

> **NOTE** As a reminder, <variable> += <value> is the same as typing <variable> = <variable> + <value>. The same goes for the subtraction version: <variable> -= <value>.

These positions, like so many other things, were a matter of trial and error. You can set the color of the material to something other than clear and see for yourself where they sit. You may want to adjust them further for your needs.

Next, add the left and right palm objects to the wrist entity contained in the handTracker. leftHandParts and handTracker.rightHandParts.

```
handTracker.leftHandParts[.wrist]!.addChild(leftPalmObject)
handTracker.rightHandParts[.wrist]!.addChild(rightPalmObject)
```

Finally, add left and right wrist entities to the RealityView content:

```
content.add(handTracker.rightHandParts[.wrist]!)
content.add(handTracker.leftHandParts[.wrist]!)
```

Adding the Finger Joint Entities

The finger joints are handled with a loop, just as you did with the Hand Tracker project. Iterate through the joint names, accessing each entity in rightHandParts and leftHandParts. For each entity, the code adds a child containing a clone of the fingerObject ModelEntity:

```
for joint in HandSkeleton.JointName.allCases {
    handTracker.rightHandParts[joint]!.addChild(
                            fingerObject.clone(recursive: true))
    handTracker.leftHandParts[joint]!.addChild(
                            fingerObject.clone(recursive: true))
    content.add(handTracker.rightHandParts[joint]!)
    content.add(handTracker.leftHandParts[joint]!)
}
```

Each entity in each hand is then added to the `RealityView` content.

Managing the User-Added Objects

Each object (sphere, cylinder, box, sphere) a user creates will be added to a parent entity named `worldObjects`. Define this variable at the top of the `ImmersiveView` struct:

```
private var worldObjects = Entity()
```

After the content additions you've already made, set `worldObjects` to be an input target for indirect gestures. This is used in conjunction with a drag gesture to move objects around. Finally, add `worldObjects` to the content:

```
worldObjects.components.set(InputTargetComponent(
                            allowedInputTypes: [.indirect]))
content.add(worldObjects)
```

As objects are added to `worldObjects`, they subsequently appear within the `RealityView`.

Adding the Scene Reconstruction Shapes

The other objects you need to include in the content are possibly the most important: the scene reconstruction model entities. Without these, user-added objects have nowhere to land, so they will fall... and fall.... and fall.

Add the `sceneReconstructor.parentEntity` to the `RealityView` code as well:

```
content.add(sceneReconstructor.parentEntity)
```

The code is in place to store user-added models, finger joints and palms, and the surfaces that make up the environment. The remainder of the project is setting up the gestures that turn the environment into a playground of shiny trinkets.

Creating Random Objects with the Tap Gesture

When a user wants to add an object to the environment, they perform a tap (pinch) gesture with either of their hands. The object is created and appears to fall from their hand position. In general, objects fall from the hand that performs the gesture—or at least the hand that is being looked at when the gesture is detected.

GESTURES AND CHIRALITY

Does that last paragraph sound non-committal to you? It should. There isn't a particularly convenient way to get which hand performed the tap gesture.

To estimate which hand performed a gesture, I chose to calculate the distance of both hands to the tap location of the gesture. Whichever is closer to the gesture location is the hand that releases the object. This doesn't always work, but it does have the helpful side effect of working quite consistently if you look at the hand you want to release the object.

Add a SpatialTapGesture after the closing brace in RealityView, as in **LISTING 8.4**.

LISTING 8.4 Detect and React to Tap Gestures

```
.gesture (
    SpatialTapGesture(count: 1)
        .targetedToAnyEntity()
        .onEnded { event in
            var releaseLocation = Transform()
            let tapLocation3D = Point3D(event.convert(event.location3D,
                                    from: .local, to: .scene))

            let distanceToRight = tapLocation3D.distance(to:
                        Point3D(handTracker.
                        rightHandParts[.indexFingerTip]!.position))
            let distanceToLeft = tapLocation3D.distance(to:
                        Point3D(handTracker.
                        leftHandParts[.indexFingerTip]!.position))

            if distanceToLeft<distanceToRight {
                releaseLocation =
                    handTracker.leftHandParts[.indexFingerTip]!.transform
            } else {
                releaseLocation =
                    handTracker.rightHandParts[.indexFingerTip]!.transform
            }

            let object = generateRandomObject()
            object.transform = releaseLocation
            object.position.y = object.position.y - 0.05

            worldObjects.addChild(object)
        }
)
```

The gesture block starts by declaring that a `SpatialTapGesture` with a count of 1 is the trigger. The gesture is then targeted to *any* entity with the `.targetedToAnyEntity()` modifier.

When the tap gesture ends (`.onEnded`), the calculations begin.

First, a release location (`releaseLocation`) for the random object is defined as an empty transformation matrix. Keep in mind that this is a transformation matrix, so it also carries orientation (rotation) information in addition to the location.

In this gesture, I make use of several instances of `Point3D`, a data structure containing x, y, and z coordinates in 3D space. `Point3D` also offers a useful `distance` function that calculates the distance to another `Point3D`.

The first use is in `tapLocation3D`, a Point3D data structure derived from the location where the spatial tap event took place, converted into world coordinates. Values `distanceToRight` and `distanceToLeft` are subsequently assigned using the Point3D `distance` function to find the distance between the `tapLocation3D` and the tip of the index finger on both the right and left hands.

If `distancetoLeft` value is larger than `distanceToRight`, you set the `releaseLocation` to be the same as the transform matrix of the left index finger entity. If not, you set it to the transform matrix of the right index finger.

Lastly, an object is generated from the `generateRandomObject` function, and its `transform` matrix is set to `releaseLocation`. For good measure, the object is lowered by adjusting its y position. This ensures that the object appears below the user's physical hand.

> **TIP** If the object is not released from a slightly lower position than the user's hand, there's a good chance it'll collide with some of the finger joint entities or the palm plane, making it bounce around. Lowering the release location reduces this possibility. You may even want to lower it further.

Finally, the object is added as a child to `worldObjects`, at which point it appears in the environment and falls to the surface below it.

The project is now in a testable state and can be launched on the Vision Pro. You should be able to add objects, interact with them, and move them around with your hands.

As I mentioned earlier, however, trying to pick up objects with your fingers can lead to frustration. You add one more gesture: an indirect drag gesture that will make it easier to grab and move any object anywhere in the environment.

Dragging Objects

The last major piece of functionality needed in the application is the ability to look at individual objects, and then drag them to other locations (including dropping them in a user's hands.) To do this, you use a second gesture—DragGesture—targeted to the worldObjects entity that contains anything a user adds to the environment.

Dragging objects that are moving or under the effect of gravity can have some strange side effects, so part of the code needs to "turn off" gravity for the duration of the drag.

Add the second gesture code block in **LISTING 8.5** directly after or before the SpatialTapGesture.

LISTING 8.5 Reposition Objects with a Drag Gesture

```
.gesture(
    DragGesture()
        .targetedToEntity(worldObjects)
        .onChanged { event in
            let object = event.entity as! ModelEntity
            object.physicsBody?.isAffectedByGravity = false
            object.physicsBody?.angularDamping = 1.0
            object.physicsBody?.linearDamping = 1.0
            object.position = event.convert(
                event.location3D, from: .local, to: .scene)
        }
        .onEnded { event in
            let object = event.entity as! ModelEntity
            object.physicsBody?.isAffectedByGravity = true
            object.physicsBody?.angularDamping = 0.1
            object.physicsBody?.linearDamping = 0.1
        }
)
```

In this gesture, you make use of both the .onChanged and .onEnded events. In .onChanged, you assign object to the entity referenced by the event (event.entity). You typecast the entity to ModelEntity because you know that the objects added are model entities, and you need to access specific features of model entities, namely the physics body.

Next, these lines "turn off" gravity and stop any spin or other motion on the object:

```
object.physicsBody?.isAffectedByGravity = false
object.physicsBody?.angularDamping = 1.0
object.physicsBody?.linearDamping = 1.0
```

If the changes to the physics body are not included, the object moves in unexpected ways while it is being dragged.

During the drag, the object's position is updated in to match the event's location3D attribute but converted to world coordinates.

When the drag gesture ends (.onEnded), you once again assign object to the entity targeted by the drag and reset its physics properties to their defaults. This means that gravity once again takes effect, and the object falls onto the nearest surface.

For an interesting effect, you can try leaving gravity disabled. Objects can then be positioned in the air and just hang in empty space. It's cool, but do you really need any new ways to make a cluttered mess of your homes and office?

Cleaning Up

One last block and you're done! After ImmersiveView is dismissed, you need to remove the entities you've added outside of the initial RealityView setup.

Add the code in **LISTING 8.6** as yet another modifier to the RealityView, similar to what you've done in other projects:

LISTING 8.6 Remove Entities from the RealityView

```
.onDisappear {
    worldObjects.children.removeAll()
    for joint in HandSkeleton.JointName.allCases {
        handTracker.rightHandParts[joint]!.children.removeAll()
        handTracker.leftHandParts[joint]!.children.removeAll()
    }
    sceneReconstructor.parentEntity.children.removeAll()
}
```

This removes all worldObjects, all finger joints, and the surfaces added by the scene reconstruction, leaving a blank canvas for when the immersive view is opened again.

Run the application on your Apple Vision Pro and try scooping, throwing, and making a mess with the randomly generated objects. Cleaning up after throwing a tantrum just got much easier!

> **TIP** For those without a paid developer account, you can load a maximum of four development applications to your device. If you hit the limit, you get a warning message and need to remove some of the apps before more can be installed.

SUMMARY

In this chapter, you learned about some of the most useful tools for visionOS: scene reconstruction and occlusion. Using scene reconstruction, you can rebuild your entire environment using the Apple Vision Pro sensors and compute power. Successfully combining the real and virtual is the lynchpin of creating compelling experiences. Although Apple hasn't made this process as easy as it *could* be, it is still simple enough to include in everyday projects with the help of the reusable `SceneReconstructor` class.

You also explored advanced hand-tracking with the `HandTracker` class. This code takes the complexities of working with the ARKit hand skeleton and, again, turns it into a reusable piece of code that makes entities available for every single joint in both of a user's hands.

While there is still more ahead, you have what you need to build some fun and functional applications. I'll round out your primary toolkit over the next two chapters, then show you how you can prepare your creations to reach as wide an audience as possible via the App Store.

Go Further

I highly recommend downloading and exploring the source code for Apple's scene reconstruction example: https://developer.apple.com/documentation/visionos/incorporating-real-world-surroundings-in-an-immersive-experience. It may give you some good ideas of how to manipulate and place objects differently from what we've done in these examples.

It would also be good practice to go back to the Chapter 7 plane detection example and add scene reconstruction for more precise placement of the objects within the environment. Plane detection is a *much* less resource-intensive operation than scene reconstruction, so don't disregard it entirely, but scene reconstruction does a significantly better job of enabling your physical environment to accommodate virtual objects.

With hand-tracking, you now have access to all the data that visionOS can provide. Experiment with ways that hands can be involved in natural direct and indirect gestures. An important goal for any AR or VR developer is to make the actions the user performs feel as natural as possible. The more you can make your virtual world feel real, the better. Just adding the ability to flick an object if you want to move it feels incredibly satisfying and can make you forget you're staring at a piece of glass and metal.

CHAPTER 9

Lights, Sounds, and Skyboxes

We're going to take a break from the last code-heavy chapters and focus on some odds and ends that you might have been wondering about, like why all the sample projects are utterly silent. In this chapter, you use both Xcode and Reality Composer Pro to add new audio and lighting effects to projects and even create a fully immersive space using nothing but a photograph.

With the Apple Vision Pro, you have access to two of the most useful senses: seeing and hearing. The more that you can do with each, the more realistic, meaningful, and fun your experiences will be. If you've run Apple's Encounter Dinosaurs application, consider how engaging it would it be if the dinosaurs were silent and flat. The roars, squeaks, and sunlight glinting off surfaces make it feel natural in a way that's difficult to describe.

In this chapter, you work with the following technologies. Each is surprisingly simple to implement, so I include plenty of hands-on examples along the way:

- **Image-based lighting:** You haven't used anything but the default lighting so far. By using the visionOS `ImageBasedLightComponent`, you can add infinite variation to your scene's lighting. The process is a bit weird, but it's surprisingly easy to accomplish. Also you'll add shadows.

- **Sounds:** What is an experience without sound? (It's quiet—very quiet.) Sight brings the primary "wow" factor of the Apple Vision Pro, but audio can make user interactions feel more natural and immersive. This chapter examines two audio components—one ambient and one spatial—that you can configure and add to scenes through Reality Composer Pro and code.

- **Skybox:** A Skybox surrounds a user with a 360-degree panorama—either a photograph or rendered scene. When used with a Progressive or Full immersive view, a Skybox can block out the monotony of the real world and place the user wherever you'd prefer.

As you've come to learn, Apple's documentation can be hit-and-miss for different topics, and these are some of the bigger "misses" (in my opinion.) Keep these code snippets in mind for your creations because trying to find them in the current documentation can be a good way to drive yourself bonkers for an afternoon.

The projects in this chapter run in the visionOS Simulator, but you won't be able to fully see or hear some of the effects. I recommend donning the headset yet again so you can experience these techniques in all their glory.

> **NOTE** Be sure to head to https://visionproforcreators.com/files/ or www.peachpit.com/visionpro to download the Chapter 9 project files.

LIGHTING

Lighting seems like a no-brainer on a platform like visionOS, and, for much of what you do, it is. The Vision Pro seamlessly blends virtual objects with your room's natural lighting, making virtual objects look like they "fit" where they are placed. Unfortunately, sometimes you don't want natural lighting; you want to make objects that look like they're being lit by disco lights, a sunset, or a cheap flickering lightbulb hanging by a single cord in a basement where terrible things are about to happen.

With the initial releases of the operating system, you have access to a single type of light—an image-based light delivered by RealityKit's `ImageBasedLightComponent`.

An image-based light component delivers the ability to generate complex lighting to a scene but can be frustrating for those who want to just place lighting entities around their scenes.

As the name implies, this is a component that gets added to an entity and... does nothing. Unlike more traditional lighting models, an image-based light consists of a high-resolution, HDR image (see **FIGURE 9.1**). This is an image applied to any entity within the scene using the `ImageBasedLightComponent`.

> **NOTE** In visionOS 2.0+, you can add directional and ambient lights directly to a scene—similarly to the way we handle sound sources later this chapter. Visit https://visionproforcreators.com for examples.

FIGURE 9.1 The default lighting image file used in visionOS

The image itself is pretty simple to understand. Imagine it wrapped around an invisible sphere that is situated directly around a RealityKit scene. Light shines through the white (or light) portions of the image but is blocked by the black areas. If color is used instead of white, the light coming through is tinted that color. If you want to represent a bright sun in the sky, you use a black rectangle with a small white circle. If you want lighting that looks like a solar eclipse, you create a thin white circle against a black background. You can even take pictures of real light sources, black out any areas not emitting or reflecting light, and use those images for realistic room lighting.

This image is applied to an entity in the scene, but the location of the entity is *meaningless*. If you apply it to a cube and put the cube on the floor, it *still* works like a giant invisible sphere surrounding your scene. So, what good is applying it to an entity at all? The answer is orientation. By rotating the entity with the light component, you can cause the light sources to move around the room or the sun to travel across the sky. This provides a simple way to make lighting dynamic using the same entity rotation/orientation techniques you've been using throughout the book.

So, you apply the `ImageBasedLightComponent` to an entity, feed it an image file, and tada! Your scene is lit, right? Nope. The light component is only half the story. You also need the

`ImageBasedLightReceiverComponent` to be attached to any entity that is *receiving* illumination from the light source. Yes, you read that right, the lighting doesn't just "happen" automatically; you must set a receiver component on any entities that should be lit by the entity with the light component.

It's not that bad, I promise.

Adding Image-Based Lighting

Adding imaging-based lighting to a scene requires three things:

- The image that will be used for lighting

- An entity with the `ImageBasedLightComponent`

- At least one entity to receive the light via the `ImageBasedLightReceiverComponent`.

Let's walk through this configuration now.

Adding the Image Resource

To create an image-based light, first generate an image file to use. How you generate this is up to you, and it's worth experimenting with the lighting design to see the different styles you can create. Apple's lighting files are 2048×1024 pixels, but larger and smaller files work as well.

For example, assume I have a file (I do!) named `RGB Lights.png`. To add this to an Xcode project as a lighting source, I first place it in a folder with the suffix ".skybox." My sample is shown in **FIGURE 9.2** and is included with the Chapter 9 project files in the Lighting.skybox folder.

FIGURE 9.2 My light source file

I then drag that folder into the Xcode project, choosing to copy the files, create groups, and add to the default target.

That's the hard part. On to the code.

Adding the `ImageBasedLightComponent`

There are three steps to setting the `ImageBasedLightComponent` on an entity. First, the image for the light must be loaded as an `EnvironmentResource`:

```
let <light resource> = try? await
                    EnvironmentResource(named: <light filename>)
```

Next, the light resource along with a brightness level (`intensityExponent`) is used to initialize the `ImageBasedLightComponent` component:

```
var <light component> = ImageBasedLightComponent(source:
                    .single(<light resource>),
                    intensityExponent: <brightness>)
```

The brightness (intensity) of the light starts at 0. The light's brightness is multiplied by 2 to the power of <brightness>. Setting this too high can quickly make objects extremely bright and washed out, so start low.

Next, a property .inheritsRotation is set to `true` on the component. This means that the rotation of the entity that holds the light component will affect the direction and orientation of the light itself. This is optional. If you want the lighting to be static, just ignore me.

```
<light component>.inheritsRotation = true
```

Lastly, the image-based light is applied to the entity:

```
<an entity>.components.set(<light component>)
```

For the sake of making this easy to understand, assume you have two entities (spheres maybe??) in your scene. One is called `imageLight` and the other is `lightMe`. The first is the source of the image-based light, and the second is the receiver of the light. The following code would set up `imageLight` with the RGB Lights.png image:

```
if let lightResource = try? await EnvironmentResource(
                    named: "RGB Lights") {
    var lightComponent = ImageBasedLightComponent(source:
                    .single(lightResource),
                    intensityExponent: 5.0)
    lightComponent.inheritsRotation = true
    imageLight.components.set(lightComponent)
    content.add(imageLight)
}
```

That takes care of creating and adding an image-based light, but, as I said, it doesn't do anything until you have a light receiver.

Adding the ImageBasedLightReceiver

There are only two steps to setting up the receiver: creating the component based on the entity that "holds" the light image and then applying it to another entity:

```
let <light receiver> = ImageBasedLightReceiverComponent(
                        imageBasedLight: <image-based light entity>)
<lit entity>.components.set(<light receiver>)
```

To add the previously defined `imageLight` so that it's lighting up the entity `lightMe`, the code would look like this:

```
let lightReceiver = ImageBasedLightReceiverComponent(
                     imageBasedLight: imageLight)
lightMe.components.set(lightReceiver)
```

All-in-all, not the worst code (or component) you've worked with. And, like many other components, lights and receivers can be set up entirely in Reality Composer Pro.

Lights and Reality Composer Pro

I have a love-hate relationship with Reality Composer Pro. It can be very helpful for quickly setting up scenes and entities without dealing with any code, but sometimes code just seems faster. With lighting it's a toss-up, so you may prefer using this method—or not.

Adding the Image Resource

If you'd rather set up lighting in a Reality Composer Pro scene, you first need to add the lighting image to the Reality Composer project. You can do this simply by dragging the image file into the Project Browser or using the File menu or Import button at the top of the Project Browser. However you do it, the file needs to be visible in the project before you can set up the components, as demonstrated in **FIGURE 9.3**.

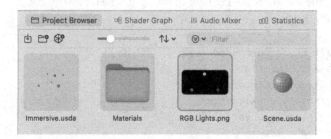

FIGURE 9.3 Adding the light image to the Reality Composer Pro project

Adding the Image-Based Light Component

Once an image is available, you can select an entity in one of your scenes and, using the button at the bottom of the Attributes Inspector, choose Add Component. In the component list that appears, choose Image Based Light, as shown in **FIGURE 9.4.**

In the Attributes Inspector, you should now see an Image Based Light panel for configuring the lighting. Use the Intensity Exponent to set a value for the brightness and then click Choose to select the lighting image file you added to the project.

Check Inherits Rotation if you want the lights to follow the rotation of the entity that holds them; leave the mode set to single (see **FIGURE 9.5**).

FIGURE 9.4 Adding the Image Based Light component

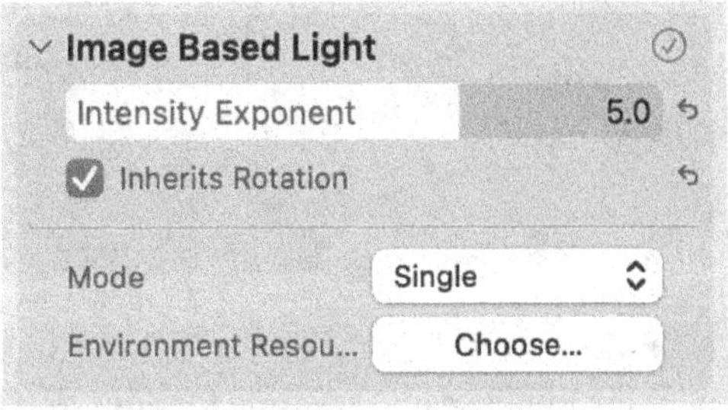

FIGURE 9.5 Configuring the Image Based Light

> **TIP** If you want to blend multiple light images, you can do that by changing the mode to Blend.

The image-based light is now ready, but you need at least one other entity set as a receiver.

Adding the Image-Based Light Receiver Component

To add the receiver component, select another entity within your scene and again click the Add Component button at the bottom of the Attributes Inspector, this time choosing the Image Based Light Receiver.

The light receiver component, shown in **FIGURE 9.6,** has a single configuration option: a drop-down (shown here as None) where you can select any other entity in the scene that has the image-based light component added.

Well, that's somewhat anticlimactic, wouldn't you say? Before you jump into some hands-on exercises, here's a quick review of a component you first added in Chapter 8, "Reconstructing Reality": shadows.

Adding Grounding Shadows

Much like lighting must be "received" on a per-entity basis, a `ShadowGroundingComponent` must also be configured for an entity for it to cast a shadow on the surfaces beneath it.

To add a shadow component in code, this is as simple as

```
shadowComponent = GroundingShadowComponent(castsShadow: true)
<entity>.components.set(shadowComponent)
```

To do the same in Reality Composer Pro, just choose an entity and add the Grounding Shadow component. Configuration is nothing more than clicking the Casts Shadows checkbox (see **FIGURE 9.7**).

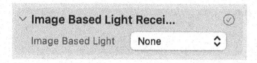

FIGURE 9.6 Choosing an entity that already has the Image-Based Light component

FIGURE 9.7 Adding shadows with a Grounding Shadows component

Okay, get your clicking finger ready! It's time for your first hands-on exercises. In the next project, you explore dynamic lighting effects entirely controlled by your hand.

HANDS-ON: HAND-LIT OBJECTS

In Hand-Lit Objects, you create a sea of shapes using a very familiar method that you've seen in different variations throughout the book. (In fact, `generateRandomObject` is the *longest* code block in this chapter.) You also use a hand AnchorEntity to attach an entity with the Image-Based Light component. **FIGURE 9.8** shows the final product.

FIGURE 9.8 With code, you can build much more expansive lighting effects.

Project Setup

Create a new project named **Hand-Lit Objects** and then follow these steps to clean things up:

1. Edit the ContentView.swift file to add an introduction screen, if desired, and update the <Project Name>App.swift file to resize the initial view to be an appropriate size.

2. Clean out the RealityView in the ImmersiveView.swift file. It should be empty before you begin.

3. Import the Lighting.skybox folder into the project by dragging the folder into the Xcode Project Navigator. Leave the default settings untouched when prompted during the import. This folder contains the RGB Lights.png file needed for the project.

Adding the Random Object Code

To create all of the floating objects in the project, you're going to use the getRandomObject and getRandomColor functions that were established in Chapter 8. Enter the code shown in **LISTING 9.1** before the closing brace of the ImmersiveView struct.

LISTING 9.1 Adding the **generateRandomObject** and **getRandomColor** to ImmersiveView

```
func generateRandomObject() -> ModelEntity {
    var object: ModelEntity
    let randomChoice = Int.random(in: 0...3)
    switch randomChoice {
```

```
        case 0:
            object = ModelEntity(mesh: .generateSphere(radius:
                        Float.random(in: 0.005...0.025)))
        case 1:
            object = ModelEntity(mesh: .generateCone(height:
                        Float.random(in: 0.01...0.09),
                        radius: Float.random(in: 0.02...0.03)))
        case 2:
            object = ModelEntity(mesh: .generateCylinder(height:
                        Float.random(in: 0.01...0.09),
                        radius: Float.random(in: 0.02...0.03)))
        default:
            object = ModelEntity(mesh: .generateBox(size:
                        Float.random(in: 0.01...0.05), cornerRadius:
                        Float.random(in: 0.0...0.009)))
        }
        let material : SimpleMaterial = SimpleMaterial(color:
                        getRandomColor(),
                        roughness: MaterialScalarParameter(floatLiteral:
                            Float.random(in: 0.0...1.0)),
                        isMetallic: Bool.random())
        object.model?.materials = [material]
        return object
}
func getRandomColor() -> UIColor {
    let red = CGFloat.random(in: 0...1)
    let green = CGFloat.random(in: 0...1)
    let blue = CGFloat.random(in: 0...1)
    let color = UIColor(red: red, green: green, blue: blue, alpha: 1.0)
    return color
}
```

This version omits any physics or input component additions because they will not be needed for the project. If you have any questions about the implementation, review Chapter 8.

Setting Up the Image-Based Light Entity

Let's begin by setting up the entity that will have the lighting component attached. Initialize a new private variable `lightingEntity` at the top of the `ImmersiveView` struct:

```
@State private var lightingEntity = Entity()
```

At the start of the `RealityView` block, add code to create a hand-targeted anchor. Load the lighting image and apply it to the `lightingEntity`. Lastly, add the `lightingEntity` to the hand anchor, and the hand anchor to the view's content:

```
let handAnchor = AnchorEntity(.hand(.right, location: .palm))
if let lightResource = try? await
                    EnvironmentResource(named: "RGB Lights") {
    var lightComponent = ImageBasedLightComponent(source:
                        .single(lightResource), intensityExponent: 5.0)
    lightComponent.inheritsRotation = true
    lightingEntity.components.set(lightComponent)
    handAnchor.addChild(lightingEntity)
}
content.add(handAnchor)
```

That takes care of the hand-anchored image-based light, now let's add a field of random objects that can receive the light.

Generating an Object Field

As you frequently do when you're creating a bunch of objects, you're going to keep them all as child entities of an objectCollection entity. Declare that entity immediately following the start of the RealityView block:

```
let objectCollection = Entity()
```

Now you need to fill the collection. In this code block, you're going generate 500 objects, rotate them randomly to make them unique, add the light receiver components, add the objects to the objectCollection, and, finally, add the objectCollection to the RealityView content.

Place this code anywhere after the definition of objectCollection within the RealityView code:

```
for _ in 1...500 {
    let object=generateRandomObject()
    object.position.x = Float.random(in: -1.5...1.5)
    object.position.z = Float.random(in: -1.5...1.5)
    object.position.y = Float.random(in: 0.5...2.5)
    let xRotation = simd_quatf(angle: Float(Angle(degrees:
                    Double.random(in: 0.0...360.0)).radians),
                    axis: SIMD3<Float>(1,0,0))
    let yRotation = simd_quatf(angle: Float(Angle(degrees:
                    Double.random(in: 0.0...360.0)).radians),
                    axis: SIMD3<Float>(0,1,0))
    let zRotation = simd_quatf(angle: Float(Angle(degrees:
                    Double.random(in: 0.0...360.0)).radians),
                    axis: SIMD3<Float>(0,0,1))
    object.transform.rotation *= xRotation
    object.transform.rotation *= yRotation
    object.transform.rotation *= zRotation
    let lightReceiver = ImageBasedLightReceiverComponent(
                        imageBasedLight: lightingEntity)
```

```
        object.components.set(lightReceiver)
        object.components.set(GroundingShadowComponent(castsShadow: true))
        objectCollection.addChild(object)
}
content.add(objectCollection)
```

The code spends most of its time randomizing the positions of the objects around the user and then rotating them by a random angle between 1 and 360. Setting up the `ImageBasedLight-ReceiverComponent` based on the `lightingEntity` established earlier happens only in the last few lines of the loop. In a final configuration step, a `GroundingShadowComponent` is added to the `object`.

Each object created is added as a child to the `objectCollection`, which in turn is added to the content at the end of the loop.

Because you're not doing anything special like adding objects outside of `RealityView`, there is no programmatic cleanup required when the user exits `ImmersiveView`.

Run the application and enjoy making hundreds of different objects react to the image-based lighting attached to your hand.

CODE-FREE LIGHTING

You can re-create the effect from Hand-Lit Objects entirely in Reality Composer Pro. To learn how, download a short tutorial, Appendix D, from www.peachpit.com/vision-pro or https://visionproforcreators.com/.

PLAYING SOUNDS

In Chapter 7, "Anchors and Planes," you added video material to an object and initiated play-back. If that video had included audio, it would have played as well. In this chapter, I formally introduce two audio components— `SpatialAudioComponent` and `AmbientAudioComponent`—that *probably* make your creations more engaging but *definitely* make them louder. When added to an entity, these components enable it to play audio, either ambient or spatial, as the names imply.

These components are different than others you've used because the component itself can be used with next to no configuration. The setup for each uses identical code, with just a minor adjustment to switch from spatial (the default) to ambient.

Before going further, perhaps you'd like a better definition of what Apple considers "ambient" vs "spatial":

- **Ambient:** Ambient audio is typically multichannel audio (stereo or higher) that plays within a scene. It does not vary in loudness based on the user's position (you can't get nearer or further from the audio) but does vary based on a user's orientation. In other words, as you spin around, your ears hear variations based on the position of the different channels being played. Ambient audio is usually recorded with a microphone array placed within an environment and is generally looped. Think of it as "background noise."

- **Spatial:** Spatial audio, while more complicated technically, is easier to explain. Spatial audio is mono audio that appears, to the listener, to emanate from a specific entity in a specific location in space. It changes in volume as a user gets closer or further away. Succinctly, you can hear where the sound is coming from and mentally identify its location.

In both cases, playing audio is dependent on an `AudioFileResource`—the file that is being played along with attributes that describe how it is played—and `AudioPlaybackController` that controls the playback itself, giving you the option to start and stop playback at will.

That might sound like a bunch of moving parts just to play a sound, so let's look at how that translates to actual code, starting with adding the audio file.

Adding Audio Resources

To play audio, the first thing you need is, surprise, audio as an AIFF, MP3, M4A, WAV, or other popular format file. Add audio files to your project by dragging them into the Xcode Project Navigator. You're prompted to copy the files, create groups, and add them to the application target. Leave these settings on their default values.

> **TIP** If adding many audio snippets to your project, you can place them in a folder first and then drag the folder into the Project Navigator.

As I show you shortly, you also can add these resources to the Reality Composer Pro package, which offers a slight advantage in the initial setup of audio playback but with a head-scratching *gotcha*.

If you're interested in loading audio dynamically from online locations, be sure to read the `AudioFileResource` documentation at https://developer.apple.com/documentation/reality-kit/audiofileresource .

Playing Ambient Audio

Once you've added an audio file and you have an entity to which the audio will be "attached," the rest is trivial. Create the `AudioFileResource` and initiate playback with a code block like this:

```
if let <audio file resource> = try? AudioFileResource.load(named:
                                  <audio filename>) {
    <entity>.ambientAudio = AmbientAudioComponent()
    let <playback controller> =
```

```
                    <entity>.prepareAudio(<audio file resource>)
    <playback controller>.play()
}
```

To adjust the relative volume for ambient audio, you can modify the ambient audio component's gain property from -.infinity (silence) to 0, which is the "normal" level at the current system volume. This value is provided in decibels. For example,

```
<entity>.ambientAudio?.gain = <gain value -.infinity to 0>
```

To play audio file drums.m4a from an entity named entity and set the gain to –5.0, I'd use this code:

```
if let audio = try? AudioFileResource.load(named: "drums") {
    entity.ambientAudio = AmbientAudioComponent()
    entity.ambientAudio?.gain = -5.0
    let drumPlaybackController = event.entity.prepareAudio(audio)
    drumPlaybackController.play()
}
```

> **TIP** If you want to load and immediately play the audio, you can shorten this code by replacing *prepareAudio* with *playAudio*. This shortcut creates the playback controller and initiates playback all at once.

If you're struggling to understand how the "entity" comes into play here, don't. The entity is just needed as an attachment point for the sound. It doesn't need to be a visible object; it can be as simple as entity = Entity(). With ambient audio, the location of the entity doesn't matter at all—but orientation (rotation) *does*. By adding audio to an entity, you can rotate the entity to change where the different audio channels are directed.

Playing Spatial Audio

Ambient audio isn't so tough, is it? Spatial audio can't be that much more difficult, can it? Nope. It takes less code. Rather than describing it in the same detail as ambient audio, let's just look at the code needed to play the "drums" audio as spatial audio coming from an entity.

```
if let audio = try? AudioFileResource.load(named: "drums") {
    let drumPlaybackController = event.entity.prepareAudio(audio)
    drumPlaybackController.play()
}
```

As you can see, this is *easier* than ambient audio. The default audio component for an entity *is* spatial audio, so there isn't anything to configure—just load and play.

To alter how the sound is played, the spatial audio component provides several properties you can adjust, such as gain, reverbLevel, and directivity.

The gain property works identically to ambient audio but accesses the spatial audio component instead:

```
<entity>.spatialAudio?.gain = <gain value -.infinity to 0>
```

The reverb property changes how full the spatial audio sounds. The smaller the value (down to -.infinity) the more the audio seems to come from a smaller, less expansive space.

```
<entity>.spatialAudio?.reverb = <reverb value -.infinity to 0>
```

The directivity of the sound is the width of the "beam" of sound coming from the entity. This value can vary from 0 (omnidirectional) to 1 (extremely targeted) and is configured like this:

```
<entity>.spatialAudio?.directivity = .beam(focus: <0 to 1>)
```

Unlike ambient audio, the location and orientation of the entity are considered when generating the sound. By default, spatial audio sources are directed along the z-axis, or away from the user's initial position. Rotating the entity will change this direction, enabling the sound to "beam" in whatever direction you want.

By altering these properties and manipulating your entities, you can create unique soundscapes where objects come alive in more than just appearance.

Looping and Other Settings

In a departure from what you learned with the video material you looped a few chapters ago, looping during audio playback is a function of the AudioFileResource rather than the playback controller. To add looping, you need to update the creation of the AudioFileResource by initializing a configuration property. For example, to loop the spatial drum audio, you update the if statement:

```
if let audio = try? AudioFileResource.load(named: "drums",
                configuration: .init(shouldLoop: true)) { … }
```

There are other useful parameters you can add to the configuration as well, such as shouldRandomizeStartTime: <true or false> that changes where the starting point of the audio will be. This can be useful when playing a single sound coming from different entities. It will make them all slightly different rather than starting simultaneously and just overlapping.

You can learn more about the AudioFileResource configuration structure and settings at https://developer.apple.com/documentation/realitykit/audiofileresource/configuration-swift.struct.

Controlling Playback

To control playback, you use the `AudioPlaybackController` created when calling `prepareAudio` or `playAudio` with the audio file resource. In many cases, you're going to just play the audio and move on, but there are additional commands and properties that you can use with the playback controller:

- `.play()`: Plays the audio

- `.stop()`: Stops the playback.

- `.pause()`: Pauses the playback

- `.isPlaying`: Returns `true` or `false` depending on whether audio is playing

The playback controller also gives you a **completion handler**, or a means of executing a block of code when playback is finished:

```
<playback controller>.completionHandler = (() -> Void)? {
    // Do something when the audio has finished playing.
}
```

HOW DID YOU KNOW TO ADD (()->VOID) FOR THE COMPLETION HANDLER?

First, it's important to understand that what this code is saying is that you could (rather than formatting the handler as we've done here) create a new function that takes zero arguments and returns nothing and set the completion handler to *that* instead. What you're doing is using a closure to handle the work rather than a separate function. You do that *all* the time, and the concept was first introduced with gestures in Chapter 5.

"Okay, John but where can I *see* the (()->Void) defined?" In the documentation, of course. Just look at the documentation for the playback controller, and you'll see it spelled out :https://developer.apple.com/documentation/realitykit/audioplaybackcontroller.

This will be used momentarily in an upcoming exercise, but first let's explore how some of the audio playback setup can be handled directly in Reality Composer Pro.

Audio and Reality Composer Pro

I want to start by making one thing clear: Reality Composer Pro is mostly useful for the setup of audio resources and the entities to which they attach. You can see the direction of the audio and adjust configuration settings without code. What you cannot do, however, is create the playback controller or initiate playback. The reason I'm telling you this is because the application offers a preview feature that looks like it *might* be doing more than it actually does.

Adding Audio Files

Adding audio file resources to Reality Composer Pro is similar to adding them to Xcode. You can access these resources very similarly to the audio added directly within Xcode, so *where* you decide to add the files is just a matter of how much you want to do in code versus what you want to do visually.

To add an audio file to Reality Composer Pro, first make sure you've opened the RealityKit-Content package and the Reality Composer Project Browser is visible. Drag the audio file (or files) into the browser. There won't be any prompts; the audio file simply appears as a new file in the Project Browser.

After you add an audio file, you need to configure the audio file resources. Recall that the AudioFileResource isn't the file itself; it references the audio file and a bunch of configuration options.

Creating Audio File Resources

To create an AudioFileResource from the files that have been added, drag the audio files into a scene that you're going to be using, such as the immersive scene. In **FIGURE 9.9**, I've added drums and tambourine sounds to an otherwise empty (except for the Root node) immersive scene.

> **NOTE** When you add the audio files to the scene, Reality Composer Pro labels them with an underscore (_) and their extension name (*m4a*)—thus, the somewhat strange names in the hierarchy.

The audio entries that appear in the hierarchy are now AudioFileResources. Select one; the Audio File pane within the Attributes Inspector reveals all the different settings that can be made to it, including looping, randomization, and more, as demonstrated in **FIGURE 9.10**. Here you can configure the resource however you'd like. No coding is required.

Jump back to the "Looping and Other Settings" section in this chapter for more information.

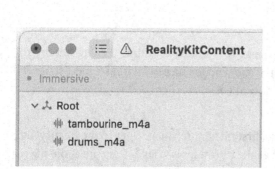

FIGURE 9.9 Adding the audio files to a scene

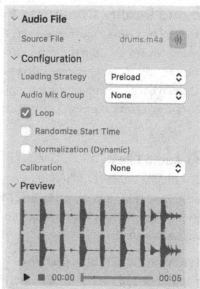

FIGURE 9.10 Configuring an audio resource within the scene

Adding the Entities and Audio Components

This is where things get weird. You have your `AudioFileResources`, and it would make sense to configure an entity with a specific resource, but that's not how it works. Instead, you can configure entities with an ambient component or spatial audio component. What's more, you can add audio-only entities (this are likely `Entity()`) that have no associated visible objects.

To add spatial or ambient audio entities, choose Insert, Audio, Spatial Audio or Insert, Audio, Ambient Audio from the File menu. These choices insert entities with the default names of SpatialAudio and AmbientAudio to the hierarchy—each containing, you guessed it, a `SpatialAudioComponent` or `AmbientAudioComponent`. You can rename them as you see fit. Each of the entities is represented with a different icon in the scene preview, as shown in **FIGURE 9.11**.

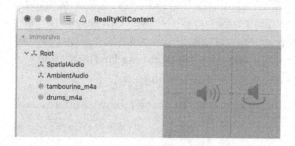

FIGURE 9.11 Audio entities are just like any other entity, there's just no object attached. Spatial audio is on the left.

Selecting the SpatialAudio entity displays the Spatial Audio configuration settings in the Attributes inspector, as demonstrated in **FIGURE 9.12**. These are the same parameters you can access via code.

Now, pay close attention to the bottom of the settings, See the dropdown where you can choose an audio resource? If you pick one (tambourine_m4a, here), you can click the arrow beside the resource and the pane expands to show all the audio resource settings. It *appears* as if you might be setting up the entity to play audio without writing any code. Be warned: This is only a preview of the audio. You can click the Play button at the top of the Attributes Inspector and hear what playback might sound like, but the entity is in no way being attached to a specific resource that magically connects all the parts. You still need to handle that in code.

If you choose to use existing entities rather than adding empty Spatial and Ambient Audio entities, the setup is the same, except you first add the Ambient or Spatial audio component via the Add Component button in the Attributes Inspector. The two components are shown in **FIGURE 9.13**.

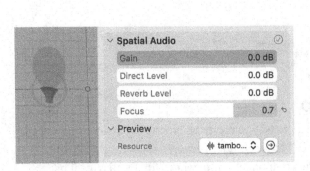

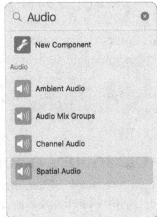

FIGURE 9.12 You control Spatial Audio settings in the Attributes Inspector. Focus (beam) changes are visualized with the gray ellipse appearing from the speaker.

FIGURE 9.13 To use your own entities, just add a Spatial or Ambient Audio component to the object.

Almost done! Now that there are configured audio resources and audio components, you can write a few lines of code to access and play the associated audio.

Coding the Playback

One of the reasons to use Reality Composer Pro is to avoid code, but it takes almost as much code to play back resources within a scene as it does to write it all in code:

```
if let <audio file resource> = try? AudioFileResource.load(named:
                                    <audio resource path>,
                                    from: <scene file>,
                                    in: realityKitContentBundle) {
    <playback controller> = <entity>.prepareAudio(<audio file resource>)
    <playback controller>.play()
}
```

For example, let's assume that you have an entity loaded from the immersive scene named entity and also there is an audio resource named drums_m4a added to the scene. I can play the sound with this code:

```
if let audio = try? AudioFileResource.load(named: "/Root/drums_m4a",
                    from: "Immersive.usda",
                    in: realityKitContentBundle) {
    playbackController = entity.prepareAudio(audio)
    playbackController.play()
}
```

"What in the world did I gain from this versus just coding it?" you ask. You gain the configuration of the entity's audio component (gain, reverb, and so on) as well as the configuration of the audio resource (looping and so on), but that's it. You still need to create the playback controller just as you would without using Reality Composer Pro.

> **NOTE** I've also omitted the code (*findEntity*) needed to access an entity in the scene, so there's more needed than what is presented here. Don't you worry, we're gonna code up an example now!

HANDS-ON: SOUNDS GOOD

Unlike the lighting example earlier, there is no way to create an interactive audio experience without code. In this exercise, you practice both techniques covered for adding audio files: configuring audio resources, setting audio components, and, whew, finally, playing it back. Apple provides many audio samples in the Reality Composer Pro Content Library. Feel free to follow along and do what I do or use your own audio choices.

In the Sounds Good project, you're just going to play around with entities and associated sounds. In my project, I'm adding a drum kit entity that, when tapped, starts playing an ambient audio drum loop and continues until it's tapped again. I'm also including a tambourine playing a spatial audio loop.

Surrounding the user, once again, is a cloud of random objects. When the user touches an object, it makes a spatial popping sound and disappears. **FIGURE 9.14** shows the finished application—unfortunately, sans audio.

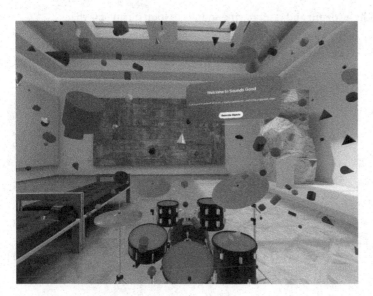

FIGURE 9.14 Tap objects and fill your head with sound.

Project Setup

Am I a broken record? I think I might be. Follow the same project setup as earlier, creating a new Mixed Immersive project named **Sounds Good**. Add an introduction screen to ContentView and update the <Project Name>App.swift file to resize the initial view to content-hugging size.

Do *not* change the ImmersiveView.swift file. You can make use of the existing code that loads the Immersive.usda scene from the RealityViewContent package.

As part of the setup, revisit **LISTING 9.1** in the "Adding the Random Object Code" section earlier in the chapter. Enter the code as described in ImmersiveView.swift. No sense in filling another page and a half with an identical listing!

Building the Reality Composer Scene

Begin this exercise by adding audio and objects to the Immersive.usda scene. Open the project's RealityViewContent package in Reality Composer Pro now.

Adding the Audio Files and Resources

Drag the drums.m4a and tambourine.m4a files from your projects folder into the Reality Composer Pro Project Browser. You now have the audio *files* included, but you need AudioFileResources. To turn the audio into usable resources, open the Immersive.usda scene and drag the two files from the Project Browser into the scene. While you're at it, delete the spheres and material from the scene. You only want the root entity and two audio resources, as shown in **FIGURE 9.15**.

In the final project, I want both the drum and tambourine sounds to loop during playback. Selecting the drum_m4a entry in the hierarchy, I use the Attributes Inspector, shown in **FIGURE 9.16** to set the Loop checkbox. This is then repeated for the tambourine_m4a audio resource.

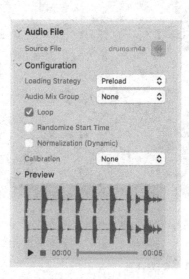

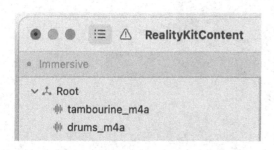

FIGURE 9.15 The immersive with just two audio resources   **FIGURE 9.16** Setting both audio resources to loop

Adding Entities

Next, use the Content Library to add the DrumKit model and Tambourine model to the Immersive scene. Using the Attributes Inspector and the Transform pane to adjust the Drum-Kit model so it is located at 0 on the x- and y-axes and about –1.5 meters on the z-axis. Set the scale of the DrumKit to 75% (0.75) or smaller (it's a large model).

Do the same for the tambourine, but place it at about 0.5 meters on the y-axis (so it floats in the air) and 1.0 meters on the z-axis (behind the user). Honestly, the positions and models aren't particularly important. You just need to get some objects added around the scene.

Setting the Audio Components

The DrumKit and Tambourine entities now need to be updated with an Ambient Audio and Spatial Audio component, respectively. Start by selecting the DrumKit, click Add Component in the Attributes Inspector, and then choose Ambient Audio from the component list.

Do the same for the Tambourine entity, but choose Spatial Audio as the component. You may now use the Attributes Inspector to change any of the presets for the audio components. Of particular interest are the Reverb Level and Focus settings (see **FIGURE 9.17**). You may want to experiment with these to see how they affect the experience.

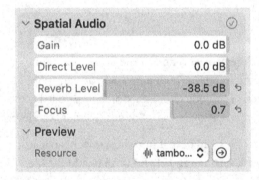

FIGURE 9.17 Play around with the reverb and focus settings to see how they change the audio experience.

Configuring the Scene for Input

Before finishing up with Reality Composer Pro, you need to add the ability to interact with the DrumKit and the Tambourine, which requires both a Collision component and an Input Target component. Select each entity and add a Collision Component, leaving the defaults as is.

To add the Input component, do something different. Select the Root node in the hierarchy and add an Input Target component (again, leaving the defaults). This component is inherited by the objects under the Root node, meaning you don't have to attach separate input components to DrumKit and Tambourine.

The final hierarchy and object layout should resemble **FIGURE 9.18**.

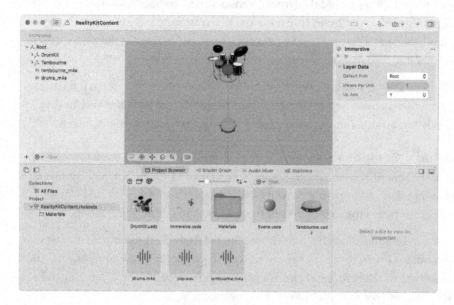

FIGURE 9.18 Completed work in Reality Composer Pro

Adding the Pop Sound

There are waaay more entities that will be part of the project than just the drums and tambourine because you'll be programmatically adding hundreds of objects that you can "pop" into oblivion. You the pop sound (pop.wav) directly in Xcode to demonstrate pure code base audio, so exit Reality Composer Pro and turn your attention back to Sounds Good in Xcode.

Now, find the pop.wav file in the Chapter 9 project files and drag it into the Project Navigator in Xcode. When prompted, leave the default import settings and click Finish to add the file.

That's it? Yep, that's it. Time to type.

Generating An(other) Object Field

Earlier in the chapter, you created a field of randomly generated objects. Now, you're going to do it again. You need to create another `objectCollection` entity to hold all of the generated objects. This time, it should be added directly after the `ImmersiveView` struct so that you can access it and manipulate the objects it contains outside of `RealityView`:

```
private let objectCollection = Entity()
```

If you don't add the line in this location, you won't experience any errors, but gestures targeted to the collection won't work properly.

Next, add a loop inside the RealityKit code block that generates the object field, adds the objects to `objectCollection`, and then finishes by adding the `objectCollection` to content.

This can be placed *after* the Immersive entity (the Reality Composer Pro scene) is loaded. The code is identical to the Hand-Lit Objects project, but also adds collision shapes and an input target to every object created.

```
for _ in 1...500 {
    let object=generateRandomObject()
    object.position.x = Float.random(in: -1.5...1.5)
    object.position.z = Float.random(in: -1.5...1.5)
    object.position.y = Float.random(in: 0.5...2.5)
    let xRotation = simd_quatf(angle: Float(Angle(degrees:
                    Double.random(in: 1.0...360.0)).radians),
                    axis: SIMD3<Float>(1,0,0))
    let yRotation = simd_quatf(angle: Float(Angle(degrees:
                    Double.random(in: 1.0...360.0)).radians),
                    axis: SIMD3<Float>(0,1,0))
    let zRotation = simd_quatf(angle: Float(Angle(degrees:
                    Double.random(in: 1.0...360.0)).radians),
                    axis: SIMD3<Float>(0,0,1))
    object.transform.rotation *= xRotation
    object.transform.rotation *= yRotation
    object.transform.rotation *= zRotation
    object.generateCollisionShapes(recursive: true)
    object.components.set(InputTargetComponent())
    objectCollection.addChild(object)
}
content.add(objectCollection)
```

If you run the application now, you see drums, a tambourine, and a few hundred of your favorite shiny shapes hanging in the air. The next step is to prepare for audio playback.

Preparing the DrumKit and Tambourine for Playback

Even with all the setup in Reality Composer Pro, you still need to add code to handle loading the audio and preparing for playback. Additionally, because you need to access the entities and the playback controllers elsewhere in the code, you need to create additional top-level variables for them.

Add these lines before or after the `objectCollection` declaration at the beginning of the immersive view:

```
@State private var drumKit = Entity()
@State private var tambourine = Entity()
```

```
@State private var drumPlaybackController : AudioPlaybackController?
@State private var tambourinePlaybackController : AudioPlaybackController?
```

This sets up drumKit and tambourine as empty entities. You reassign them to the appropriate Reality Composer Pro entities next. It also declares a drumPlaybackController and tambourinePlaybackController, which you also create and use in a few gestures. You can't initialize these without already having an audio resource, so they are just declared with the variable type (AudioPlaybackController) and a ? to indicate that they may (or may not) contain a value during execution.

Now you need to load the audio resources and use the tambourine and drum entities to create the playback controllers. Piece of cake, huh?

Add the following code as part of the if statement that checks to see whether the immersive scene can be loaded. There's no point in bothering with loading sounds if the scene doesn't even load!

```
if let drumKitEntity = scene.findEntity(named: "DrumKit") {
    drumKit = drumKitEntity
    if let audio = try? AudioFileResource.load(named: "/Root/drums_m4a",
                    from: "Immersive.usda", in: realityKitContentBundle) {
        drumPlaybackController = drumKit.prepareAudio(audio)
    }


}
if let tambourineEntity = scene.findEntity(named: "Tambourine") {
    tambourine = tambourineEntity
    if let audio = try? AudioFileResource.load(named:
                        "/Root/tambourine_m4a",
                        from: "Immersive.usda",
                        in: realityKitContentBundle) {
        tambourinePlaybackController = tambourine.prepareAudio(audio)
    }
}
```

To set up audio for the drums and tambourine, the first step is to use findEntity to grab the individual entities (DrumKit and Tambourine) from the scene. Because the entities need to be used outside of this code block, the variables drumKit and tambourine, which were previously defined, are set to the retrieved entities. Finally, the audio resource is created, and prepareAudio generates the playback controller, which is stored in the drumPlaybackController and tambourinePlaybackController variables, which were also defined earlier.

You have a scene with plenty of entities and playback controllers for the drums and tambourine. The last step is creating the reaction to gestures to control the audio and "pop" the entities.

Adding the Gestures

There are three required tap gestures in this project. One for the drums, one for the tambourine, and a third for everything else. The drum and tambourine toggle between audio "playing" and "not playing" states when tapped. Let's start there.

Add these two gesture modifiers to the RealityView (after the final brace):

```
.gesture(
    TapGesture(count: 1)
        .targetedToEntity(drumKit)
        .onEnded { event in
            if let playing = drumPlaybackController?.isPlaying {
                if playing {
                    drumPlaybackController?.stop()
                } else {
                    drumPlaybackController?.play()
                }
            }
        }
)
.gesture(
    TapGesture(count: 1)
        .targetedToEntity(tambourine)
        .onEnded { event in
            if let playing = tambourinePlaybackController?.isPlaying {
                if playing {
                    tambourinePlaybackController?.stop()
                } else {
                    tambourinePlaybackController?.play()
                }
            }
        }
)
```

The logic is easy to follow. A TapGesture is added, targeted to the respective drumKit and tambourine entities. When a tap is detected, you attempt to retrieve the playback status from the playback controllers with .isPlaying. If the controller *is* playing, it's told to stop. If it isn't, it's told to play. The controller variables are referenced (unwrapped) with ? because you had to define them without values, and you must acknowledge that they might not exist if something has gone wrong.

The final gesture is targeted to the `objectCollection` entity, which contains all the different random objects added to the scene. When a tap is detected on an entity, the pop.wav audio file is played, and the entity is removed from the scene. Add the third gesture now:

```
.gesture(
    TapGesture(count: 1)
        .targetedToEntity(objectCollection)
        .onEnded { event in
            if let audio = try? AudioFileResource.load(named: "pop") {
                let popPlaybackController =
                            event.entity.prepareAudio(audio)
                event.entity.spatialAudio?.gain = -5.0
                popPlaybackController.completionHandler = (() -> Void)? {
                    event.entity.removeFromParent()
                }
                popPlaybackController.play()
            }
        }
)
```

In this gesture, when a tap is detected, the code loads the "pop" audio file into an audio file resource (`audio`) and creates a playback controller (`popPlaybackController`) for the entity that received the tap (`event.entity`). The gain is set to –5.0 (it's a rather loud sound) and a completion handler is created that, after the sound plays, executes `event.entity.removeFromParent()`, which removes the targeted entity from the scene (that is, it disappears). Lastly, the pop sound is played.

Cleaning Up

The `objectCollection` entity needed to be defined at the top level of the `ImmersiveView` struct so that it could be accessed by gestures and its children could be manipulated outside of the initial `RealityView` setup. This means you have some cleanup to do.

Add an `.onDisappear{}` modifier directly after the `RealityView` code block (before the gestures) that removes everything added to `objectCollection`:

```
.onDisappear{
    objectCollection.children.removeAll()
}
```

The project is complete.

Now that you've used both a Reality Composer Pro–centric and code-centric approach, which do you feel is better? My opinion doesn't matter, but I'll just casually note that you handled all the spatial audio playback for hundreds of entities with the code just within that last gesture...

That's it for sound. Let's move on to something more visual to finish up.

BUILDING A SKYBOX

When building your immersive environments, you have the option of choosing between mixed (what you've been using) and progressive or full. In progressive and full spaces, your job is to build out a space, presumably with a floor, objects, and everything else a user sees. This can be daunting, as you're effectively creating a digital world. Thankfully, there is a common technique, called a **skybox**, that makes implementing full and partially immersive spaces much more manageable. A skybox takes a photograph and wraps it around the user, enabling them to look around and see *something* in all directions. This is exactly what happens when you use the digital crown to immerse yourself in one of Apple's Vision Pro environments.

You've kinda sorta encountered a skybox when implementing the image-based lighting (even adding .skybox to the end of a folder name.) This is because the image-based lighting is effectively creating a skybox wrapped around a scene where only certain areas allow light to shine through. You don't see this skybox, but it's there.

Unfortunately, RealityKit is currently missing skybox functions for visionOS. Apple has provided code to make a skybox manually, so that's what you do in this final section.

NO, IT'S NOT A BOX!

Traditionally, a skybox has consisted of photographs constructed in the shape of an unfolded cube that is then reconstructed around the viewer. Apple's implementation is a giant sphere where the image is rendered on the inside of the sphere and the user sits in the middle. Is this a skybox? Not really. Do I call it a skybox because Apple does? Absolutely.

Skybox Images

To create a skybox, you need an image to serve as a `TextureResource` for a sphere. Apple has not provided any real guidance on the preparation of the image, but, because it is being wrapped onto a sphere, you should expect some visual distortion with images containing strong geometric figures. Additionally, the left and right edges of the image should match as closely as possible; otherwise, you see a seam where the edges come together.

In my experience, natural panoramic settings work the best. As a quick and dirty trick for getting the edges to align, you can mirror the image and place it beside the original. For example, **FIGURE 9.19** had closely aligned edges to begin with, but, by mirroring the image and making it twice as wide, it is both higher resolution on the Vision Pro and entirely seamless.

The maximum size you can use for a `TextureResource` is 8192×8192, so the image needs to fall within that range.

FIGURE 9.19 Skybox images should be panoramic with aligning edges.

NOTE If you're interested in using AI for the job, visit https://blog.kuula.co/ai-panoramas for a quick overview of some technologies (free and otherwise) that can help get you started.

Adding Texture Assets

To add a texture to an Xcode project, you make use of the Assets catalog. This is a central location where you can drop images and other files to keep them organized in your project. To add a Texture asset to an Xcode project, click the Assets icon in Xcode project navigator (see **FIGURE 9.20**). By default, the only asset established in a new project is the AppIcon (application icon), which I talk about more later in the book.

To add a new Texture asset, click the + button at the bottom of the asset list, choose AR and Textures and then Texture Set, as shown in **FIGURE 9.21**.

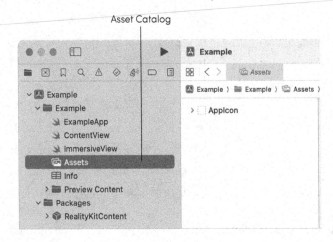

FIGURE 9.20 The Asset Catalog can hold image-related resources for your projects.

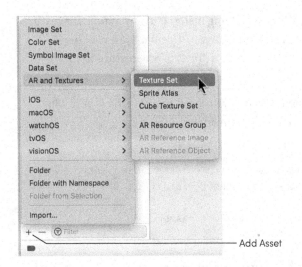

FIGURE 9.21 Using the Asset Catalog to add a new Texture Set

A new entry appears in the Asset Catalog. You can name this anything you want. This is the name by which you refer to the asset in code and *doesn't* need to match the image filename.

You add the image to the asset by dragging it into the image well on the right side of the Xcode window. **FIGURE 9.22** shows an example of a new texture asset waiting for the image to be added.

Asset name   Image well

FIGURE 9.22 Name the asset and add the corresponding image by dragging it into the image well.

All that is needed now is some code to create the Skybox.

Coding the Skybox

The code for a skybox is very similar to creating and adding material to any entity. The texture is loaded and applied to a very large sphere as an unlit material. The one "unusual" step is applying a –1 scaling factor to the x-axis of the sphere. This "inverts" the texture so that it's located on the inside of the sphere.

Depending on your texture image orientation, you may also need to rotate the sphere 180 degrees along the x-axis so that the texture appears right-side-up.

```
if let <texture resource> = try? await
                        TextureResource.init(named: <texture asset>) {
    let <skybox> = ModelEntity(mesh: .generateSphere(radius: 500.0))
    var <material> = UnlitMaterial()
    <material>.color = .init(texture: .init(<texture resource>))
    <skybox>.model?.materials = [<material>]
    <skybox>.scale = .init(x: -1, y: 1, z: 1)
    let <x rotation> = simd_quatf(angle: Float(Angle(degrees:
                        180.0).radians), axis: SIMD3<Float>(1,0,0))
    skyBox.transform.rotation *= <x rotation>
    content.add(<skybox>)
}
```

Following this pattern should make it pretty painless to add skyboxes to your creations. Incidentally, this creates a 1000-meter-wide sphere. I've seen higher and lower numbers used, but anything over a few meters wide (enough to encompass the entire scene you want to build) should be plenty.

NOTE In visionOS 2.0+, Apple is adding the ability to create skyboxes in Reality Composer Pro. Just choose Insert, Environment, Sky Dome or Sky Sphere from the menu to add a half or full sphere skybox; then adjust their material to an image of your choice. See an example at https://visionproforcreators.com/.

(Mini) Hands-On: SkyBox It

In this project, you create a skybox in a progressive or fully immersive project (your choice!). You can even use the digital crown to adjust the immersion level of the experience. I've provided an image named Skybox Texture.png that you can use, or you can find a different panoramic image and try it instead. The final experience works on both the simulator and the headset and resembles **FIGURE 9.23**.

FIGURE 9.23 Create a skybox so that you can stand peacefully in a picturesque field. Careful, it looks like rain!

Project Setup

Create a new immersive project named **SkyBox It** using the Progressive or Full style (you've been using Mixed). I prefer to use Progressive because the user has the opportunity to choose to "go full" using the digital crown.

Follow the usual steps of adding an optional welcome screen and updating the size of the ContentView window. Or don't—it's optional!

In the ImmersiveView file, clean out the RealityView code block so that it is empty. You add the skybox code here.

Adding the Texture

Using the Asset Catalog in Xcode, create a new Texture Set asset named **nature**. Drag the Skybox Image provided in the Chapter 9 projects folder into the image well in the catalog. Your catalog should resemble **FIGURE 9.24**.

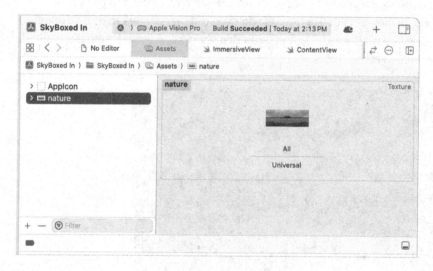

FIGURE 9.24 Your texture resource configuration should look like this.

Generating the Skybox

Use the code block established in this section to finish off the project. Within the ImmersiveView RealityView code block, you load a texture named nature, apply it as an unlit material to a large sphere, use the scale property of the sphere to turn the texture "outside in," and then rotate the sphere 180 degrees on the x-axis (so the sky is up.) Finally, you add the sphere to the content.

```
if let texture = try? await TextureResource.init(named: "nature") {
    let skyBox = ModelEntity(mesh: .generateSphere(radius: 500.0))
    var material = UnlitMaterial()
    material.color = .init(texture: .init(texture))
    skyBox.model?.materials = [material]
    skyBox.scale = .init(x: -1, y: 1, z: 1)
    let xRotation = simd_quatf(angle: Float(Angle(degrees:
                    180.0).radians), axis: SIMD3<Float>(1,0,0))
```

```
    skyBox.transform.rotation *= xRotation
    content.add(skyBox)
}
```

Enter the code and try running the application. As you look around, think about all the ambient sounds you can add to your new outdoor field simulator.

> **NOTE** Progressive and Fully Immersive projects prompt the user to make sure they're aware of their surroundings. This is automatic for these project types.

SUMMARY

In this chapter, you learned about entirely new features that can literally light up your experiences. Using the `ImageBasedLightComponent`, you can create lighting schemes that match the environment that you're creating. You explored the somewhat bewildering nuance that image-based lights require both an entity that "holds" a lighting image and one or more "light receivers" that to be lit. At present, there is no way to apply a light to all the objects in a scene, but I suspect the feature will be coming soon.

You also worked through two different ways to apply spatial and ambient audio to your work: directly in code or with a mix of code and Reality Composer Pro. A combination of an `Audio-FileResource`, `SpatialAudioComponent` (or `AmbientAudioComponent`), and `AudioPlaybackController` are the only things you need to start playing sweet, sweet music in your applications.

You ended on a fun note by reviewing the purpose of a skybox and even created an immersive application that generates a 360-degree view of the outdoors.

If you're reading between the lines, you may conclude that I'm slightly dissatisfied with the implementation of the technology in these topics—and you'd be right. I fully expect Apple to update almost everything discussed in future releases for visionOS. At the very least, the platform should be brought up to par with macOS, iOS, and iPadOS, all of which offer features that are beyond what RealityKit and ARKit provide on Apple Vision Pro today.

Go Further

When it comes to sound, you may want to read more about some additional components, like the `ChannelAudioComponent` (https://developer.apple.com/documentation/realitykit/channelaudiocomponent), which provides a means of playing audio "normally" through the device without taking location or orientation into account. You may also be interested in `AudioMix-Group` (https://developer.apple.com/documentation/realitykit/audiomixgroup) for handling audio mixing.

With lighting, the key is the image used for the lights. Try different colors and different patterns. Take a photo of the lights in your ceiling, black out everything but the lights, and try *that* image. Take a photograph of the night sky, including the moon, and use it for an outdoor experience. You won't understand what's possible until you go beyond the provided samples.

I recommend taking each one of the technologies that you used in this lesson and apply it to a previous project. Make sounds, create environments, and light things up. Previously in the book, I implored you to practice. Now, with significantly more tools available to use, practice is even more important. It's the combination of these tools and techniques that can make a product memorable.

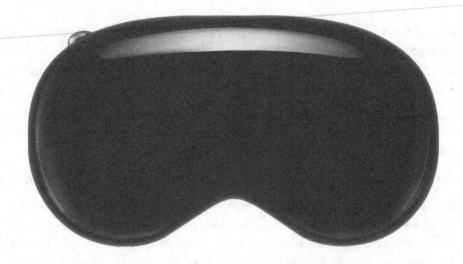

Components, Systems, and the Kitchen Sink

Good job! You've made it to Chapter 10! This is the last major coding chapter before before things wrap up in the two online chapters - Chapter 11, "Thoughtful Design," and Chapter 12, "Sharing Your Creations." You've absorbed much on this journey, and this lesson is going to pull many of those topics together with the help of a few new technologies.

You've been using components now for quite a while—adding physics, input, hover effects, and more. This is great if you can find a component for everything you need, but chances are, just throwing a physics component on some objects isn't going to lead to the depth of interactions you want in an immersive product—certainly not a powerhouse like the Apple Vision Pro.

What if you could write components that do whatever you want? Animate objects, take care of background tasks, and so on? Well, you can, and you will! You also find out more about the systems that work with components to make the magic.

To add to the fun, I take you on an exploration of collisions. No, not just for gestures. I show you how to identify and react to collisions between objects. Using collisions, objects can interact with each other and (when coupled with the scene reconstruction from Chapter 8, "Reconstructing Reality") the environment.

The focus is a single project—the largest in the book—that implements an actual game from the ground up. Almost every line of code is something you've already seen, but now you get to watch how it comes together into something truly useful and fun.

By the end of the chapter, you'll be able to use these new elements in all your future creations:

- **Components:** Components store information associated with an entity. Not a good enough definition for you? I agree. Components offer a way to store configuration information about how you want something to act. If you want an object to spin, for example, a component might store how quickly and along what axis an object should spin.

- **Systems:** A system works hand in hand with a component to implement the behaviors described in a component configuration. Sure, you can create a component that describes how to spin an object, but you still have to do it! That's the job of a system.

- **Collisions:** Collisions can take a meh experience and raise it to a yay! experience. If you want to implement a sword fighting game, you certainly know how to add a sword to your hand and even add targets for the sword to hit, but how would you detect the hits? Collisions, my friend... collisions.

- **Singletons:** Previously in the book I showed you a few ways to share information between different areas of an application. Now that you've gotten your feet wet with more classes and structures than you can shake a stick at, I'm introducing a final (and my favorite) approach to data sharing that is so simple you'll want to applaud.

If you aren't feeling excited by the end of this chapter, I recommend a teaspoon or two of sugar. This is some cool stuff, and it's going to be so easy for you to use that you'll wonder why you've taken so long to start programming for AR and VR. (Probably because it took so long for Apple to make a headset!)

Unfortunately, very little of what I'm discussing has a visual component, so this chapter focuses mostly on code. You'll still turn to your old frenemy Reality Composer Pro, but only for a few minutes.

> **NOTE** Visit https://visionproforcreators.com/files/ or www.peachpit.com/visionpro to download the Chapter 10 project files before starting.

COMPONENTS AND SYSTEMS

After just introducing components and systems as two separate topics, why am I putting them together in a single section? Because these two parts of the Entity-Component-System (ECS) paradigm are rarely not used together. Components say "what" to do, and a system describes "how" to do it.

You can create components without a corresponding system if you just want to store information relevant to an entity, but, as you'll see, in most cases you want both to exist together. Thankfully, the code is going to do a better job of describing this than I can, so let's take a look.

Components

A component is a structure (`struct`) that stores information associated with an entity. When you've been configuring components throughout the book, the component isn't making anything happen. It's just holding information that a system can then act upon. Although you can add logic to a component, this is not recommended unless it is related to managing the configuration data.

Defining a Component

Components are usually defined within a standalone Swift file (File, New, File from the menu bar) that may or may not also contain a corresponding system.

A component definition typically has a syntax like this:

```swift
import SwiftUI
import RealityKit

public struct <component name>: Component[, Codable] {
    var <variable name> = <value>
    ...
    public init() {}
}
```

Define the component name and variables and you're done. You can also add an `init()` method that takes parameters and uses them to initialize the variables in the component.

Because this code fragment is so little to go on, let's look at a hypothetical component—one that stores how quickly an object should spin (`rotation`) and whether it is spinning (`isSpinning`).

```swift
import SwiftUI
import RealityKit

public struct SpinBehaviorComponent: Component, Codable {
    var rotation = 1.0
    var isSpinning = true
```

```
    public init() {}
    public init(rotation: Double, isSpinning: Bool) {
        self.rotation = rotation
        self.isSpinning = isSpinning
    }
}
```

For now, don't worry about how this would be implemented. That's the job of the system that works with a component. All this is doing is defining a SpinBehaviorComponent that stores a rotation Double and an isSpinning Boolean. The default value for rotation is 1.0, whereas isSpinning is true. As an extra convenience to the developer (you), the component includes an initialization function that enables you to set these values when it is added to an entity.

WHAT'S CODABLE?

Codable indicates that the data stored in this structure can be encoded and decoded into an "external representation." In other words, it isn't so complicated that it can't just be written or read from a file. Complex data types are *not* codable and cannot be used in the component if this keyword is specified.

The reason for making the structure codable is so that it can be used to generate an interface in Reality Composer Pro. If you have no intention of using custom components in Reality Composer Pro, it is entirely unnecessary.

For a list of the variable types that conform to the codable standard, visit https://developer.apple.com/documentation/swift/encodable.

Registering Components

Before a component can be used in a project, it needs to be registered. This can happen anywhere in your application, as long as it occurs before the component is used. To register a component, call .registerComponent() on the component you've defined. For the SpinBehaviorComponent, this would be

```
SpinBehaviorComponent.registerComponent()
```

Now the component is ready to be used.

Adding the Component to an Entity

You've done this so many times with the built-in components, I'm just going to skip the explanation. *Kidding.* Once a component has been defined and registered, you can add it to an entity with this syntax:

```
<entity>.components.set(<component name([parameters])>)
```

For example, to add the spin behavior component to an entity named `entity`, I could use this:

```
entity.components.set(SpinBehaviorComponent())
```

This code establishes the component with the default variable values established in the code: `rotation = 1.0` and `isSpinning = true`.

If I want to set the variables by way of parameters, I could use

```
entity.components.set(SpinBehaviorComponent(rotation: 2.0,
                                   isSpinning: false))
```

Interacting with Components

After a component has been added to an entity, you can manipulate the values through two approaches. First, you can access the variables in the component directly with this syntax:

```
<entity>.components[<component name>.self]?.<variable> = <value>
```

To set the spin component so that `isSpinning` is true, I type:

```
entity.components[SpinBehaviorComponent.self]?.isSpinning = true
```

An entity can have only one copy of a given type of component applied at any time. In many cases, it may be easier to re-add the component to the entity with the values that you want than set each variable individually.

Removing Components

Components can be used for any length of time and then be removed if they are no longer relevant. To delete a component from an entity, you can use the `remove` function:

```
<entity>.components.remove(<component name>.self)
```

If you want to remove *all* the components from an entity, you can use the `removeAll` command. This, however, is rarely something you will want to do because just about everything useful about an entity is contained in a component.

Defining and Adding Components via Reality Composer Pro

Apple has added a way to define components in Reality Composer Pro that also links them directly to the user interface.

To create a custom component via Reality Composer Pro, open a scene and select an object to which you want to add a new component. This is the same as adding any other component. Click Add Component at the bottom of the Attributes Inspector, and, when prompted, double-click New Component in the list that appears as shown in **FIGURE 10.1**.

After double-clicking New Component, Reality Composer Pro asks for a name for the component. By default "Component" is automatically added to the name you specify. If you were recreating the SpinBehaviorComponent, you'd type **SpinBehavior** and click Create, as shown in **FIGURE 10.2**.

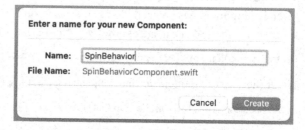

FIGURE 10.1 Adding a new component via Reality Composer Pro

FIGURE 10.2 Creating the new Swift file for the component

The component file is created using an Apple template and is *not* stored with your main source code files but inside of the RealityKit Content package. **FIGURE 10.3** displays the location of the new source file within Xcode.

By default, Apple's component template adds a single variable, count, to the component. This isn't useful (unless you need a count value), so you want to remove it and replace the content with the source for your component using the syntax I've just covered.

After editing the source, you see your custom component in Reality Composer Pro each time you go to add a new component, as shown in **FIGURE 10.4**.

When the component is added to an object, Reality Composer Pro generates a nice configuration screen with all the variables that can be adjusted (see **FIGURE 10.5**).

TIP If you've already written components that are located elsewhere in the Xcode project, use the Project Navigator in Xcode to drag the Swift file into the location shown in Figure 10.3. Once moved, it appears as a custom component in Reality Composer Pro.

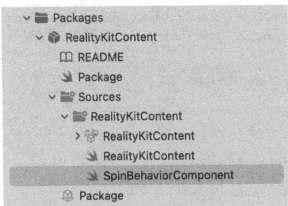

FIGURE 10.3 Drilling down into the RealityKit Content package to find the new component

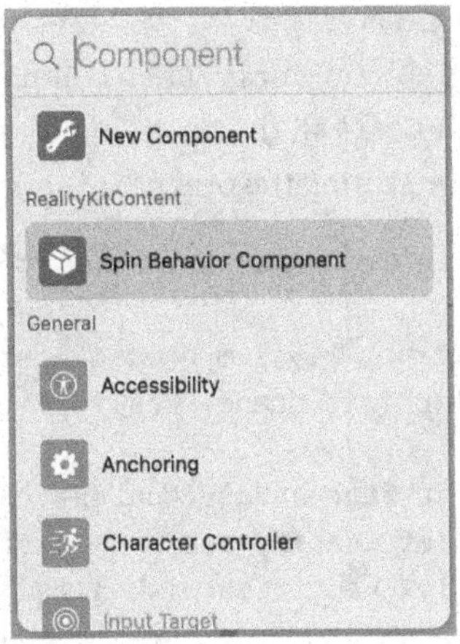

FIGURE 10.4 The custom component in the Add Component list

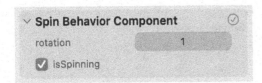

FIGURE 10.5 You can visually add and configure the component directly within Reality Composer Pro.

One note of caution: If you do *not* define the component as Codable, you're in for a world of pain, even if you haven't used any advanced data structures. Reality Composer, rather than displaying an error, will crash randomly and the component will not be visible in the interface. Bleh.

That about does it for components, but what about systems? Presumably, if I'm creating a spin behavior component, I also want to define a system that, just maybe, makes an entity spin.

Systems

A system works hand in hand with a component to perform actions on an entity. It can read information from a component as well as get and set information about the entity to which the component has been added. A system is called at each frame update for the Apple Vision Pro, meaning that it can change the behavior of an entity in real time as it is being rendered to the screen. This, as you might expect, is a resource-intensive activity, so you want to test your systems before just assuming you can apply them to every single object in a scene without any slowdown.

Defining a System

Because a system works with a component, I highly recommend using the same code file for each. That keeps all the functionality together and, when you're editing one, you're *likely* going to be editing the other.

The structure of a system (another struct) looks like this:

```
public struct <system name>: System {
    public init(scene: RealityKit.Scene) {}

    public func update(context: SceneUpdateContext) {
        let <entity query> = EntityQuery(where: .has(<component name>) )
        let <entities with named component> =
                            context.scene.performQuery(<entity query>)

        for <entity> in <entities with named component> {
            if var <component> = <entity>.components[
                                    <component name>.self] {
                // Do something with the <entity>
                <entity>.components.set(<component name>)
            }
        }
    }
}
```

This code pattern is required, so don't change it. You want to focus on the implementation of the update function, which handles all the real work. This function is called each time the scene is updated and includes some new syntax that turns out to be very helpful.

Rather than looping through all the entities manually and trying to figure out which ones have a given component and might need to be updated, these two lines handle that:

```
let <entity query> = EntityQuery(where: .has(<component name>) )
let <entities with named component> =
                        context.scene.performQuery(<entity query>)
```

An **entity query** is defined to select all the entities in a scene that have a given component name. When the query is performed, it returns a collection of those entities that can be looped through and modified as needed by the system.

> **TIP** Entity queries can also perform Boolean logic to check for entities with multiple components that are (or aren't) defined. To learn more about entity queries, read the documentation at https://developer.apple.com/documentation/realitykit/entityquery.

With the collection of entities in hand, the code loops through them, accesses the component in each, and then executes whatever arbitrary code you'd like. An optional line

```
<entity>.components.set(<component name>)
```

ensures that any changes you've made to component values are saved back to the component.

To implement the logic for the SpinBehaviorComponent, you might implement it like this:

```
public struct SpinBehaviorSystem: System {
    public init(scene: RealityKit.Scene) {}
    public func update(context: SceneUpdateContext) {
        let spinQuery = EntityQuery(where:
                        .has(SpinBehaviorComponent.self) )
        let spinners = context.scene.performQuery(spinQuery)

        for spinner in spinners {
            if var spinComponent =
                spinner.components[SpinBehaviorComponent.self] {
                if spinComponent.isSpinning {
                    spinner.orientation *= simd_quatf(angle:
                    Float(Angle(degrees: spinComponent.rotation).radians),
                    axis: SIMD3<Float>(1,0,0))
                }
                if spinComponent.rotation == 0 {
                    spinComponent.isSpinning = false
                } else {
                    spinComponent.isSpinning = true
                }
                spinner.components.set(spinComponent)
            }
        }
    }
}
```

In this system structure, named SpinBehaviorSystem, a spinQuery is created to grab all the entities with the SpinBehaviorComponent. The query is performed, returning a collection of entities in the variable spinners.

The code then loops over spinners, storing each entity in a variable named spinner. The SpinBehaviorComponent is retrieved for each entity and stored in spinComponent.

Finally, the logic is implemented: If the spinComponent.isSpinning variable is set, the entity's (spinner) orientation is multiplied by a rotation component along the x-axis. The angle of the rotation is Float(Angle(degrees: spinComponent.rotation).radians), which is a complicated way of saying "take the rotation in degrees stored in spinComponent.rotation and then convert to radians because that's what Xcode wants."

The second if-then-else block makes sure that if the spinnerComponent's rotation is set to 0, then isSpinning is set to false. If the rotation value *isn't* 0, then isSpinning is set to true.

The combination of both logic statements means that the spinnerComponent's isSpinning and rotation values are always in sync. If a user sets the rotation to a non-zero value, isSpinning is set to true. If a user changes isSpinning to false, the rotation value is set to 0.

Registering Systems

When you're finished with your system and want to use it, you must register it in much the same way as you did for the component, using the .registerSystem() function. For the SpinBehaviorSystem, the registration would be

```
SpinBehaviorSystem.registerSystem()
```

Once registered, anything with a properly configured SpinBehaviorComponent starts working. Add spin to anything you want either in code or through the Reality Composer Pro interface.

I'm hoping this sparks an aha! moment for you. With this new knowledge, you can create objects that take on new characteristics and carry out actions "on their own." The system becomes the brain of whatever entity employs a corresponding component. Multiple different components equals multiple different brains.

COLLISIONS

Collisions aren't generally something that people look forward to in real-life (with the exceptions of billiards and bumper cars). On the Apple Vision Pro, however, collisions can give way to fabulous interactivity that goes far beyond what a gesture can do. You've seen (and probably ooooh'd over) collisions in several of our projects, thanks to the physics component, but those aren't collisions that we're controlling. Imagine trying to write a game where you pop balloons with a pin, but you have to perform the tap gesture each time the virtual pin contacts a balloon. Sorta takes something out of the experience, in my opinion.

By detecting a collision between a pin object and a balloon, you can pop the balloon quite naturally. Heck, just being able to detect collisions between an object anchored to your hand and other virtual models opens up a realm of possibilities that aren't relying on a PhysicsBodyComponent.

To handle collisions between objects, you create an EventSubscription variable and subscribe it to an event called CollisionEvents. Each time a collision occurs, a block of code is executed, much like a gesture. The code is simply

```
@State private var <subscription>: EventSubscription?
...
<subscription> = content.subscribe(to: CollisionEvents.<event type>.self,
                        on: <entity>) { event in
    // Do something with event.entityA and event.entityB
}
```

The event type is one of three values—Began, Ended, and Updated—corresponding to the collision beginning, ending, or still in progress.

Looks easy enough, doesn't it? As an example, consider a situation where I want to see when my sword entity collides with an evilPumpkin entity. Let's also assume both entities have their names set accordingly, either with <entity>.name ="<a name>" or within the Reality Composer Pro scene hierarchy.

The code becomes

```
@State private var swordCollision: EventSubscription?
...
swordCollision = content.subscribe(to: CollisionEvents.Began.self,
                        on: sword) { event in
    // Do something with event.entityA and event.entityB
    if (event.entityA.name == "evilPumpkin" ||
        event.entityB.name == "evilPumpkin") {
        // Your sword has hit evilPumpkin!
    }
}
```

Notice that the collision event subscription is set up to look for all collisions on the sword entity. If I want to monitor *all* collisions taking place between *all* entities, I could just replace the on: <entity> parameter with on: nil.

When a collision takes place, the two entities involved are returned in event.entityA and event.entityB. You can check the names of the entities or compare the event entities against known entities in your code to understand what was involved in the collision. In this example, the collision event subscription is targeting the sword entity, but we still need to check both `entityA` and `entityB` to see if one of them has a name that matches `evilPumpkin`. If not, the sword struck something else.

Time to move on to our last big topic of the lesson: singletons.

SINGLETONS

A **singleton** is a concept, not a specific Swift command or data type. A singleton offers a single location where data can be stored and retrieved while an application is running—*anywhere* in the application. Back in the Plane Detection project in Chapter 7, "Anchors and Planes," you created two instances of the `PlaneDetector` class. The first was added to `ContentView` so that you could display a classification label for the planes the Vision Pro saw. The second, in `ImmersiveView`, was used to detect and add the planes to the environment.

This worked, but it wasn't good form because two copies of the `PlaneDetector` code were running simultaneously—not a particularly efficient thing to do. Using a singleton, you could have made the information available to whatever `view`, `class`, `struct`, or anything else in our application—like a global variable but without the risks.

Although this isn't a book on object-oriented programming, you have created some classes over the past few chapters, and you're going to need to do it one more time to create a singleton.

Creating a Singleton Class

Singletons are just a Swift class structure, with a very special difference: the inclusion of an instance of the class stored *within* the class itself. This is typically named `shared`, although it can be anything you'd like. Like components, classes are typically stored in a separate Swift file but can be mixed with any of your other files if you prefer.

Again, starting with the syntax, this looks like

```
import Foundation

class <class name>[: ObservableObject]  {
    static let shared = <class name>()
    [@Published ]var <variable> = <initial value>
    ...
}
```

The `import Foundation` command is needed *only* in the case the class is in a standalone file. This imports the `Foundation` framework, which provides much of Swift's core functionality. Without it, Swift won't even know what a class *is*.

If, however, you add the class to another file you've already been coding, the existing `import` statements almost certainly include *other* frameworks that already `import Foundation`.

The class code block kicks off by first defining a class name. If you want your views to begin an update automatically when the class updates, you should append : ObservableObject after the class name.

Next, the "singleton" is created by initializing the class *within itself*. Finally, you define the variables you want to store data along with the initial values you want them to have.

For example, I want a singleton that helps me store the score and the amount of "hits" a character has taken in a game. I could define a ScoreKeeper singleton like this:

```
class ScoreKeeper {
    static let shared = ScoreKeeper()
    var score: Int = 0
    var hits: Int = 0
}
```

Now let's see how we can *use* it.

Accessing a Singleton Class

To access the class, initialize a constant to the <class name>.shared and then you can use the syntax <variable>.<class variable> to access each variable stored in the singleton. With the ScoreKeeper class, for example, I can increment the score with this code:

```
let scoreKeeper = ScoreKeeper.shared
scoreKeeper.score += 1
```

What's more, I can use this anywhere in any file in my project. The code will have access to the same values and can read and write to them as needed.

If I want to use these values in a view and have them updated in real time, I update the class file to include the ObservableObject and @Published syntax described earlier and define a scoreKeeper variable at the start of the view definition (such as the ImmersiveView or ContentView structs) and add the @ObservedObject wrapper:

```
@ObservedObject var scoreKeeper = ScoreKeeper.shared
```

NOTE Only variables (*var*), not constants (*let*), can be used with the *@ObservedObject* wrapper, thus, the additional change in the definition.

Singletons are tremendously useful when you want different parts of your code to access and process the same values. A singleton class can even define functions that access and manipulate that same shared data or that are globally available and can be accessed anywhere in your code just by typing <class name>.shared.<function([parameters])>. This presents a convenient way to write and access utility functions available anywhere in an application. Future versions of the visionOS templates include an AppModel.swift file that can be used to share values in a similar manner to what I cover in Chapter 3, "Adding an Environment Object for Settings." I, however, prefer this approach.

THE KITCHEN SINK

Throughout this book, I've tried to throw in nifty features that might not be necessary for a project but can be useful. We already know *almost* everything for the upcoming hands-on example, but, since this is the grand finale, there are a few more esoteric things you should know before starting.

Physics Forces

You've used the `PhysicsBodyComponent` many times. During its use, you've observed the force of gravity on objects and movement that you've induced through the physical act of batting objects around with hand tracking. What you *haven't* done, however, is *programmatically* make something move.

This is done through the application of forces to an object. If a physics body is set, you can apply the programming equivalent of a "tap" on an object to get it moving.

Applying a Linear Impulse

A **linear impulse** sets an object moving in a straight direction. It can be applied to a model entity with a dynamic mode physics body with

```
<model entity>.applyLinearImpulse(SIMD3<Float>(<x-axis force>,
                                  <y-axis force>, <z-axis force>),
                                  relativeTo: <entity or nil>)
```

The force along each axis is given in **Newton-seconds**—not a preowned Apple Newton, but a standard unit of force that you can read about at https://en.wikipedia.org/wiki/Newton-second. Not feeling up to a physics lesson? Just consider the force value to be a tap: the bigger the number (start at around 0.5), the harder the tap.

The direction of the force is further influenced by the `relativeTo:` parameter. If nil, the force is relative to the world coordinates. If an entity is used instead, the force is applied based on the coordinate system of that entity.

To control how quickly a linear force dissipates (such as slowing down when moving through the air, water, and so on), you can adjust the physics body's `linearDampening` value. The higher the number, the quicker it slows down. If set to 0.0, the entity just keeps going and going:

```
<model entity>.physicsBody?.linearDamping = 1.0
```

Applying an Angular Force

An angular force works like a linear impulse but is a push that starts an object spinning. To add an angular impulse, do the same thing, but with a slightly different method:

```
<model entity>.applyAngularImpulse(SIMD3<Float>(<x-axis force>,
                                   <y-axis force>, <z-axis force>),
                               relativeTo: <entity or nil>)
```

Control the speed the angular force diminishes with the angular dampening value within the physics body:

```
<model entity>.physicsBody?.angularDamping = 1.0
```

Turning off Gravity

Gravity is always acting on the objects in dynamic mode physics simulation—unless you turn it off for a specific object:

```
<model entity>.physicsBody?.isAffectedByGravity = <true|false>
```

By setting the linear and angular dampening to 0.0 and turning off gravity, you effectively put an object in kinematic physics mode (the mode where the developer applies all forces to an object manually.)

Why is this important? Because if you set the physics mode to kinematic when establishing the physics component, none of these functions will work!

Motion in kinematic mode requires a `PhysicsMotionComponent` added to an entity (in *addition* to the `PhysicsBodyComponent`). You can perform similar actions in a physics kinematic mode, but you need to add a `PhysicsMotionComponent` (along with the physics body component) to each entity and use the linear and angular acceleration methods described here: https://developer.apple.com/documentation/realitykit/hasphysicsbody/.

APPLYING CONSTANT FORCE

If you'd prefer a steady application of force to induce motion rather than a quick smack against an object, you can configure entities to receive a constant force for the duration of an entire frame of a scene refresh with the addForce (linear) and addTorque (angular) methods. These are functions you might use within a Component System to accelerate bodies at a steady rate over time. Learn more at https://developer.apple.com/documentation/realitykit/hasphysicsbody/.

Relative Scale

Whenever you've needed to set the scale of an entity, you've used one of two ways: adjusting the individual x, y, z components of an entity's `scale` value or setting the `scale` property all at once

```
<entity>.scale.x = <x scale>
<entity>.scale.y = <y scale>
<entity>.scale.z = <z scale>
```

or

```
<entity>.scale = SIMD3<Float>(<x scale>, <y scale>, <z scale>)
```

When you use either of these formats, you're setting the scale of the entity *relative to its parent*. With one-off models that you're adding to a scene, this works great. If the entity is part of a larger parent collection, however, the scale is going to act in a way you didn't anticipate— most likely making the entity MUCH larger than you were hoping.

To scale an entity that is a child in a collection of entities, you can use the `setScale` function:

```
<entity>.setScale(SIMD3<Float>(<x scale>, <y scale>, <z scale>),
                relativeTo: <entity>)
```

Aside from the slightly different syntax, this variation includes a `relativeTo:` parameter. Usually, when you've encountered `relativeTo`, it's been related to setting the coordinates relative to a specific entity's coordinate system or `nil` for world coordinates. In this case, the *scale* is set relative to a given entity rather than an overall value.

If I want an entity to reduce its size in half each time something happens, I could use this:

```
entity.setScale(SIMD3<Float>(0.5,0.5,0.5), relativeTo: entity)
```

When first called, this sets the entity to half its original size. Calling it again sets the entity to half its size *relative to* its current size—so half of 0.5, or 0.25. Subsequent calls do the same thing, making it half as large each time.

> **TIP** When setting a *SIMD3<Float>* value for an object's *scale*, chances are you want to keep the scale uniform across *x, y,* and *z*. Rather than type the entire three values, you can repeat a single value across each component. Substitute the code *.init(repeating: <value>)* in place of the entire *SIMD3<Float>* declaration, and you've saved yourself some typing.

Absolute Values

In the upcoming project, you're going to be checking objects to see if they are a certain distance away along the different axes. This is simple enough; just check the **absolute value** of the distance. The absolute value, returned by the abs(<value>) function, given a positive number, returns that number as is. Given a negative number, it returns the number without its sign.

abs(-3), for example, is equal to 3. Using absolute values makes it easier to compare distances without having to account for where on an axis they are located. An object a meter in front of you is the same distance away as one a meter behind you.

String Comparisons

You've used string comparisons before, and you'll use them again, but when you need to check whether a string is "sorta" like another one, you can use the `<string>.contains("<substring>")` comparison to offer more "fuzzy" logic.

At its simplest, this enables you to check whether a string is contained within another

```
myName.contains("John")
```

returns `true` if a string variable `myName` contains any value with the name "John." For a case-insensitive comparison, you can combine this with the `lowercase` (or `uppercase`) functions. These take a string value and return the upper or lowercase equivalents:

```
lowercase(myName).contains(lowercase("John"))
```

evaluates as `true` if `myName` contains "JOHN", "jOhn", or any other variation.

REGULAR EXPRESSIONS

If you'd like to match a string against more complex patterns, such as repetition, optional content, or position within another string, you need to turn to **regular expressions** or (**regex**). Regular expressions, which are built into the Swift language, can be very complex, but also very useful. Learn the basics with this convenient Wikipedia page: https://en.wikipedia.org/wiki/Regular_expression. You can get started using them in Swift with the documentation at https://developer.apple.com/documentation/swift/regex.

That's it. You've got everything you need to be able to be able to create the upcoming project on your own. Of course, it's not quite that easy, and we'll work through it together. That said, you should only be seeing code that you've been using throughout the book.

HANDS-ON: SPATIAL SPECIAL

You've been through a ton of hands-on and mini hands-on activities throughout the book. I've started each with an introductory paragraph like this, then a short description of how the project should function. This time, it's going to be different. I give you a quick look at what you're building and then do a more detailed breakdown. For an application of this complexity, you want to have more than a vague idea of how the pieces fit together.

In Spatial Special, you create a game from scratch. It includes a rotating asteroid belt that surrounds the user. The asteroids spin and tumble as they move through their orbits. The user, using a spaceship attached to their hand, can shoot at the asteroids, but in doing so, they cause additional debris fields to appear. By carefully navigating their ship through the asteroids, the user can dock with an orbiting space station, thereby winning the game. Shooting asteroids gains points. Colliding with asteroids causes damage to your ship and reduces your score. Too many collisions, and you lose.

Just typing that sounds like a lot, but I assure you that this is a very manageable project that demonstrates how you can create a fully engaging user experience with what you've learned. **FIGURE 10.6** shows the finished project.

FIGURE 10.6 Spatial Special: an asteroid-shootin', space station-dockin' experience

So how will you create this project? Using components, systems, collisions, a hand tracker, and a tad of old-fashioned cleverness. Let's review what this translates to in code.

Project Description

In this project, several areas of functionality need to be addressed during development: working with the visuals and handling collisions, gestures, and score tracking. Let's review each of these now.

Visual Features

The most obvious piece of this project is its visuals. Rather than cramming all the work into a RealityView code block, you use a combination of functions and components to keep things organized.

- **Models:** The project makes use of several asteroid models, Apple's Toy Rocket model, and a space station model stored in the Reality Composer Pro package. These are loaded using a function `loadModels()`.

- **The asteroid belt:** Once asteroid models are loaded, an asteroid belt is generated using the asteroid models and the function `generateAsteroidBelt()`. Each model is cloned, sized, and positioned randomly around the user. Positioning happens by way of Orbit-BehaviorComponent—a component and system that place each asteroid in an animated orbit around the user.

- **The spaceship:** The "hero" object of the game is a toy rocket anchored to the user's wrist using the `HandTracker` class you created a few chapters ago.

- **Shots:** When the user touches their fingers in a typical tap gesture, a `generateShot()` function is invoked that propels a yellow sphere from the front of the ship. This is your ship's weapon.

- **Debris:** If a shot collides with an asteroid, the asteroid "explodes" into smaller pieces that scatter around the area. The explosion and placement of the debris are added in a `generateDebris()` function.

- **A space station:** A space station is added to the scene in an orbit just outside of the asteroid belt. It also contains the `OrbitBehaviorComponent` to set its position and add an orbiting animation.

- **Head sphere:** One of the challenges of this project is making a standard tap gesture work no matter where you're looking. Because a gesture must be detected on an entity, you can ensure that this always works by creating a bit transparent sphere around the user's head with a `generateHeadSphere()` function.

- **Game over:** When a game ends, the objects—except for the space station, which remains slowly rotating—are removed from the scene, and a final game-over message is displayed using a `gameOver()` function. Removing the head sphere is a must; otherwise, the sphere continues to intercept all your taps, so you can't exit the immersive space.

- **Spin:** Objects in space don't just orbit, they also spin. Using a `SpinBehaviorComponent` and corresponding system, you add more animation to the asteroids, spaceship, and space station.

- **Object cleanup:** When an asteroid is shot by the spaceship, its debris expands out from the center. Sometimes this debris may get far enough away that it really shouldn't be included in the scene. The same goes for the shots that miss an asteroid. There's no point in watching them fly forever. A third component, `ObjectCleanupComponent`, monitors entities to see how far away they are and then removes them from the scene if they exceed a maximum distance.

Collision Detection

There are three types of objects in the game: the spaceship, the space station, and, of course, asteroids. The three types of collisions you need to account for and the actions they perform are

- **Ship-asteroid:** When the ship collides with an asteroid, it will take damage and the score is reduced. This is tracked with a `ScoreKeeper` singleton class. Additionally, the ship starts to spin faster and faster on the user's wrist as damage accumulates. If damage hits a predefined limit, `gameOver()` is called and the user loses.

- **Ship–space station:** The ship colliding with the space station is a good thing! It means that the user has won. The score is increased and the `gameOver()` function is called.

- **Shot-asteroid:** If the ship fires a shot via `generateShot()`, and the shot collides with an asteroid, the `generateDebris()` function is called, and the original asteroid and shot are both removed from the scene.

Gestures

A single gesture—`TapGesture`—is needed for the project. When the user taps their fingers, `generateShot()` is called. The user pilots the ship with their hand and activates the firing with the gesture. No other controls are needed.

Scoring

To keep track of the score, damage, and update a status message displayed to the user, you create a singleton `class` named `ScoreKeeper`. You use it with the window created in ContentView. swift to display a live readout of how the user is performing in the game.

Yes, there will be a few odds and ends here and there that occur in addition to these functions, but nothing you haven't seen before. Let's get this show on the road.

Project Setup

You know the drill. Begin by creating a new Mixed Immersive project, naming it **Spatial Special**.

Do not bother editing the ContentView.swift file. You use the window it creates as a status display, so you'll modify it later. Clean out the RealityView code block in the ImmersiveView. swift file so that you have a nice clean slate.

Lastly, set the ContentView to resize appropriately to your content. Update SpatialSpecialApp.swift to include .windowResizability(.contentSize) following the ContentView WindowGroup.

Adding Hand-Tracking

This project uses hand-tracking and the HandTracker class. Because this requires the user's permission, select the Info file in the Xcode Project Navigator and edit it to include the NSHandsTrackingUsageDescription key and an appropriate string value prompt, as shown in **FIGURE 10.7**.

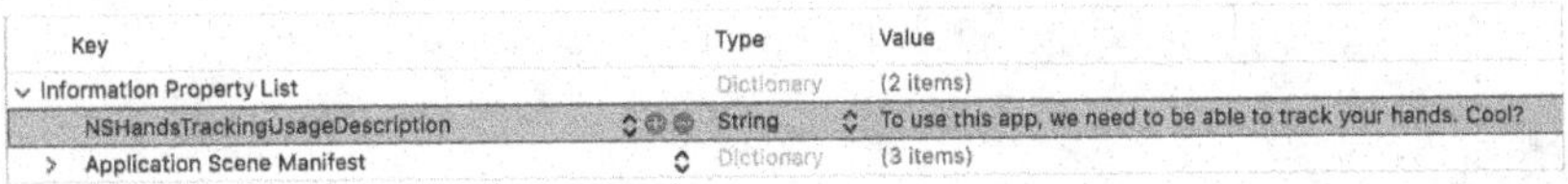

Key	Type	Value
∨ Information Property List	Dictionary	(2 items)
NSHandsTrackingUsageDescription	String	To use this app, we need to be able to track your hands. Cool?
> Application Scene Manifest	Dictionary	(3 items)

FIGURE 10.7 Adding the hand-tracking prompt to the project

Now, drag the HandTracker.swift file from Chapter 8 into the project. I've included it with this chapter's project files so you don't have to go digging for it. Choose to copy items and add the file to the Spatial Special target (all the defaults) when prompted.

Next, edit ImmersiveView.swift to initialize a variable, handTracker, to an instance of the HandTracker class. Place this line immediately inside the ImmersiveView struct:

```
@ObservedObject var handTracker = HandTracker()
```

Lastly, add a task to start running the hand tracker after the closing brace in the RealityView block:

```
.task() {
    await handTracker.startHandTracking()
}
```

Baby steps, but you're making progress!

Adding Model Assets to Reality Composer Pro

The last part of the project setup (before you get into real code) is importing the models that you're going to be using for the asteroids, spaceship, and space station. Open the project's RealityKitContent in Reality Composer Pro.

Located in the included project folder you see several "rock" .usdz files and a spacestation. usdz file. Drag all these into the Project Browser pane of Reality Composer Pro.

Next, using the Content Library, add a copy of the RocketToy1.usdz file (search for "rocket") to the Project Browser by dragging it from the library. Feel free to leave or delete the materials and scenes that Xcode creates by default.

When finished, your Reality Composer Pro Project Browser should resemble **FIGURE 10.8**.

Now you can jump out of "prep" mode and get into the code. I know it seems like a lot, but this is going to go much faster than you expect. You begin with the components, systems, and the singleton ScoreKeeper class. My reasoning for this is simple: These are all standalone pieces of code that can be reused in *any* project. There is nothing about them that is specific to Spatial Special.

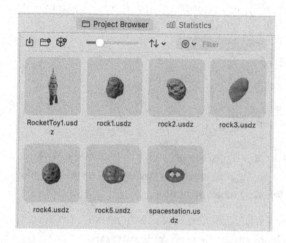

FIGURE 10.8 Adding the model resources to Reality Composer Pro

Creating the Components

I'm reviewing each component one at a time. How you choose to create them—either through Reality Composer Pro or just by adding a file in Xcode—is up to you. I'm choosing to go the Xcode route because it's simpler, and I can just drag the files into the RealityKitContent sources folder later if I want the custom components to appear in the Reality Composer Pro interface.

The Orbit Behavior Component and System

Start with the most complicated component: the orbit behavior component. Choose File, New, File from the menu bar and add a new visionOS Swift file, OrbitBehaviorComponent. swift to the project, as shown in **FIGURE 10.9**.

Open the new swift file in the Xcode editor and get down to business. Start with the "component" part of the component and system. There are four values you want to track:

- **orbitRadius:** The radius of the orbit—that is, how big of a circle the object should track as it is moving around.

- **orbitStart:** A location around the perimeter of a circle, in degrees, where the object in the orbit should be located. This enables you to place objects around an orbit, rather than them just starting in the same place.

- **orbitSpeed:** The speed of the object in the orbit. This is measured in degrees per frame. In other words, for each frame rendered, how many degrees should the object move along the circle?

- **orbitCenter:** A SIMD3<Float> value that contains the x, y, and z coordinates for the location of the center of the orbit.

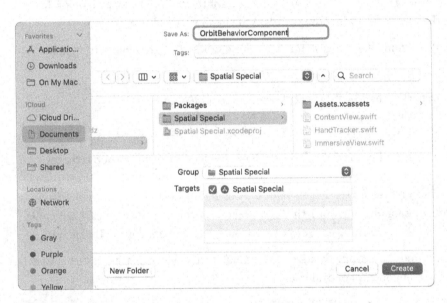

FIGURE 10.9 Adding the new OrbitBehaviorComponent file to the project

Enter the code in **LISTING 10.1** into the OrbitBehaviorComponent.swift file.

LISTING 10.1 Storing Several Parameters for Defining an Orbit

```
import SwiftUI
import RealityKit

public struct OrbitBehaviorComponent: Component, Codable {
    var orbitRadius = 0.0
    var orbitStart = 270.0
    var orbitSpeed = -0.1
    var orbitCenter = SIMD3<Float>(0.0,1.0,0.0)
```

```
    public init() {}
    public init(orbitRadius: Double = 2.0, orbitStart: Double = 270.0,
                orbitSpeed: Double = 0.1,
                orbitCenter: SIMD3<Float> = SIMD3<Float>(0.0,1.0,0.0)) {
        self.orbitRadius = orbitRadius
        self.orbitStart = orbitStart
        self.orbitSpeed = orbitSpeed
        self.orbitCenter = orbitCenter
    }
}
```

The code follows the pattern you established for components. It defines the needed properties and sets them to default values. Why these defaults? Why not? There's nothing special about them except for the orbitCenter. With that value, I want the orbit to be located off of the floor, so I set the y value to 1.0 (in other words, 1 meter above the floor).

Notice that I also include the ability to initialize these values directly when setting up the component:

```
public init(orbitRadius: Double = 2.0, orbitStart: Double = 270.0,
            orbitSpeed: Double = 0.1,
            orbitCenter: SIMD3<Float> = SIMD3<Float>(0.0,1.0,0.0)) { … }
```

This gives you the flexibility to establish the orbit component in one fell swoop rather than accessing each property independently and setting it. Another thing to note is that in defining this initialization, I've *also* set default values. By including default values when defining a parameter (this goes for *any* function), those parameters become optional, meaning I could include orbitRadius and nothing else, or just orbitSpeed, and so on. You get the picture.

If the developer chooses to explicitly state the parameters, those values are copied back to the properties in the component. For example,

```
self.<variable name> = <parameter name>
```

Okay, that was the easy part. Now the system! Add the code in **LISTING 10.2** after the component:

LISTING 10.2 Implementing Orbiting Based on the Component Properties

```
struct OrbitBehaviorSystem: System {
    public init(scene: RealityKit.Scene) {}

    func update(context: SceneUpdateContext) {
        let orbitQuery = EntityQuery(where:
                            .has(OrbitBehaviorComponent.self) )
        let orbits = context.scene.performQuery(orbitQuery)
```

```
        for entity in orbits {
            if var orbitComponent =
                    entity.components[OrbitBehaviorComponent.self] {

                orbitComponent.orbitStart += orbitComponent.orbitSpeed

                let xPosition =
                    orbitComponent.orbitRadius *
                    cos(Angle(degrees: orbitComponent.orbitStart).radians)
                let zPosition = orbitComponent.orbitRadius *
                    sin(Angle(degrees: orbitComponent.orbitStart).radians)

                entity.position.x = Float(xPosition) +
                                    orbitComponent.orbitCenter.x
                entity.position.z = Float(zPosition) +
                                    orbitComponent.orbitCenter.z
                entity.position.y = orbitComponent.orbitCenter.y

                entity.components.set(orbitComponent)
            }
        }
    }
}
```

Like the component portion of the code, this follows the pattern established for systems.
The work is performed in the update function. All the entities in the scene are queried
(orbitQuery) to see if they have the OrbitBehaviorComponent applied. Those that do are
returned as a collection in the orbits variable.

You then loop through orbits, working on one orbiting entity per iteration. The
OrbitBehaviorComponent is retrieved for each object with orbitComponent = orbit.
components[OrbitBehaviorComponent.self], giving a convenient way to access the properties
stored in the component.

The starting place for the object's location around the orbit circle, orbitStart, is incremented
by orbitSpeed. This moves the object orbitSpeed degrees around the circle for each refresh.

Next, the heavy lifting of determining where an object should be placed within an orbit is
executed. The equation of a circle, based on an angle, is

```
<x-location> = <radius> * cos(<angle>)
<z-location> = <radius> * sin(<angle>)
```

NOTE Typically, a circle is defined with x and y coordinates. Because you want the orbit to appear horizontal,
not as a hoop, you set the z-location. If you do want hoops, the assignment would set a y-location.

Translating this into code becomes

```
let xPosition = orbitComponent.orbitRadius *
                cos(Angle(degrees: orbitComponent.orbitStart).radians)
let zPosition = orbitComponent.orbitRadius *
                sin(Angle(degrees: orbitComponent.orbitStart).radians)
```

Once calculated, the position of the `entity` that's orbiting is set using the calculated positions plus any offsets in the `orbitCenter` component property. The y value of the entity's position is the same in `orbitCenter` because it doesn't change during the orbit.

That completes the `OrbitBehaviorComponent`. It was the worst, so the rest is going to fly by.

The Spin Behavior Component and System

To create the `SpinBehaviorComponent`, follow the same steps described for the orbit component. Create another new Swift file, this time naming it SpinBehaviorComponent.swift.

In this component, you only track three values:

- **xRotation:** The rotation in degrees around the x-axis to add during each refresh.

- **yRotation:** The rotation in degrees around the y-axis to add during each refresh.

- **zRotation:** The rotation in degrees around the z-axis to add during each refresh.

You may experience a bit of déjà vu because this component is the same as the example spin component described earlier. The only difference is that it can spin an object around all three axes.

Define the component in the new file as shown in **LISTING 10.3**.

LISTING 10.3 A Spin Component That Tracks Rotation Values on All Three Axes

```
import SwiftUI
import RealityKit

public struct SpinBehaviorComponent: Component, Codable {
    var xRotation = 0.1
    var yRotation = 0.1
    var zRotation = 0.1
    public init() {}
    public init(xRotation: Double = 0.1,
                yRotation: Double = 0.1, zRotation: Double = 0.1) {
        self.xRotation = xRotation
        self.yRotation = yRotation
        self.zRotation = zRotation
    }
}
```

Nothing new to see here folks—just setting up some default values for the rotation properties. If you're wondering, I use Double rather than Float because when you use a floating-point value in your code (for example, **let** number = 1.0) it *is* a double-precision floating-point number unless you specify otherwise. Using Double here prevents you from having to do a bunch of pointless conversions between Float and Double in your code.

Add the system to implement the spin behavior by placing the code in **LISTING 10.4** directly following the spin component:

LISTING 10.4 Rotating the Entities with the SpinBehaviorComponent Added

```
struct SpinBehaviorSystem: System {
    public init(scene: RealityKit.Scene) {}

    func update(context: SceneUpdateContext) {
        let spinQuery = EntityQuery(where:
                        .has(SpinBehaviorComponent.self) )
        let spinners = context.scene.performQuery(spinQuery)

        for spinner in spinners {
            if let spinComponent =
                    spinner.components[SpinBehaviorComponent.self] {
                if spinComponent.xRotation != 0 {
                    spinner.orientation *= simd_quatf(angle:
                    Float(Angle(degrees:
                        spinComponent.xRotation).radians),
                        axis: SIMD3<Float>(1,0,0))
                }
                if spinComponent.yRotation != 0 {
                    spinner.orientation *= simd_quatf(angle:
                    Float(Angle(degrees:
                        spinComponent.yRotation).radians),
                        axis: SIMD3<Float>(0,1,0))
                }
                if spinComponent.zRotation != 0 {
                    spinner.orientation *= simd_quatf(angle:
                    Float(Angle(degrees:
                        spinComponent.zRotation).radians),
                        axis: SIMD3<Float>(0,0,1))
                }
                spinner.components.set(spinComponent)
            }
        }
    }
}
```

The logic is the same as the example spin component reviewed earlier but now for each axis. A query is performed to return all the entities (`spinners`) with a `SpinBehaviorComponent`. For each `spinner` entity in the collection, it rotated `xRotation` degrees around the x-axis, `yRotation` degrees around the y-axis, and `zRotation` degrees around the z-axis.

You're on to the last component you need for the project: the cleanup component.

The Object Cleanup Component and System

In the final component for this chapter, `ObjectCleanupComponent`, you track a single value: `maxDistance`. This is the distance an object is allowed to travel away from the origin point. The system checks each object to see whether it exceeds that distance along any axis. If it does, the object is removed from the scene. For the y-axis, you also add the restriction that no object is allowed to exist with -y coordinates. Rendering things under the floor or ground is a waste of processing power.

Set up a new `ObjectCleanupComponent.swift` file within your project and add the component code, as in **LISTING 10.5**.

LISTING 10.5 A Simple Cleanup Component

```
import SwiftUI
import RealityKit

public struct ObjectCleanupComponent: Component, Codable {
    var maxDistance : Float = 5.0
    public init() {}
    public init(maxDistance: Float) {
        self.maxDistance = maxDistance
    }
}
```

If the component is initialized without a `maxDistance` parameter set, it defaults to 5.0 meters from the origin.

The system is equally simple. Grab all the objects with the object cleanup component and get their position in world space. If any object's x, y, or z position values are greater than `maxDistance`, it's outta here (that is, you call `.removeFromParent()`)

Enter **LISTING 10.6** after the `ObjectCleanupComponent` definition.

LISTING 10.6 Comparing an Object's World Position to the maxDistance

```
struct ObjectCleanupSystem: System {
    public init(scene: RealityKit.Scene) {}
```

```
func update(context: SceneUpdateContext) {
    let objectQuery = EntityQuery(where:
                        .has(ObjectCleanupComponent.self) )
    let objects = context.scene.performQuery(objectQuery)

    for object in objects {
        if let cleanupComponent =
                object.components[ObjectCleanupComponent.self] {
            let position = object.position(relativeTo: nil)
            let maxDistance = cleanupComponent.maxDistance
            if abs(position.x) > maxDistance ||
                abs(position.y) > maxDistance ||
                abs(position.z) > maxDistance ||
                position.y < 0 {
                object.removeFromParent()
            }
        }
    }
}
```

Notice that you use the absolute value function here (abs) because you're looking at the object's position relative to the origin (0,0,0). An object 5 meters away on the right is reported with a position of position.x==5.0. If it is an equal distance away on the left, it is position. x==-5.0. In both cases, it's 5.0 meters away, so you don't care about the negative sign.

All of the components are finished and ready to be used. It's time to move on to one other reusable chunk of code: the ScoreKeeper singleton.

Creating the ScoreKeeper Singleton

The ScoreKeeper singleton class manages three values that you want to be able to access anywhere in an application. These are set as @Published variables and the class itself as Observable; you want the views containing these values to update when the value changes:

- **score:** The user's score in a game

- **hits:** The number of hits (damage) a user has taken

- **message:** A status message that can be updated in the game at any time

The score and hits properties are initialized as integers with the value 0, whereas message is a string that just reads "Play!"

Crack your knuckles and settle in. There's some typing ahead. Create another new Swift file, the same as the components. This time, name it **ScoreKeeper** and add the code shown in
LISTING 10.7.

```swift
import Foundation

class ScoreKeeper: ObservableObject  {
    static let shared = ScoreKeeper()
    @Published var score: Int = 0
    @Published var hits: Int = 0
    @Published var message: String = "Play!"
}
```

Okay, I said there was *some* typing ahead, not that it would be long. The ScoreKeeper class is now finished. You can now work your way through the implementation of Spatial Special itself. You build the needed functions (see "Project Description") as you get to them so as not to break the flow of the logic.

Let's begin.

Initializing the Variables

You have several pieces of information that needs to be tracked throughout the project: a hand tracker, a score keeper, collisions, asteroids, ships, and more. You need these through-out your code in the ImmersiveView file, so add the following initializers directly after the ImmersiveView struct:

```swift
@ObservedObject var scoreKeeper = ScoreKeeper.shared
@State private var sceneCollision: EventSubscription?
@State private var shipCollision: EventSubscription?
@State private var asteroidBelt = Entity()
@State private var asteroids : [Entity] = []
@State private var spaceship = Entity()
@State private var handAnchor =  Entity()
@State private var headSphere = ModelEntity()
@State private var headAnchor = AnchorEntity(.head)
@State private var spaceStation = Entity()
@State private var shots = Entity()
```

While the names are largely self-explanatory, I'll quickly define each so that there is no confusion later on.

- handTracker: An instance of the hand-tracking data provider class.

- scoreKeeper: A reference to the ScoreKeeper's shared singleton instance.

- sceneCollision: A subscription to all the "Began" collision events within the scene. This is used for handling all but the ship-asteroid collisions.

- **shipCollision**: A subscription to the scene's "Ended" collision events, used for ship-asteroid collisions.

- **asteroidBelt**: An entity that holds all of the asteroids added to the scene.

- **asteroids**: An array of the different asteroid entities you can add to the scene. You use this to randomly choose an asteroid, clone it, and then add it to the scene.

- **spaceship**: The spaceship attached to the user's hand.

- **handAnchor**: The hand anchor that holds the spaceship.

- **headSphere**: A sphere ModelEntity that wraps around the user's head to help detect taps.

- **headAnchor**: An AnchorEntity targeting the user's head to which the headSphere is added.

- **spaceStation**: The space station that orbits the asteroid belt.

- **shots**: More than one shot can be fired at a time, so all are managed as children of this entity.

Note that while I could just state that a variable *will* hold an entity (or whatever) like this

```
@State private var headSphere : ModelEntity?
```

I've instead chosen to initialize them to empty entities where possible. This enables you to test the code during implementation because the variables are initialized to *something*, even if it isn't what they will eventually reference.

Registering the Components and Systems

The next step is to register all the components and systems within the RealityView code block. Enter the following lines at the top of the RealityView block:

```
OrbitBehaviorComponent.registerComponent()
OrbitBehaviorSystem.registerSystem()
SpinBehaviorComponent.registerComponent()
SpinBehaviorSystem.registerSystem()
ObjectCleanupComponent.registerComponent()
ObjectCleanupSystem.registerSystem()
```

Now the components are ready to use with any entities you create.

Initializing the Singleton

The scoreKeeper singleton is next on this list. But wait! The code for the singleton already initializes its values to perfectly acceptable values. That's true, but it does it *once*. When the game is running and is keeping score, those values change. If the game ends and the user decides to *restart* the game, the values need to be initialized again.

Add these lines next:

```
scoreKeeper.message = "Play!"
scoreKeeper.hits = 0
scoreKeeper.score = 0
```

Setting Up a Hand Anchor

You couldn't fully initialize handAnchor at the start because RealityView hadn't loaded yet. Thus, the .task that starts hand tracking hadn't executed. You can do it now, in the RealityView block, targeting the wrist on the user's right hand:

```
handAnchor = handTracker.rightHandParts[.wrist]!
```

If you don't recall the data structure set up by the HandTracker class, review **Chapter 8** for the implementation details.

Adding and Anchoring the Head Sphere

You're breezing right along, but you've just hit the first function you need to create. This function generates the headSphere and adds it to the headAnchor. Remember that you need this so that any tap gestures, regardless of whether the user is looking at something, can be detected. You *could* add this code directly in the RealityView code block, but the goal is to keep things a tad cleaner and more modular. Add the function in **LISTING 10.7** directly after the RealityView block.

LISTING 10.7 Creating a Head-Anchored Sphere

```
private func generateHeadSphere() {
    headSphere = ModelEntity(mesh: .generateSphere(radius: 1.0))
    let headSphereMaterial = UnlitMaterial(color: .clear)
    headSphere.model?.materials = [headSphereMaterial]
    headSphere.generateCollisionShapes(recursive: true)
    headSphere.components.
        set(InputTargetComponent(allowedInputTypes: [.indirect]))
    headSphere.position.y = 0.5
    headAnchor.addChild(headSphere)
}
```

The function defines the headSphere model entity as a sphere with a one-meter radius and clear unlit material. Collision shapes are generated for the sphere (so it can detect gestures). An indirect InputTargetComponent is also added for gesture support. The sphere is positioned up half a meter and added to the headAnchor.

If you *just* add the sphere to headAnchor without setting a position first, you probably find it to be too low and not covering your head. How can you tell? Set the color to something other than .clear (such as .red) and see how the sphere "fits" for you.

Of course, for the sphere to be part of the scene, the function must be called and the headAnchor added to the content. Return to the top of the RealityView code block and add the following lines after the handAnchor assignment:

```
generateHeadSphere()
content.add(headAnchor)
```

Congrats! You've added the first entity to the scene. It's the most boring entity possible, but it's now out of the way, so you can move on to more exciting things.

Loading the Models

The next step, before you can display anything beyond an entirely invisible head sphere, is to load the rest of the models that you use in Spatial Special, specifically the asteroids, the spaceship, and the space station. Add another new function, loadModels following the generateHeadSphere code, as shown in **LISTING 10.8**.

LISTING 10.8 Loading the Asteroid, Spaceship, and Space Station Models

```
private func loadModels() async {
    for count in 1...30 {
        if let asteroid = try? await
            Entity(named: "rock\(count)", in: realityKitContentBundle) {
            asteroid.generateCollisionShapes(recursive: true)
            asteroid.children[0].name="asteroid"
            asteroids.append(asteroid)
        } else {
            continue
        }
    }
    if let spaceStationEntity = try? await
        Entity(named: "spacestation", in: realityKitContentBundle) {
        spaceStationEntity.generateCollisionShapes(recursive: true)
        spaceStationEntity.children[0].name="spacestation"
        spaceStationEntity.components.set(
            OrbitBehaviorComponent(orbitRadius: 3.5, orbitSpeed: 0.2,
                                   orbitCenter: SIMD3<Float>(0.0,1.5,0.0)))
        spaceStationEntity.components.set(
            SpinBehaviorComponent(xRotation: 0.1,yRotation: 0.5))
        spaceStationEntity.scale=SIMD3<Float>(0.03,0.03,0.03)
        spaceStation = spaceStationEntity
    }
```

```
if let spaceshipEntity = try? await
    Entity(named: "RocketToy1", in: realityKitContentBundle) {
    spaceshipEntity.generateCollisionShapes(recursive: true)
    spaceshipEntity.children[0].name="spaceship"
    spaceshipEntity.position.y = 0.1
    spaceshipEntity.position.x = -0.15
    spaceshipEntity.orientation = simd_quatf(angle:
                    Float(Angle(degrees: 120.0).radians), axis:
                    SIMD3<Float>(0,0,1))
    spaceship = spaceshipEntity
    handAnchor.addChild(spaceship)
    }
}
```

This function definition includes the async keyword (indicating it can run asynchronously) because the functions to load the entities are also asynchronous, so the overall function must match. This is easy to miss, but Xcode complains if you don't added it.

The Asteroids

The initial for loop populates the asteroids[] array in a rather clever way (if I dare say so myself). The count value during the loop is set to integers between 1 and 30, corresponding to rock1, rock2, rock3, and so on. To generate the unique name string of each rock entity and attempt to load it, I use rock\(count) as the string for the name. The \(count) syntax performs a substitution for the value of count, so the loop effectively tries to load up to 30 rocks. There are only 5 included with the exercise, but you can add up to 25 more just by importing the model to Reality Composer Pro and setting the name to a different number in the sequence— for example, rock6, rock7, and so on.

Assuming the rock model is found, it's stored in the constant asteroid and collision shapes are generated. The name property of the entity's ModelEntity (asteroid.children[0]) is set to "asteroid" so you can easily tell what object you're dealing with in collisions. Lastly, the asteroid entity is appended to the asteroids[] array. This will become a very useful way of storing the entities when you need to pick one randomly in the (very) near future.

The Space Station

After the asteroid array is created, you load the space station model into spaceStationEntity, calculate the collision shapes, and set the ModelEntity name to "spacestation" (again, for handling collisions).

The OrbitBehaviorComponent is added so that the space station slowly orbits 3.5 meters away from the origin point (where the user is initially standing) at a height of 1.5 meters. The space station moves 0.2 degrees along its orbit for each frame that is rendered. The

`SpinBehaviorComponent` is also added with a slow rotation around the x-axis (0.1) and a faster rotation around the y-axis (0.5).

The `spaceStationEntity` is scaled to a fraction of its original size (which is *huge*) so that it fits properly in the scene. Finally, `spaceStation` is assigned the value of `spaceStationEntity`, making it available throughout the `ImmersiveView` structure.

> **NOTE** If you're questioning why I didn't use *.init(repeating: 0.03)* to set *spaceStationEntity.scale*, it's because the amount of typing it would have saved me is next to nothing. It makes more sense to use this when you've got the contents of a variable you want to use in a *SIMD3<Float>* definition.

The Spaceship

You follow a similar process for the spaceship. The model is loaded into `spaceshipEntity` from the RocketToy1.usda file. Collision shapes are generated, and the position and rotation are adjusted so that the rocket looks okay attached to the user's wrist. How do I know these values look okay? Trial and error. It took some tweaking everything to make it look just right.

The spaceship is assigned the value of `spaceshipEntity` and is added to the `handAnchor` you've already created.

This takes care of almost everything. As a last step, add a new line that calls the `loadModels` function and waits for it to complete. This should be added to the RealityView block following the addition of the `headAnchor`:

```
await loadModels()
```

ALL THESE NUMBERS? WHERE DO YOU GET THEM?!

The numbers you see when defining the different entities are what I call "values John found aesthetically pleasing." There's no deep math going on; it's just a matter of trying a value and seeing how it looks when the application is running. You may want to change them to something else entirely, and that's perfectly fine!

Generating the Asteroid Belt

Oooh! Guess what time it is?? Time to generate the stars (errr... asteroids) of the show: the asteroid belt. This is where things start getting fun because you can see the project coming together. The asteroid belt is generated through a function `generateAsteroidBelt`. The function takes a single integer parameter (`count`) and executes a loop to select a random asteroid model, clone it, size it randomly, and then add randomly configured `OrbitBehaviorComponent` and `SpinBehaviorComponent` components. Each asteroid created is added to the `asteroidBelt` entity so that they can be managed as a single group.

You've already entered the largest code listing in the project when loading the models, so it's just going to get simpler(ish) from here. Enter the new function, `generateAsteroidBelt` (shown in **LISTING 10.9**) following the previous two functions.

LISTING 10.9 Randomly Generating Asteroids with Orbit and Spin Components

```
private func generateAsteroidBelt(count: Int) {
    for _ in 1...count {
        let asteroid = asteroids[Int.random(in:
                    0...(asteroids.count-1))].clone(recursive: true)
        asteroid.scale = SIMD3<Float>(.init(repeating:
                                    Float.random(in: 0.01...0.03)))
        asteroid.generateCollisionShapes(recursive: true)
        asteroid.components.set(SpinBehaviorComponent(
                    xRotation: Double.random(in: -2.0...2.0),
                    yRotation: Double.random(in: -2.0...2.0),
                    zRotation: Double.random(in: -2.0...2.0)))
        asteroid.components.set(OrbitBehaviorComponent(
                    orbitRadius: Double.random(in: 1.5...2.75),
                    orbitStart: Double.random(in: 1.0...360),
                    orbitSpeed: Double.random(in: -0.75...0.75),
                    orbitCenter: SIMD3<Float>(0.0,Float.random(in:
                                0.5...2.5),0.0)))
        asteroidBelt.addChild(asteroid)
    }
}
```

The function loops from 1 to count. In each iteration of the loop, an asteroid is chosen randomly from the `asteroids` array. How is the choice made randomly? By indexing into the array with a random integer. A count of the values stored in an array is accessed with the code: `<array name>.count`. Using that, I can select a random asteroid like this:

```
<random asteroid> = asteroids[Int.random(in: 0...(asteroids.count-1))]
```

Because an array starts at index 0, you must subtract 1 from the count of elements; otherwise, the random number generation may produce an index 1 higher than the total number of elements stored in the array.

Once you've indexed into the array appropriately with a random integer, you use clone to generate a copy of the chosen asteroid, which is stored in `asteroid`. Next, the asteroid is scaled down a random amount. Like the space station, the asteroid models are huge.

Spin and Orbit behavior components are added using random values for each of the component properties. The most important random properties are the `orbitStart` value, which defines where the object is starting (and later, where it is) in the orbit, the `orbitRadius`, and the `orbitCenter`. Generating a random angle between 1 and 360 degrees for the `orbitStart` places objects all around the user. Randomizing `orbitRadius` varies the width of the orbits—meaning some are closer to the user and some farther away—1.5 to 2.75 meters. Lastly, generating a random y value for the `orbitCenter` ensures that asteroids appear at varying heights—from 0.5 meters above the floor up to 2.5 meters.

As each `asteroid` is generated, it is added as a child to `asteroidBelt`. This can mean only one thing: It's time to add `asteroidBelt` to the content!

Add two lines to the end of the RealityView code you've entered so far—one to call the generateAsteroids function and another to add the resulting `asteroidBelt` to the content:

```
generateAsteroidBelt(count: 75)
content.add(asteroidBelt)
```

While you're at it, add the rest of the objects you need as well:

```
content.add(spaceStation)
content.add(handAnchor)
content.add(shots)
```

This adds the orbiting space station (`spaceStation`), the spaceship (by way of `handAnchor`), and the entity that will eventually hold the shots fired by the ship (`shots`). That's it for adding to the scene's content.

If you run the project, you see that it now generates and displays 75 tumbling asteroids moving around your position along with an orbiting space station and a spaceship anchored to your wrist. It looks pretty cool, so give it a try. Unfortunately, looks aren't everything. You still need to add the final pieces to enable interaction, starting with the gesture and code that makes the spaceship shoot.

Creating the Ship's Weapon

The spaceship in Spatial Special is armed with the latest and greatest "yellow sphere thrower" system. Asteroids stand no chance against these yellow metallic spheres! When the user performs a tap gesture, the `generateShot()` function is called.

This function serves three purposes:

First, it generates a shot (`ModelEntity`) with a sphere mesh. Second, it positions the shot in front of the spaceship model. Third, it creates an impulse force on shot that propels it away from the spaceship.

Positioning the Shot

When initially working on this application, I was having trouble applying transformations to get the shot to appear properly aligned with the spaceship. It eventually struck me that, because I have a handAnchor, I don't have to do anything special—just add the shot to the handAnchor and poof, it's aligned.

Once anchored, I can make a few adjustments to make sure the ball is properly oriented such that it can receive an impulse force along the x-axis and shoot into space (or your living room.) Finally, I remove the sphere from the handAnchor, apply the force, and away it goes.

Enter generateShot(), shown in **LISTING 10.10**, alongside the other functions you've added.

LISTING 10.10 Generating a Shot and Propelling It away from the Ship

```
private func generateShot() {
    let shot = ModelEntity(mesh: .generateSphere(radius: 0.02))
    let material = SimpleMaterial(color: .yellow, isMetallic: true)
    shot.model?.materials = [material]
    shot.components.set(PhysicsBodyComponent(mode: .dynamic))
    shot.physicsBody?.isAffectedByGravity = false
    shot.generateCollisionShapes(recursive: true)
    shot.name = "shot"
    shot.orientation = simd_quatf(angle: Float(Angle(degrees:
                       30.0).radians), axis: SIMD3<Float>(0,0,1))
    shot.position.x = -0.375
    handAnchor.addChild(shot)
    shot.removeFromParent(preservingWorldTransform: true)
    shot.components.set(ObjectCleanupComponent(maxDistance: 4.5))
    shot.applyLinearImpulse(SIMD3<Float>(-3.5,0.0,0.0), relativeTo: shot)
    shots.addChild(shot, preservingWorldTransform: true)
}
```

There's nothing unusual in the preparation of the shot ModelEntity, but it is somewhat extensive. A small sphere (shot) is created, and a yellow metallic material is applied.

For a force to have any impact on the shot, a PhysicsBodyComponent is required (and added) to shot. Gravity's effect on shot is disabled (because this is supposed to be outer space!).

Next, collision shapes are generated for the shot, and its name is set to "shot."

I ended up tweaking the orientation with a small rotation around the z-axis and set the position to -0.375 meters on the x-axis (out past the tip of the ship). Huh? Wouldn't negative x be to the right? Not here. You're about to add the ship to a hand anchor, so the positioning is within that entity's coordinate system.

Recall that with hands, the axes for anchor points are all over the place. In this situation, the negative x-axis happens to point along the back of the hand, thus the weirdness in the positioning.

The main anchor point axes are described in **"Hand Target Anchors" in Chapter 7.**

Once positioned and added to the `handAnchor`, `shot` is immediately removed from the anchor, preserving its location. The `ObjectCleanupComponent` is applied with a maximum distance of 4.5 meters; shots automatically disappear after they've exceeded this distance.

The `shot` is propelled forward with a 3.5 newton-second impulse force along the `shot`'s negative x-axis.

Lastly, `shot` is added as a child to the `shots` entity. You already added this to the `RealityView` content, so everything is ready to go, aside from not having any means of firing the gun.

Adding the Gesture

To enable the firing of the ship's weapon, you need a tap gesture that calls `generateShot()`. Add the code for a single tap gesture detector after the `.task` block at the end of `RealityView`:

```
.gesture(
    TapGesture(count: 1)
        .targetedToAnyEntity()
        .onEnded({ event in
            generateShot()
        })
)
```

Start the application again, aim your spaceship, and try the tap gesture. Each tap should result in a shot coming from the ship extending out past the asteroid belt, then disappearing from view.

The final missing logic is entirely related to collisions. You're in the home stretch, so let's finish this thing off.

Handling Ship-Asteroid Collisions

Earlier in the chapter, you saw that you can subscribe to collision events and react when two objects start or end a collision. It's time to put that into practice with the three collision types I identified at the start of this project.

The first collision type is the spaceship with an asteroid. This interaction causes damage to the ship. If that damage exceeds a limit, the game ends with a call to `gameOver()`. You start with this function because collision handling is dependent on its existence.

Implementing Game Over

Whether a game ends in a win or a loss, the gameOver() function works in the same way. It removes the hand and head anchors and stops the spaceStation from orbiting by removing the OrbitBehaviorComponent.

To clear out the asteroids, it loops through the child entities in asteroidBelt. For each asteroid, a PhysicsBodyComponent is added along with an ObjectCleanupComponent, and gravity is turned on. The effect is that the asteroids fall to the ground and disappear. It's a dramatic end to the game.

> **NOTE** I chose to leave the space station in place and rotating when the game ends. It's intended as a callback to old arcade games where the screen might freeze except for one object that keeps animating in some manner.

Add the gameOver() function, shown in **LISTING 10.11**, after the end of the other functions.

LISTING 10.11 Ending the Game and Removing the Entities

```
private func gameOver() {
    headAnchor.removeFromParent()
    handAnchor.removeFromParent()
    spaceStation.components.remove(OrbitBehaviorComponent.self)
    for object in asteroidBelt.children {
        if object.children.count > 0 {
            if let asteroidEntity =
                    object.children[0] as? ModelEntity {
                        asteroidEntity.components.set(
                        PhysicsBodyComponent(mode: .dynamic))
                asteroidEntity.components.set(
                    ObjectCleanupComponent(maxDistance: 3.5))
                asteroidEntity.physicsBody?.isAffectedByGravity = true
            }
        }
    }
}
```

PhysicsBodyComponents can only be attached to model entities, which is why you use .children[0] to grab the first child of each asteroid (its ModelEntity) and store it in asteroidEntity. You can then work with asteroidEntity, adding the physics body, and applying gravity.

You don't even need to worry about removing the asteroids from the view because the ObjectCleanupComponent takes care of that automatically.

Detecting the Ship-Asteroid Collision

When a ship collides with an asteroid, more happens than just calling gameOver()—especially if the game *isn't* over. The collision processing code must increment the hits variable in the scoreKeeper singleton. To add insult to injury, it also reduces scorekeeper.score by 2.

The collision must also show damage to the spaceship. I found that an effective and simple way to do that is to rotate the ship increasingly quickly along its y-axis with a tiny rotation along the x-axis to add wobble. The faster it spins, the more trouble you're in.

Lastly, if the damage of the ship becomes too high (hits>10) the gameOver() function is called and the game ends.

I've chosen to implement the shipCollision event subscription for when a collision event has *ended*. I've experienced multiple collision *began* events when first colliding with an object. Using the ended event type helps prevent unnecessary damage from being registered.

Enter the shipCollision event subscription code found in **LISTING 10.12** to the end of the RealityView code block.

LISTING 10.12 Processing Ship-Asteroid Collisions

```
shipCollision = content.subscribe(to:
                CollisionEvents.Ended.self, on: nil) { event in
    if (event.entityA.name.contains("rocket") ||
            event.entityB.name.contains("rocket")) &&
            (event.entityA.name == "asteroid" ||
            event.entityB.name == "asteroid") {
        scoreKeeper.hits += 1
        scoreKeeper.score -= 2
        spaceship.components.set(SpinBehaviorComponent(xRotation: 0.2,
                                yRotation:Double(scoreKeeper.hits)))
        if scoreKeeper.hits>=10 {
            scoreKeeper.message = "Game Over! You Lost."
            gameOver()
        }
    }
}
```

The code, at first glance, seems obvious. If a collision between the rocket and an asteroid occurs, the scoreKeeper hits and score properties are updated and a SpinBehaviorComponent is set with a y-rotation speed based on the number of hits the spaceship has received.

If the number of hits exceeds 10, the code sets the message Game Over! You Lost. for the user and ends the game by calling gameOver().

At a second glance, you may find that I've glossed over something quite annoying. For whatever reason, I'm unable to assign a name to the `ModelEntity` child of the spaceship entity. Because of this, I'm unable to refer to the toy rocket model as "spaceship"; instead, it's identified by a string that includes the word "rocket." I can work around this by checking each of the entities involved in the collision to see if the name contains "rocket" If it does, the spaceship (also known as "rocket") has been hit.

Perhaps more annoying, I'm unable to subscribe to events involving only the spaceship entity, so the `shipCollision` subscription monitors *all* ended collision events on *everything* (on: `nil`). It isn't efficient, but it works.

WHY CAN'T I NAME THE ROCKET?

Oh, believe me, I've called it a few names during the project. I discovered the problem with the spaceship name by trying to ram it into asteroids, but nothing would happen. To see what was going on, I printed the names of the entities involved in the collision. One was "asteroid" and the other "rocket_toy_tin_1_base_realistic_lo0."

Using the hierarchy inspector in Reality Composer Pro (the lower-right corner pane, visible in **FIGURE 10.10**) you can drill down to find the model entity that is being detected in the collision. You can see that the hierarchy is extensive—not just a single layer—so to actually set the name, I'd need to work with the child of a child of a child... and that's just not worth the effort.

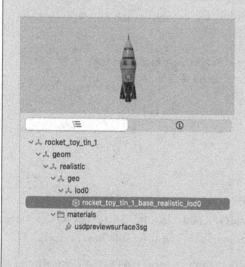

FIGURE 10.10 The toy rocket has many layers before you find the model itself.

Try running the application again and pilot your ship into a few asteroids. When each collision ends, you'll notice that the spaceship is rotating faster. When you exceed 10 hits, the gameOver() function runs and the objects, aside from the space station, are removed.

Handling Spaceship–Space Station Collisions

The second type of collision that you detect is between the spaceship and spaceStation entities. When this occurs, scoreKeeper.score gets updated with an additional 100 bonus points and the message Docked! You Win! is set for the user in scoreKeeper.message. Lastly, gameOver() is called to close out the game.

The detection and reaction of this collision occurs in the sceneCollision event subscription at the *began* event—again targeted to all entities in the scene.

> **NOTE** This same subscription also handles shots hitting asteroids—thus, the generalized *sceneCollision* name.

Add the code in **LISTING 10.13** after the previous event subscription.

LISTING 10.13 Processing Spaceship–Space Station Collisions

```
sceneCollision = content.subscribe(to: CollisionEvents.Began.self,
                              on: nil) { event in
    if (event.entityA.name.contains("rocket") ||
        event.entityB.name.contains("rocket")) &&
        (event.entityA.name == "spacestation" ||
        event.entityB.name == "spacestation") {
          scoreKeeper.score += 100
          scoreKeeper.message = "Docked! You win!"
          gameOver()
    }
}
```

Once again, I've had to match against the string "rocket" to determine if the spaceship has been involved in the collision.

You've reached the last collision type and the last function you need in the code. The light at the end of the tunnel is *not* a train, I swear.

Handling Shot-Asteroid Collisions

Don't get me wrong: The other two collision types are important, but they hardly bring the same satisfaction as blowing up giant space rockets.

When a shot collides with an asteroid, you need to do something dramatic. The generateDebris() function's sole purpose is to make an explosionlike effect, scattering debris into the environment.

Implementing Debris Generation

This function generates a random number (between 2 and 8) of "mini asteroids" using the same randomized asteroid selection as the `generateAsteroidBelt()` function.

Each of these entities is called a `shardEntity` and is randomly located near the site of the collision based on the shot's position (`shot.position`). The `ModelEntity` of each `shardEntity` is retrieved with `.children[0]` and assigned to the variable `shard`. Using `shard`, a physics body is applied, gravity is turned off, and moderate angular and linear dampening is configured. An impulse force in a random direction is applied to each `shard`, making it fly away from the asteroid that was struck. They fly for a short while, stop, and begin spinning—by way of a `SpinBehaviorComponent`.

The `generateDebris` function requires two input parameters: the `shot` that was fired and the asteroid that was struck. These entities are necessary to place the debris in the scene and to create shards that are smaller in size, relative to the destroyed asteroid.

After a `shardEntity` and its associated `shard` are fully configured, the `shardEntity` is added to the `asteroidBelt` entity and displayed to the user. Although the shards don't have the same orbit component as other asteroids, they otherwise behave like asteroids—reacting to shots and ship collisions as expected.

Enter **LISTING 10.14** along with the other functions. This is the last function needed in the project!

LISTING 10.14 Generating Shards That Radiate from the Collision Point

```
private func generateDebris(shot: Entity, asteroid: Entity) {
    for _ in 1...Int.random(in: 2...8) {
        let shardEntity = asteroids[Int.random(in:
                    0...(asteroids.count-1))].clone(recursive: true)
        let shard = shardEntity.children[0] as! ModelEntity
        shardEntity.position = shot.position
        shardEntity.setScale(SIMD3<Float>(0.5,0.5,0.5),
                    relativeTo: asteroid)
        shardEntity.setPosition(SIMD3<Float>(
                    Float.random(in: -0.1...0.1),
                    Float.random(in: -0.1...0.1),
                    Float.random(in: -0.1...0.1)), relativeTo: shot)
        shard.components.set(PhysicsBodyComponent(mode: .dynamic))
        shard.physicsBody?.isAffectedByGravity = false
        shard.applyLinearImpulse(SIMD3<Float>(
                    Float.random(in: -0.0003...0.0003),
                    Float.random(in: -0.0003...0.0003),
                    Float.random(in: -0.0003...0.0003)),
                    relativeTo: nil)
        shard.physicsBody?.angularDamping = 1.0
        shard.physicsBody?.linearDamping = 4.0
```

```
            shard.components.set(SpinBehaviorComponent(
                    xRotation: Double.random(in: -2.0...2.0),
                    yRotation: Double.random(in: -2.0...2.0),
                    zRotation: Double.random(in: -2.0...2.0)))
        asteroidBelt.addChild(shardEntity)
    }
}
```

The values for scaling, positioning, the impulse force, and the spin behavior component are all randomized. This means that each explosion will be different from the last. Not bad for about a dozen lines of code (counted without the wrapping, mind you.)

Detecting the Shot-Asteroid Collision

To finish up the collision detection, you add another if-then statement to the existing sceneCollision subscription in **LISTING 10.13**. This statement looks for collisions between entities named "shot" and "asteroid" (no darn "rocket" to worry about this time!). If a collision is detected, the code assigns the entity containing the shot to a variable shot, and the asteroid entity to asteroid. These are passed to the generateDebris() function, which does its magic and creates new debris that the user must navigate around.

In addition to creating the debris field, the scoreKeeper.score value is incremented, and both the entities involved in the collision (the shot and the asteroid) are removed from their respective entity collections.

Update the code in **Listing 10.13** to add this new functionality. The completed event subscription is shown in **LISTING 10.14**.

LISTING 10.14 The Completed Event Subscription Logic

```
sceneCollision = content.subscribe(to: CollisionEvents.Began.self,
                                   on: nil) { event in
    if (event.entityA.name.contains("rocket") ||
        event.entityB.name.contains("rocket")) &&
        (event.entityA.name == "spacestation" ||
        event.entityB.name == "spacestation") {
      scoreKeeper.score += 100
      scoreKeeper.message = "Docked! You win!"
      gameOver()
    }

    if (event.entityA.name == "shot" ||
        event.entityB.name == "shot") &&
        (event.entityA.name == "asteroid" ||
        event.entityB.name == "asteroid") {
      var asteroid : Entity!
      var shot : Entity!
```

```
        if event.entityA.name == "asteroid" {
            asteroid = event.entityA
            shot = event.entityB
        } else {
            asteroid = event.entityB
            shot = event.entityA
        }

        generateDebris(shot: shot, asteroid: asteroid)
        scoreKeeper.score += 1
        shot.removeFromParent()
        asteroid.removeFromParent()
    }
}
```

Run the application again and give all the features a try. Shot asteroids, try to dodge them, dock with space station—you know, *play the game*. Everything should function, but there are still two things that need to be added so that it is feature-complete: cleaning up the scene and creating a scoreboard.

Cleaning Up the Immersive Space

Like many other immersive spaces, you need to do some cleanup when the user exits the space. Implement the following .onDisappear modifier for RealityView after the .gesture modifier:

```
.onDisappear{
    shots.children.removeAll()
    asteroidBelt.children.removeAll()
    spaceStation.removeFromParent()
}
```

This removes the remaining entities that hadn't already been removed in the gameOver() function.

> **TIP** In general, if I'm working with a collection of entities, I remove the children from the entity (*children. removeAll()*). If it's just a single entity or anchor (such as *spaceStation*), I use *removeFromParent()*.

Adding the Score Screen

You've diligently set and updated scoreKeeper.score as needed throughout the project, as well as the number of asteroid "hits" the spaceship has suffered. Unfortunately, these don't just appear somewhere on their own; you need to configure the application to display them.

You use the ContentView window for this purpose. Before you can add the values, however, the ContentView must be able to access the ScoreKeeper shared singleton. In ContentView. swift, immediately after the ContentView struct begins, define a scoreKeeper variable to access the singleton. This is identical to what you did in ImmersiveView:

```
@ObservedObject var scoreKeeper = ScoreKeeper.shared
```

Finally (and I mean this sincerely), update the ContentView content VStack to include an introductory message along with the scoreKeeper score, hits, and message properties.

My SwiftUI code for ContentView looks like this, but you can style yours however you'd like:

```
VStack {
    Text("Welcome to Spatial Special")
        .font(.largeTitle)
        .padding(40)
    Text("Avoid contact with the asteroids. Shoot them,
        but beware of debris.")
    Text("Pilot your ship through the asteroid field
        to reach the space station.")
    Text("\(scoreKeeper.message)")
        .font(.largeTitle)
        .padding(20)
        .foregroundStyle(.blue)
    Text("Score: \(scoreKeeper.score)")
        .font(.largeTitle)
        .padding(20)
        .foregroundStyle(.green)
    Text("Damage: \(scoreKeeper.hits)")
        .font(.largeTitle)
        .padding(20)
        .foregroundStyle(.red)
Toggle("Play Game", isOn: $showImmersiveSpace)
    .toggleStyle(.button)
    .padding(.top, 50)
//In upcoming versions of visionOS templates, the preceding 3 lines
//will be replaced with ToggleImmersiveSpaceButton()
}
```

You. Are. Done. Play the game, drop the mic, do a dance. It's time to celebrate. You've gone from creating a few simple 3D layers to a complex animated application in just 10 chapters. It's an accomplishment!

SUMMARY

This chapter used many tools and techniques that you've been learning since you began the book. By using custom components and systems, suddenly your creations can do so much more. Components give your entities additional configuration settings, whereas systems can access these settings and use them to create autonomous behaviors. You witnessed this firsthand with the `OrbitBehaviorComponent`, `SpinBehaviorComponent`, and `ObjectCleanupComponent` implementations. Each of these components (and corresponding systems) enables you to set up an entity feature, such as orbiting a location, and then just forget about it. The components and systems continue to drive the behavior of their entities until the components are removed.

You also learned more about physics and applied forces. By applying forces to objects in the environment, you can create motion that isn't simply due to gravity. This came in handy in the Spatial Special project for launching projectiles from the spaceship and creating the effect of an asteroid exploding into pieces when it is shot.

Collisions also came into play with the newfound capability of subscribing to event notifications. Using event subscriptions, you can run arbitrary code when a collision occurs between two objects. This opens up new avenues of development by providing ways to interact with the environment and for the objects in an environment to interact with each other.

Possibly the most important takeaway is the experience of working through Spatial Special. By taking the time to break down all the key features and necessary components and functions before delving into the code, you were able to create easily digestible code that, on its own, performed small actions, but, working as part of the larger application, made the entire experience possible.

Go Further

You've rounded out your knowledge of the ECS paradigm, but there's always more to learn. Expand your knowledge of entities, components, and systems with the Apple documentation at

- https://developer.apple.com/documentation/realitykit/entity

- https://developer.apple.com/documentation/realitykit/component

- https://developer.apple.com/documentation/realitykit/realitykit-systems

Collisions are also worth some additional exploration. I covered the basics, but you can do some cool things with collision triggers, masks, and filters, giving you far more control of what can and will generate a collision. Read through https://developer.apple.com/documentation/realitykit/collision-detection to get started on some of these advanced concepts.

INDEX

Navigator panel, 13
    Issue Navigator, 15–16
    Project Navigator, 13–15
    Search Navigator, 15
Newton-seconds, 380
nodes
    adding, 159–160
    graphs, 140, 150–151
    Fractal3D, 159
    surface shaders, 169–170

O

Object Capture, Reality Composer, xvi, 142
    bounding box, 144
    guided capture, 143–146
    household items, 142
    lighting, 143
    model, resizing, 146
    objects, white dot, 144
    point clouds, 145
object cleanup component, Spatial Special project, 394–395
objects
    adding to environments, 121
    bounding boxes, 144
    classes, 120
    dragging, Reconstruction project, 327, 329
    entities
        creating, 205–206
        packaged, 204
    environment objects, 120
        Snow Globe project, 131–132
    interactive, 186
    mass, 245
    point clouds, 145
    random object generation, 320–322
    user-added, Reconstruction project, 325
    viewing, 122
observable classes, 262
occlusion, 302, 311
occlusion materials, 312
occlusion meshes, 312
Opacity component, 252–253
orbit behavior component, Spatial Special project, 388–392
orbitCenter value, 389
orbitRadius value, 389

orbitSpeed value, 389
orbitStart value, 389
Organizational Identifier, 10
orientation. *See also* rotation
    lighting and, 333
Outputs node, 154

P

.palm location, 265
parameters (SwiftUI), 53
    shaders, 201–202
parent entities, relative scale and, 382
parentheses, 50
particle emitters, 106–108
    Snow Globe project, 128–129
permissions
    ARKit, 279
    Information Property List, 280
photogrammetry, 140–141
physics, 230, 244
physics bodies, 380
    angular force, 381
    constant force, 381
    gravity, 381
    kinematics physics mode, 381
    linear forces, linear impulses, 380
PhysicsBody component, 244
    PhysicsBodyMode, 246
    PhysicsMassProperties, 245
    PhysicsMaterialResource, 245
    Reality Composer Pro and, 246–252
plain windows, 113
Plane Detection project, 285
    ContentView window, planeLabel, 295
    Plane Detector class
        anchor updates, monitoring, 290
        forgetting planes, 294
        internal variables, 290
        output, defining, 289
        planeLabel, 291
        removePlane, 294
        structure, 289
        updatePlane, 291–294
    Reality Composer Pro assets, 287
    setup, 286–287
    spatial taps, ImmersiveView, 296–299